GOD HAS SKIN IN THE GAME

How a New Understanding of Politics and the Soul Could Change America

Sean J. O'Reilly

House of a Thousand Suns
An Imprint of Auriga Ltd.

Published by the House of a Thousand Suns
An imprint of Auriga Limited

Copyright 2016: First edition
Copyright 2019: Second edition

Printed by CreateSpace in the United States

Jacket design by Mainsail Digital Design
The Pillars of Creation in the Eagle Nebula, or M16
http://www.mainsaildigitaldesign.com

ISBN-13: 978-0-9708647-6-5
ISBN-10: 0-9708647-6-0

Non-Fiction
Categories: Philosophy, Politics, Self-Help, New Age
BISAC: New Thinking
Original Copyright 1993
Politics and the Soul: Adventures on the River of Gold

ALSO BY SEAN J. O'REILLY

The Road Within
with James O'Reilly and Tim O'Reilly

Pilgrimage
with James O'Reilly and Larry Habegger

How to Manage Your D.I.C.K.*
Redirect Sexual Energy and Discover
Your More Spiritually Enlightened, Evolved Self

Fifth Access:
Cyber Therapy and Quantum Cyberdynamics

30 Days in the South Pacific
with James O'Reilly and Larry Habegger

Authority, Creativity and the Third Imperium:
Why God's Knowing Himself, Outside Himself, Matters

* An acronym for Destructive Impulses (with) Cyber Kinetics

"The mind is not a vessel to be filled but a fire to be kindled."

—Plutarch

TABLE OF CONTENTS

PART III

EXISTENCE AND THE SOUL

PART IV

REFLECTIONS ON THE MORAL CONTINUUM

PART V

THE FOUNDERS' CODE

AUTHOR'S ACKNOWLEDGMENTS

I would like to thank my wife Brenda for her patience and valuable suggestions regarding the title and various sections of the text. The solipsist nature of my intellectual life would not be possible without her. I would also like to thank my brother James and his wife Wenda for both their encouragement and support. The following offered invaluable editorial help: Peg Balka, Dennis Helming, Rev. Edward Berbusse, S.J., James O'Reilly, Tim O'Reilly, Henri Dixon, Kate O'Reilly, Sue Caulfield, editor extraordinare, and many others for their encouragement and thoughtful comments. Special thanks to the Estrella Community College in Glendale, Arizona for the use of computer library facilities in 1994.

Additional thanks are in order as follows: George Simon for his early guidance; Frederick D. Wilhelmsen whose legendary lectures at the University of Dallas imbued me with a passionate belief in the power of metaphysics; Dr. Paul Eidelberg for showing me what thinking outside the box looked like; Professor Lyle Novinski for teaching me to love art history; the Department of Psychology for inadvertently showing me the limitations of Phenomenology; the Rev. Thomas Cumiskey, O.P. for kindly sharing the Albert the Great Priory in Irving, Texas with a poor student during a summer long ago; Fr. Damian Fandal, O.P. for displaying the joy and power of the priestly life; Monsignor Gerald Hughes for his uncanny discernment; Haviv

Shieber for fighting for America, a country that never accepted him; my father for demonstrating spiritual values in his life and work as a neurologist; my mother for never being anything but her unusual and irrepressible self; my brothers and sisters and my sons Clement, Seumas, Liam, Tobias, Declan and beautiful daughter Joan Marie who all, in one way, shape, form or fashion have helped me to more clearly understand the marvelous universe we live in.

Dedicated to All Those Yet to Come

INTRODUCTION TO SOME
NEW IDEAS

"The modern age began to come to an end when men discovered
that they could no longer understand themselves
by the theory professed by the age."

—Walker Percy,
The Message in a Bottle

God Has Skin In The Game is a new way of thinking about America, God, the human soul and politics. Creatively promenading down the avenues of time, history, science and philosophy, this deep examination of the relationship between politics and the soul is also the blueprint for a moral revolution. What is missing from contemporary political and moral discourse is which concept of existence underlies our common thinking and our institutions. Understanding how we think about Existence, as either a transcendental reality or a discontinuous process, affects the entire social order. How a culture frames the question of Existence determines whether or not values will be conceived as being merely subjective and relative, or whether they might be connected objectively, to a higher order that might compel or incline the human heart to goodness.

This is, in fact, the fault line between Empiricism and Rationalism. "The dispute between rationalism and empiricism concerns the extent to which we are dependent upon sense experience in our effort to gain knowledge. Rationalists claim that there are significant ways in which our concepts and knowledge are gained *independently* of sense experience. Empiricists claim that sense experience is the ultimate source of all our concepts and knowledge...The dispute between rationalism and empiricism takes place within epistemology, the branch of philosophy devoted to studying the nature, sources and limits of knowledge."[1]

At present, the distinction between empiricism and rationalism has become so obscured by an over-reliance on empirical data that few people, outside of academia, are even concerned about the meaning or the distinction between Empiricism and Rationalism. Empiricism, when applied to law, results in an intellectual severance between law and morality by making law self-referential or simply the product of what might be termed various cooperation agreements.[2] Empiricism, when applied to politics, results in moral distortions such as slavery, Communism, Nazism, legal abortion and homosexual marriage.

Rationalism looks, by default, to Existence for answers to the meaning of life and good conduct. Empiricism dismisses moral questions or concerns as merely subjective considerations that must be dismissed in the absence of hard evidence to the contrary. Moral relativism is the ultimate by-product of empiricism. Is it any wonder that American politics has been reduced to shouting matches between newly tribalized factions, who like the Black Lives Matter movement, or

---

1   *Rationalism Versus Empiricism* by Peter Markie http://plato.stanford.edu/entries/rationalism-empiricism/
2   Yuval Noah Harari, *Sapiens: A Brief History of Humankind,* Harper Collins, NY. Y.N. Harari is a recent expositor of the notion that inter-subjectivity and imagination are the sole source of belief and what we call truth

white supremacists want what they want with little or no reference to morality or even the public good?

The American political system was not founded by empiricists but by rationalists, who were, at the very least concerned about God, religion and morality. The attempt of atheists to "walk back" moral values to some imagined and radical separation of church and state is entirely contrary to the intentions of the Founding Fathers, the Constitution and the Declaration of Independence.

John Adams voiced a rationalist concern, for example, in 1811, when he noted the relationship between good governance, religion and morality. "Religion and virtue are the only foundations, not only of Republicanism and of all free government, but of social felicity under all governments and in all the combinations of human society."[3] We cannot imagine, in today's moral climate, anyone with either fully empirical or liberal leanings making such a statement. In order to fully understand what Adams meant by this, when the common understanding today is one of an absolute and empirical separation of Church and State, a broad investigation into the metaphysical and moral heritage of the West is both useful and necessary.

Metaphysics, by itself, is a dry science but when sharpened by political ideas and heated in the flame of moral passion, it becomes a weapon of astonishing power. One has only to reflect on the Christian Crusades of the Middle Ages or the influence of Marxist Hegelianism, underpinning Communist ideology in the 20th century, to realize the truth of this proposition. Islamic Jihad is, if nothing else, the application of an incomplete concept of Existence, translated to the political order. We laugh, for example, at the idea that suicide bombers think they will be rewarded for immoral, terrorist acts with virgins in heaven but is this any odder than the notion that the entire human race would have warranted divine punishment for the actions of two individuals? [4]The notion that human nature was so perfectly formed in Adam

3   *The Works of John Adams—Second President of the United States,* Boston, Little and Brown and Co.,1854, page 101 (Harper Brothers edition, 1958)

4   *The Works of John Adams—Second President of the United States,* Boston, Little and

and Eve that their choices affected all who came after them is logically consistent but the premise is never challenged. Without an original state of perfection, the argument collapses and without proof, this is an extraordinary assertion. What we think about Existence and human origins is directly connected to how we perceive the political order.

The American Founding Fathers, for example, departed from the notion of the Divine Right of Kings[5] in order to ascertain the God-given rights that might be secured from the predations of men with insufficient ideas regarding human liberty and the nature of Existence. The "Divine Right" was based on the very old notion that God and the political order must be linked in order for society to be the proper and correct means of bringing men into the right relationship with God. The purpose of government should be to bring men and women into harmony with both themselves and the fundamental realities, which may have brought them into existence. This tends not to occur, however, when Existence is hijacked by one religion to the exclusion of all other understandings regarding the nature of Divinity. The Founding Fathers, were for the most part Deists, i.e., they believed in a Supreme Being without the trappings of any specific religion. Consequently, their understanding of Existence was more open to a variety of interpretations.

Recent decisions by the Supreme Court of the United States regarding abortion and the right to same-sex marriage were made upon an understanding of the meaning of Existence that was not shared by the Founding Fathers but upon an atheistic agenda that delinks moral goodness from the Divine enterprise. There are many who claim, on the other side of the Deist argument, that the 1857 Dred Scott Decision of the Supreme Court was caused by Christian prejudice. The Court, in an extraordinary moral and political contortion, argued that whether free or enslaved, a black individual could not be a citizen of

---

Brown and Co.,1854, page 101 (Harper Brothers edition, 1958)

5 The idea that kings derive their authority directly from God, not from their subjects, from which it might follow that rebellion could be thought of as the worst of political crimes.

the United States. The radical failure of Christians to enact laws that reflected the universality of the teachings of Jesus, in regards to all members of humanity, was not only a failure to more fully understand the nature of Existence, it was a failure to understand themselves.

We tend to forget that the Founding Fathers had a public philosophy, well subscribed to by most of the populace, which we refer to in retrospect, as Christian morality. This moral code was never properly informed by the complete teachings of Jesus but by a kind of convenient cherry picking of salient doctrines and racially biased conventions. Christ's mandate: "Go therefore and make disciples of all nations, baptizing them in the name of the Father and of the Son and of the Holy Spirit, and teaching them to obey everything I have commanded you" means just that—all nations, which includes all human beings. How enslaving your neighbor might be included in this dynamic is surely one of the greatest ironies of Christianity.

THE REALITY DYSFUNCTION

Many of the ideas presented in this book may seem shocking and possibly intolerant but they can lead you on an intellectual adventure that will change your life. In order to recover the power of the foundational doctrines of the Declaration of Independence and the Constitution, we are going to explore where the religion and ideas of the Founders came from. You will learn new things that the Founding Fathers never knew but would have loved to have known. You will also learn those truths that the Founders were familiar with and that you should know.

During this journey you will discover what America needs to do, culturally, in order to reinstitute the public philosophy of the Founders but in a larger and more comprehensive manner that may enable a new form of world governance[6] based on American ideals. You will also learn about new concepts in philosophy that the Founding Fa-

---

6   Sean J. O'Reilly, *Authority, Creativity and the Third Imperium: Why God's Knowing Himself, Outside Himself, Matters*, House of a Thousand Suns, 2015

thers were not familiar with. You may view, with some incredulity, the *Reality Dysfunction*[7] or *Tsimtsum*[8] whereby Existence, paradoxically, withdraws without movement or change in its Eternal Nature and creates time, derivatively and virtually, also without movement, as force and information (be-ing) in billions and trillions of variations in one astonishing moment that science refers to as the Big Bang. You will not be disappointed, however, in the richness and complexity of the ideas presented. You may even find yourself, instead of being confused, shouting with enthusiasm as concepts are linked to problems in a way that explains life in a novel and compelling way.

Existence, under the labels God, Jehova, Brahman, Tao, the Divine, Holy One, Allah, or Source has been described as uncreated, unchangeable, utterly transcendent and outside of time by many religions. Existence, under the label of energy is viewed by science, according to the First Law of Thermodynamics, as being neither created nor destroyed. Existence, consequently, viewed as simply energy and "process" by modern philosophers (embracing the metaphysics of Hegel) often degenerates into the kind of relativity that has become commonplace in public discourse.

Existence and energy, when considered from the perspective of metaphysics and modern physics, are eerily similar. Both energy and Existence are considered to be uncreated but there are dramatic consequences, depending on which view is selected. This bifurcation of meaning between the older metaphysical view of Existence as the Divinity and the newer understanding of energy, with different manifestations, as supplanting the notions of Existence and being, marks the real distinction between previous ages and modern thinking. What used to be understood as a distinction between Existence and being, or what is uncreated and created, is now simply seen as a manifestation of energetic relations unconnected to an intelligent ordering of the universe.

---

7   This concept is borrowed from Peter Hamilton's excellent science fiction series of the same name. The use of the term here is significantly different.

8   Tsimtsum: A notion from the Jewish *Kabbalah* whereby God withdraws from Himself in order for something else to exist.

What is common to all discussions about Existence and energy is how they affect our understanding of time, motion and the direction of life. If time is related to Divinity, then time is viewed as being interpenetrated by spirit and moral obligation. There is, in other words, an unknown delta,[9] dialectic,[10] or algorithm between time and eternity. How can we describe this unknown delta or algorithm in such a way as to shed more light on human existence?

"Algorithm" is defined by David Berlinski, in his wonderful book, *The Advent of the Algorithm: The Idea That Rules The World* as, "an effective procedure, a way of getting something done in a finite number of discrete steps." An algorithm can be as simple as the steps we take between waking up and going to work or the complex algorithms that make ordering a book from Amazon or a vehicle through UBER so simple and easy. The prime question for those who believe in God might be: how does He do it? What is the algorithm between the Eternal's unchanging Nature and all that is made? Is it just by fiat or magic, or are there transcendental algorithms that will reveal the nature of Existence in a new way?

On the other side of the coin, time viewed, simply, as the unfolding of energetic relations, or motion not associated with a Creator, results in time being seen simply as clock time with no embedded moral or spiritual affiliation or direction. There are new algorithms between matter and energy to be discovered within the atheistic understanding that energy is neither created nor destroyed but those algorithms terminate in a view of reality that might be thought of as being entirely accidental or without a chain of causation that reaches backwards or forwards to an ultimate intelligence or ordering principle in the universe.

---

9   Change of any changeable quantity, in mathematics and the sciences

10 The process especially associated with Hegel of arriving at the truth by stating a thesis, developing a contradictory antithesis and combining and resolving them into a coherent synthesis… the Marxian process of change through the conflict of opposing forces, whereby a given contradiction is characterized by a primary and a secondary aspect, the secondary succumbing to the primary, which is then transformed into a new contradiction. http://www.thefreedictionary.com/dialectic

How we understand Existence is fundamentally related to our understanding of time and motion. It goes without saying that there can be no motion in God (at least as we understand motion) because there is no time in God. There is no motion or interval of time between what He thinks and what He does. This was first understood by Aristotle who described Existence as the Unmoved Mover. The great medieval theologian, Thomas Aquinas, following the thinking of Aristotle, postulated that God's knowing of anything, given the unity of the Divine Nature, creates through what he called *approbation*.[11] This means there is no interval or separation in God between God's thoughts and His actions. The separation or delta occurs in time but how is this even possible without movement, unless that movement is external to Existence conceived of as God?

Almost all human discussions about value and meaning revolve around how we understand the relationship between Existence and time. Existence, understood from the perspective of classical metaphysics, is the Unmoved Mover of Aristotle. The Unmoved Mover creates time without a corresponding algorithmic motion in Itself or does it? Aristotle understood the Unmoved Mover to make everything exist through the almost incomprehensible nature of its Actuality but was never, as far as we know, able to explain how something that did not exist, as all other things exist, was able to make everything else exist without motion. Why would Existence bother to make anything but Itself exist? Without personhood being tied to Existence there would seem to be little reason to make anything else besides Itself exist. The notion of Existence sharing its existence, contingently, with everything that exists was a notion that was not fully developed until Christianity appeared on the scene.

Existence doesn't exist.[12] All things that are said to exist do so out of some matrix. Existence, ultimately, can only be described by

---

11 Meaning that because He knows Himself in all the ways that He might be imitated, His very knowledge brings about their algorithmic creation in time.

12 Wilhelmsen, Frederick, *The Paradoxical Structure of Existence*, University of Dallas Press, 1970

using the word "Is". In order to have some means, some way of describing something that doesn't exist but makes all things exist, we must first call it Existence—understanding that it can only be called Existence because it is that by which all things that exist come into being. This notion of contingency or the dependence of being on Being was first clearly articulated by Aristotle and is implicit in the Chinese concept of the Tao[13] and in some of the early Sanskrit theology[14] of India. The notion of an Unmoved Mover still tends to fall into the semantic trap of subject and object. Existence is neither a subject nor an object, except to Itself, and even then that is an improper way of thinking about Existence.[15]

This kind of algorithmic "movement", whereby things come into existence due to the influence of something that doesn't exist, is almost impossible to conceive. All we can do is point at it and try to use a variety of analogies to give us some purchase on the sheer cliffs presented by an Act, which involves no motion or time. Think of it as an *unknown algorithm* or exchange between Existence and all things that exist because of Existence. The notion of contingency (meaning that all things depend on Existence to exist) does not explain how this kind of participation in Existence actually works. Think of contingent existence as having a lower case "e". Imagine something that could move without moving, think without thinking, create without motion and you begin to get the idea of how radical Existence (the big "E") really is in relation to all human constructs.

---

13 Tao (pronounced "dao") means literally "the path" or "the way." It is a universal principle that underlies everything from the creation of galaxies to the interaction of human beings. The workings of Tao are vast and often beyond human logic. In order to understand Tao, reasoning alone will not suffice. One must also apply intuition. http://www.taoism.net/articles/what_tao.htm Lao Tze, who probably codified and perfected an existing tradition, is said to have lived in the sixth century B.C.

14 Sanskrit is the classical language of India and the liturgical language of Hinduism, Buddhism, and Jainism. It is also one of the 22 official languages of India. The name Sanskrit means "refined", "consecrated" and "sanctified". [WP]

15 All items in italics are call-outs for important information and if not attributed to an outside source are the work of this author.

Time, as the measure of motion, or as a delta for velocity, is many things and how we approach or treat it will be based on our understanding of Existence. If time is created, it is an artifact of such stupendous proportions that an extraordinary kind of causality is hinted at. Existence is, so to speak, the elephant in the room but it must be adverted to and evaluated for meaning when considering the many ways in which values, in relation to time, may be understood. What might the algorithm between time and eternity look like if Existence Itself doesn't exist?

How might we characterize the ratio or relationship between Existence and contingent existence? The metaphysics of both Aristotle and Aquinas are, together, one very long attempt to understand this algorithm. Their solution was the notion of matter and form, with form being the invisible and derivative component of Existence conceived of as a kind of directed potential or potential with information. We will dig into this idea and see why it works conceptually but needs to be revised based on what we have learned in the past one hundred years from empirical science in the form of quantum mechanics.

THE TIME WAR AND RELIGION

As we look at the landscape of emotion and belief, it is apparent that how we conceive of, or deny the relationship between time and existence, is a result of different understandings of Existence and its imputed relation to time and motion. These different perspectives are at the root of many of our religious and political differences. How many wars and how much blood has been shed over differing understandings of the meaning of Existence in relation to moral and religious ideas? The notion that human behavior might be conditioned by or be accountable to a Divine being is probably the oldest formulation of the relationship between an eternal Entity and mankind. This relationship might be posed as a simple question. Does God care about how we behave, or why we behave, is He simply uninterested or must we try to understand the imputed relationship in a new way?

If we query the notion of "interest" it can be noted that the word means: "the state of wanting to know or learn about something or someone." This state cannot apply to God because He already, presumably, knows and understands all outcomes, everywhere and for all time. What God wishes cannot change and what He wishes can only be that all things *exist* in all the ways that are appropriate to what they *are* relative to the eternal vision that has called them forth. A dog is not called to be more than a dog or less than a dog. A man or woman is not called to be less than a man or woman but they are called, if we are to believe the Old and New Testaments and many other sacred scriptures, to be more than human beings. They are, if we were to distill the fundamental message of the New Testament, to be like the sons and daughters of God. So what needs to be queried, ultimately, is what it means to be like God.

The requested sacrifice of the beloved Isaac, by Abraham, at God's request is emblematic of a certain common authoritarianism[16] at the heart of western culture, as found in orthodox Judaism, Christianity and Islam. This authoritarianism is a particular interpretation of the relationship of Existence to humanity indicating that Existence is always conceived as a primary values driver based on punishment for non-compliance with the prescribed algorithms for a return to the Deity. How we conceive of our relationship with Existence, from within time, is translated by religion and belief (and that includes atheism) into a multiplicity of conflicting viewpoints.

If God cares about how we behave, how does humanity express that in terms of law and culture? Judaism, for example, claims a moral and spiritual descent from a covenant that God Himself made with Abraham[17] (2000-1900 B.C.) and the Jewish people. Islam has a highly theocentric system that is governed by the notion that God wants all of mankind to believe in Allah, the one, true God. This assertion is based on the notion of a specific revelation to the prophet Mohammed

---

16 Hockney, Mike, *The Last Man Who Knew Everything,* Hyperreality Books, July 14, 2012
17 When Abram was 99 years old, the Lord appeared to Abram and said to him, "I am El Shaddai. Walk with me and be trustworthy. I will make a covenant between us and I will give you many many descendants." https://http://www.biblegateway.com/passage/?search=Genesis+17&version=CEB

(580-632 A.D.) Unfortunately, Mohammed was not the first to claim divine appointment as God's spokesman, despite his claim to be the "seal" or final revelation of the prophets. Who but God could say that prophecy or revelation, for that matter, has come to an end?

Mohammed was one of a long line of desert prophets going all the way back through the Old Testament to the Egyptian Pharaoh Ikhanaton, who ruled from 1353 to 1336 B.C. Ikhanaton was one of the first historical figures that we know of, aside from Abraham, to propose that there was only one God. Ikhanaton, sometimes referred to as Akhenaten, was, if current dating is to be believed, a contemporary of Moses, and it is possible that there was a confluence of ideas about monotheism, at that time, among a larger group of people than would have been represented by the Chosen People. Moses (1393-1273 B.C.) was said to have been spoken to by God in a burning bush and been given moral and spiritual instruction with the Ten Commandments, which were said to have been written in stone by the finger of God. Jesus, who arrived on the scene nearly six hundred years before Mohammed, claimed to be the Son of God, performed miracles and was crucified by the Jews for asserting that He and the eternal Father were One.

What are we to make of these competing claims? Is one right and the other one wrong or are we better instructed to consider all such claims *as a continuing revelation* by God of Who He is? If we take this position, how might we describe the relationship between God and mankind? Should it only be understood as establishing one way of behaving or should the relationship be thought of as consisting of many different paths? Clearly, there are many strongly-held opinions in this regard. Orthodox Jews believe that the Messiah has yet to come and that Jesus was just another prophet. Christians believe that Jesus, due to his Divine Nature, is the final authority on revelation with revelation coming to a full stop. Islam believes that Jesus was just prophet and that Mohammed was the final prophet whose words cannot be contradicted.

The pattern of authoritarian displacement by one set of revelatory beliefs over another is commonplace in history. This is part of the moral spectrum of the Time War, whereby belief is attached to God in such a way as to justify many different kinds of behavior towards God and to neighbor. This behavior is sometimes beneficial but often creates friction between various groups of believers. All of this is very obvious to the modern mind but it is helpful, sometimes, to raise questions that are almost superficial in order to grasp the kind of collective lunacy mankind sometimes evinces in relation to strongly held beliefs tied to the notion of revealed truths.

What we can say in the most respectful way possible is that revelation can seldom be tested because it is always located somewhere in the past and must be accepted on faith. The merits of accepting some spiritual ideas on the basis of faith cannot be overly questioned but revelation itself is singularly resistant to scientific examination and a great deal hinges on whether or not exaggeration or delusion might be involved in some instances. One can sympathize with atheists and empiricists who simply deal with what they can see, touch and feel.

The apparent power of human beings to create dynamic and comprehensive belief systems based on sometimes questionable information, yields a baseline for what a civil society can accept or put aside from revelation. This may be an important tool in maintaining the relative separation of Church and State intended by the Founding Fathers. A society that does not see God as being aligned with the notion of moral goodness and the fair and equitable treatment of all human beings, for example, may be missing a fundamental truth about Existence.

The primary claim of many religions is that they have been given a unique mission directly from God that is at variance with other religions making the same claim. Can God be recruited by any organization, as either its founder or its mouthpiece, or should we take a larger view of the Divinity and Its actions in the world? If the former, we will have to settle on one religion as foundational. If the latter, we will have to formulate a different way of dealing with strong religious opinions and beliefs. The solution of the Founding Fathers was religious tolerance and it was not a solution that entailed separation of God from the

State but a separation of Church and religious modality from the State. We would be wise to reconsider this uniquely American proposition and seek ways to enforce it.

The notion of religious freedom, which enables God to enter human life as a competitor, so to speak, for faith means very simply, one thing: the religion that has the most compelling set of circumstances and offerings will be the one that will attract the hearts and minds of men and women. Faith is part of the continuing revelation of the Divine and it requires the free assent of human beings to be effective. Faith is the ongoing revelation of God to the human heart and this will, in the larger sense, not be in opposition to the revelation of theology but will, rather, perfect it.

> *The Time War, which pits one understanding of the relationship between time and eternity against another, requires for its continuance, the assertion that there can only be one way to God or, in the case of science, only one way of thinking about reality. The Time War is a metaphor for a certain discontinuity or incongruity in human thinking about Existence. Existence does not exist in any format that can be formulated in such a way as to be completely definitive. It's relationship to any religion can only be by way of attribution of goodness. The notion that God might require anything other than goodness from humanity is a moral, political and spiritual discontinuity.*

RESOLUTION THEORY

"Gregory David Roberts' philosophical and cosmological model, known as Resolution Theory, is presented through Khader Bhai, the Indian Mafia-style don, in his book, *Shantaram: A Novel*".[18] Resolution Theory begins to get at the complexity engendered by Existence in a novel way.

---

18 Bennet, Juliet http://www.julietbennett.com/2010/10/22/a-deeper-exploration-of -resolution-theory/

"The whole universe is moving toward some ultimate complexity. This has been going on since the universe began, and physicists call it the tendency toward complexity. And...anything that kicks this along and helps it is good, and anything that hinders it is evil...

"And this final complexity...it can be called God or the Universal Spirit, or the Ultimate Complexity, as you please. For myself, there is no problem in calling it God. The whole universe is moving toward God, in a tendency toward the ultimate complexity that God is..."

"In order to know about any act or intention or consequence, we must first ask two questions. One, what would happen if everyone did this thing? Two, would this help or hinder the movement toward complexity [God]?"

(Roberts 2007:550-551.) [19]

Relating such philosophies to the various religious traditions Roberts says:

"Every guru you meet and every teacher, every prophet and every philosopher should answer these two questions for you: What is an objective, universally acceptable definition of good and evil? And What is the relationship between consciousness and matter?...This is a test that you should apply to every man who tells you that he knows the meaning of life."

(Roberts 2007:708.) [20]

The relationship between consciousness and matter is mediated by the splintering effect of the Reality Dysfunction and the eternity of Di-

---

19 Ibid
20 Ibid

vine consciousness that attracts creation back to Itself. The "reditus" or return of creation to the Creator is something new in creation but it is not new to God. Resolution theory, then attempts to understand the relationship between God and man in a new way. Religion is a vehicle of resolution, generated as possibility by the power of Existence, which attracts all things to Itself. It is a means, not an end. Would you prefer to return to Existence in a luxury vehicle or a spiritual jalopy? Regardless of what you may choose, focusing on one means, to the exclusion of others, can sometimes be a distraction.

Have you ever noticed how many people who claim to be religious are, often, not particularly spiritual? This is because they are so focused on the means that they miss the end, which is an encounter with a living Being that is fundamentally transformative of human experience. We should stop wasting time worrying about how other people encounter God and instead focus on our own relationship with the Divinity. It is always easier, as Jesus indicated, (with some humor I suspect) to see the splinter in our brother's eye but to miss the timber that might be sticking out of our own eyes.

The Time War, which is both the indicator and symptom of a misunderstood delta (or algorithm) between time and eternity that has different and sometimes radical interpretations, is the ultimate cause of most ideological conflicts. Think about the present day squabbling between Israelis and Islamic Palestinians over access to the Dome of the Rock. It is sacred to the Jews as being part of the original first temple of Solomon and it is sacred to Islam, as this is the point where Mohammed is said to have ascended to heaven on his horse. Even now, Christian religious orders squabble over who gets to administer the various holy places. Anyone who has been to the ostensible site of Jesus's tomb in Jerusalem can witness first- hand an almost absurd religious tourism, whereby the faithful are herded through by tired monks—often with bad manners.

These kinds of conflicts over holy places and religious meanings can only be ameliorated if and when humanity is willing to reach a collective agreement about the meaning of Existence. A deeper un-

derstanding of God, as Existence, may help remove the anthropomor-
phisms[21] that commonly drive religious thinking. God is here now and
available at any time to each one of us—no matter where we are or
what we have done.[22] We must purge ourselves of the notion that God
is some sort of cosmic and religious administrator, who can be accessed
in some sort of special way by visiting holy sites. While it is certainly
beneficial to reverence holy places, forgetting that God is not bound
to space and time in any way, is not helpful. This is also the larger
purpose of this book: to help bring an end to The Time War, which
is largely caused by a failure to understand the meaning of Existence.

THE JUMPING OFF POINT

The earliest common western meaning of the word "religion" comes
from the Latin *religare*, which means to bind.[23] Using this general definition, any set of beliefs about the universe or God, or human behavior
might be considered binding or "religious" in nature. Existence, considered apart from organized religion, can only be understood by referring
to Existence Itself and its relationship to time. There is no motion in
God, if God is understood as Aristotle's Unmoved Mover ("that which
moves without being moved") yet motion occurs wherever there is time
or potential. The Unmoved Mover has an extraordinary influence over
everything in the visible universe. Not existing in the way that anything
else exists, it makes everything in the universe exist.

---

21 "Anthropomorphism is the attribution of human traits, emotions, and intentions to
non-human entities and is considered to be an innate tendency of human psychology."
[WP]
22 This is not to eschew traditional Christian spirituality that limits itself to participation
in sacrament and ritual; it is only to remind the religious that God is not limited by
either religion or circumstance. God's participation in sacramental systems, by either
direct action or existential modality, is neither affirmed or denied in this book, in
order to maintain an even hand in the description of spiritual systems.
23 The English word "*religion*" is derived from the Middle English "*religioun*" which came
from the Old French "*religion*." It may have been originally derived from the Latin
word "*religo*" which means "*good faith*," "*ritual*," and other similar meanings. Or it may
have come from the Latin "*religàre*" which means "*to tie fast*," or "bind together." http://
www.religioustolerance.org/rel_defn1.htm

What this means is that even though the Unmoved Mover is invisible, its affects cannot be said not to exist. We are so used to being able to see technological cause and effect that attempting to deal with a cause that is only visible in its effects, leaves us gibbering like monkeys over a fallen banana that has been pulled up into the trees by a piece of clear fishing line. Claiming that what we don't understand is caused by random events related to sub-atomic particle attractions is no different than the discontented noises of monkeys over the disappearance of the banana. It is an emotional reaction against something—that if accepted—would require a radically different approach to the goals of science.

What is the algorithm—remembering that an algorithm is just a series of discrete and finite steps in getting something done—between Existence as the Unmoved Mover and that which is moved? God's knowing Himself, *outside Himself*, in the metaphor of the Reality Dysfunction, creates both motion and time simultaneously in a delta that did not previously exist. (This unique concept, which functions as an alternative explanation for the fall of man will be explained in greater detail as the book unfolds.)

> *An analogy between the quantum wave and the collapse that occurs with observation that is known in physics as decoherence[24] may provide an answer. Science has discovered that observation changes the outcome of what is observed at the experimental level of quantum activity. What science has not done, except by way of dismissal,[25] is ask what would happen if an eternal observer, who could see and know everything, collapsed the continuum. What sort of special decoherence would occur for all of quantum reality*

24 Decoherence then, results in the collapse of the quantum wave function and the settling of a particle into its observed state under classical physics, its transition from quantum to classical behavior. http://www.physicsoftheuniverse.com/topics_quantum _superposition.html

25 This was noted in The Atlantic in an August 29, 2016 article entitled, *The Multiverse Idea is Rotting Culture* by Sam Kriss. The author asserts that the German Theologian, Karl Heim, postulated that an eternal observer was responsible for the collapse of the quantum wave in 1951. Kriss noted that physicist Stephen Hawking claimed the idea was merely "trivially true", [thereby consigning it to irrelevancy].

if there was always a universal observer? **The Reality Dysfunction is simply the decoherence of the universe that appears
to have taken place in the "Big Bang".**[26] *Decoherence is, in
fact, a transcendental algorithm or ratio that can be queried for
metaphysical and empirical meaning.*

"The singularity [said to be responsible] for the Big Bang is the
center of a black hole, which is a gravitational singularity, a one-dimensional point which contains a huge mass in an infinitely small
space, where density and gravity become infinite and space-time curves
infinitely, and where the laws of physics as we know them cease to
operate."[27] So where does the first singularity come from? Physicists,
in a sleight of hand worthy of a magician, simply assert that it was just
there or always had been due to the idea that energy is neither created
nor destroyed. They claim that "according to the "cosmic censorship"
hypothesis, a black hole's singularity remains hidden behind its event
horizon, in that it is always surrounded by an area which does not
allow light to escape, and therefore cannot be directly observed. The
only exception the hypothesis allows (known as a "naked" singularity)
is the initial Big Bang itself."[28] This might be thought of as the intellectual jumping-off point between physics and metaphysics.

What can be said with certainty is that with the hypotheses of
"cosmic censorship", the first singularity and the subsequent Big Bang,
physics has said almost all that it can say without lapsing into metaphysics, and it is at this point where the Reality Dysfunction can be invoked in order to further explicate the relationship between Existence

---

26 The Big Bang Theory is the leading explanation about how the universe began. At its
    simplest, it talks about the universe as we know it starting with a small singularity,
    then inflating over the next 13.8 billion years to the cosmos that we know today. Be-
    cause current instruments don't allow astronomers to peer back at the universe's birth,
    much of what we understand about the Big Bang Theory comes from mathemati-
    cal theory and models. Astronomers can, however, see the "echo" of the expansion
    through a phenomenon known as the cosmic microwave background. http://www
    .space.com/25126-big-bang-theory.html
27 http://www.physicsoftheuniverse.com/topics_blackholes_singularities.html
28 http://www.physicsoftheuniverse.com/topics_blackholes_singularities.html

and the visible universe. What would cause the singularity to expand? Why wouldn't it remain a singularity? Atheistic science is very busy trying to squirm off the hook that has been baited by the "naked" singularity and subsequent String Theory. Why should there be anything at all if there is no additional layer of causality between matter and energy and time and space?

A conversation that physicist Abraham Pais recalled having with Albert Einstein regarding quantum theory and the nature of reality is illuminating in this context. This exchange has been noted by a number of different story tellers. "We often discussed his notions on objective reality. I recall that during one walk Einstein suddenly stopped, turned to me and asked whether I really believed that the moon exists only when I look at it."[29] Physicist, Tom McFarlane, argues that Einstein was incorrect, stating, "although the moon is not there when nobody looks, it acts as if it is."[30] This indicates a certain annoying and almost smug version of the paradox that Samuel Johnson dispensed with in the mid-1700's when refuting Bishop Berkeley. Bishop Berkeley believed that God caused all things to exist in such a way that material reality was an illusion. This is an early version of a similar but different error that physicists make by asserting that things don't really exist until they are observed by human beings.

Boswell recounts the incident in his book, *Life of Samuel Johnson*, as follows: "After we came out of the church, we stood talking for some time together of Bishop Berkeley's ingenious sophistry to prove the non-existence of matter, and that everything in the universe is merely ideal. I observed, that though we are satisfied his doctrine is not true, it is impossible to refute it. I never shall forget the alacrity with which Johnson answered, striking his foot with mighty force against a large stone, till he rebounded from it—"I refute it thus."

29 McFarlane, Tom https://http://www.quora.com/Is-the-moon-there-when-nobody-looks
   Rev. Mod. Phys. 51, 863–914 (1979), p. 907
30 Ibid

COSMOLOGICAL ARGUMENTS

The metaphysical error of asserting that things don't really exist or don't possess contingent existence will be explored in this book. Understanding that Existence makes all things be or possess what might be called contingent existence is part of two different metaphysical cosmological arguments.[31] A cosmological argument, in the broadest sense of the word, is a theory that deals with the origin and development of the universe. There are metaphysical cosmological arguments and scientific cosmological arguments. The scientific (astronomical) models of cosmology deal with the origin, structure and space-time relationships of the universe. Consequently, there are four major cosmological arguments: two metaphysical cosmological arguments and two (or more) scientific cosmological arguments.

"The modal cosmological argument or "argument from contingency" is a metaphysical argument from the contingency of the world or universe to the existence of God. The argument from contingency is the most prominent form of cosmological argument historically. The classical statements of the cosmological argument in the works of Plato…and of Leibniz are generally statements of the modal form of the argument."[32] "What distinguishes the modal cosmological argument from the Kalam cosmological argument is that it is consistent with the idea that the universe has an infinite past. The Kalam cosmological argument rests on the controversial claim that the universe has a beginning in time. The Modal argument from contingency, in contrast and paradoxically, is consistent with the universe having existed from eternity."[33] This may appear to be a superficial distinction, but a beginning in time, as apposed to no beginning in time, are two very different things. The "Big Bang" and the Steady State Theory are the two primary sci-

---

31 An argument for the existence of God that claims that all things depend on something else for their existence (i.e., are contingent), and that the whole universe must therefore itself depend on a being that exists independently or necessarily.

32 http://www.philosophyofreligion.info/theistic-proofs/the-cosmological-argument/the -argument-from-contingency/

33 Ibid. This is, essentially, a view held by both Christians and Moslems.

entific cosmological arguments. They are closely followed by various modalities of String Theory involving multiple dimensions but they all have a number of puzzling elements that may be better answered with metaphysics. The Big Bang, for example, assumes the existence of a singularity beyond space and time that explodes in a "Big Bang". The "why" this expansion (inflation) happens with the naked singularity is never clearly answered except to say that it is part of an eternal expansion and contraction of energy that is science's substitute for Existence. Let's look at this again for emphasis.

> *"The singularity [said to be responsible] for the Big Bang is the center of a black hole, which is a gravitational singularity, a one-dimensional point which contains a huge mass in an infinitely small space, where density and gravity become infinite and space-time curves infinitely, and where the laws of physics as we know them cease to operate."*[34] *The laws of physics might be said to "cease to operate" in the presence of God in the same way that they would cease to operate within a black hole. Why kick the can into an unknown hole when God's Existence in the Reality Dysfunction may provide a more compelling answer?*

The QSSC or Quasi Steady State Theory of Cosmology postulates that creation might be continuous with particles constantly being born out of nothing. We will look at the Steady State Theory again but first let's look at one of the peculiarities of the Big Bang.

> *If we accept the Theory of Relativity, "the Big Bang is not an event at all. An event takes place within a space-time context. But the Big Bang has no space-time context; there is neither time prior to the Big Bang nor a space in which the Big Bang occurs. Hence, the Big Bang cannot be considered as a physical event occurring at a moment of time. As Hawking notes, the finite*

---

34 http://www.physicsoftheuniverse.com/topics_blackholes_singularities.html

universe has no space-time boundaries and hence lacks singu-
larity and a beginning (Hawking 116, 136). Time might be
multi-dimensional or imaginary, in which case one asymptot-
ically approaches a beginning singularity but never reaches it.
And without a beginning the universe requires no cause. The best
one can say is that the universe is finite with respect to the past,
not that it was an event with a beginning." [35]

This argument is, from a metaphysical perspective, limited. Time has a beginning relative to something that has no beginning; i.e., Existence. Within metaphysics, the Modal Cosmological Argument anticipates Hawking's concern in that relative to God's Existence time may not *appear* to have a cause. However, taking refuge in a counter-intuitive, infinite regression marked by the non-existence of time's beginning is the kind of discontinuous proposition that science tends to embrace because the only other conclusion would be to accept a metaphysical argument for cosmology. Might there be another way of looking at all the data, both metaphysical and scientific, and recasting the cosmological question?

The existence of two different metaphysical cosmological arguments based on contingency and two or more different scientific cosmological arguments, contain with them an extraordinary, unexplored gem, which is the basis for understanding the Reality Dysfunction. Imagine, if you will, two giant pools of water. One pool is called Energy and the other pool is called Existence. Both pools "contain" the potential for everything that will ever be. This is, generally speaking, the difference between the cosmological models of science and those of metaphysics. It is also, and unfortunately, the fault line between atheism and religion. The giant pool of Energy has no personality and no moral values, other than those that are

---

35 Cosmological Argument, http://plato.stanford.edu/entries/cosmological-argument/
    #5.4

self-referential, and it does not care. The only values to be discovered are scientific. The pool that we are calling Existence is the source of objective, as opposed to relative or subjective moral values, and it is also the source of all religious belief.

Existence is, then, for science pure, undifferentiated energy and Existence for metaphysicians is, generally speaking, God. What is the mechanism which makes the energy pool be anything but undifferentiated energy? Physics has yet to determine a clear answer to this question, despite theories about energy exchanges between white and black holes and inflation and deflation of multiple universes. The other pool, Existence or what the theologians call God, can be queried with a substantial question. How can an unchanging God, who knows everything, create in time without first creating time or create without some change, occurring in Himself? This question can be explored using decoherence as a scientific metaphor for the coming into existence of all things that God knows by knowing Himself and all the ways that He can be known.

Can God decohere Himself through an observation of Himself as other than Himself? Might this not be thought of as a possible and algorithmic cause of the original singularity?

God doesn't change in this scenario; He creates Himself, in motion without motion, as the derivative "beingness" we call energy in the very first instance of time. This might be thought of as the primary transcendental algorithm or the way that Existence relates to the universe. The paradox is that there can never have been a time when God did not know Himself in this way. It can be argued that God doesn't need to know Himself derivatively, in this way, as He is His Own Knowledge of Himself but a set of relations does occur in time—in reference to the Divine Essence—once decohered by the Divine Act that automatically adjusts all things, algorithmically to Itself. Expressed as a mathematical analogy, at point zero, there is nothing but the moment something exists contingently, point zero might be thought of as existing in relation to whatever is not point zero.[36]

Creation, in other words, makes God relational to creation in a way that He was not relational prior to creation. This can only occur in time through a derivation of Divine Existence that exists in relation to creation. God creates Himself, *as what we call God,* by creating the universe. This is why Existence can be called the Creator but it doesn't add anything to what Existence already Is—the addition occurs in time—at our end. We call this the Reality Dysfunction because it represents an original flaw or imbalance in the structure of the universe relative to the perfect Source that created it.

Perfection and eternity cannot enter time without a kind of asynchronous or disproportionate ratio between what is created and that which creates. This asynchronicity does not assume a perfect relationship between that which creates and that which is created. The asynchronicity is simply seen as a consequence of relation between that which is infinite and that which is finite. Imperfection is translated as an expression of the ratio between Existence and contingent existence. No original state of perfection is assumed or necessary within the dynamics of the Reality Dysfunction.

The Reality Dysfunction, then, is a cosmological argument that fuses elements of both metaphysical and scientific cosmological arguments. This *asynchronicity* between eternity and time does not exist in the religious tradition of the West except as a consequence of the fall of man from an original state of grace. The idea that God could not create something imperfect in relation to Himself serves as the basis for finding the fault in man rather than elsewhere. The Realty Dysfunction is consonant with the universe as we observe it—not as we may want it to be from any particular religious perspective.

The Islamic scholar, Ibn Rushd, better known in the West as Averroes, notes in his *Decisive Treatise* (written in the 12th century AD) that "the apparent meaning of Scripture is that there was a being and time

---

36 Hockney, Mike, *The Last Man Who Knew Everything*, Hyperreality Books, July 14, 2012

before God created the present being and time. Thus the theologians' interpretation is allegorical and does not command unanimous agreement." This creation of "a being and time" before the present being and time is the derivative consciousness of God in relation to Himself as Existence. This knowing Himself, outside Himself, does not add anything to God; it is a modality of Divine self-knowledge in time.

There is, therefore, an imbalance of proportion between an Infinite Being and the finite universe, by which He understands Himself, outside Himself. This "understanding" is only derivative because it necessarily becomes relational in time. God's Existence does not depend on this relational understanding. This "understanding" is a derived relation between all of contingent being and the derivative consciousness[37] in time that comprehends and orders contingent reality. This, rather than the fall of man, postulated in scripture, is responsible for evolution and our present condition. This might be seen as rank heresy among some religious groups but this new philosophy cannot spare the metaphysical and religious sensibilities of either liberals or conservatives as it seeks to uncover the metaphysical origins of western civilization and its relationship to politics and the soul.

The explosion of being and consciousness, in the "Big Bang" of the Reality Dysfunction leads to a kind of splintering effect that may be the basis for the cultural, political and religious wars that are referred to collectively, in this book, as the Time War. The creation of time and space is not an entirely benign event. An original unity appears to have manifested in a derivative format that desperately desires its original unity and Source. Human existence, from this perspective, seems more like a shipwreck than a well-prepared arrival in a safe harbor. What we tell ourselves about life and how we actually experience it are sometimes at odds, in a curious kind of cognitive dissonance, whereby what we believe is contradicted by various forms of scientific or anecdotal evidence.

---

37 The ancients referred to this consciousness as the Demiurge or the One. We will visit this concept in detail as the chapters unfold.

Do we really believe, for example, that God infused souls into Adam and Eve 6,000 years ago, when all the scientific evidence indicates something more gradual may have occurred during much longer evolutionary timelines? How on earth could Jesus or Mohammed have ascended to Heaven and Mary have been assumed into Heaven, if Heaven were not a created place? Jesus could not come back to Existence and add anything new to God that He does not already possess. The legend of Mohammed ascending to heaven on a horse from the Dome of the Rock may have been a didactic way of giving to Mohammed the same legitimacy or pedigree attributed to Christ and His Ascension. This tendency, found in all religions, to amplify events in order to create additional legitimacy for tenuous ideas has a long history and must be watched carefully for ideological distortion. Coming back to God in physical form would imply change in God and that is not possible based on the metaphysics of Aristotle, Aquinas and the Islamic philosopher, Averroes, (Ibn Rushd) who, it is said, was enormously cosmopolitan in his understanding of Existence.

"Ibn Rushd contended that the claim of many Muslim theologians that philosophers were outside the fold of Islam had no base in scripture. His novel exegesis of seminal Quranic verses made the case for three valid "paths" of arriving at religious truths, and that philosophy was one if not the best of them, therefore its study should not be prohibited. He also challenged Asharite, Mutazilite, Sufi, and "literalist" conceptions of God's attributes and actions, noting the philosophical issues that arise out of their notions of occasionalism, divine speech, and explanations of the origin of the world. Ibn Rushd strived to demonstrate that without engaging religion critically and philosophically, deeper meanings of the tradition can be lost, ultimately leading to deviant and incorrect understandings of the divine."[38]

---

38 http://www.iep.utm.edu/ibnrushd/

It should be noted that "The verses of the Qur'an make it clear that the very name Allah existed in the *Jahiliyya* or pre-Islamic Arabia. Certain pagan tribes believed in a god whom they called 'Allah' and whom they believed to be the creator of heaven and earth and holder of the highest rank in the hierarchy of the gods. It is well known that the Quraish as well as other tribes believed in Allah, whom they designated as the 'Lord of the House' (i.e., of the Ka'ba)...[which was also worshipped before the rise of Mohammed]. It is therefore clear that the Qur'anic conception of Allah is not entirely new."[39] Mohammed himself did not come to found a new religion but to testify to the truth of the older tradition.

The literalist conceptions of religion that Averroes and others have warned against can only occur in a derivative or virtual reality, which is entirely real to us but not so to God. It should be clear from any comparative study of religion that the spiritual traditions, which we have inherited today have a very long history, which is sometimes at odds with the hagiographies of present pieties. We will explore the notion that creation is similar to a virtual or holographic universe and the kinds of tempering of religious concepts that this notion tends to provide or engender.

Existence, for example, can be seen as either personal or impersonal depending on whether you are looking at Existence from the perspective of metaphysics and theology or the hard sciences. Within time, existence can appear to be a neutral process that is part of the appearance and departure of things. Existence thought of as appearance, instead of being or essence, is one of the differences between modern and ancient philosophy. This distinction is also the fault line, as indicated earlier, between Rationalism and Empiricism. As appearance, being is relegated to process, and ultimately to subjective irrelevancy. Existence, considered outside of eternity is, as this book will attempt to outline, the nature and workings of a Divine Person or Persons

---

39 *A Guide to the Contents of the Qur'an*, Faruq Sherif, (Reading, 1995), pgs. 21-22., [Muslim Scholars' notation]

engaged with reality in a unique manner that has only previously been hinted at and never fully described.

What empiricism has shown us, however, is that the universe is much more fully connected than even the ancients may have thought. The complex interrelationships between energy and matter, between quantum wave and particle manifestations, pointed to by modern physics, show a world that is not incompatible, as we will see, with the metaphysical world-view of Socrates, Plato, Aristotle and Aquinas.

THE ALGORITHMS OF EXISTENCE

The hypothesis behind superstrings, according to physicist Michio Kaku, involves the existence of nine dimensions of space and one dimension of time (a total of 10). According to this notion, we observe only three spatial dimensions and one time dimension because the other six spatial dimensions are "curled up" or "compactified." According to Superstring Theory, all of the elementary particles in the universe are composed of vibrating, one-dimensional mathematical objects known as strings [which vibrate *and* rotate at the speed of light]. The theory does not explicitly state what the strings are made of or where they come from; rather, they are proposed as geometric ideals. Each string has a length of 1035 meters, many times smaller than the diameter of the nucleus of an atom.[40] They are said to be a multi-dimensional expression of the original singularity responsible for the Big Bang.

What would happen, however, if we were to add two other dimensions of "time" to the mix, in addition to the clock time we are familiar with? The first would be time with a beginning but no end (aveternity) and the second would be eternal "time". The Reality Dysfunction indicates how multi-dimensional theory can be used to explain the relationship between the One Nature of Existence and the secondary reality of created or contingent being, and different

---

40 http://mkaku.org/home/articles/hyperspace-and-a-theory-of-everything/

kinds of time and dimension. The fundamental and relational algorithm that comes into existence, as a result of Divine Consciousness translating Infinity into finitude, is one way of understanding the Reality Dysfunction.

The Infinite Source cannot be translated by the finite and this results in a quasi-disproportion of relation between the infinite power of Existence and what is created. Think of Existence, within time, working somewhat like the browser on a computer; it translates *Source Code* into something else.

> *This translated disproportion between what God knows, as He Is in the Divine Essence, and what He knows in a secondary or derived manner is the Reality Dysfunction, which manifests as what the Christian understands as a fallen universe. God is in no way affected by the Reality Dysfunction, rather the Reality Dysfunction is an effect of creation—a relation of abstract reason necessitated by the way the human mind works and nothing more. God remains utterly free and transcendent and is no more bound by the processes of the Reality Dysfunction than He would be by the chemical reactions between hydrogen and oxygen that produce water. The Reality Dysfunction simply discloses an additional level of causality, caused by Existence, within both the classical and the scientific understanding of time and space.*

A new way, then, may be required to describe how God operates within time. The Greek word for helmsmen or pilot is "cyber" and "kinesis" is defined by Aristotle as: "Change (motion) the actuality of that which potentially is, qua such"[41] or what we would call process, which is the movement between what is potential and what is actual. In the sciences, kinetics is a term for the branch of classical mechanics

---

41 From S. Marc Cohen's reiteration and explanation of Aristotle's definition of kinesis: https://faculty.washington.edu/smcohen/433/KinesisLecture.pdf

that deals with the relationship between motion and its causes, namely forces and torques. "Dynamics" is often used in place of the word "kinesis" in many of the hard sciences.

> *Dimensionally Interactive Cyber Kinesis, which in a nutshell might be defined as the energy of God's self-aware Existence, decohering time and space in the Reality Dysfunction might also be thought of as how atoms "think." Cyber-Kinesis[42] is the metaphysical analog to what physicists call superstrings, which are particles (hadrons) rotating at the speed of light and moving in and out of multiple dimensions—also at the speed of light. Cyber-Kinesis is Superstring Theory personalized and applied to metaphysics, religion and science, and represents a new way of thinking about God, the forms, (or the Divine Ideas) and the concept of Universal Mind.*

God knows everything as it relates to Himself but God does not *have* thoughts; He *Is* His thoughts, as the great Thomas Aquinas states on multiple occasions. God having thoughts, as we understand thinking, might be said to be the beginning of space, time and matter or what is commonly known as creation. These "thoughts" can only occur outside of the unity of God's eternal Nature and are responsible for the world as we know it. These "thoughts" must extend between all forms of time and dimension but how can this be if there can be no change in Existence?

According to Aquinas, "an idea in God is identical to His Essence." This results in God taking the first "hit" by eternally withdrawing from His own Infinity to express Himself in a new way, in time.

---

42 This term was originally developed to understand how immoral acts might affect the matrix of our moral and spiritual consciousness in the 2001 book by Sean J. O'Reilly, *How to Manage Your Destructive Impulses with Cyber Kinetics: Redirect Sexual Energy and Discover Your More Spiritually Enlightened, Evolved Self,* 10 Speed Press, 2001.

> "Since therefore God is the effective cause of things, the perfection's of all things must pre-exist in God in a more eminent way...Inasmuch as He knows His own Essence perfectly, He knows it according to every mode in which it can be known... Now it can be known not only as it is in itself, but as it can be participated in by creatures...God does not understand things according to an idea existing outside Himself. Thus Aristotle (Metaph IX) rejects the opinion of Plato, who held that ideas existed of themselves, and not in the intellect. God is the similitude of all things according to His Essence; therefore, an idea in God is identical with His Essence." [43]

The Reality Dysfunction then, is the result of an infinite Being, *knowing Itself from the perspective of limitation*, or as to how It might be known or not known; imitated or not imitated; loved or not loved, etc. God's understanding does not occur outside Himself but the manifestation of this understanding, in term of relation, occurs outside Himself. This is the original "singularity" responsible for the Big Bang. The manifestation of the singularity is a translation of what God knows eternally—expressed within time. God's knowledge of Himself, perforce, includes all possibilities and all dimensions but possibility involves potential, which is not possible in Existence. Possibility, then, can only exist in a reality external to the Divine Mind.

UNIVOCITY AND EQUIVOCITY

All potentialities for good and evil are made possible by the Reality Dysfunction in a singular moment of Divine Consciousness in time that occurs *external* to God's Nature. There is some mysterious proportionality that occurs between God's eternal Existence and what is created in time. Aquinas referred to this as *proper proportionality*. Stephen Long, a Professor of Systematic Theology at Marquette University

---

43 Aquinas, Thomas, *Summa Theologica*, Q. 15, Art 3, Pt.1

who specializes in systematic theology, Christian ethics, and political theology notes that:

> "*Analogy, as understood by Aquinas, is a point between univocity (sameness) and equivocity (difference). So, Thomistic analogy holds together similarity and difference in such a way that the analogates cannot be reduced to either of these conditions.*"[44] *Trabbic notes that:* "*Analogy of (extrinsic) attribution introduces a relationship between the analogates; this is something that is missing from the analogy of proper proportionality but that would seem to be key in theology since creatures are really related to God as their cause.*"[45]

The difference between extrinsic and intrinsic analogy may seem like investigating the number of angels dancing on the head of a pin but the distinction is real enough. Intrinsic attribution of terms is univocal[46] whereas extrinsic attribution is equivocal.[47] Let us move beyond what the theologians are adept at repeating and attempt to understand these distinctions in a new way.

> *What God knows in a univocal way, in and through His eternal Nature, is manifested in time equivocally. This equivocal manifestation cannot occur in God, whose Nature, Mind and Affections are One but only externally in reference to His Nature. This is what we are calling the Reality Dysfunction. The Reality Dysfunction represents God's thoughts, as it were, understood or translated imperfectly, outside the Divine Essence, which is univocal.*

---

44 Trabbic Joseph, *The Analogy of Proper Proportionality in Steven Long's "Analogia Entis"*, page 1 http://www.academia.edu/16460175/The_Analogy_of_Proper_Proportionality_in_Steven_A._Longs_Analogia_Entis_
45 Ibid, page 3
46 Univocal Term: A term that has only one meaning. That is, it signifies only one thought, and therefore corresponds to only one definition.
47 Equivocal Term: A term that has a variety of different meanings. An equivocal term has completely different intentions once it's used. For instance, the term "state" can mean one of the American states or it can mean a state of mind or a state of matter, etc.

After the creation, God is said to have observed (in Genesis) that all that He made was good. (He did not say, however, that it was perfect.) Clearly this "goodness" of the creation was known from eternity but what makes it different is that it is now known within time, albeit in an equivocal and necessarily imperfect manner, in reference to a Nature where thoughts are equivalent to One Act of Existence. The idea that God's creation was perfect, as He might be said to be perfect, is not born out by what we see around us. The extraordinarily curious reference in Genesis 1:26 where God says: "Let us make them in our image" might be thought of as an early reference to the Divine Persons later identified within Christianity as the Trinity but it may also refer to the notion of an image as being derivative—for no image is the exact equivalent to what is reflected.

The question that any good theologian would ask is: why does God need to know Himself, outside Himself? The answer is that He doesn't. God creates, as it were, a derivative image of Himself, in creation, in order to be related to something—other than what He is—in His eternal Nature. God cannot change; he does not make things in one minute and the next not do so. He is not at once the Creator within Eternity and then the creator inside of time—the "then" does not exist for God. He also does not create evil within the Reality Dysfunction; it is simply the unfortunate result of allowing for freedom of choice—the gift of His own freedom, which is allowed within the context of less than perfect knowledge.

The Reality Dysfunction is God knowing Himself Outside Himself—in all ways—not because He has to but because He knows Himself eternally in all ways. This does not limit God in any way; it is simply a conscious aggregation of the entire essential order, as a contingent and derivative set, relative to and external to Existence in time. Much like a prism, the Reality Dysfunction simply separates Existence into "colors" in time. There is never anything but one form of eternal light, One Source, behind the manifestation of any contingent reality.[48]

---

48 The "real" is traditionally asserted to be composed of all that is potential and all that is actual.

Another way of thinking about it is, by analogy, like attempting to pour the ocean into a teacup. The Big Bang, caused by a "naked" singularity, to repeat the definition for emphasis, "is a one-dimensional point which contains a huge mass in an infinitely small space, where density and gravity become infinite and space-time curves infinitely, and where the laws of physics as we know them cease to operate."[49] The notion of a singularity, in this context, and even from the point of view of physics is not empirical science but philosophy that has been backed into, almost inadvertently, by physicists. The force of Existence, from a metaphysical perspective, is behind the singularity but the vessel cannot fully accept what it is receiving. This results in a kind of distortion between what can be received by matter in a three and four-dimensional configuration and multi-dimensional forces that are working within matter to more fully express the power of Existence.

*Even the notion of the singularity as a one-dimensional point containing an infinite amount of energy, **"not subject to the laws of physics"** is an analog to what might be better described metaphysically as the Reality Dysfunction. The difference being that the singularity is governed by a set of laws currently outside the purview of physics. These "laws" are part of a derivative consciousness that is produced by Existence "knowing Itself outside Itself." The algorithms between univocal and equivocal consciousness that create the singularity are subject to metaphysical inquiry and are part of the treasure house of philosophy.*

Energy is defined as "the capacity of a physical system to perform work." The infinite amount of energy and mass, possessed by the "naked" singularity, once it unfolds, creates dimensions effortlessly as infinite energy "works" to express Existence, which is its cause. This is the hidden meaning behind the forces of evolution augmented by natural selection, and it is the Reality Dysfunction, rather than the fall

---

49 http://www.physicsoftheuniverse.com/topics_blackholes_singularities.html

of man that is the source of our sorrows. The fundamental limitation of beings who do not possess perfect knowledge but seek it, due to the infinite force of Existence behind their contingency, are the circumstances that we find ourselves in within the Reality Dysfunction. God, in this scenario, has skin in the game. In my opinion, this is why Existence chose to incarnate as the Second Person of the Trinity and was crucified. It was not done just to expiate our "sins" but to make up for an original condition that is intimately related to both the creation and our freedom as sons and daughters of God. This teaching, hopefully, will enable mankind to understand God, who is Existence, in a new light.

God cannot possibly be concerned with how we approach or acknowledge Him. All ways are His ways, except those that are in contradiction to his goodness. Clearly, some ways of approaching God are more clearly aligned with what we know, relatively speaking, about God's goodness but the notion that we must kill others to ensure some correct understanding about God is so absurd that it must be forbidden by all religions. Any religion that does not allow God to compete for souls is not a religion that is in full alignment with the will of God. God cannot will evil but men can. Bringing ourselves and our culture into alignment with Existence and goodness is the essential political task of this millennium.

I

WHY THINGS ARE THE WAY THEY ARE

"There is only one science that could produce blindness on so large a scale, the science whose job it was to provide men with sight: philosophy. Since modern philosophy, in essence, is a concerted attack against the conceptual level of man's consciousness—a sustained attempt to invalidate reason, abstractions, generalizations, and any integration of knowledge—men have been emerging from universities, for many decades past, with the helplessness of epistemological savages, with no inkling of the nature, function, or practical application of principles. These men have been groping blindly for some direction through the bewildering mass of (to them) incomprehensible concretes in the daily life of a complex industrial civilization—groping, struggling, failing, giving up and perishing, unable to know in what manner they had acted as their own destroyers."

—Ayn Rand,
The Anatomy of Compromise

Chapter 1

THE METAPHYSICS OF LIGHT

*"All matter has an internal property of energy. This energy is related to the electrons traveling in orbits around the nucleus of the atoms. As the electrons change orbital levels, energy is emitted or absorbed. For example, if we burn a sheet of paper, energy is given off, which we see as a flame. The matter in the filament of a light bulb emits light when it is excited by an electrical current. The term that we use for emitting energy from matter is called radiation. Radiation is often referred to as electromagnetic radiation because the emitting energy has both electrical and magnetic properties. The emitted energy is trans-mitted at a wavelength determined by the nature of the matter and the forces acting on it. **The human eye can only detect a very small range of wavelengths of radiation.** What it detects we call light. Physicists often refer to it as visible light.[1] "*
What this means is that we live in a sea of electromagnetic radiation—most of which we cannot see.

---

1   *What is Light and How Is It Produced?* G. A. Davis, J. D. Keller, Pearson Allyn, Bacon Prentice Hall

3

THE FORCE OF LIGHT

Light functions as a metaphor for goodness throughout the world's spiritual literature, and darkness as the absence of light, is usually thought of as a metaphor for evil. Light commonly indicates an energy source, whereas darkness is the absence of this source energy. Light is, therefore, often associated with Existence as the visible manifestation of that which is hidden. The Rig-Veda of India (1500 B.C.) uses the image of the sun as a metaphor for Divinity.

> *"Behold the rays of Dawn, like heralds, lead on high*
> *The Sun, that men may see the great all-knowing god.*
> *The stars slink off like thieves, in company with Night,*
> *Before the all-seeing eye, whose beams reveal his presence." [2]*

The ratio between Divine Light, as the manifestation of an energy Source, and its relationship with contingent existence is the subject of the metaphysics of light. This relationship is another way of understanding the dynamic between Existence considered as the ultimate Source and the participated existence of being, which is dependent on this Source. Light is a secondary effect, in other words, of a process. The sun, for example, produces light as a by-product of the fusion of four hydrogen atoms, which fuse under the immense pressure and weight of hydrogen within the sun, to become one atom of helium. The extra energy that is released during this process is the electromagnetic radiation that we see as visible light. Philosophers and theologians have long used the dynamics of visible light to express analogies involving derivative or secondary aspects of existence that appear to be contingent or dependent on a Source.

"Plato's Idea of the Good is not spoken of figuratively; it is the spiritual light. However, it was Plotinus who first developed a metaphysics of light, considering light no longer as a physical substance.

---

2   http://www.sacred-texts.com/hin/hmvp/hmvp10.htm

From the One emanates immaterial light, radiating outward, growing dimmer and dimmer until it shades off into darkness (a privation of light), which is matter. From the One also proceeds Nous (thought, mind), which knows all things simultaneously in an eternal now. From Nous emanates the world soul; from the latter emanate human souls and finally material beings. They do not lack light completely, for they are illumined by form, which is considered the exteriorization of the intelligible. Here light starts its ecstatic return to its origin and proves that the sensible and the intelligible are bound together. Such unity allows for mystical and prophetical experience and knowledge…In later centuries an amalgamation of Christian, Jewish, and Arabian thought led to a fuller development of the metaphysics of light. Some Arabian and Jewish philosophers saw light as a substance or a power. The literature of the Talmud and Midrash speaks of light as the garment of God…Through a good moral life man participates in the light of the Intelligence. Similar doctrines were held by the Arabs, mainly by Alfarabi, Avicenna, and Algazel, who combined Aristotelian, Neoplatonic, and Oriental thought."[3]

We can only understand the following quote from Corinthians 2, 3:18, for example, by mentally invoking the dynamics of light as the image of something more profound.

> *"We all, with unveiled face, beholding as in a mirror the glory of the Lord, are being transformed into the same image from glory to glory, all this comes from the Lord who is the Spirit."*

Looking at the Reality Dysfunction from the perspective of physics, there is a metaphysical utility that can be derived, analogically, in order to further the theological and philosophical concerns of almost all the major religions. We see, for example, that energy equals mass times the speed of light squared ($E=mc2$). Why do we have to square

---

3   Schultzinger, Carolyn Ewa *"Light, Metaphysics of"* New Catholic Encyclopedia, 2nd. ed. vol. 8 (Detroit: Gale, 2003), pp. 583-584. ©2013 Catholic University of America

the speed of light? "It has to do with the nature of energy. **When something is moving four times as fast as something else, it doesn't have four times the energy but rather 16 times the energy**—in other words, that figure is squared. So the speed of light squared is the conversion factor that decides just how much energy lies within a walnut or any other chunk of matter. And because the speed of light squared is a huge number—90,000,000,000 (km/sec)^2—the amount of energy bound up into even the smallest mass is truly mind-boggling."[4]

"Here's an example. If you could turn every one of the atoms in a paper clip into pure energy—leaving no mass whatsoever—the paper clip would yield 18 kilotons of TNT. That's roughly the size of the bomb that destroyed Hiroshima in 1945. On Earth, however, there is no practical way to convert a paper clip or any other object entirely to energy. It would require temperatures and pressures greater than those at the core of our sun."[5] These incredible figures are also mirrored in the energy present in each cubic centimeter of space. The energy that creates space and time is even more dramatic than that which creates matter.

> "When physicists calculate the minimum amount of energy in a wave form, they find that every cubic centimeter of [empty] space has more energy than the total energy of all the matter in the known universe."[6]

Where is all this energy coming from? Why does this *conversion factor* between energy and matter that appears to take place at 4 times the speed of light and with at least 16 times the force of the speed of light even exist?

> The convertibility of matter and energy, (E=mc^2) first described by Einstein, might also be thought of, analogously, as the signature equation of the Reality Dysfunction, whereby Existence in

4 http://www.pbs.org/wgbh/nova/einstein/lrk-hand-emc2expl.html#fea_top
5 Ibid
6 Talbot, Michael, *The Holographic Universe*, Harper Perennial 1991, pg. 51

the form of Infinite energy, creates matter, time and space in one single movement outside of Itself. This is a movement of infinite expansion moving at least 4 times the speed of light and with enormous compression at 16 times the force of the speed of light,[7] which, in short, is the micro and the macro universes made and understood in one glance—exterior to the nature of Existence.

This might be thought of as the ultimate meaning of the "Big Bang", an idea which was first developed—not by Edwin Hubble—as it is often misattributed but in 1927 by the Belgian Catholic priest Georges Lemaître. "He proposed an expanding model for the universe to explain the observed redshifts[8] of spiral nebulae, and calculated the Hubble law [before Hubble confirmed the same findings]. He based his theory on the work of Einstein and De Sitter, and independently derived Friedmann's equations[9] for an expanding universe."[10] Einstein greatly admired Lemaître, and after listening to a lecture by Lemaître in California in 1933, he publically stated that "This is the most beautiful and satisfactory explanation of creation to which I have ever listened."[11]

Lemaître noted that "If the world has begun with a single quantum, the notions of space and time would altogether fail to have any meaning at the beginning; they would only begin to have a sensible meaning when the original quantum had been divided into a sufficient number of quanta. If this suggestion is correct, the beginning of the world happened a little before the beginning of space and time."[12] This

---

7   Ibid
8   "Redshift" is the observed phenomenon of longer wave lengths of light in relation to age and speed. Redder means an increase in wavelength which can be algorithmically related to distance.
9   "The Friedmann equations are a set of equations in physical cosmology that govern the expansion of space in homogeneous and isotropic models of the universe within the context of general relativity." WP
10 WP
11 http://www.catholiceducation.org/en/science/faith-and-science/a-day-without-yester-day-georges-lemaitre-amp-the-big-bang.html
12 Ibid

"beginning" is, in fact, metaphysical evidence for the Reality Dysfunction or something very like it.

Lemaître understood, using both science and theology, that the creation of time and space must be a reflection of an eternal understanding of God within an incomprehensible matrix that we can only approach via its effects. The potentiality of matter and energy, and the creation of time and space exists in relation to something that is pure Actuality, by way of non-possession of anything but Itself. Existence, energy and mass then, appear to be dynamically related. (We will explore this concept in detail as the book unfolds.)

UNIVERSAL MIND AND SOURCE CODE

Universal Mind is what the ancients also referred to as the Demiurge or the Nous of Plotinus: a derivative form of Divine Consciousness that is limited by the total set of relations that constitute the created universe in relation to the Divine Essence. The word "demiurge" is an English word from a Latinized form of the Greek, which means literally "public worker", and which was originally a common noun meaning "craftsman" or "artisan", but gradually it came to mean "producer" and eventually "creator". The philosophical usage and the proper noun derive from Plato's Timaeus, written c. 360 BC, in which the demiurge is presented as the creator of the universe." [13]

Universal Mind might be thought of as the first synthesis of the Reality Dysfunction, as Divine Consciousness, after exploding in being to the farthest star, in the most distant universe, and across all time begins to return, *in time,* to its point of no origin, which is Itself. The *reality function* is an expression of Universal Mind, as the all seeks to return to the All, by bringing the universe back into a deeper and more profound alignment with the Creator. This *reditus* or "return" is modulated by God's knowledge of Himself outside Himself. This modulation is based on a ratio between Divine Consciousness that is

13 (http://montalk.net/gnosis/171/corruption-of-the-demiurge)

equivocal in time, to a univocal Eternal consciousness, which is outside of time.

> *This ratio, which is equivocal, might be thought of as an "exchange" or transcendental algorithm that operates in multiple dimensions, between something that does not exist, which paradoxically, makes everything exist.*

The only rational alternative to this idea is that Existence operates by fiat or by magic with no intermediary processes of any kind. However, based on the evidence that metaphysics and science presents, this does not appear to be the case.

This "exchange" may be modulated by the complex interactions of the quantum world and String Theory described by physicists, which has not yet articulated the algorithm between that world and the hidden world of Existence. The complex relations between particles that might be considered local and non-local (as quantum waves) or manifest and un-manifested, operate through a multi-dimensional interface that likely has an operative set of principles that goes beyond the stochastic model offered by physicists. Operating at 4 times the speed of light and with 16 time the force of the speed of light,[14] we might think of this as Existence's stamp on reality and when more concrete evidence for it is discovered, it will change the way we understand the world around us. Sri Aurobindo described this derivative form of Divine Existence as the Overmind and as an "ocean of stable lightning."[15] Whether described as Universal Mind or Overmind, the principle is the same: Existence Itself cannot change. What changes is some manifestation of Itself in space and time.

Universal Mind/Overmind cannot download, so to speak, Existence and so is limited *in relation* to Existence. This set of algorithmic relations or *Source Code* is so complex and yet so effortlessly engaged

14 http://www.pbs.org/wgbh/nova/einstein/lrk-hand-emc2expl.html#fea_top
15 Satprem, Sri Aurobindo, *The Adventure of Consciousness*, Sri Aurobindo, Ashram Trust, 1968

by Existence that it can be easily mistaken for God. What many people think of as God is not God at all but rather an effect or a way that we think about what we know about God, albeit in a limited way. The ancient Jewish prohibition and current Islamic prohibition of representing God as a graven image is not without justification or merit. The tendency to equate God with what we know about God is a perennial human temptation. What we know about God is what we know; it is derivative and can never correspond exactly to what God Is. Infinite energy, consciousness and love cannot be comprehended or captured in a net of concepts and presented as "this". There is no "this", "that" or "there" where God is concerned. "This", "that" and "there" exist only in relation to something that is beyond our ability to comprehend, except in some sort of derivative or abstract format. The ancient Chinese attempted to describe this puzzling relationship in the *Tao* or the Ta-Hua, which was known as the Great Becoming. The Ta-Hua indicates a dynamic relationship between Existence, space and time. This dynamism is now being rediscovered by physicists within the parameters suggested by String Theory.

> *"Ta-Hua (Tao) makes every modality of being in the universe a dynamic change rather than a static structure. A piece of stone, a blade of grass, a horse, a human being, a spirit and Heaven all form a continuum. They are all integrated by the pervasive Ch'i (vital force and material force which constitutes both matter and energy) that penetrates every dimension of existence and functions as the constitutive element for each modality of being."* [16]

Why is any of this important to an understanding of politics and the soul in the twenty-first century? We cannot articulate the importance of the invisible world of spiritual and moral values without articulating or contrasting it with the limited world presented by empirical science. As the great Walker Percy noted:

---

16 Eliade, Mircea; *Encyclopedia of Religion*

"...The shattering of the old dream of the Enlightenment—that an objective-explanatory-causal science can discover and set forth all the knowledge of which man is capable...that dream is drawing to a close. The existentialists have taught us that what man is cannot be grasped by the sciences of man. The case is rather that man's science is one of the things that man does, a mode of existence. Another mode is speech. Man is not merely a higher organism responding to and controlling his environment. He is, in Heidegger's words, that [*being in the world*] whose calling it is to find a name for Being, to give testimony to it, and to provide for it a clearing."[17] Our work in this world is, however, more than just providing a clearing for being. Teilhard de Chardin, for example, shows how "all human efforts to create a better world are really ways to further God's ...project, and so our actions are much more significant than just ways for us to get higher grades on our heavenly report card, as some traditional [forms of spirituality] would infer."[18]

Chardin's view of the universe, as moving towards and being part of a larger Divine project, indicates "that In addition to the two classical ways of picturing God—either far away in heaven (transcendent) or living within your heart (immanent)— [a new view of] spirituality presents a third, much more comprehensive way to view our relationship with God. God is the One in whom we live and move and have our being. This is a way that was recognized in ancient times but never [fully] emphasized by formal religions."[19]

METAPHYSICAL AMNESIA

At this point, and as you read some of the italicized asides,[20] you may be thinking that the author is an unhinged polymath, but please be

---

17 Percy Walker, *The Message in a Bottle*, pg. 158, Picador, (Farrar, Straus and Giroux), New York, NY.
18 http://www.teilhardforbeginners.com/
19 Ibid
20 All items in italics that are not referenced are the author's thoughts expressed from the perspective of a deeper and more creative sense of self that may be thought of (in the possible sense) of being linked to Universal Mind.

aware that the distinctions, so dear to many theologians and metaphysicians, are being recast in order to harness the full power of metaphysics. All of these seemingly odd concepts will be explained as the chapters unfold and we examine the treasure house of philosophy. The Greek notions of matter and form, for example, are ways of understanding how patterns in the mind of God enable potential to exist. This is, of course, completely foreign to the empirical mind, which only admits to the existence of energy and various quantum processes between sub-atomic particles.

The *hylomorphism*[21] of Aristotle and the Greeks was a way of metaphysically describing how change occurs in matter when the potential pattern exists in a higher state than can be observed. This is classical Rationalism as the "form" cannot be touched, tasted or heard. The idea of form is, instead, imputed by both intuition and deduction much in the same way that atoms were hypothesized by the Greeks to be the building blocks of matter. The notion of "form" or what is also known as "essence" was a way of describing a pattern that seems to be held in common by things that possessive repetitive commonalities. All cats, for instance, seem to participate in what might be called "catness" but what is catness? Is it merely a random association of patterns and energetic relations that have evolved over time, in response to environmental stimuli, or are the patterns augmented or guided by a timeless intelligence?

Many of the ancients seemed to take it for granted that there would be a relationship between the natures of different existing things and the mind of the Divinity. This is an early form of Rationalism. Trying to understand this relationship between things that both endure and change, and the mind of the God, which cannot be said to change was a concept that preoccupied many early Greek metaphysicians. Not all Greek philosophers, however, subscribed to the view that a Divine

---

21 Hylomorphism (or hylemorphism) is a philosophical theory developed by Aristotle, which conceives being (ousia) as a compound of matter and form (essence). The word is a 19th-century term formed from the Greek words ὕλη hyle, "wood, matter" and μορφή, morphē, "form." [WP]

force was behind all existing things. Democritus, a pre-Socratic philosopher who lived in the period 460 to 370 B.C. and his mentor Leucippas were, as nearly as history can tell, the founders of the notion of atomism. Their early version of atomic theory stated:

> *"The universe is composed of two elements: the atoms and the void in which they exist and move." According to Democritus atoms were miniscule quantities of matter. Democritus hypothesized that atoms cannot be destroyed, differ in size, shape and temperature, are always moving, and are invisible."* [22]

There were, of course, no electrons or protons hypothesized since the Greeks did not have the tools of high energy physics but this is an astounding example of a metaphysical idea that anticipated modern physics by several thousand years. Democritus also did not believe that any sort of causality, outside of the mathematical relationships between atoms, was responsible for the world we see around us. Democritus was an early scientific agnostic and could be said to be the father of empiricism. The Roman poet Lucretius, who lived around 50 B.C. was the first to re-introduce the ideas of Democritus and Epicurus to the Roman public in his six-part poem *De Rerum Natura* (On the Nature of Things). This book, when recovered by Poggio Bracciolini from a medieval monastery and translated, had a powerful impact on Renaissance thinking. Epicurus believed that a focus on the afterlife and the potential wrath of the Gods for misbehavior was the cause of much human unhappiness.

This message fell upon many receptive ears in a post-medieval culture steeped in an inordinate fear of God. The subsequent cultural influence of this translation was documented in Stephen Greenblatt's wonderful book, *The Swerve: How the World Became Modern*, which shows how the emergence of the scientific frame of mind came from a fusion of ancient and new ideas that began with the recovery of the wisdom of pre-Christian philosophers. An unkinder interpretation of the "swerve" would be to see it as the beginning of a movement away from Rationalism or the first steps towards an unqualified academic acceptance of Empiricism.

What the ancient philosophers, (aside from Democritus, Leucippas and Lucretius) understood as essence or form and the Chinese understood as an essential dynamism between nature and Existence, we understand as various multi-dimensional relations between subatomic particles or phase changes between quantum states. These concepts are not as far off from each other as they might seem at first glance. The Schrödinger Equation, which will be discussed later, describes how change occurs between quantum states over time. The Schrödinger Equation might be thought of as a kind of modern equivalent to both atomism and hylomorphism. Form, in its simplest iteration, is a potential pattern within Existence that can be copied or changed. It is interesting to note, in this context, that Democritus believed that free will was caused by the tendency or ability of atoms to "swerve."[23]

The recovery of independent thinking, brought about by the Renaissance's dipping into the treasures of the past and holding them up as a mirror to the light of truth, unobscured by ritual and religious pieties, simultaneously freed the human mind from ideas that were no longer working but also enslaved the incipient modern mind to a new set of ideas that would later obscure the same light that was revealed by the ancients. Empirical science, by focusing solely on the results of experimental evidence, suppressed rational thought by making it subject to a limited dimensionality. Who has ever seen love for example? We all know, intuitively, what it is but it is also part of a hidden but very real world that science, generally speaking, cannot not access.

The reframing of the concepts of essence and Existence, as algorithms of Dimensionally Interactive Cyber Kinesis, within the context of a new understanding of time afforded by the Reality Dysfunction,

23 Greenblatt, Stephen, *The Swerve: How the World Became Modern*, W. W. Norton & Company, September 4, 2012

might be thought of as one of the more significant developments in metaphysics to have occurred since The Renaissance; it also represents the rebirth of a new kind of Rationalism. In this new epistemology, our minds and God's "mind" are on a proportioned continuum of being and energy in the Reality Dysfunction.

This makes the understanding of what "being" and Existence are and how they might be understood as being qualitatively different from their matter and energy twin, a critical human and cultural enterprise. Terms like "essence" and "form" sound alien to modern ears, when the world is understood to be made up of matter and energy but what will be revealed to the reader is that the ancient ideas of matter and form are concepts that have new relevance in the context of multi-dimensional theory (we will get to that) and the quantum decoherence that occurs in the Reality Dysfunction.

Superstring Theory, which describes particles as rotating and moving in and out of dimensions at the speed of light, and the notion of "branes"[24] or points that can be ascribed to different dimensional locations, take physics back beyond atomism to the notions of essence, form and *substance*[25] with substance being the composition of matter and form. While the metaphysical iteration may not exactly match the science, there is a sufficient overlap to indicate a certain complementarity of viewpoint that is worth exploring. The notion of "branes" as being the twenty-first century non-local equivalent of "form" or essence will help you to understand how close metaphysics and physics really are to a revolutionary, new understanding of reality based on the metaphysics of light.

The idea that superstrings might be thought of as a product of, or metaphor for Dimensionally Interactive Cyber-Kinesis[26] will,

---

24 Branes are mathematical objects created by superstrings. "In string theory and related theories such as supergravity theories, a brane is a physical object that generalizes the notion of a point particle to higher dimensions. For example, a point particle can be viewed as a brane of dimension zero, while a string can be viewed as a brane of dimension one." [WP]

25 "that which stands under"

26 Sean J. O'Reilly, *How to Manage Your Destructive Impulses with Cyber Kinetics: Redirect*

no doubt, outrage many scientists but they won't be the only ones. If you are a philosophical or theological conservative, you may want to shake your fist at the author for his audacity in defining "being" as *Dimensionally Interactive Cyber Kinesis* in the same breath that essence and Existence are presented. You may want to shout out that God cannot change and that to suggest that *movement without movement* or that transcendental algorithms enable God to affect a seemingly virtual or decohered reality is ontological gibberish.

You would claim that being and time could not possibly be the result of the Reality Dysfunction but you might begin to wonder. Then you would hear about the proposed Fifth Law of Thermodynamics and your ears would prick up. Later you would hear about the deconstruction of causality by Thomas Hobbes, John Locke, Bishop Berkeley, David Hume, Immanuel Kant, Alfred Korzybski and Jacques Derrida and you would pause. Then you would see, later on, the assault on modern psychology, which is described as a form of *psycho-bondage* and you might sniff with approval. And finally, when you see that the ideas presented in this book are based not only on concepts developed by John Scottus Eriugena but on some of the foundational ideas of Aristotle and Thomas Aquinas, then you might be moved by a grudging curiosity and you would read on.

Political conservatives, in some circles, might be disturbed at this book's linking of the political concepts of the Founding Fathers to arguments first generated by Catholic medieval philosophers. However, the ideas of the Founding Fathers grew out of a deeper and richer soil than the deliberations of John Locke or the brilliance of Washington, Jefferson and Adams. Psychologists and sociologists, likewise, may bristle at the presentation of Freud's concepts of the id and the unconscious as superficial explanations of human behavior in relation to the more detailed understanding of human nature held by Plato, Aristotle and Aquinas. The ideas of "relation" and the

"divine energies" are so far off the modern map as to be virtually unknown outside of specialized philosophical circles. Our civilization
suffers from amnesia when it comes to metaphysics[27] and this book
will attempt to show the reader why.

HOW THIS BOOK BEGAN

I began to formulate and explore the practical application of metaphysical and philosophical ideas as a member of a Boy Scout Explorer
post in 1967. This group was led by New Age pioneer George Simon,
who believed as many of us did in the 1960's, in the congruence between eastern religions and many Christian values. Many years later,
as a volunteer teacher of Ethics at the former Lorton Penitentiary in
Virginia, in 1989, I saw a way of using metaphysics to help change
lives. Teaching at Lorton gave me a first-hand opportunity to see how
philosophical ideas from ancient sources might still have the power to
motivate the human mind. I later took some of these proven concepts,
and by engaging some of the more vexing philosophical and moral
problems, much like "outlier" or outside-the-box thinkers Walter Rus-
sell, Gustaf Stromberg, Colin Wilson, L. Ron Hubbard, Peter Tomp-
kins, Allan Watts, Fred Alan Wolf, Gary Zukav, Ken Wilber, Howard
Bloom, and Jared Diamond, attempted to create a useful synthesis that
would function as a time-spanning message from the past to the future.

I originally developed and wrote most of this book during the early 1990's. Twenty-two years later, based on current moral and political
trends, many of the original ideas have been reworked and updated
with more recent information. The original title was, *Politics and the
Soul: Adventures on the River of Gold.* This was the precursor to the
more controversial book that followed: *How to Manage Your Destructive Impulses with Cyber-Kinetics* published in 2001. The first chapter
of the current book, entitled, *The Metaphysics of Light* serves to provide

---

27 Metaphysics attempts to clarify the fundamental ideas by which people understand
the world, e.g., existence, objects and their properties, space and time, cause and effect,
and possibility.

a context for some transforming and complex ideas, which the original work never fully developed. The second chapter, *How We Understand Existence*, introduces the reader to the metaphysical background of Existence and the third chapter, *The Time War and Two Kinds of Physics*, introduces new ideas not commonly seen in either metaphysics or physics. The fourth chapter, *Politics and the Soul*, is the first chapter of the older book but it too has been modified to reflect more current thinking.

I am certainly not the only writer to attempt to link the great minds of the past and the absence of their ideas to our current political and social difficulties. Ayn Rand, Taylor Caldwell, Walter Lipmann, Walker Percy, Richard Hofstadter, George Gilder, Allen Bloom, E.D. Hirsh Jr., Michael Savage, Bill O'Reilly, Andrew P. Napolitano, Ann Coulter, Mark Bauerlein and Michael Walsh, to name a few, have all decried the anti-intellectualism that characterizes both academia and the media to the detriment of rational political policy. Few of them, however, seem to have found and elaborated on the root cause of almost all social incoherence and disorder: the failure to identify and advert to what theory of causality and Existence motivates our intellectual, moral and political views.

This problem, as previously stated, recapitulates the fundamental divide between Empiricism and Rationalism. This divide has a significant history that is worth reflecting on. The utility and benefits of empiricism cannot be doubted for civilization but it cannot be allowed to trample, without restraint, on metaphysical and rational systems of thought that have taken several thousand years to develop. The moral vacuum created by empirical science makes the recovery of rationalism a moral and political priority.

Brian Davies, the series editor for *Great Medieval Thinkers*, notes that "The origins of modern science lie in the conviction that the world is open to rational investigation and is orderly rather than chaotic—a conviction that came fully to birth, and was systematically explored and developed during the Middle Ages (600 to 1500 AD). And it is in medieval thinking that we find some of the most sophisticated and rigorous discussions in the area of philosophy and theology ever offered for human consumption." [28]

There have been many thinkers who have covered some but not all of the same territory in what might be called the high country between morality and Existence. Socrates, Aristotle, Plato, Scotus Eriugena, Avicenna, Aquinas, Duns Scotus, Bishop Berkeley, John Locke, Hegel, Sri Aurobindo, Martin Heidegger, Alfred N. Whitehead, Etienne Gilson, Joseph Pieper, Kung and Karl Rahner, to name a few of the more famous and well-known philosophers and theologians, have all grappled with the effect God's knowledge may or may not have on the material universe.

> *Understanding how an immutable or unchangeable Being can act within and without time, or affect change without changing Itself, might be said to be the puzzle of the ages. It is no wonder that the modern mind dispenses with the problem altogether by asserting that energy is neither created nor destroyed, thus ending the religious dichotomy between created and uncreated, or essence and Existence.*

Relating a Divine Person or Persons to observable and scientific processes is no small enterprise but the attempt, if metaphysics, science and theology are to move forward and have greater moral and political relevance, outside of the confines of their respective disciplines, must be made.

The word exist means "to have being in a specified place or under certain conditions." In philosophical circles, to exist means to exist out of something or by virtue of something else, but what is existence? Both Aristotle and Aquinas argued that God's existence is self-caused. The former argued for an Unmoved Mover, the latter for the "Ipsum Esse", an essence which is its own existence. Existence, as philosopher

---

28 John Scottus Eriugena, Carabine, Diedre, Professor and Director of the Institute of Ethics and Development Studies, Uganda Martyrs University; Oxford University Press, copyright 2000, page VIIII

Frederick D. Wilhelmsen argued, does not exist. It *is* pure act or what he referred to as 'radical extramentality' in his book, *The Paradoxical Structure of Existence.* The universe exists, according to Wilhelmsen, through something that does not itself exist out of any known matrix other than itself. Everything that we see in the universe has existence; "it has being in a specific place or under certain conditions." God's being has no specific place, nor does it have conditions other than Itself.

The historically affiliated notion of "essence" or 'form' is simply one way of trying to algorithmically describe how Existence imparts be-ing to existing things. Another way of looking at this is to ask, "How does Being (with a capital "B") as in Existence (which makes Itself exist) make be-ings, which only possess existence?" The notion of Cyber-Kinesis enables us to think about the relationship between the Divine Ideas and the forms as a Transcendental Algorithm. Understanding the relationship between matter and form in this way may seem like mere panpsychism[29] but it is backed up by what we see occurring in nature through the lens of modern physics.

The First Law of Thermodynamics, for example, is a version of the law of conservation of energy, adapted for thermodynamic systems. The law of conservation of energy states that the total energy of an isolated system is constant; energy can be transformed from one form to another, but cannot be created or destroyed. Note that the idea is based on 'an isolated system'. *What if the system is not isolated?* The First Law of Thermodynamics, commonly understood to be that energy is neither created nor destroyed, removes the metaphysical dichotomy between essence and Existence but it tends to impoverish philosophical discourse. If energy is neither created nor destroyed what else is there to be said about it other than discovering the laws of mathematics and physics? God, as His own Existence and the First Law of Thermodynamics, whereby energy is neither created nor destroyed are ideas that are almost mirror images of each other, except for the moral and

---

29 "In philosophy, panpsychism is the view that consciousness, mind or soul (psyche) is a universal feature of all things, and the primordial feature from which all others are derived." [WP]

intellectual consequences which follow from adopting either position.

How we think about the concept of existence, consequently, affects how we think about both morality and politics. As Bill Clinton once famously remarked, in a different but related context, "it depends on what you mean by 'is'." Indeed, it does! This book attempts to outline an answer about the relationship of Existence to morality and politics for the modern, educated reader and also provides a vital philosophy based on the Code[30] of the Founding Fathers and many other cultural sources for effective social change.

There seems to be an impetus in every era, where multiple individuals unconnected with each other, (at least from their point of view) seem to converge on the same subject. As I reviewed the original manuscript in the light of more recent scholarship, it became clear to me that some of the work in this book independently developed some of the ideas of John Scottus Eriugena, a ninth century Irish philosopher; aspects of Process Philosophy based on Hegelian insights; Kenotic Theology; and the work of Karl Rahner—without my previously being familiar with what was already well-underway in this area—even more than twenty years ago. This is not due to any special ability on my part; it simply shows how useful ideas will converge and continue to re-emerge until they are resolved.

My own understanding and formulation of the dynamic relationship between the classical Greek concepts of essence and Existence is based on a life-long fascination with the relation of unchangeable Ideas in the Divine mind and their effect on the material order, which is subject to change. Philosophers have tried to understand this imputed relationship between the uncreated Creator and the created in many ways over the centuries. The notions of essence and Existence and matter and form are, in the simplest iteration, ways of understanding and framing how the One can produce the Many.

Physicists understand matter and form in an entirely different

---

30 The Founders' Code, as it is referred to towards the end of this book, is the moral 'system' that the Founding Fathers used to create the Declaration of Independence and the Constitution. It represents the common moral inheritance of the western world.

way. The idea of sub-atomic particles, known collectively as *hadrons*, manifesting as both wave and particles is a similar attempt to understand how the One can be many. All are trying to grasp the mechanics of how things appear in the world. In the words of the Irish poet, Dylan Thomas, they are trying to comprehend, "the force that through the green fuse drives the flower."

EXISTENCE AND THE REALITY DYSFUNCTION

Aristotle states that the Unmoved Mover ("that which moves without being moved") is a self-caused being without potentiality. The complexities of the visible world, which are clearly in flux and temporal are not self-caused but dependent in some way on the Unmoved Mover. One way of thinking about essence and Existence is to assert that Existence is the ultimate source that underlies the universe but that the algorithmic transmission and translation of Existence into the particular and finite still remains hidden and mysterious.

What does the metaphysical 'system' between the motor of the universe and the four wheels of reality really look like? Is there a kind of 'transmission' or does it work like magic with the Divine simply creating out of nothing with no intermediary process or algorithm of transformation to observe and catalog? Plato believed the forms were Ideas in the mind of God that existed separately in their own eternal universe and influenced the world of men. Plato and Aristotle were both well aware that there could be no change in God (otherwise God would not be God) but that change had to be accounted for by some rational process. Both Plato's "Ideas" and Aristotle's, later hylomorphic theory, which mediated change through the forms, were early attempts to describe the linkage between heaven and earth or between the universe and an Entity that does not change.

The opinion of many Christian philosophers is that neither Plato nor Aristotle completely succeeded because they didn't sufficiently link the transmission of Existence, via a process, to existing things. The

Christian perspective, if put in a nutshell, would be that God powers the Ideas or the forms—that they are contingent upon His Existence in order to enjoy a derivative or secondary kind of existence. God is, unfortunately, and from this perspective often thought of, whether we like it or not, as "the ghost in the machine." This was not what Aquinas intended, although it is hard to see how this characterization can be avoided.

Aquinas spoke of relations that were real to the creature but not so to God. This was closer to the Aristotelian position in that the Unmoved Mover, by the excellence of its Existence, simply attracted the rest of reality to imitate It without any change occurring in Itself. The great Aquinas, who stood on Aristotle's shoulders, can also be queried from the perspective afforded by modern physics. How are essences linked to God's Existence? What are the algorithms between essence and Existence? Aquinas claims that Existence posits things into Existence based on its knowledge and love of Itself and that God and His ideas are One in the Divine Nature but no further mechanism of participation is described or sought. What Aquinas did with his particular formulation of essence and Existence was to create a believable algorithm between time and eternity!

Aquinas' notion of a *proper proportionality* between Existence and being is simply an algorithmic restatement of the relationship between matter and form from the perspective of the Divine Ideas.[31] The translation or primary mechanism, if you will, of how proportionality might occur between the Mind of God and existing things does not seem to be adequately reflected on by metaphysicians bent on merely reproducing old ideas as clearly as possible for future generations. The Reality Dysfunction, or the notion of God knowing Himself, Outside Himself in the creation of time makes it possible to understand the

---

31 There is a long discussion of this subject in: Steven A. Long, *Analogia Entis: On The Analogy of Being, Metaphysics, and the Act of Faith*, University of Notre Dame Press, 2011, 146 pp. A link to an abbreviated analysis by Thomas Osbourne Jr. is here: http://ndpr.nd.edu/news/30849-analogia-entis-on-the-analogy-of-being-metaphysics-and-the-act-of-faith/

notion of proper proportionality in an entirely different way.

The complexity of particle physics, particularly as it might be articulated by Super String Theory, makes a deeper understanding of proper proportionality necessary. It is not simply enough for the Jewish, Christian or Islamic theologian to say that God makes all things be without change or motion as if He were simply a giant, invisible magnet attracting and repelling. The physical universe seems to operate on a coherent and discoverable system of some kind. How can creation be understood from both a scientific and a metaphysical perspective that doesn't simply repeat the old pieties?

> *"The task, is not so much so see what no one has yet seen, but to think what nobody has yet thought, about that which everybody sees."*
>
> —Erwin Shrödinger

Is it possible, without ever fully understanding the Mind of God, to approach the problem of the One and the Many from an entirely different angle? Metaphysically speaking, this is a very difficult enterprise. Aquinas, for example, states: "I agree unqualifiedly that God actually knows an infinity of things, absolutely."[32] He goes on to indicate that "the infinity of items that God knows is in no way adequate ontologically to the infinity which He himself is."[33] What Aquinas is stating is that there is a ratio between what God knows and what He is—at least in terms of how we might speak about God. Thomistic metaphysicians would argue that there is no need for God to "excogitate"[34] Himself in

---

32 Dewan, Lawrence, O.P.; *St. Thomas, James Ross, and Exemplarism* from The American Catholic Philosophical Quarterly, Volume LXV, Spring 1991, Issue no. 2, pg. 231, Catholic University of America, Washington D.C. 20064.Citation DV 2, 9 (DV refers to the *Quaestiones Disputatae de Vertitate*)

33 Ibid

34 Maurer, Armand, *James Ross on the Divine Ideas: A Reply*; American Catholic Philosophical Quarterly, Volume LXV, Spring 1991, Issue no. 2, pg. 213, Catholic University of America, Washington D.C. 20064

that an idea in the mind of God is identical to the Divine Essence but acknowledge that what God is, ultimately, can be distinguished, if only for purposes of argument, from what He knows.

There has never been, as near as can be determined, a satisfactory answer as to how God can know things other than Himself through Himself without simultaneously asserting that His knowledge of things that *might be* can only be mediated proportionately through His Essence. Proportionately how? In other words, God knows all things that might be through His own excellence or through His own eternal knowledge of how He might be imitated. What God knows is identical to the Divine Essence and yet does not exist before it exists. God is His own Existence and things only exist contingently because of His Existence.

This is, of course, the standard Thomistic and Catholic answer to the question of God's foreknowledge of creation. It is, however, also a circular answer to a metaphysical question that may have additional layers of meaning and causality. Postulating that God can know Himself, outside Himself, in the Reality Dysfunction, provides a compelling explanation for the world as we experience it and the evolutionary processes observed by science. Time and space are, from the perspective of the Reality Dysfunction, created by the Divine's eternal knowledge of Itself—in reference to Itself. In other words, God knows Himself, not only as He is in Himself but outside Himself, as other than Himself. Whether or not this is necessary or consequential, in reference to His Nature, are two different questions, which due to the voluminous literature on the subject, we will not attempt to answer in detail.

What can be safely asserted is that time is either eternal, as Aristotle may have thought, or it was created, and before it was created it was nothing. However, the kind of movement required to create a "before" creation and "after" suggests that before and after are already eternally known or are, simply, a consequence of the creation that cannot be adequately penetrated by the human mind. A creation out of nothing, or *ex nihilo*, also tends to create an unbridgeable gap between God and the creation in that the distance between ourselves and God, for example, is precisely nothing.

The notion of a *participation* in Existence, as a bridge between our nothingness and God, creates a link between God's eternal knowledge and His creation that is not entirely explained by the metaphysics of Aquinas (1225-1274 A.D.) What Aquinas does say, rather cryptically, is that the "creatables" do not "have in themselves determinate being, still they are *determinately* in the divine knowing."[35] This is consonant with the teaching of Augustine who maintained, like Plato, that there were archetypal ideas in the mind of God, according to which the world was created.

Duns Scotus, known as the Subtle Doctor (1236-1308 A.D.) claimed that God's foreknowledge of all things was an *ens diminutum* or little being but at the same time he denied that there was a real distinction between essence and existence. The doctrine of the *univocity of being* in Duns Scotus' works implies the denial of a real distinction between essence and existence in the natural world. Aquinas had argued that in all finite being (i.e., all except God), the essence of a thing is distinct from its existence. Scotus rejected this distinction.

Scotus argued that we cannot conceive of what it is to be something, without conceiving it as existing in some way. We should not make any distinction between whether a thing exists potentially and what it actually is for we never know whether something exists, unless we have some concept of what we know to exist.[36] In other words, what we know only discloses what actually is. Prior to being it is nothing but this is also complicated by the notion that God's Existence doesn't exist either. Trying to get a grasp on Existence and how it operates in the visible universe is a frustrating exercise. Whatever algorithms might exist between the Divine Ideas, which are One, and the external universe are almost impossible to conceive, except by inference.

---

35 Dewan, Lawrence, O.P.; *St. Thomas, James Ross, and Exemplarism* from The American Catholic Philosophical Quarterly, Volume LXV, Spring 1991, Issue no. 2, pg. 232, Catholic University of America, Washington D.C. 20064. (Referencing DV 3 6 ad1)
36 WP

What Aquinas did, prior to the work of Duns Scotus, was to feather the notion of essence in such a way as to lift it from the "tarring" of an actual pre-existence, coming into existence from some sort of fixed state of possibility, instead of nothing. Aquinas did not want God to be constrained by any exterior, pre-existing layer of causality that the metaphysics of Plato and the later Gnostics would have indicated as being necessary. Aquinas absolutely preserves the freedom of Existence from creation or any kind of pre-determinism but may have left an intellectual gap in the process. Aquinas' matchless zeal for understanding the freedom of God may have neglected God's ultimate and equal freedom to also be what He is not.

Duns Scotus, likewise, attempted to keep God free from any entangling distinctions. Duns Scotus appears not to have fallen into the trap of asserting the unchangeable Nature of God and then re-inserting time through the back door via metaphysical discussion. He did, however, seem to leave room for the notion that there might be some way of thinking about the *difference* between Univocal Being and Equivocal being, which always involves some sort of composition. This "difference" may be interpreted metaphysically, in terms of some kind of algorithm, to reveal new distinctions and shades of meaning.

The notion of univocity can be thought of in two ways. Being is univocal from God's point of view but equivocal in reference to nature. In other words, univocity is a restatement of the notion of relation. Being is not a real relation in God but the relation between Existence and the created is a real relation.

Being is equivocal in the Reality Dysfunction but it is driven by the univocal reality of Existence. How this can possibly be requires new ways of thinking in order to understand what sort of algorithm is possible between Univocal and Equivocal or between un-composed and composed being. There is little evidence of continuous creation in the four dimensional construct of the universe that we inhabit. The "location" that can be interrogated for transitional algorithms might only be found in multi-dimensional analytics or Superstring Theory.

There is a kind of circularity of cause and effect that occurs when God's Essence is invoked by the scholastics as being the source of His knowledge about what is possible in time. This is similar in concept to the argument that matter is neither created nor destroyed. You can't get beyond the concept because the concept has already, a-priori, shut out the possibility of any further penetration of meaning. This difficulty can be ameliorated with the hypothesis of the Reality Dysfunction or God's eternal knowing of Himself, outside Himself, in a way that is simultaneously consonant and proportionate to the infinity and eternity of His Existence.

God's knowledge of Himself, outside Himself, does not diminish either His freedom or His transcendence. The Reality Dysfunction is a result of God's eternal Nature, or what He Is, and nothing else. Infinities proceed from the Divine, in the Reality Dysfunction, like rays from the sun. How these infinities might, ultimately, be unified by a Being that Is its Own Existence is a paradox that we can only work to reduce by degree. The notion of transcendental algorithms created by the Reality Dysfunction is simply another way of trying to get some traction on extremely difficult concepts. The metaphysics of light and transcendental algorithms, considered in the most preliminary way, are an indication that the univocal light of Existence is different from but related to equivocal or created light. All forms of creationism then, might be said to involve the metaphysics of light.

Science has an odd parallel algorithm to creationism. Scientists, using a model of the universe known as QSSC or Quasi Steady State Cosmology, used to think that creation might be continuous with particles constantly being born out of nothing. This was replaced by the notion of the Big Bang for which there is evidence based on background radiation from some cataclysmic explosion fifteen billion years ago. What is not clear is why the notion of the Big Bang is really that much different, from the point of view of origin, than the former notion of Continuous Creation.

*"Though the Big Bang has become the prevailing paradigm, a challenge to its role as a dominant theory of the universe has been made and is known as the Quasi Steady State Cosmology (**QSSC**) proposed by scientists Fred Hoyle, Geoffrey Burbridge, and Jayant V. Narlikar. The QSSC proposes the continuous creation of matter in space rather than a single event and proposes to account for observations that seem to strain the limits of the Big Bang model. Other proposed cosmologies suggest that our universe is just one in a chain of reproducing universes. That the substance of the universe seems to come from nowhere is a continuing mystery and is the edge where physics fumbles for answers...Some recent correspondence hints that [alleged] anomalous appearances and disappearances[37] of matter [may] have taken place without accountability.[38] If verified, this could put a whole new spin on the creation process and suggest that either matter and energy can be created or there is a bridge to some other physical dimension that permits the transfer of matter and energy into our universe. This also bumps up against the edge of another mystery, the mystery and role of consciousness in the universe."[39]*

In the case of both hypotheses, Continuous Creation and in the Big Bang, something comes from nothing. What if Aquinas' notion of "relation" were a proximation of what we think of today as a virtual reality or the decoherence of quantum reality caused by an eternal

---

37 "In email exchanges physicist Robert Neil Boyd noted an anomalous phenomenon in a vacuum chamber. "That was our first thought, that the hydrogen was migrating through the walls of the containment chamber. But we were rapidly disabused of this notion by the sheer volume and persistence of the hydrogen density. Regardless of how many times we ionized the chamber and swept the chamber clean, we still had the same amount of hydrogen we started with. And we could count how much hydrogen we had removed from the chamber. So it was obvious what was going on. Hydrogen was being created in the chamber. Our observations informed us that this process did not occur until a certain level of vacuum had been obtained. But from then on, it was hopeless to try to obtain our "perfect vacuum". So we gave up and worked with what we had." http://www.bibliotecapleyades.net/ciencia/ciencia_astrosciences02.htm
38 http://www.bibliotecapleyades.net/ciencia/ciencia_astrosciences02.htm
39 Ibid

observer? The Big Bang could then be categorized as a result of the Reality Dysfunction (God knowing Himself, outside Himself, in the creation of time which is a kind of algorithm) as easily as it could be attributed to the emergence of something from a white hole.[40] Is there a link between the universe, as we know it, and Existence that might be further explicated in order to better understand morality and politics and its awkward relation to science?

A NEW PERSPECTIVE ON THE POLITICAL ORDER

The radical approach of analyzing the political order, from the perspective provided by metaphysics, is significantly different from many previous attempts in this direction, by the so-called culture warriors. This is not a traditional work of scholarship; it is more like guerilla metaphysics whereby intellectual weapons, recovered from the treasure house of history, are used to attack and excise socially, intellectually and morally bad ideas.

The ancient notion that both moral and immoral behavior, for example, can have an effect on the human soul and spirit has been largely lost in the scientific degrading of values that were formerly associated with spiritual and divine things related to the concept of Existence. The association of 'good' behavior with moral and intellectual excellence has been eclipsed in modern society by focusing, solely on the development of intellectual skills, in lieu of cultivating both moral and intellectual habits as being complimentary. Allan Bloom, who could only be described as a rationalist, noted this trend in his influential book, *The Closing of the American Mind: How Higher Education Has Failed Democracy and Impoverished the Souls of Today's Students*. His claim that the classics contained universal truths and timeless values, which were being ignored by cultural relativists and

---

40 "In general relativity, a white hole is a hypothetical region of space-time which cannot be entered from the outside, although matter and light can escape from it. In this sense, it is the reverse of a black hole, which can only be entered from the outside, from which nothing, including light, can escape." [WP]

empirical science, is a theme that this book continues and develops more deeply.

God Has Skin In The Game: How a New Understanding of Politics and the Soul Could Change America, attempts to differentiate some of the metaphysical differences between the left and the right so that the reader can formulate a rational response to the growing irrationality and anti-intellectualism unfolding within the American social and political order. Americans have, increasingly, become unable to hold common discourse on the most elemental topics based on various ideological taboos instituted largely by political correctness. Unfortunately, and from the perspective of an atheistic understanding of existence— that energy is neither created nor destroyed—the moral consequence of much political correctness makes many moral choices relative to personal preference or to social contract. There is no compelling reason to be good or to invite others to be morally good in this scenario, other than for reasons personally chosen.

Political correctness is, ultimately, the result of adopting either empiricism or nihilism as the default position for moral judgement. The approach of Rationalism, which *may* consider moral excellence in relation to Existence, as the bedrock for interpreting human behavior, is able to use a compelling moral schema to explain why people should behave in one way more than another. Virtue or acquired moral and intellectual excellence are two of the most powerful tools available to the Rationalist. These tools can be used to intellectually skewer those promoting the empirical vagaries of moral relativism.

The intellectual virtues[41] of science, wisdom, understanding, prudence and art (understood as craftsmanship or sport) are not more important for civilization than the moral virtues [42] of courage, continence (self-restraint in general), liberality, magnificence (the ability to spend money wisely on great civic projects), magnanimity (giving without regard for gain), honor (a state of character which is a result of the prac-

---

41 Virtue is defined as a good habit or acting in accordance with right reason.
42 Moral virtues are good habits of the will while intellectual virtues are good habits of mind. Both are needed for complete human excellence.

tice of moral virtue) gentleness, friendship, temperance (self-restraint in regards to pleasure), resolution, kindness, truthfulness, and justice, etc.,. The idea that what someone does or does not do, for example, with his or her genitals, might have an affect/effect on the quality of their souls and emotional states is, currently, a notion in intellectual suspended animation in the West.

SEX AND CIVILIZATION

Jumping from the heavy details of metaphysics and physics to the slippery subject of masturbation may seem like an odd leap but masturbation, and sex in general, may have a hidden impact on the human psyche that is directly related to the mysterious junction or disjunction between univocal and equivocal states of being. Excessive sexual activity, in terms of its negative spiritual effects, may reveal a great deal about the hidden aspects of human nature. Masturbation, for example, was referred to for centuries by philosophers and theologians as a form of moral pollution. Today, masturbation and most forms of casual sex are simply thought of as toilet functions having no moral or spiritual significance. Science, however, now provides some concrete evidence for what the moralists of the past intuitively understood.

"Dr. Norman Doidge, author of *The Brain that Changes Itself,* says there are two separate pleasure systems in our brains: one for exciting pleasure and another for satisfying pleasure. Masturbating to fantasies and especially pornography activates the exciting system, but leaves the satisfying system starved for "the real thing."

The exciting system is fueled by the neurochemical dopamine. Dopamine focuses our attention, giving our brain a little feel-good reward, helping us become sexually aroused, gearing up for sex. The satisfying system involves actually having sex—touching, kissing, caressing, and really connecting with someone—which provides a calming, fulfilling pleasure. The problem with masturbation is that the satisfying system is never activated.

The more one masturbates to porn, the more dopamine is released in the brain. Eventually dopamine receptors and signals [become] fatigued, leaving the viewer wanting more but unable to reach a level of satisfaction. This desensitization in turn impacts the prefrontal cortex—the "executive control" center of the brain— causing what is called hypofrontality. **This means a loss of self-control and a propensity to addictive behavior."** [43]

Addictive sexual and other behaviors can run counter to what psychologists primly refer to as "delayed gratification". Education, work and social activities all require some consensus on restraining impulsive activity. Maintaining a demanding school schedule is much more difficult, if not impossible, when students need to spend more time sleeping to recover from excessive "partying". Toilet sexuality is no more morally neutral, in this regard, than any other form of uninhibited behavior. There can be no significant analysis, for example, of the growth of homosexuality and its relation to pornography without understanding that masturbation (despite what anyone might be imagining) is essentially same-sex sexuality.

Same-sex attraction, aside from psychological issues, might be characterized as masturbation on steroids. Prison rape, for example, is often not practiced just by homosexuals but by straight men who want to "get off". A reminder of the plasticity of sexual behavior, when there are no objective moral standards other than personal preference, was noted many years ago by Gore Vidal, who stated that "being bisexual doubles your chances of getting a date." Gore Vidal, to his credit, did not believe that same-sex attraction was anything other than a personal choice, irrespective of inclination or orientation.

The larger and more compelling issue is that there is, at the present time, no hard scientific evidence for a gay gene or any other biological indicators for homosexual behavior. We would be wise to drop the separation of human beings into "gay" and "straight" categories and

---

43 http://www.covenanteyes.com/2015/04/13/the-great-masturbation-hoax-is-not-masturbating-unhealthy-for-you/#comment-2668437

simply understand that human beings are profoundly pansexual from the point of view of appetitive biology.

How sexuality is expressed is a result of complex psychological, physiological, moral and spiritual factors that must be differentiated if there is ever to be consensus on homosexual behavior. Same-sex attraction or any of the other LBGT issues are choices resulting from a mélange of psychological, moral, physical and spiritual inclinations. There is no scientific proof otherwise and it was a profoundly unconsidered position that the APA engaged, in 1973, when homosexuality was taken off the list of mental disorders.[44] At the very least, homosexuality is a moral and spiritual anomaly and until it is proven otherwise, same-sex relations should remain morally and psychologically suspect.

The current debate and assertion that same-sex attractions are innate and unchangeable is more ideological than scientific. A closer look at homosexual behavior indicates that the root cause of all sexual misbehavior, including homosexuality, is related to assumptions about the morally neutral repercussions of masturbation. Given the continuum of moral disorders that include pederasty, necrophilia and a host of other bizarre sexual behaviors, taking masturbation off the list of moral problems only makes the defining of sexual misconduct more difficult.

The proponents of same-sex attraction have consistently sought equality of consideration for morally and intellectually suspect behavior. This is not a rational reason, however, to grant legal or political "consideration". The Supreme Court's 5 to 4 decision regarding gay "marriage" indicated a profound legal and moral disagreement from the perspective of American jurisprudence. No serious student of Constitutional law could discover and assert an undiscovered right that has lain dormant for two hundred years. That those schooled in the law could come to such a conclusion is a blanket condemnation of the mentality of the universities that produced them.

---

44 *When Homosexuality Was a Mental Illness*, http://www.dailykos.com/story/2011/04/26/970357/-When-homosexuality-was-mental-illness#

How could any liberal, supportive of unrestricted masturbation and pornography on demand, reproductive "rights" or homosexual and transgendered rights, really understand or want to understand the following quote from Edmund Burke? "Men are qualified for civil liberty in exact proportion to their disposition to put moral chains upon their appetites...society cannot exist unless a controlling power upon will and appetite be placed somewhere *and the less of it there is within, the more there must be without.* It is ordained in the eternal constitution of things that men of intemperate minds cannot be free. Their passions forge their fetters." The answer is that they would, in the words of Nietzsche, "blink".

The Freudian assertion that sublimation of the sexual impulse was essential for the development of civilization was not a religious concept for Freud but a scientific observation. Sexual energy has to come from somewhere and be stored if it is not to be immediately expended. What is the mechanism for the storage or sexual energy? Historically speaking, civilized behavior is based on the common understanding that biological impulses must be intellectually and morally restrained less they dissipate too much energy in frivolous pursuit of satisfaction. Sexual energy, much like any other form of energy, such as that generated by falling water or sunlight can be harnessed and converted. This ancient conversion, known as sublimation, seems to have been completely ignored by modern psychology and pop culture as sex has been relentlessly reduced to a toilet function of no consequence. There are, however, some very serious psychological consequences that come about from viewing sexuality as a toilet function.

CONNECTING THE DOTS

When we further examine the disparity, in America, between intellectual excellence, and the lack of moral excellence, we can reflect more critically on statistical data that indicates that there are large numbers of people in the United States and in the rest of the civilized world who suffer from depression and other psychological disorders.[45] Robert Whittaker, in his article, *Anatomy of an Epidemic*, notes that in 1987 there were 1.25 million adults in the United States who were receiving disability checks because of a mental or a psychological disorder.[46] In 2011 that number had risen to 4.8 million adults or 1 in 65 of all Americans. Surely both academia and the media are not adverting to all the parts of this story.

The rise of mental disabilities is not simply a result of better reporting but more likely, a result of the increased availability of sex without responsibility, porn and the public abandonment of privately held spiritual principles. Depression, as one example, and when it is not a result of biological dysfunction or economic or personal suffering, can mask the root cause of feeling badly, which is more often than not, caused by moral failures such as unkindness, greed, envy, jealousy, gluttony, sexual excess, (including the mindless consumption of pornography) and violence rather than some sort of psychological 'disorder' of dubious origins. Guilt, in other words, can lurk within depression as a cause that is not properly adverted to. As an outlier metaphysician, moralist and psychologist, I find many of the characterizations of psychological and social issues by the 'sciences' of psychology and sociology to be ignorant of the moral and spiritual dimensions of the human person.

A clear understanding of what constitutes moral and intellectual excellence tends to clarify psychological, political and social issues. Racism, for example, is frequently portrayed as some sort of social position taken by various groups independent of either moral or intellectual analysis. Racism, in point of fact, tends to be the default emotional position for people who react viscerally to behavior but who do not have a moral map to analyze that behavior. People of all races who do not plan for

---

45 Globally, and according to the World Health Organization (WHO) more than 350 million people of all ages suffer from depression. Depression is the leading cause of disability worldwide, and is a major contributor to the global burden of disease. More women are affected by depression than men.

46 As cited in Mark Bauerlein and Adam Bellow's *The State of the American Mind,* Templeton Press, PA, 2015, page 88

the future, who are unable to delay gratification, who talk loudly and uninhibitedly, who engage in sexual innuendo at every opportunity and who spend their time in pursuit of alcohol, recreational drugs, sex and violence are, by common understanding, vice-ridden. No one talks about this because we have forgotten that the word "vicious" means vice-ridden. Racism, like the term "homophobia", is often (although certainly not always) an attempt to map bad behavior with pejorative language, in lieu of having the proper moral terminology to express such sentiments. The color of one's skin is irrelevant or should be irrelevant in a moral society. As Martin Luther King once remarked, "he would rather be judged by the content of his character than the color of his skin."

Sexual orientation, by itself, should condemn no one. However, the persistence in maintaining sexual orientations that are inconsistent with both right reason and biology are on a continuum with vice. Only by distinguishing the moral from the intellectual virtues, and by grasping the ontological difference between good and bad habits, will we ever be able to bridge the gap between the divide of belief and opinion caused by two very different understandings of the meaning of existence. Existence either has a transcendental source or it doesn't. There are consequences, up and down the social order to whichever position is adopted.

The association of a moral order solely with religion is a profound mistake. Morality, in its purest form, addresses the management of biological impulses by both the intellect and the will; it is, fundamentally, an energy management system based on the metaphysics of light. This energy management system, more commonly known as sublimation, should be part of the sexual and moral ecology of any rational civilization.

> *"Sublimation is the transformation of unwanted impulses [this includes sexual impulses] into something less harmful. This can simply be a distracting release or may be a constructive and valuable piece of work. When we are faced with the dissonance of uncomfortable thoughts, [including but not limited to anger,*

jealousy, envy and lust] we create psychic energy. This has to go somewhere. Sublimation channels this energy away from destructive acts and into something that is socially acceptable and/or creatively effective. Many sports and games are sublimations of aggressive urges, as we sublimate the desire to fight into the ritualistic activities of formal competition." [47]

Biology and impulse cannot be managed by the mind alone as the observations from Robert Pirsig indicate in Chapter 19 of this book. The law, in the form of the police and military, need to be invoked where self-governance of human appetite and impulse fails. Most calls to 911 are the result of some failure of moral self-governance and are not simply just a violation of the law. The conversion of sexual energy into something more constructive cannot be seen but its absence is made manifest by crime. Sublimation is part of the invisible yet powerful realm of impulse management. The conversion of impulse is, simply, the conversion of one form of energy into another but without the notion of a moral structure that can help focus and transform this energy, the very idea of self-control can become largely meaningless.

One of the greatest aspects of the Declaration of Independence and the Constitution was that the Founding Fathers, knowing the moral failures of human nature, attempted to create a system to compensate for and offset those failures. They understood that human impulses had to be converted through virtuous action or vice would prevail. The embracing of moral turpitude[48] by the Supreme Court in recent decisions relating to abortion and same-sex attraction are repugnant to the original enterprise of the Founding Fathers and should be repealed and condemned as a moral and political aberration.

The failure of modern psychology, in a similar vein, to properly understand the relationship of the will to the intellect is a further

---

47 http://changingminds.org/explanations/behaviors/coping/sublimation.htm
48 Moral turpitude is a legal concept in the United States and some other countries that refers to "conduct that is considered contrary to community standards of justice, honesty or good morals." (WP) What can be said, however, when community standards are corrupt?

reflection of the inability to distinguish between the consequences of differing ideas about the meaning of Existence and the moral consequences that occur due to whichever position is favored. The "intellect must not," in the words of Herman Melville's *Billy Budd*, be "the lawyer to his will".

The fundamental insight of liberalism is that values must be appropriated authentically and in a free state of mind. This is sometimes referred to as *agency*, although scholars might also refer to this as *sovereignty*. Agency or sovereignty can be understood in two ways. It can be described as a kind of secular authenticity based on a balanced psychology of insight and personal behavior, or it may be described as a progressive unfolding of awareness and self-identity related to the notion of 'soul' and a higher form of existence than is posited by the First Law of Thermodynamics.

However *agency* might be conceived, the essential conservative insight is that there are fundamental values given to us by Divine Existence that must be adverted to in the formation of any personal value system or civil society. The reality is that both positions are intellectually valid, or at least consistent, as long as the operative concept of existence behind the assumptions is adverted to. It has been said that the first duty of a critical mind is to examine its assumptions. This is nowhere more true than in regards to our understanding of Existence.

A fundamental question and issue involves understanding what increases *agency* and what decreases it. Common observation indicates that vice tends to decrease agency and virtue tends to increase it. Poor people, for example, are often poor not just due to lack of money or work but due to a lack of moral agency, which keeps them in the grip of bad habits. Those who wish to define their own values cannot be allowed, by default, to make those the values of a country that was not founded on the moral algorithm of existence as simply "energy that is neither created nor destroyed". The notion that values should be subjectively and authentically subscribed to should never, in other words, be allowed to shoulder aside the notion that there are real values to be objectively affirmed, by each individual, in a civilized society.

Jack London had a unique and early "take" on the concept of agency, which he would not have known but certainly understood from his own adventurous perspective. The freedom to choose, and particularly the freedom to choose what is good, is fundamental to human life. We might also suggest that it is one of the building blocks of a rational civilization.

> *"**The ultimate word is 'I Like.'** It lies beneath philosophy, and is twined about the heart of life. When philosophy has maundered ponderously for a month, telling the individual what he must do, the individual says, in an instant, 'I Like,' and does something else..."*[49]

The cultured individual understands that the art of living consists of a dialogue between Existence (however conceived) and the human person and that each dialogue is different and unique. The important thing is that each person be empowered to understand what concept of existence it is that they are engaging and what the consequences are of their choices. As Jack London indicates, the choice is not always clear but we all have an internal compass that directs our sense of agency and that compass is always rooted in the freedom of Existence.

---

49 Eschenroeder, Kyle http://www.artofmanliness.com/2016/08/15/what-do-you-want-to-want/? citing Jack London's explanation of why he wanted to build a boat

Chapter 2

HOW WE UNDERSTAND EXISTENCE

"If value is a function of scarcity then what is most scarce in our culture is long, thoughtful, patient, deliberate analysis of questions that do not have obvious or easy answers." [1]

—Leon Wieseltier

Many of the concepts in this book have been around for a very long time and have been abandoned by modern thinkers. Books, like civilizations, have mega concepts or "big ideas" that drive the engines of both creativity and decay. Virtue and vice are two big ideas that have empowered generations of American and European political thinkers. Senator Daniel Webster (1782-1852), in his famous Plymouth Rock oration noted, "...Our ancestors established their system

---

1   As cited in Steve Wasserman's essay, *In Defense of Difficulty*, pg. 180, as found in *The State of the American Mind* by Mark Bauerlein and Adam Bellow, Templeton Press, PA, 2015

of government on morality and religious sentiment. Moral habits, they believed, cannot safely be on any other foundation than religious principle, nor any government be secure which is not supported by moral habits." For Webster and many other uniquely American thinkers, virtue or acting in accordance with right reason was taken for granted. That such virtue could exist without a notional asset to religion would have been unthinkable.

Few contemporary scholars focus on the meaning and origin of virtue[2] and its relationship to time and what the philosophers refer to as "Existence" or, as Aristotle put it, the Unmoved Mover. When we think of time, we often only associate it with the commonly understood meaning of past, present and future. But what if time had a fourth component—something at right angles to our experience of it? What if our concept of future time had an unknown causal element that was exerting evolutionary pressure on the present?

How we describe and understand time and its relation to Existence has consequences, so understanding the models that we use or default to can illuminate or even darken the journey. If Christians and Muslims consider life a preparation for an afterlife and adapt their behavior accordingly, relative to the "requirements" of the final destination, then that is a model that has consequences up and down for the social order. The Islamic notion of Sharia,[3] for example, is little different from the non-separation of Church and state that occurred in Western Europe prior to the Reformation. The consequences were and are, largely, the same in that an external order is used to suppress various activities as being un-conducive to the temporal and eternal goals of human life.

Atheism, on the other side of the coin, poses the question of how to behave in the present when no reward or form of condemnation ex-

---

2 Virtue or the Greek 'Arete' means "excellence of any kind". The term may also mean "moral virtue". In its earliest appearance in Greek, this notion of excellence was ultimately related to the notion of the fulfillment of purpose or function: the act of living up to one's full potential.

3 The term means "way" or "path"; it is the legal framework within which the public and some private aspects of life are regulated for those living in a legal system based on Islam. [WP]

ists after death. This point of view also has consequences up and down for the social order. Is there a third way to model our understanding of time between the extremes of religious fundamentalism and the rigors of scientific atheism?

Our present concept of time may be at odds, for example, with an evolutionary and even more invisible form and force more significant than time itself. Aristotle, one of the first scientists of the ancient world, argued that *final causality*, in addition to three other kinds of causality: material, formal and efficient[4] was a dynamism caused by an *Unmoved Mover* (a self-caused being) that exerted force beyond and across time to make all things exist. Aristotle's thinking on the Four Causes formed the basis for centuries of speculative thought on the relationship between time and something that appeared to be outside of time.

Aristotle, like Socrates before him, believed that a knowledge of causality was essential—essential to politics as it was to philosophy. If politicians wanted to make the people, "good and obedient to the laws,"[5] then an understanding of human behavior, based on a knowledge of what made a human being "good" through sound intellectual and moral habits, was essential. The linkage between understanding causality, as Existence, and virtue and vice, as ways of being either in conformity or at odds with Existence or the will of the gods was well known to the philosophers of the ancient world. Even the ancients understood that goodness might be linked to Existence by way of an attraction exerted in human affairs. The best human response then, as

---

4   The famous Four Causes are: formal, material, efficient and final causality. A table, for example, is first of all being a table—that is the *formal* cause—the idea that is behind the organization of its parts. Secondly, it is made of various materials prior to its organization into what we call "table"; that is the *material* cause. Third, it is conceived and made by man, who is the *efficient* cause. Finally, it has a purpose, an 'end' for which it was made; this is the *final* cause. These four causes are intimately related to each other, as they are all events that occur in the generation of what we call reality. The formal cause was ultimately said by Plato to reside in the mind of God as an eternal form or essence. For Aristotle, the form was an act, a *suppositum*, so to speak, of Existence that combined matter and form into substance. Note that the Act of Existence, Itself, cannot exist anywhere.

5   Aristotle, *Nichomachean Ethics*, Bk. 1: Ch. 12

it is now, is a fundamental reverence or piety towards what is perceived to be a divinely related attraction to goodness. How we conceive of and understand our obligation to the "call" or impetus of goodness is the essence of both the ethical and spiritual life. This obligation cannot be properly understood without some understanding of the nature of Existence and that is where the troubles begin.

God, it has been said, cannot will evil; He can only will what is good, although what God may consider good and what we might consider good are, likely, coming from two very different perspectives. Our limited understanding of "goodness" is based on a much narrower timeline than that of eternity, where goodness, down multiple timelines, may take on forms that we cannot even begin to fully understand. Much in the same way that a child may not understand the "good" that is being offered by school or proper eating habits, we may not understand the nature of goodness as it is present to the mind of the Divine and offered to us in life.

The notion of an Unmoved Mover has a great deal in common[6] with scientific atheism and the First Law of Thermodynamics, which states simply that energy is neither created nor destroyed. There is, however, a metaphysical back door in this definition.

> *"The First Law of Thermodynamics:[7] a version of the law of conservation of energy, adapted for thermodynamic systems. The law of conservation of energy states that the total energy of an isolated system is constant; energy can be transformed from one form to another, but cannot be created or destroyed."*

Note that the idea is based on 'an isolated system'. What if the system is not isolated? What if all energy systems in the physical universe are dependent on something else? The primary metaphysical argument of the ancients, in its simplest form, was that the finite was contingent

---

6   Sean J. O'Reilly, *Authority, Creativity and the Third Imperium: Why God's Knowing Himself, Outside Himself, Matters*, pg. 65, House of a Thousand Suns, 2015

7   Officially, there are only Four Laws of Thermodynamics.

upon the infinite. Arguing that God makes Himself be, or is His own Existence, is just one rung above the notion that energy is neither created nor destroyed but the political and social consequences of holding to one or the other of these two different ideas are enormous.

A God Who is His Own Existence leads inexorably to either the Aristotelian notion of the Unmoved Mover ("that which moves without being moved") an impersonal entity removed from human experience, or to a highly personal God who, like the Christian God, is said to be involved in human affairs or, at the very least, aligned intentionally with what might be described as moral goodness. Alternatively, holding to the scientific point of view that energy is neither created nor destroyed leads, ultimately, to the kind of positivism[8] that we are currently seeing in our political and legal system. Abortion and capital punishment, for example, are not understood in terms of any moral or intellectual values other than those made by collective agreement.

The moral disjunction between those who support abortion and yet at the same time cannot seem to understand the value of capital punishment is striking. If human beings can be killed for the sake of convenience, then surely human beings who have illegally taken the lives of others might also be thought of as worthy of execution. Existence, taken as a simple given or without reference to a higher context, is simply like artists' clay to be shaped in any way that common agreement sees fit. Existence, from this perspective, has no power to shape human moral or spiritual life—except as a neutral motor force translated into various and relativistic belief systems.

It is, perhaps, an indication of how far both camps may have drifted from the truth when neither can admit to the essential similarity of the basic argument, which is in the very broadest sense that Existence (or energy on the other side of the coin) is not created. Existence can be assumed as a given but the failure to interrogate existence for further intelligibility is no less reprehensible on the part of atheists than it is

---

8 Positivism, as it is applied to law, means that the law is self-referential. There is no adverting to objective moral rules or Natural Law in positivism.

by clerics who use it as a kind of super glue to make all the bits stick together. The notion of ultimate causality for both atheists and theists has become, in practice, a largely dead-end street. For the former, the only questions to be answered are scientific and for the latter, all the answers have already been discovered. Both groups, in my opinion, have obscured some of the dynamic truths about Existence.

The temptation of science to assert that energy is neither created nor destroyed is Occam's Razor[9] applied to the thorny and difficult questions posed by the nature of existence. This principle goes back at least as far as Aristotle, who wrote "Nature operates in the shortest way possible."[10] This is why it is important to understand the causal interface between Existence and the natural order. Understanding cause and effect might be said to be the purest of all forms of rational activity. There are, as can be readily seen, political and social consequences when Existence is rationally understood or not understood by a culture.

Communist and Nazi ideologies, which were both based to some extent on the philosophy of Hegel, proceeded from a literal understanding that energy (which from their perspective was Spirit) is neither created nor destroyed. The *Geist* or Spirit of Hegel's dialectic, manifesting as a kind of universal concretization of spirit in matter, through a procession of oppositions and over-comings, didn't just destroy the transcendental aspect of Divine consciousness and concomitant values pointed to by Christianity, it reduced them, simply, to an expression of history. The Marxist Hegelians, in the old Soviet Union, consequently and euphemistically referred to violence as, "surgery on the body of history." As many as 100 million people (according to the Walker Report) may have been killed in the 20th century by these vicious ideologies implemented by Stalin and later by Mao.

Meaning and values, as an expression of the First Law of Thermo-

---

9   Occam's razor is a principle attributed to the 14th century logician and Franciscan friar
     William of Ockham. Ockham was the village in the English county of Surrey where he
     was born. The principle states that "Entities should not be multiplied unnecessarily."
10   (http://math.ucr.edu/home/baez/physics/General/occam.html)

dynamics, can only be relative to whatever agreements might be made among men as there are no fundamental moral constants or laws (as in Natural Law)[11] to be observed. The existentialism of Sartre, by way of additional illustration, is the metaphysic that necessarily flows from adopting the First Law of Thermodynamics as a default philosophy. There is, generally speaking, very little objective moral reality for those who literally believe in the First Law of Thermodynamics (that energy is neither created nor destroyed) other than various kinds of utilitarianism and self-interest codified by collective or personal agreement. The well-known psychological anguish attested to by existentialists is based on the ostensible meaninglessness of the universe versus the personal meanings that we attempt to impose on it, which are, in the final analysis a kind of tragedy.

THE FIFTH LAW OF THERMODYNAMICS

There are, at present, only four laws of thermodynamics acknowledged by science. A recent book, deeply rooted in the four laws but going in a new direction is, *Design in Nature: How the Constructal Law Governs Evolution in Biology, Physics, Technology and Social Organization.*

Written by leading thermodynamics theorist Adrian Bejan and J. Peder Zane, this is probably one of the most important books on the social and political aspects of thermodynamics written in the past ten years but for two very different reasons. One: the author brilliantly describes an implicit law or potential first principle of nature, the *Constructal Law*, which describes how the tendency for an increasing and more efficient movement of mass and energy through time is ruled by a physical law. This, the book asserts, naturally creates many complex designs that we see in nature that do not violate the laws of thermodynamics. The second reason, which is not quite so flattering, is that his

---

11 A principle or body of laws considered as derived from nature, right reason, or religion and as ethically binding in human society. This is distinguished from 'positive' law which is self-referential and based on social contract or whatever people can agree should be ethically binding.

book clearly describes the approach of the modern mind—that despite all his arguing to the contrary, points in the direction that consciousness is either a feature of matter and energy or "the designer" cannot be conceived properly using the imagery of Bejan's schoolboy God.

Bejan absolutely fails to describe what should be obvious to all but not to those who refuse to look: that the universe is, from the point of view of common sense, not unintelligently self-assembling and that a postulated Fifth Law, negentropy, which assumes some sort of teleology in the universe, really needs to be looked at more closely for a more accurate and scientific accounting of the universe.

Let's look closely at what Bejan says:

> "*Of course, there is no conscious intelligence behind these patterns, no Divine Architect churning out brilliant blueprints. To pre-empt any confusion, let me make this perfectly clear: The constructal law is not headed toward a creationist argument, and in no way does it support the claims of those who promulgate the fantasy of intelligent design... [How can he possibly know this from a scientific perspective? Better to take a more agnostic and humble position as in: "we don't know-period"]. Bejan goes on to say:* **this raises the question: How come? What causes the constructal law? The short answer: we don't know.** *The constructal law is what is known in science as a first principle, an idea that cannot be deduced or derived from other laws (if it could, it would be a theorem.* **It just is—a law of physics** *that governs the emergence of macroscopic shape and structure in nature. The constructal law tells us why those patterns arise and empowers us to predict how they should change in the future. It reveals that it is not love or money that makes the world go round but flow and design.*" [12]

12 Design in Nature: How the Constructal Law Governs Evolution in Biology, Physics, Technology and Social Organization, Adrian Bejan and J. Peder Zane, pg. 14, Anchor Books, 2012

This is quite amusing from a metaphysical perspective. He knows that intelligent design is a "fantasy" but he doesn't know why the constructal law works. Just make up first principles and poof—no need to inquire further. This sort of argument, much like natural selection being pimped as the only motor of evolution, is a **partial explanation posing as a final theory**.

Entropy does create efficient dispersion patterns from original energy sources, and it is also observably true that all flow systems tend to generate better and more complex conduits for the currents that flow through them due to relational factors such as gravity, pressure, time and temperature. This "tendency" simply described doesn't tell us why such systems should accumulate ever increasing amounts of energy, but it does very well describe the energy output of vice. The tendency of flow systems *towards* complex arrangements for dispersal, and even self-organization, does not adequately describe moral and intellectual excellence or the human tendency to invest enormous amounts of energy into beliefs and other systems, except as a kind of contextual background for the way all material things behave.

If we took Bejan's analysis seriously, we would have to conclude that all human activity was simply a way of dispersing excess energy— perhaps more like a complex drainage system than the kind of meaning typically ascribed to human activity. What would be the point of organisms, considered as a whole, to harvest energy in ever more complex ways only to then disperse or get rid of it? There is no sense of teleology in Bejan's system, although he would probably ascribe such meaning to the complex interplay of various forms of energy. His argument might be likened to showing up at a sumptuous, palace banquet with thousands of well-dressed guests in attendance and arguing that there is no host.

The tendency to invest energy into complex systems of machinery and thought might be thought of as being somewhat alien to the constructal law, except by way of appearance, and much more closely related to *negentropy* or the tendency to wind things up. Note how negative entropy is described in the dictionary: "Negative entropy, or **negentropy**, roughly refers to the degree of order or organization within a closed system." That is only part of what negentropy might mean.

Here is an alternative scientific opinion.

"There are, technically speaking, only Four Laws of Thermodynamics but a Fifth Law of Thermodynamics[13] has been proposed by physicist Philip Carr:

> "The missing link in thermodynamics as taught in schools today seems to be a concise explanation of why order and structures abound in a universe purported to be driven by a Second Law [popularly known as the Law of Entropy] that states that disorder increases, always and everywhere. This short note is provided in order to stimulate discussion around a possible Fifth Law which predicts what we observe, which is that order and structures should actually predominate in the world in which we live." [14] Based on this model and observations the proposed 5th Law of Thermodynamics criticizes the notion of stochastically generated order.

> "An open system containing a large mixture of similar automatons, placed in contact with a non-equilibrated environment, has a finite probability of supporting the spontaneous generation and growth of self-constructing machines of unlimited complexity." [15]

This proposed Fifth Law of Thermodynamics is also known, in some circles, as negentropy. Negentropy was proposed by the physicist Schrödinger as a kind of free energy that accumulates within systems that store energy[16] but it is facetious to assume that the storage of ex-

13 http://www.canadaconnects.ca/quantumphysics/10078/
14 http://www.canadaconnects.ca/quantumphysics/10078/
15 Ibid
16 http://www.i-sis.org.uk/negentr.php

tra energy might necessarily result in greater order, (and complexity) except by way of increasing the means of storage. The Fifth Law of Thermodynamics supports the notion of creation by an outside force such as the Unmoved Mover or the non-local intelligence referred to as God.

So, let's get back to Existence and the two ways our culture tends understand Existence. Existence can be understood simply as energy that is neither created nor destroyed or it can be understood as being contingent on something else. Existence does NOT exist—it IS. Something that does not exist generates all that exists. Energy and mass exist. Therefore, there are only two possible directions to consider. One: energy is eternal, and concomitantly, consciousness and self-organization may only be a higher order feature of energy and mass. This is the position of an elevated atheism. Two: all that exists depends on something that does not exist. This is the philosophical and metaphysical explanation of Aristotle and St. Thomas Aquinas that leaves the door open to providence, grace, honor and beauty. The stochastic universe of the materialist is a closed universe going nowhere. When you die you return to energy for re-cycling. End of story.

The world of negentropy, rooted in something that does not exist in a way that we can fully understand, preserves a universe where honor, beauty and goodness are desirable for more than just subjective reasons. Where is the goodness and beauty in the cold atheism of abortion or the moral weirdness of sexual perversion? The desire for a stochastic or randomly generated universe is a moral-free universe from the perspective of objective morality. A stochastic universe fits the process morality of pure subjectivity and is the universal choice of moralists on the left.

Make no mistake about it. The present political tension in the US is really about atheistic morality versus the flawed but traditional morality of the Founders. Conservatives, for all their faults, tend to support the intent of the Founders. What the left thinks it is supporting, in regards to many issues, is nothing but entropy in the guise of concern. It is revelatory that many of our friends on the left have an implicit dislike of moral structures, strict laws, border fences and anything that smacks of top-down order. Their preference appears to be for a kind of amorphous, bottom-up order that they think will somehow emerge from a herd-like consensus that largely seems to consist of hides rubbing together to generate direction—that is the constructal law in action.

Throw a set of marbles down and watch them roll. They will describe a random pattern of energy dispersion based on various resistances of friction, gravity, direction, etc. What the pattern does not tell you is who threw the marbles.

Conservative Christianity is based on the notion of God as being His Own Existence with the moral and material order flowing from His goodness, which is based on His knowledge of everything that was, is and will ever be. Here, again, there are consequences up and down the social order that come from not holding to metaphysical and moral positions developed over two millennia. Science simply assumes that negentropy of the sort represented by God's Existence cannot exit. This bias is entirely unscientific and represents a radical failure of imagination.

Islam is based on yet another interpretation of God as His own Existence. The metaphysical position of Islam, based on thirteen centuries of philosophic and religious speculation, much like Judaism, has been faithful to the notion of God's essential Oneness in contradistinction to the Three-in-One formulation of Christianity.

The rift between Christianity, Judaism and Islam is based on a false dichotomy of understanding. God is not more One than He is Three. God's nature is paradoxically One, consisting of three separate Persons within orthodox Christianity. Islam's faithfulness to the oneness of God is admirable but is, contrary to some extent, to Christian revelation, which discloses the existence of Three Persons with one Nature.

Clearly then, how we think about God's nature or the nature of the universe forms the backbone upon which our moral, political and social thinking is built. While this may seem obvious, what may not be as clear are the assumptions that every religious, political or moral system is built on. How we politically understand the meaning of Existence is, in this respect, more important than almost any single ideology or religion.

GOD AND THE DIVINE IDEAS

What the ancient Greek philosophers and the later medieval theologians described as, God and the Divine Ideas, is another very old "big idea" at the root of western civilization. Time could only exist for the ancients with eternity as an obvious, transcendent backdrop. "Time—what are you?" asks St. Augustine. One senses, in that almost personal question, a hint of a more modern understanding of time. How we model time and space is often how we model the philosophy of our life's conduct. Time and space can be viewed as being completely neutral or they can be viewed as being interpenetrated by hidden forces and intelligence. Time is, as this book will suggest, a manifestation of God's own knowledge of Himself, as other than Himself.

The "Ideas" of an eternal God, as the medieval theologians John Scotus Eriugena[17] (815-877 AD), Thomas Aquinas (1225-1274 AD) and Duns Scotus (1266-1308 AD) argued, are not other than Himself except from the perspective of time. This is a profound concept that was taken from the older Aristotelian perspective, whereby a form of causality *that caused itself*—the Unmoved Mover—was postulated. God does not change. Change occurs in time and in what is "moved" or created. If this is accepted as a postulate, then the issue of understanding how this external change occurs in relation to the Divine Nature becomes one of paramount importance. Clearly there would have to be some sort of astonishing internal proportionality involved

---

17 "Johannes Scottus Eriugena was an Irishman, educated in Ireland. He moved to France (about 845 AD) and took over the Palatine Academy at the invitation of Carolingian King Charles the Bald. He followed Alcuin of York (735–804 AD) as head of the Palace School." (WP)

in a creation that balanced all the nuances of hundreds of billions of galaxies, each containing hundreds of billions of stars and at least one (our own planet) that is inhabited by many thousands of different life forms.

Existence, then, must have some sort of internal organizational intelligence that operates in a way that is simply off the charts of anything that we recognize as thought. The notion of a Being Whose thoughts and ideas are all "part" of One Act of Existence that doesn't even seem to exist, except by way of abstraction, is simply incomprehensible to the human mind and is far easier to dismiss as an impossibility.

How does the notion of a God with a Univocal Nature square with the anthropomorphic God of the Old Testament who creates in seven days, speaks to Adam and Eve in the Garden of Paradise, forbids the eating of a certain fruit and then sends his Son, in the New Testament, to assume human nature and be born as a man? God, it would seem, cannot decide to create and operate in this manner because this would imply a before and after in God, which is not possible for an unchangeable being.

What is more likely, based on what we know about evolutionary anthropology, is that the Biblical account is simply an early theological attempt to understand and model the relationship between man, God, and the universe. Given that the biblical account tends to be at odds with science, it is more likely that the former is imperfect and the latter is unfinished. If there was no "fall" then it would be logical to assume that there would need to be no Redemption—at least as it is presently understood. The notion that we would need the assistance of God, regardless of whether or not there was a fall of man, would seem to be obvious, if all human beings are seen as the children of God.

What conclusions might we come to if the whole matter of creation were misunderstood or mischaracterized by both theologians and scientists? Is it possible that the fall of man is based on an original defect of creation or on an apparent ontological[18] contradiction that required the creation of time and space to occur? Whatever the case, it is nearly self-evident that by making God the source of all goodness, in an absolute manner, the source of all evil has to be located elsewhere, which produces a starker dichotomy of the faults of human nature than reality may indicate. It should be evident from evolutionary biology that nature is not at all entirely benign and likely never was under any scenario that might be imagined prior to the fall of man. It is unlikely that an original state of perfection ever existed except in the minds of the writers of Genesis. The notion that God cannot create something that is imperfect is not the same argument as creating something that is unfinished and requires time and action for its perfection.

The concept of an *Unmoved Mover* bypasses some of the religious aspects of salvation history and allows us to attempt to understand how an Unmoved Mover can "move" or create movement without change occurring in the Unmoved Mover. Getting a relative, conceptual separation between the God of religion and the God of Aristotle enables us to reframe our metaphysical political and religious thoughts in a more useful and less ideological manner. The Unmoved Mover can only be postulated and not completely demonstrated. In order to grasp the concept of an Unmoved Mover, and its relation to excellence, a certain amount of forward thinking is required. That such a thing *could be so* can be registered by an open mind, as a working possibility, rather than an article of faith.

NEGENTROPY AND EVOLUTION

Science, in general, acknowledges the principle of entropic decay but gives little assent to the notion of *negentropy,* or some force, or set of algorithmic forces that wind the universe up, as opposed to winding it down. The universe, as we see and experience it, makes much more

---

18 Ontology is the philosophical study of the nature of being, becoming, existence, or reality, as well as the basic categories of being and their relations.

sense when both concepts are employed. The philosopher Martin Heidegger, quoting Leibniz, expressed this sentiment when he said, "Why is there something rather than nothing?"

Clearly there is an element of stochastic (random) aggregation at work in the universe but there also appears to be a non-stochastic principle that may be operating on something very like Aristotle's final causality. Whether we call this negentropic principle the Unmoved Mover, God, Master of the Universe, Intelligent Designer, Actuality, the Holy Trinity or simply the Divine is not particularly important. Acknowledging that there *may be* a principle or force of intelligence within evolution, in addition to either natural selection or the aggregation favored by entropy, enables us to think outside the box when it comes to reflecting on the nature of reality.

The notion of *conatus* or a "habit of continuing to exist or live or continuing to seek improvement" is noted by Mike Hockney "as embracing both habit and will to power and therefore provides a good concept for explaining how the universe operates."[19] Conatus, however, cannot exist without something negentropic (opposing the natural disorder of the Law of Entropy) behind it such as Existence. Hockney also notes that Rupert Sheldrake's *morphic fields*[20] have been hypothesized to create a resonance that drives evolution but the same principle applies. Why are these principles operative at all? There are a variety of mechanisms and ways of describing how negentropy works but there must be a larger metaphysical explanation for the existence of negentropic activity to begin with.

The action of negentropy, whether described as conatus, morphic resonance, essence or the preferred term of this book: Dimensionally Interactive Cyber Kinesis—it is that which is the driving force behind evolution. As an aside, it is interesting to note that Dimensionally Interactive Cyber Kinesis nicely fits the gap between Darwin's notion of random selection and the theories of Jean-Bap-

19 Hockney, Mike, *The Last Man Who Knew Everything,* Hyperreality Books, July 14, 2012, location 4986
20 Ibid, location 5056

tiste Lamarck, who maintained that evolution was, in part, driven by the relationship between the organism and its environment in a purposeful manner.[21]

THE ONE AND THE MANY

Philosophers and theologians assert that God knows everything and that God does not change because He is an eternal being. God's knowledge is also changeless. God is, according to Aristotle and theologians down through the ages, a self-caused being or a Being Who Is His Own Act of Existence. According to Thomas Aquinas, God *is* His Ideas and is said to create by *approbation*—meaning that because He knows Himself in all the ways that He might be imitated, His very knowledge brings about their creation in time. In other words, God and His Ideas are One but clearly they are not entirely one, in time, or one in the same way that they might be said to be One in the Mind of God. There is a proportionality between God's Existence and His eternal knowledge of how and when things will be. The problem of God and His Ideas is as old as philosophy. It is the problem of the One and the Many. How can the One be reconciled with the Many? This is sometimes referred to as the problem of Universals.[22]

The problem of Universals or the One and the Many is frequently

---

21 In the modern era, Lamarck is widely remembered for a theory of inheritance of acquired characteristics, called soft inheritance, Lamarckism or use/disuse theory, which he described in his 1809 *Philosophie Zoologique*. However, his idea of soft inheritance was, perhaps, a reflection of the wisdom of the time accepted by many natural historians. Lamarck's contribution to evolutionary theory consisted of the first truly cohesive theory of evolution,[7] in which an alchemical complexifying force drove organisms up a ladder of complexity, and a second environmental force adapted them to local environments through *use and disuse* of characteristics, differentiating them from other organisms. Scientists have debated whether advances in the field of transgenerational epigenetics mean that Lamarck was to an extent correct, or not. https://en.wikipedia. org/wiki/Jean-Baptiste_Lamarck

22 Gonzalo Roderiquez-Pereyra, Mind, 2000, 109 (434) *What is the Problem of Universals?* pp. 255-273. "The Problem of Universals is considered to be the problem of showing how numerically different particulars can have the same properties, as when white particulars share the property of being white, hot particulars the property of being hot, square particulars the property of being square and so on."

approached as if it were simply an abstraction without a source. When the One and the Many is examined from the perspective of a phenomenology of Divine Consciousness, a very different picture emerges. What God knows must occur without change in God. Existence creates essences (patterns in subsistent being) out of nothing and without movement. Existence also considers nothing pre-existing in creating; we cannot add time in through the back door to God when considering Him as an Eternal being acting within time but "from" eternity. All we see are the effects of eternity that are generated in the present. However, Existence does consider Itself, so to speak, in all that it creates and what It knows is part of the paradoxical "structure" of eternity. An analogical way of understanding this, using terms from modern physics, would be to say that God's knowledge of Himself is what causes the de-cohering and "localizing" of the quantum wave function that results in the universe that we see around us. God de-coheres Himself in the Reality Dysfunction. What is decohered is not God.

Rather than considering creation, in relation to God's nature, as simply nothing brought into being, we might consider the Divine Ideas *and* the One and the Many as profoundly relational within Existence Itself. These are what I would call Transcendental Acts, whereby what is known from Eternity is part of a larger tapestry of Existence, in that the *affect* of Existence, which while not reducible to anything pre-existing, is relational to Itself. This relation to Itself is like a diamond prism that creates time, space, matter and energy as both an affect and effect of the Divine nature, at right angles to Itself, in the Reality Dysfunction.

CREATED OR UNCREATED?

Consider, for example, the light at Mount Tabor. Jesus Christ was said to have been transfigured there, in light, according to the eyewitness account of the disciples. The question theologians have asked is this:

was the light of the Transfiguration created or uncreated?[23] At first glance this might seem like an irrelevant question but there are metaphysical consequences to whichever position is taken. If the light was created, then God may have engaged in some sort of special intervention in time. If the light was uncreated then how did it manage to manifest in time? The mechanism, so to speak, of engagement for the Eternal within time is not clear based on theological speculation. Stating that it is the prerogative of the Eternal to manifest in time does not explain, rationally, how this is possible within the context of our present understanding of time, space, eternity and aseity.[24]

How can we understand the algorithm (if there is one) whereby the Eternal can enter or manipulate time without any change occurring in the Eternal's Nature? We can hypothesize that there are functions that the Divine can engage within time but only indirectly or through a third party. A function is defined as relating an output to an input. In God there should be no real distinction between the input and the output from the perspective of origin but this seems not to be the case when the Divine operates in time. The output seems to come from an input that doesn't exist or cannot be located in space and time.

One metaphysical solution is to posit, as previously indicated, the existence of a delta point that we are calling the *Reality Dysfunction*[25] whereby God limits Himself in some mysterious way, in creation, to the confines of what is less than Himself in space and time and yet never loses His absolute transcendence. The Kabbalists refer to this

23 A. N. Williams, *The Ground of Union: Deification in Aquinas and Palamas*, Oxford University Press, 1999
24 "Aseity (from Latin *a* "from" and *se* "self", plus-*ity*) refers to the property by which a being exists in and of itself, from itself, or exists as so-and-such of and from itself. The word is often used to refer to the Christian belief that God contains within himself the cause of himself, is the first cause, or rather is simply uncaused, though many Jewish and Muslim theologians have also believed God to be independent in this way. Notions of aseity as the highest principle go back at least to Plato and have been in wide circulation since Augustine, though the use of the word 'aseity' began only in the Middle Ages." (WP)
25 From Peter Hamilton's excellent science fiction series of the same name. The use of the term, in this book, is significantly different.

as *Tsimtsum* or a way of being absent in presence. It is the way God withdraws so that something else can even begin to exist in the overpowering presence of His Existence. This is to be distinguished from the Hegelian notion of a God who is, so to speak, dissolved in both matter and history and seeking his transcendence. Tsimtsum allows God, metaphysically speaking, to retain his transcendence while paradoxically engaging time. This is not a Hegelian reduction of Spirit to the energy of the First Law of Thermodynamics.

From a Christian perspective, what we may know at any given point in time—as to how God's knowledge and intentions might be known—can be at variance with the transcendental and final totality of God's knowledge of Himself, as the Alpha and the Omega or the beginning and end of all things. God's own knowledge of Himself, within time and from this perspective, can be at variance with His eternal knowledge but only by way of relation.

God's Existence is a form of non-existence and this is said to distinguish that which originates existence from that which possesses existence. The possession of knowledge, *decohered in time,* is secondary to being that knowledge in the eternity of Divine Consciousness. It is *Tsimtsum,* perhaps, rather than the fall of man described in the Bible that may be responsible for the difficulty that human beings have in understanding their own relationship to good and evil. The Reality Dysfunction represents a division between human and Divine understanding that can be bridged through reason and revelation.

God, in other words, acting within time seems different to us from God's Existence, as we might imagine It, outside of time. How can this be if God does not change? Within time, the Divine seems to be subject to a self-imposed limitation, as it seems impossible to understand how Eternity can be contained in, or enter time unmodified.[26]

---

26 It is possible that eternity shoulders time aside in any theophany but that "shouldering" is itself, it would seem, an alteration or action within time. It could also be that Existence subsumes time in such a way that asking whether or not God can "enter" time is an irrelevant question. As my son Tobias noted, when presented with this argument, "how could God *not* enter time?"

The possession of existence in time, versus the origination of Existence, which occurs outside of time, is the delta point at which God "has skin in the game". It is also the indirect cause of the Time War. The *Reality Dysfunction* is both an *affect and effect* of the delta that God's own knowledge of Himself, within time, generates. The Reality Dysfunction is a *relation* brought about by a disproportion between the non-Existent existence of God and everything that exists contingently. The presence of an Infinite Force that englobes matter and time is not without consequence. As Walker Percy noted, so beautifully, in *The Message in a Bottle:*

> *"In the beginning was alpha, the end is omega, but somewhere in between came Delta, man himself. Man became man by breaking into the daylight of language—whether by good fortune or bad fortune, whether by pure chance, or by the touch of God, it is not for me to say here."*

Within the differentiation caused by the Reality Dysfunction, each one of us represents God knowing Himself, outside himself, in a unique and exclusive way. Our knowledge of Him, conversely, is equally unique, and while not exclusive, is extraordinarily nuanced by the creativity and power of each human being. It is this extraordinary variety that contributes to the vast difference and kind of opinion that we find in the world at large. Progressives tend to "get this" in outline better than conservatives, although there is a difference between variety and license that conservatives tend to make their primary focus. It is for this reason that moral distinctions are critical in honoring the vastness of the human enterprise. Both liberals and conservatives often assert what could be complimentary truths, if the proper distinctions are observed.

THREE TRANSCENDENTAL ALGORITHMS

Creation then might be described, metaphysically, as being brought about by a kind of ratio[27] between time and eternity. Given that God cannot be thought of as a quantity, which is usually ascribed to ratios, this can only function as an analogy between what we understand as a relationship between one thing and another. In this particular case it is a ratio between the finite and the infinite. This Existence/existence (Being/be-ing) ratio of E/e (once "e" is created) creates an imbalance between what is created and that which brings it into being.

> *The Infinite cannot be fully contained by time and space and so a certain lack of equivalent functionality exists between the finite and the infinite, in terms of force and consciousness, as expressed in the material order.[28] The finite, decohered and powered by infinite Existence, has an exponential force multiplier behind it that cannot be measured. It is this exponential force multiplier, created by the Reality Dysfunction (God knowing Himself outside Himself) that we are calling the **EFM Algorithm** (Exponential Force Multiplying Algorithm). This might be thought of as the second of three Transcendental algorithms. The first Transcendental algorithm is the **Reality Dysfunction** itself. The third Transcendental algorithm might be thought of as the **Infinity Differential** when infinity is known by Infinity in time.*

E/e, as the possibility of all things, becomes in the first iteration of the Reality Dysfunction, e/E or "being" powered by Existence. The infinite, not being containable by either space or time, lends itself to distortions of pressure created by an exponential explosion of existing things that Divine Consciousness, being constrained by time and dimension, cannot keep up with. Infinite consciousness attempts to keep up with

---

27 The result of one number or quantity divided by another. Ratios are the among the simplest mathematical tools that reveal significant relationships.

28 Physics: the quantitative difference between two or more forces, motions, etc.

infinite force but as an infinity it is already one step below Existence, as something known, *outside of Itself.* It is interesting to note, particularly in this context, that the Swiss mathematician Euler (1707-1783) described natural exponentials, such as are found in compounded interest rates and later used in the Richter Scale[29] for earthquakes, mathematically as "e".

Mathematics and consequently, all numbers and ratios are generated by the three *Transcendental Algorithms.* Pi, ("π") for example, is a natural exponential found in geometry. Using π as an example of the effect of the infinity differential, imagine a circle expanding at an infinite rate and the diameter of that circle expanding one hundred and eighty degrees, also at an infinite rate. Once the circle is formed, the diameter, since it starts its rate of progression in relation to the circle, *after* its formation, will never catch up. Pi, if you will recall, is the ratio 3.14159265...which is the circumference divided by its diameter.

The Golden Ratio (1.61803...) or the similarly sounding letter Phi (Φ) is also a natural exponential. "The Fibonacci Series of numbers *(0, 1, 1, 2, 3, 5, 8, 13, 21... etc., each number is the sum of the two numbers before it)* is closely related to the Golden Ratio. When we take any two successive *(one after the other)* Fibonacci Numbers, their ratio is very close to the Golden Ratio."[30] The arrangement of leaves on a plant, known as phyllotaxis, follows both the Golden Ratio and the Fibonacci series of numbers. The relationship between natural phenomenon and perceptions of beauty[31] involving the Golden Ratio and the Fibonacci Numbers are too numerous to comment on but the profound relationship of number to the rest of the material universe practically shouts the words algorithm and ratio. The ratio between the Infinite and the finite in the *Reality Dysfunction* is also a ratio—a

---

29 On the Richter Scale, each number represents ten times the force of the previous number. An earthquake of ten on the Richter Scale is ten times greater than nine on the same scale but many times exponentially higher than, say, two on the Richter Scale.

30 Golden Ratio: https://www.mathsisfun.com/numbers/nature-golden-ratio-fibonacci.html

31 The Parthenon appears to have been built on the Golden Ratio as have many other aesthetically pleasing buildings. The most beautiful human faces and bodies also, generally speaking, follow this ratio in terms of the arrangement of facial and limb dimensions

metaphysical ratio. The Infinite is constantly and effortlessly generating what is finite out of its own infinite superabundance.

> *Existence is an infinity generator. It also differentiates what is infinite in time, infinitely, without change to Itself in the Reality Dysfunction, which is its algorithmic delta. An infinite number of forms is required to mirror the infinite Source of everything.*

What God knows and does, He knows and does infinitely and simultaneously. In considering Himself infinitely, and in all the ways in which He can be known, this knowledge necessarily involves an infinite knowledge about Himself that is also infinitely finite in time and nature. Creation is part of this infinity, in all its aspects, considered and known from all eternity within the eternal and transcendental Act of Divine consciousness.

> *God's knowledge of Himself, outside Himself, in time is what creates all potential. Imagine a form of Existence so powerful that it calls things into existence simply through its Nature—in and outside of time. The Reality Dysfunction is simply a metaphor to attempt to understand the signification of a kind of Existence that deposits, as it were, all things into existence, both potentially and actually, without any sort of change occurring in Itself. This presents a complete paradox to the human mind but is consonant with the notion of a Fifth Law of Thermodynamics.*

What God knows does not become manifest until its fullness in time, which has always been known—not as something in itself but as something that is part of the continuum of infinite Being and Existence that is God. Time, in this respect, is an accident[32] relative to God's Nature.

---

32 A hat, for example, has a certain meaning regardless of *shape, size, color* or *location,* etc. Similarly, *quantity, quality, relation, place, time, position, state, action, affection* and *substance* are all accidents, or categories, i.e., they are things that are predicated of something more fundamental.

THE CONTINUUM HYPOTHESIS

The physicist, Edward Teller, made the astonishing assertion that "the extinction of the human race will come from its inability to understand the exponential function." This was a revision of a quote by fellow physicist Al Bartlett, who was only interested in applying the notion of exponential growth negatively, i.e., as it might apply to population growth and other ostensible human problems. What we can say about Teller's more interesting interpretation is that exponential growth is *where the rate of change is itself changing,* so there is no baseline, except relatively speaking between arbitrarily marked and abstract intervals of change.

What this means, in terms of metaphysics and metaphor, is that God's nature, via the construct of time, creates exponentially. God's Essence, derivatively configured in time, from the fullness of His Existence by the *Reality Dysfunction,* in freely choosing to know Himself, outside Himself, is powered by infinite force but derivative consciousness—even transdimensional consciousness—cannot keep up with the *force* of Existence from God's first look, so to speak. This is an unequal ratio of force to consciousness within time. Much like attempting to pour the ocean into a teacup, consciousness, in all its dimensional forms, cannot contain Existence. e/E always results in more of e and not more of E. What e/E does is multiply the number of cups or the number of ways whereby this infinite force, self-sequestered by time, might be comprehended. Expressed as a logarithm,[33] "e" to the power of "E" is mediated by finite numbers that continue infinitely.

> *Why do numbers even exist as possibilities? The only answer that makes sense is that something that is not generated is doing the generating both at the heart of matter and in time.* **Furthermore, the presence of zero as a number may indicate that something that is not a number is related to**

---

33 A logarithm is a mathematical way of deriving the exponent when you only know what the product of the base and the exponent is. The "log" of 100, for example, is 10 when the base is ten.

*number by its absence. It is no accident, perhaps, that com-
puter code is primarily composed of meanings based almost
entirely on a binary series consisting of zeroes and ones.*[34]
*Zero then may be a mathematical clue pointing in the direc-
tion of Existence.*

This "generation" is reflected in both mathematics and life in
multiple ways. **The Continuum Hypothesis** (CH), first developed
by George Cantor, suggests that there are non-continuous relations
between various sets of numbers. The infinite set of real numbers, i.e.,
those numbers that are generated by adding the number one to itself
or to itself one or more times does not have a real or one-to-one correspondence to, or with [all] real numbers, which include the rational
and irrational numbers.[35] This suggests that there are different kinds
of infinity at work in mathematical sets.

The Continuum Hypothesis is considered one of the most important open problems in set theory. It is rumored[36] that George Cantor received a letter from a student when he was at Cambridge University in England. The student asked:

*"Consider a set that is a collection of all the sets that do not con-
tain themselves. Does this set contain itself?"*

A set such as this that would not contain itself is a good mathematical analog to the paradox of Existence as it was understood by
Aristotle. Looking at the Continuum Hypothesis metaphysically, it
appears that something is generating different kinds of infinity from

---

34 I am indebted to Mike Hockney's book about Mozart, *The Last Man That Knew
Everything* for this insight, which he asserts is central to the claims of Illuminism. I do
not agree, however, that God is a mathematician, only that mathematics exists because
intelligence is fused with Existence in the unimaginable reality of the Divine Mind,
as it exists in a derived form. An Existence, which is its own Essence, is so far off the
charts of human comprehension that God can only be said to be a mathematician by
analogy.

35 *The Continuum Hypothesis,* by Wilzchek, Frank, May 23, 2013

36 This anecdote was passed on to me by physicist and friend, Ken Matusow.

the perspective of sets. The complexities of the real world mirror the stupendous extent of Divine self-knowledge as it leaves its signature, so to speak, on mathematics and physics. Infinite force is attempting to reunite with the Infinite consciousness and joy of the Eternal by expressing Itself in as many ways as possible. This is another example of the existence, in derivative form, of Divine algorithms between time and eternity.

Using multiple or serial processors to crack complex problems is analogous to what life does in all its permutations. This is ultimate meaning of the Reality Dysfunction: equivocal consciousness is constantly trying to play catch-up with the univocal power of Existence. We are here as the old Baltimore Catechism stated: "to know, love and serve God". However, we first have to overcome some of the problems caused by God's knowing Himself, outside Himself. God is trying to share the infinity of His Existence with creation. He has put Himself into the process[37] derivatively and paradoxically; he has "skin in the game".

This means that life is not just a recovery operation from a mythical fall of man but a real engagement of man and God with the reality that God has created. Creation is an effect and an affect simultaneously. The "effect" whether described as creation or a virtual reality, is a result of the *affect* of ideas in the mind of God as they are "affected" by other Divine Ideas. In other words, within the mind of God, there is a continuum of algorithmic effects that only take place within time. In God they are not effects but affects within the unchangeable Divine Nature that are proportionally related amongst themselves by the Divine Nature's own self-existent reality. This represents an extraordinary set of non-relations, whereby Ideas in the Mind of God, which cannot be distinct from His Essence, are distinct from each other only by the mediation of time in the Reality Dysfunction.

When we take a good hard look at nature and reality, the notion of a God who is identified with goodness, as we understand it, is hard to grasp. The "eat or be eaten" modality of nature and the billions of

---

37 Process: a series of actions, changes, or functions bringing about a result

beings, (both animal and human) killed, or destroyed in various calamities does not reflect well upon a provident and concerned God, as He is portrayed by the Bible. What we do see and experience is much closer to what might be expected from the Reality Dysfunction, whereby what God is in eternity is not quite how He expresses Himself in time. The effect seems to be not commensurate with the cause.

There are really only two conclusions that can be arrived at. One is the traditional biblical view that says everything that God created was good and it was Mankind's sin that deranged what was originally intended by God to be a blessed state is correct. This view, however, simply doesn't align with what we know about evolution and biology and the strain is telling. The second conclusion is that our "condition" is not the result of any kind of "Fall" but rather due to an evolutionary condition created by the Reality Dysfunction and the way that Ideas in the Mind of God generate multiple *effects* in time from *affects* that are unitary and eternal by nature.

An "affect" in the mind of God is translated into "effect" at an infinite and exponential rate that is equivalent to God's Nature, as it might be understood, as being self-limited, within the Reality Dysfunction. From the point of view of physics, it might be said that the decoherence of quantum reality by an Infinite Observer produces infinite effects. How do you pin down something that is not, equivocally speaking, anything but is also infinite in all other ways? Infinite Affect produces infinite effects, without change occurring within Itself. The fundamental relationship between man and God is one of an Infinite and Eternal Affect bringing about change in all things through an infinite set of algorithms that are mediated by Its own knowledge of Itself. The Eternal, then, is as infinitely relational as it is not.

Christianity is in danger of losing its relevance by insisting that old models of understanding the universe must be grafted onto the story of salvation to be meaningful. The opposite, in fact, seems to be happening. Ireland, the land of saints and scholars, recently voted for gay marriage. This is an indication that Christianity, in the form of the Catholic Church, is losing its grip on the western mind. A new understanding of salvation grounded in the meaning of the Reality Dysfunction will not make the message of Jesus any less relevant. We are in need of spiritual and moral redemption regardless of whether or not the fall of man ever occurred. The insistence that God could not have created something that was not originally perfect blinds us to seeing the reality around us.

RECONSIDERING THE MEANING OF RELATION

According to Aquinas, God Himself doesn't change in bringing about creation and sharing His life. He brings about this change by creating *ex nihilo* or out of nothing, which causes everything to change, *relationally*, in reference to the infinite power of His non-existent Existence. That relation is, for all intents and purposes, a virtual construct—an artifact of eternity—a translation of something that by its non-existence makes everything else exist. (God exists, so to speak at a right angle to the linear way in which we think and conceive of time, space and causality.)

> *What this means is that secondary forms of existence or be-ings that have their existence through God's own Existence, via participation, are not real to God in terms of subject-object relationships but rather they are what we would think of as a kind of virtual reality. St. Thomas Aquinas referred to this as "relation", which was the only word available to him at the time. It means that God's Existence is so dynamic that participated[38] forms of*

---

38 Thomas Aquinas, to my knowledge, does not exhaustively describe what participation is, although for him it would no doubt be considered a derivative or secondary form of existence in relation to the *Ipsum Esse* or self-caused existence of God. What he does say, goes something like this: "Thirdly, an effect can be said to participate in its cause, especially when the effect is not equal to the power of that cause. The effect particu-

existence are not directly real to Him, although they most certainly are for us. Conversely, we have a real relation to God but that relation for God is simply a construct, an interface between God's operating system, which we might call the E-System and our relation to that system, which might be termed an e-system (with a lower case "e"). This virtual reality enables God to interact with creation without change occurring in Himself. It is movement without movement and interval without interval, as Existence completely bypasses derived or participated forms of existence to produce change, via the participated reality, without change in Itself. This might be said to be the ultimate meaning of Tsimtsum, although the Kabbalists might formulate the metaphysical direction of the idea differently. The difference between the notion of Tsimtsum and the Reality Dysfunction is that the Reality Dysfunction is the result of the action of a Divine Person or Persons and not simply an abstract process of the One.

The E-System of the Divine Essence affects the universe through an unknown set of force dynamics that the ancients tried to describe as essence or form and that science describes as decoherence of the quantum wave function. We are calling it the Reality Dysfunction because an eternal observer can never fully enter time. There is always an algorithmic disproportion between what God knows in eternity (the E-system) and what He knows, derivatively, within the e-system. God knows Himself, *outside Himself,* in this virtual or decohered construct, which can also be described very loosely as the ratio of E/e in eternity and e/E outside of eternity. This is, ultimately, the metaphysical basis for Philip Carr's proposed Fifth Law of Thermodynamics.

There is a disproportion between God's self-knowledge as it is

---

larizes and determines the scope of the cause; for the effect acts as the determinate recipient of the power of the cause. The effect receives from its cause only that which is necessary for the production of the effect. It is in this way that a cause is participated in by its effect." (as quoted by Gaven Kerr in his presentation on the metaphysics of Aquinas) in the Ipsum Esse (His self-caused Existence) and how He knows Himself, derivatively, within the decohered construct of space and time. This disproportion of e/E might also be described in terms of energy and consciousness as, *Dimensionally Interactive Cyber Kinesis,*[39] in that infinite force and consciousness considers Itself *infinitely* within the virtual construct of time and simultaneously and infinitely, outside of time, as It considers Itself from eternity. Cyber-kinetic energy[40] then has an infinite source at one end, so to speak, of the manifestation and a decohered manifestation that is evident in the many forms of kinetic energy that are described by particle physics and Superstring Theory at the other end. (The notional relationship of cyber-kinetic energy to the concepts of locality, non-locality and superstrings will be examined shortly.)

The notion of atoms or subatomic particles having "consciousness" in terms of a rudimentary awareness of an "inside" and an "outside" mirrors the fundamental dynamics of the Reality Dysfunction. Consciousness, as we know it, is eternity considering Itself, infinitely, from within the self-created finitude of matter.

> *Imagine a sphere that is finite on the outside but paradoxically infinite on the inside. Consciousness is the relationship or ratio between the two expressed in the vast multitude of matter and dimension that makes up the universe. Dimensionally Interactive Cyber Kinesis is a four-dimensional representation or metaphor for the algorithm of change that exists between two different spheres or forms of existence.*

In the same way that Sri Aurobindo described matter[41] as con-

---

39 Sean J. O'Reilly, *How to Manage Your Destructive Impulses with Cyber Kinetics: Redirect Sexual Energy and Discover Your More Spiritually Enlightened, Evolved Self,* 10 Speed Press, 2001.

40 Kinetic energy is the energy of motion, observable as the movement of an object, particle, or set of particles. Any object in motion is using kinetic energy.

41 Satprem, *Sri Aurobindo, The Adventure of Consciousness,* Sri Aurobindo, Ashram Trust, 1968

sciousness/force, *Dimensionally Interactive Cyber Kinesis* is conscious from the bottom up and from the top down in varying degrees of intensity and in a bewildering number of dimensions all at once. The kind of physical aggregates that we see in all forms of life represent this fundamental consciousness at work. This, rather than the idea of an outside agency controlling evolution is, in fact, the basis for natural selection and evolution in general. Intelligence, diffused as it may be at the atomic level, aggregates matter according to rules laid down in the Reality Dysfunction by the Divine Intelligence. This decoherence of the quantum wave function is a result of God knowing Himself, as other than Himself, in time.

The Infinity Differential or exponential function between these two "systems" is caused by the Reality Dysfunction. There is a constant existential pressure between higher consciousness, as it is diffused in the Reality Dysfunction, and consciousness that increases in clarity, power and intensity the further up the ladder of being you go. They are asynchronous (from our perspective) to the degree that what is finite cannot fully contain what is infinite even through various modes of divinely sponsored participation. How these modes of participation (and that includes grace) actually function on the quantum level, or can be metaphorically described can take many forms as the foregoing indicates. The notion that Existence would *not* have a measurable hierarchical or cascading effect/affect on the material order is a non-rational proposition at odds with the entire metaphysical enterprise.

The foregoing description of our relationship with God in the metaphysical strangeness of the Reality Dysfunction might be considered by some as being the ravings of a lunatic but attempting to understand God's Existence without adverting to the Reality Dysfunction and the Infinity Differential turns theology into thaumaturgy. The work of the philosopher and theologian can never be merely defensive. Exploring and describing the *radical extramentality* of God is a job that will never be completed. It is the only task of humanity that will constantly produce additional information the more the concept is examined.

If we dig into some of these ideas we must consider that the creation of being, as a relational artifact or virtual reality, is simultaneous with the creation of time; being necessarily exists in time. The paradox might be stated as follows: could there ever have been a time when God did not know about His own creation? That knowledge constitutes a unique relationship of time *in reference* to the Divine Nature. The creation of time then represents a natural opposition or proportion between eternal knowledge and the temporal derivations of that knowledge that are utilized within dimensional limits by all created beings.

What God knows can never be fully translated within the limited context of created being and so each conclusion that occurs within the human time-frame functions as a premise for a new set of considerations to understand what is beyond our full ability to grasp. This is mirrored in our own version of the Reality Dysfunction in which the immediacy of biological desires are at war with our understanding of what is good or more desirable, in terms of outcome, over the long-term.

Our knowledge of God and ourselves, and God's knowledge of Himself, in time, are dynamically related in a curious and disproportionate ratio. Infinite Act, in which consciousness, existence and love are simultaneous, exerts an infinite, yet proportional[42] pressure upon whatever can possibly exist in relation to that Act. This "pressure" can be postulated as being translated by an unknowable matrix or transcendental algorithm that can be understood by both religion and science.

This matrix, as we are suggesting, is caused by God knowing Himself, outside Himself in the *Reality Dysfunction*. The adventure for us is discovering why and how He does it! Things have existence, in

---

42 This is different from what St. Thomas referred to as proper proportionality. The proper proportionality that he refers to is, from a larger point of view, a *proportioned disproportion* between the Divine Essence and everything that participates in the Existence of the Divine Essence. The assumption is that this proportionality is functionally perfect relative to the nature of a thing and to some extent this is true. There is, however, a fundamental disproportion between finitude and infinity and between time and eternity that is expressed in the Reality Dysfunction. The essential order is not perfectly translated in time, as its perfection can only be found on the other side of Eternity.

other words, because something else exists supremely. Existence makes things *be* by virtue of what it *is* and what it "is", in translation (in be-ing), is a proportion of "Is" to is-ing. A proportion is usually understood in terms of division or multiplication; it is a function, and as such, is expressible in terms of the analogical language of metaphysics and in the more exact scientific language of mathematics and physics.

The "isness" of this kind of proportionality is radically different from how we presently understand cause and effect. "Is" generates causes and effects across time, in a non-linear manner, just by being what it Is. "Is" generates potential due to a superabundance of being. "Is" creates or generates potential simultaneously in the past, present and future *as it draws the expression of Itself in time to Itself in eternity.* There is no past; there is no present and there is no future in God. An infinite number of possibilities and permutations are continuously generated across time by the Divine Mind in the *movement without movement* of the Divine's own eternal Act of self-knowledge.

The entire physical universe of hundreds of millions of galaxies and billions of suns, and the astonishing amount of energy it contains, is the reflection of an infinite force considering Itself infinitely. This is also the ultimate meaning of negentropy or the Fifth Law of Thermodynamics. Indian philosophers refer to this as the world of *Satchitananda,* which is the compound Sanskrit word for Existence, Consciousness and Bliss.

A divine paradox in regards to God's knowing Himself, outside Himself, might be stated as follows: could God choose not to be Himself? If He could not choose not to be God would He still be God? The staggering vistas of God's freedom are the gift that is extended to mankind in creation.

Chapter 3

THE TIME WAR AND
TWO KINDS OF PHYSICS

"Reason finds it sweeter to exercise her skill in the hidden straights of the ocean of divinity than idly to bask in smooth and open waters where she cannot display her power." [1]

—John Scotus Eriugena

Physics is defined as "knowledge of nature and is the natural science that involves the study of matter and its motion through space and time, along with related concepts such as energy and force." [2]Metaphysics is defined as "the branch of philosophy that deals with

---

1 *John Scottus Eriugena,* Diedre Carabine, Professor and Director of the Institute of Ethics and Development Studies, Uganda Martyrs University; Oxford University Press, copyright 2000, page 19
2 WP

the first principles of things, including abstract concepts such as being, knowing, substance, cause, identity, time, and space." [3] The linkage between the two disciplines is obvious and overlapping. It has taken a very long time, however, for the two disciplines to see that they have much more in common than not. Time, space and energy are common areas for both sciences and are constituent elements of the *Reality Dysfunction* and the Time War.

What we know and what God knows will always be somewhat at variance, or out of kilter, within the context of time. This is the basis for the Time War, which is the historical consequence or a temporal effect of the Reality Dysfunction. What we see as the Reality Dysfunction, however, is not a dysfunction at all from God's perspective. It is simply an adventure, a turn, known from eternity and manifested in time and space by an infinite and free consciousness. There never was a time when God did not know about the creation. Considering this is complicated by the idea that God doesn't *have* to know anything—as we understand knowing between one thing and another. There is no relationship between one thing and another in the Mind of God; there is only the blinding reality of an Act in which thought and Existence are one and inseparable except within time. God's Existence might be thought of as being radically or infinitely orthogonal (at right angles) to our own. The Divine is so far outside the realm of our understanding that all we can do is point in certain directions through analogy and metaphor and hope that we can get some traction on pieces of the picture.

As a metaphor, the Time War indicates that God's knowledge of Himself, *outside Himself,* in what for Him is a virtual or decohered[4] reality, is at the root of many human difficulties and some extraordinary opportunities. Grasping that the *Reality Dysfunction* is based on God's consciousness in time and space, in *relative* opposition to His eternal

---

3   Ibid
4   Remember that decoherence results in the collapse of the quantum wave function and the settling of a particle into its observed state under classical physics, its transition from quantum to classical behavior.

knowledge in the Act of Existence, enables human beings to understand history and evolution in an entirely different way. God knowing Himself, *outside Himself*, creates multiple dimensions of intention and meaning throughout time and is the driving force and algorithm of change that we understand and characterize as evolution. The Reality Dysfunction, consequently and as a delta point between time and eternity, has three effects:

One: It has a splintering or dysfunctional effect in terms of multiple perceptions caused by God's own knowing of Himself in trillions of different ways, across different time lines and in different worlds all in the same eternal moment but separated from Him because he knows them, not just as they are in Himself, which is in eternity but as they are in themselves—in time.

Two: God's knowing of Himself, *as other than Himself*, results in the creation of a derivative form of existence; a being and beings who know or are themselves in terms of *knowledge and possession* rather than directly through the Act of Divine Existence.[5] This was noted by John Scottus Eriugena in the ninth century and theologian Henry of Ghent in the thirteenth century. Scotus Eriugena claimed that while uncreated, *God creates God's self* as a creature.[6] This means that God, as cause, is the essence of all things. Eriugena's reasoning was based, in part, on the established teaching of the Neo-Platonist Proclus (412-485 AD) who asserted that "every effect remains in its cause, proceeds from it and returns to it."[7]

---

5   The followers of St. Thomas would claim that this is a false distinction but the burden of proof, in terms of what we see in the world around us, has yet to be demonstrated.

6   *John Scottus Eriugena*, Diedre Carabine, Professor and Director of the Institute of Ethics and Development Studies, Uganda Martyrs University; Oxford University Press, copyright 2000, pages 34 and 117

7   Ibid

Henry of Ghent argued that the possession of the Divine Essence was a primary actuality and that the secondary actuality of considering the Divine Essence was in potency to the first.[8] The possession of the Divine Essence is what we might refer to, analogically, as the decoherence of Existence in quantum reality.

The first of this creation is known as "God" by way of abstraction or concept, instead of what He is, which is an Act of such overwhelming light and power that it cannot be known by finite beings without the mediated assistance of that same God. God manifests, so to speak, in an abstract form that we can understand and this is done through the mediation of the Reality Dysfunction. It is not, however, the self-existent God that we perceive. What we see are abstractions of an abstraction, the first born of all creation, the Son of God, the Demiurge or Kali.[9] The Indian philosopher, Sri Aurobindo referred to this first born of creation in his book, *The Life Divine*, as "Supermind" and the Kabbalists refer to it as "Ari".

The notion of Gods that are, perhaps, symbols of another deeper or more fundamental reality, probably goes back at least 10,000 years to pre-historical times. Brahman was the fundamental Being of the Hindus from whom all other Gods came forth. There was also Amon, (also known as Amon-Ra) the supreme God of the Egyptians, the primordial and underlying reality of the Tao of Lao Tse, the Unmoved Mover of Aristotle, the One of Plotinus and many teachings of the Neo-Platonists and later Gnostics that also point in this direction. By extension, what the Bible calls "angels" are also derivative beings—beings whose essences are limited only by the Divine Essence itself. My favorite angels, in this regard, are the Seraphim—the "burning ones"—those closest to the impossible radiance of the Divine.

---

8   William Owen Duba, *Seeing God: Theology, Beatitude and Cognition in the Thirteenth Century*, page 250

9   The name of Kali means "black one" and "force of time"; she is therefore called the Goddess of Time, Change, Power, Creation, Preservation, and Destruction. [WP]

Three: God's eternal knowing of His nature, as He has always been and will always be, has a unifying and compelling effect, in time and space, akin to gravity. This is the negentropic activity of the *reality function*.[10] Aristotle described this as a kind of attraction that the Unmoved Mover exerted on the rest of the universe. The reality function results from an ordered decoherence of quantum reality by an eternal observer as it brings reality back towards Itself. Teilhard de Chardin refers to this process as "centration". The name, however, is not important. Understanding the reality function or centration as an algorithm between Existence and contingent existence makes it possible to talk about God's relationship to the universe in a new way.

The splintering effect of the *Reality Dysfunction* results in an observable moral and spiritual Tower of Babel, which is the subject of this book. The unifying effect of the *reality function* involves an expansion of our self-knowledge in reference to an infinite source. The *reditus* or the return of the infinite to the Infinite is the basis for the negentropic and evolutionary activity that is characteristic of the proposed Fifth Law of Thermodynamics. There is a constant, negentropic evolutionary pressure, as it were, from God's eternal knowledge, which seeks to bring perfection into the present by bridging what we know and understand with the shining reality of what God knows. The stochastic[11] element of evolution is natural selection. The hidden, causal element of evolution is the design brought about by God's knowledge of how all things can imitate His consciousness. From our perspective this infinite differential seems almost like a fault but from God's perspective it is simply an expression, in time, of a greater perfection and continuum that is already known in the One Act of Divine Consciousness.

---

10 A function simply relates an input to an output.
11 Randomly determined; having a random probability distribution or pattern that may be analyzed statistically but may not be predicted precisely.

What seems to be part of the Reality Dysfunction might be more authentically described as the reality function of the Divine Mind, i.e., God creates both the actual and the possible in the reality function. The ancients referred to pure possibility as prime matter or matter without an act that would make it into something specific. Sri Aurobindo described one of the derivative Acts of the Divine intelligence as the Overmind. He called it "an ocean of stable lightning." [12]Our perception of what is one function, on the basis of observable positive and negative results, splits what is one reality into two functions. The reality function is exerting constant, negentropic pressure in the present time in order to bring the universe into alignment with God's eternal purpose. The Reality Dysfunction, from this perspective, is a kind of hiccup in time (but not in eternity) based on an original and voluntary act of self-abnegation that is part, so to speak, of the Divine Nature.[13] What changes is reality in relation to Existence. God does not change but brings about change through the sheer force, so to speak, of what He is not. Whatever God knows, He knows infinitely. Knowing Himself, as other than Himself, He also knows Himself infinitely as possibility. This is a metaphysical conundrum but it is also an attempt to grasp the radical difference between God's Existence and our own, which is a pale imitation.

The ancient Norse, in a primitive but useful line of reasoning, believed in a rainbow bridge between heaven and earth. The Bifrost Bridge connected Asgard (heaven) with earth (Midgard). "In the pre-Christian worldview, the invisible, religious modality of existence doesn't lie in a realm of absolute remove from the material world, as

---

12 Satprem, *Sri Aurobindo, The Adventure of Consciousness*, Sri Aurobindo, Ashram Trust, 1968

13 Abnegation is a noun that means renunciation of one's own interests in favor of others. When you purposely deny yourself something, especially in favor of the needs of others, you would describe this act as an abnegation.

in monotheistic religions. Rather, it lies *within* or *behind* the every-day, material world."[14] This view is compatible with the concept of an Unmoved Mover who draws the world to Himself, via the power of attraction, or what might be called the *reality function*. The reality function is also the basis for morality. All of morality is based on the notion that to be "good" is to imitate the excellence of the Divine. But what is goodness? The philosophical and theological development of the concepts of virtue and vice, over the past two thousand years, is one long attempt to answer that question.

What we believe about God is often at variance with what we know or intuit about God but do not necessarily advert to or, as is the case in many instances, are unable to advert to due to the prevalence of conflicting ideas generated by the intuitive knowledge of the soul and the activities of rational classification. In other words, the way the universe actually operates, as opposed to our model of how we think it should operate, can be at variance.

This conflict, or time war, is specifically related to our under-standing of time and causality. If causality is simply stochastic (random) then time can be considered as a neutral box in which random things can happen based on various material fluxes. If time is related to eternity, then the picture of causality is radically different. The attempt of science, for example, to suppress the notion of intelligent design appears to be non-rational and rooted in a desire for moral and spiritual non-accountability. It is also a very good example of one aspect of the time war. God knows that He will be known *as not existing* and He knows what that will and does feel like in the secondary construct of His knowledge that occurs in time.

Currently, atheists and many "progressive" thinkers subscribe to

---

14 "If Bifröst is correct, however, the meaning would be something akin to "the shaking or trembling rainbow." In either case, the word points to the ephemeral and fragile nature of the bridge. All rainbows, of course, are "fleeting." In the pre-Christian… worldview, the invisible, religious modality of existence doesn't lie in a realm of abso-lute remove from the material world, as in monotheistic religions. Rather, it lies within or behind the everyday, material world." (http://norse-mythology.org/cosmology/bi-frost/) (WP)

the notion that time has only the meanings that we give it, as opposed to any significance imposed by an eternal intelligence. Conservatives, typically, align themselves with a view of time that is sponsored or driven by a divine intelligence. The adherents of random mutation, as the sole cause of evolution, are at odds with those who would claim that there are different kinds of causality at work in the universe.

THEOPHANIES AND CREATION

The kind of causality that we are said to effect is called *extrinsic causality*. Material causality and the making of things (efficient causality) fall into this category. *Intrinsic causality*, on the other hand, is an internal property of time, space and matter. God's causality is said to be intrinsic, as is formal causality, which might also be thought of as being negentropic or resisting and opposing the entropy of the Second Law of Thermodynamics.

The God of Christianity is affirmed to be, paradoxically, One Nature and Three Persons. While it is not traditional Christian teaching to say that the Three Persons are an emanation of the One it might be argued that God, as Three distinct Persons, would seem by necessity to possess a temporal element, and that it might be more appropriate to describe the Persons of God, as a kind of temporal derivation that is the expression of a greater unity of Persons, within Existence, than can presently be comprehended.

Fr. Jerome Fasano,[15] in a recent sermon, employed the metaphor of the sun to explain the Trinity. God the Father is the sun; Jesus Christ might be likened to the rays of the sun and the Holy Spirit corresponds to the heat of the sun. Aside from the obvious beauty of this analogy, the danger of this image is that both the Son of God and the Holy Spirit might be thought of as effects or emanations of the Father. However, God is most certainly "more" One outside

---

15 Pastor of St. John's Catholic Church in Front Royal, Virginia

of time, no matter how we conceived of the relations[16] between the Persons of the Trinity, than within the temporal manifold. It is for this reason that I like to think of the Trinity in terms of the Sanskrit formulation: Existence as the Father, Consciousness as the Son and Bliss as the Holy Spirit. How God or this Trinity of Being might be thought of or understood within time is part of the focus of the Reality Dysfunction.

God's knowledge from within time might be thought of, from our perspective, as trinary. He knows Himself always, as He is eternally; secondly, God knows how He might be known or imitated and thirdly, He loves Himself in the profusion of His One Nature, which is paradoxically a community of Persons and a vast contingent reality. In other words, in order for God to know and love something other than the blinding reality of His own Existence—within eternity—whereby being, knowledge and love is fused in an incomprehensible, unified Act (whether One Nature, or Three Persons with One nature) a derivative or virtual reality, in which God understands Himself as *an abstraction*, can be understood or postulated as requiring the creation of space and time.[17]

This abstraction involves no change in God. What changes is the entire order of reality in reference to the incomprehensible Act of Existence, which posits creation and all possibility as a proportional relation to Itself in Dimensionally Interactive Cyber Kinesis. These relations, which collectively can be thought of as a virtual reality, have no real existence in the mind of God but are an expression of what Exis-

---

16 Aquinas, for example, in discussing the four relations of the Trinity: Paternity, Filiation, Spiration and Procession makes it clear that these are ways for us to understand something that is an expression of a greater unity than metaphysical discussion can allow. Without evaluating the theological meaning of these four relations, it is sufficient to say that Aquinas specifically states that "it is manifest that relation really existing in God is really the same as His essence and only differs in its mode of intelligibility... thus it is clear that in God relation and essence do not differ from each other but are one and the same." Aquinas, Thomas, *Summa Theologica*, The Blessed Trinity, Q. 28, Art. 4, Pt. 1, pg. 153, Benziger Brothers Edition, 1947.

17 Kenotic Christology covers some of this ground but the relationship of time to eternity in Kenotic Theology does not, to my knowledge, understand time as a virtual reality, created by eternity's complete and utter transcendence.

tence makes possible, as it considers Itself, outside Itself, in the Reality Dysfunction. Potential is made possible in reference to something that is so actual that it creates all possibility effortlessly and without motion.

This is also why Aristotle referred to the soul as "the first act of a body having life-potential." All things for Aristotle had potential only in relation to something that was itself pure actuality. Time has no beginning *in time* because it has always been known; it has, however, a beginning in relation to Existence or what might be more properly called non-existent Existence. That relation is one of creation from no-thing. The creation out of nothing, likewise, has no beginning for there could not be a time before there was nothing. For Aristotle, the futurity of the essential order was intimately connected to Actuality in which past, present and future had to be thought of as being present to the Unmoved Mover. Potential, in this respect, was simply a manifestation of the future as it might be known by the Unmoved Mover. (This will be discussed in greater detail in later chapters.) The failure to understand Aristotle in this regard is to misunderstand his greatest contribution to human intellection: that of Act ordering time and space to Itself—due to an idea of Itself or what we might call today a virtual reality. This idea may be hard to tease out of what we currently know about Aristotle's extant works (of which we have precious few) but the broad outlines can be seen in the existing works.

The Neoplatonists and some of the medieval theologians, particularly John Scotus Eriugena, in the ninth century and in order to better understand how there can be a relation between change and God referred to this virtual reality as a theopany[18] or manifestation of God in time. Eriugena states:

> *"The divine nature allows itself to appear in its theophanies,*
> *willing to emerge from the most hidden recesses of its nature in*

---

18 "Theophany, meaning "appearance of a god," refers to the appearance of a deity to a human or other being."

which it is unknown even to itself, that is, knows itself in noth-
ing because it is infinite and supernatural and super-essential
and beyond everything that can and cannot be understood; but
descending into the principles of things and, as it were, creating
itself, it begins to know itself in something." [19]

The "Fall" in the larger sense (the sensus plenior of the biblical scholar) may be the "fall" that God took in choosing to bring man into the fullness of His consciousness through the vast adventure that is time, space and energy. The notion that God can know Himself, *as other than Himself,* in the theophany of creation, [which we are calling the Reality Dysfunction] is a powerful metaphorical tool for understanding the nature of God in relation to our own existence. When creation is understood from this perspective, time is necessarily involved in creating. So while it can be argued, as Christians maintain, that God creates out of nothing, the result is *something* that begins to exist in time, does so, only by virtue of God's actuality made visible in a specific way. If we think of all of creation as a kind of virtual reality, in which "being" comes to exist, then God's existence within time can also be understood as derivative. This does not detract in any way from the eternal unity of Persons but makes it understandable how an impassible and immutable God can create at all.

Creation is, from this perspective, not other than God but part
of the mystery of God's own Eternal life and consciousness. Rath-
er than being simple pantheism, the Reality Dysfunction is an
eternal paradox. God's knowledge of Himself, outside Himself,
does not constitute something new to God; it is simply part of
the spectrum of the Divine Ideas in the incomprehensible fu-
sion of Existence and Consciousness that is the Transcendent Di-
vine Mind. Many of the problems of traditional theology revolve

19 *John Scottus Eriugena,* Carabine, Diedre, Professor and Director of the Institute of Ethics and Development Studies, Uganda Martyrs University; Oxford University Press, copyright 2000, page 31 citing P.1482B

around asserting a radical polarity between God and creation and then trying to bridge that polarity. Trying to understand creation in terms of cause and effect in time is missing the meaning of the original dynamic, outside of time, that even makes that possible. Metaphysical reasoning cannot proceed by taking time out of eternity and then bringing it in through the back door through metaphysical posturing via analogy. Existence must be understood as being radically outside of human consciousness. The problem is that we insist on thinking of ourselves as "here" and imagining God as "there" in some way. There is no "there" for God, although we are certainly "here".

INTERFERENCE PATTERNS

There is some evidence for the excogitation of Divine Ideas, associated with the Reality Dysfunction, in modern day holography. As demonstrated in Michael Talbot's excellent book, *The Holographic Universe*, a hologram involves the use of one laser beam that is split into two beams. The first beam is bounced off an object to be imaged, then the second beam is allowed to collide with the reflected light of the first. When this happens, an *interference pattern* is generated that can be recorded on a piece of film. As soon as a light beam is shined through the previously recorded film, a three dimensional image is formed. It is for this reason that a number of prominent scientists, including physicist David Bohm and neurosurgeon Karl Pribham, believe that the universe may be a kind of hologram.

We also have some common sense evidence for interference patterns occurring in everyday life. When you walk into a room with extremely happy people you may feel inexplicably happy; when you walk into a room full of angry people, you may begin to feel unreasoning hostility towards those around you. If you are in the presence of a very high energy person, you may feel yourself being energized and uplifted in a way that might feel good but isn't quite your normal state of mind. We often refer to this as sensing good or bad "vibes" but it isn't vibrations in the general sense that you may be feeling—it is the vibratory pattern created by the interference of two different energy patterns that creates a third and derivative state that is felt as the "vibe".

Using the analogy of a laser generated hologram, it is possible to hypothesize that God's knowledge of Himself, *outside Himself,* is roughly analogous to an interference pattern that is used to produce a holographic image. The interference pattern might be thought of as an analog for what the philosophers referred to, in their metaphysical speculations, as "form" or 'essence," or an idea from the mind of God *translating* into material reality as *be-ing* (being) and, more specifically, as a unique combination of two different kinds of be-ing in matter and form. This algorithmic combination of two different kinds of being, matter and form, is what the ancients called *substance.* Think of matter as the potential element, and form as the actuating principle, which specifies how potential will manifest.

LOCALITY AND NON-LOCALITY

Physicist David Bohm, in 1952, referred to a new field on the sub-quantum level as the *quantum potential* and theorized that it pervaded all space and all time.[20] He theorized that at the level the quantum potential operated it was *non-local* meaning that location ceased to exist. Physicists ascribe *non-locality* to the wave form and *locality* to the particle manifestation in three and four dimensions of the wave form when it is observed and *decohered.* At the non-local or un-decohered level of reality everything is connected.

"Non-locality describes the apparent ability of objects/particles to instantaneously know about each other's state, even when sepa-

---

20 Talbot, Michael, *The Holographic Universe,* Harper Perennial 1991, pg. 41

rated by large distances (potentially even billions of light years), almost as if the universe at large instantaneously arranges its particles in anticipation of future events." [21] Superpositioning, [22] as a corollary idea in physics, indicates that particles can also be located in a potentially unlimited number of places all at the same time. Superpositioning then, might be thought of, metaphysically, as the algorithmic activity of Dimensionally Interactive Cyber-Kinesis. It is truly enough to make your head swim!

Bohm further developed the idea of non-locality with the notion of *implicate* and *explicate* order. The implicate order is the non-local order, which is non-manifest at the physical level but still subject to various sets of rules at the implicate or non-local level of reality. At the physical level the order is explicate or manifest. What we see in the physical world with our senses is the explicate or local order, which is rooted in the non-local order.

A deeper question can be asked at this point: why does non-locality exist at all? It would appear that non-locality is an expression of an infinite consciousness that cannot be localized because it is outside of time. Non-locality is the one phenomenon that is, perhaps, a direct indication or signature of the activity of Existence, which does not exist in the way that any other existent thing manifests in space and time. Ideas in the mind of God can only exist in two ways. One: *non-locally* in the divine consciousness, which is One and two: derivatively, superimposed[23] as existent things in what we know as *locality* or the three

21 (http://www.physicsoftheuniverse.com/topics_quantum_nonlocality.html)
22 Part of the problem of observing and measuring superpositions is known as decoherence. Any attempt to measure or obtain knowledge of quantum superpositions by the outside world (or indeed any kind of interaction with their environment, even with just a single photon) causes them to decohere, effectively destroying the superposition and reducing it to a single location or state, and also destroying the ability of its individual states to interfere with each other. Decoherence then, results in the collapse of the quantum wave function and the settling of a particle into its observed state under classical physics, its transition from quantum to classical behavior. http://www.physicsoftheuniverse.com/topics_quantum_superposition.html
23 This is to be distinguished from the concept of superpositioning in physics, which means: the possibility of a potentially unlimited number of superposed waves, which

and four dimensions of space and time. The particle-wave duality discovered by science then, may be an indicator of divine consciousness. The words of a song from the 1960's, *There is a Mountain*, by the singer Donovan come to mind:

> *"First there is a mountain*
> *Then there is no mountain,*
> *Then there is.*
> *Oh Juanita,*
> *Oh Juanita,*
> *I call your name."*

The notion of the decoherence of the quantum wave, by observation, parallels the ancient's understanding of *form* as not specifically existing in time and space, as we know it, but existing *relationally* and in reference to the mind of an observer as a kind of mini-act or "is-ing" pattern. Translating the intention behind the idea of form in more modern terms, we might say that the form is a non-local relation and that as embodied human beings we are the local manifestation of the form. Using Bohm's language[24] of implicate and explicate, we might say that the form is implicate and that substance (the combination of matter and form) is explicate or manifested in some way.

---

means that microscopic particles can theoretically be located in a potentially unlimited number of places at once, and to behave in a potentially unlimited number of different ways.

24 "Physicists today remain largely unaware of the fact that quantum mechanics is perfectly choreographed by the mathematics of the de Broglie-Bohm theory, otherwise known as Bohmian mechanics. Despite the fact that Bohm's formalism is entirely deterministic, and less vague than the standard interpretation of quantum mechanics, so far it has only been widely recognized and embraced among philosophers of physics…There are several historical events, or "unfortunate accidents," that have led to the present ignorance of the superior mathematical clarity Bohm's formalism offers. Understanding this historical posture goes a long way towards explaining why the orthodox or "standard" interpretation of quantum mechanics is still held by the majority of physicists today—something that I would argue is one of the greatest intellectual tragedies of our time." Thad Roberts, https://www.quora.com/Why-dont-more-physicists-subscribe-to-pilot-wave-theory

The human and individual soul, from this local and non-local perspective, might be thought of as an extension or algorithmic translation of God's knowledge, as to how He might be seen and understood as, *other than Himself,* within space and time or as a kind of interference pattern generated between local and non-local Divine consciousness.

> *This interference pattern, which we are calling the Reality Dysfunction, might be thought of as a kind of superordinate intermediary, which translates Divine non-locality into locality. This is the eternal observer that mediates the functioning of the universe according to a non-local blueprint. Everything in the universe is relational, in reference to Existence, even our understanding of the idea of God.*

Divine non-locality, consequently, might be thought of as a kind of super-non-locality whereby knowledge, consciousness and act are simultaneous and eternal, *non-locally,* and *local* or decohered as a temporal manifestation in the Reality Dysfunction.

Martin Heidegger, in my opinion, was moving towards a similar notion of a complex interrelationship between the implicate and explicate orders when he articulated human existence as *dasein* or a "being there" (as in presence). Dasein might be thought of as a kind of non-local verb whereby who we are is called into being by Existence. It is on a continuum, from this perspective, with God's own *Dasein* in the Reality Dysfunction. If existence is as neutral as, or analogous to undifferentiated raw energy, then who we are, is as the existentialists might argue, a product of what we choose to be and not a product, so to speak, of a partnership between ourselves and the Divine.

Each one of us is, derivatively, from the perspective of the arguments presented in this book, a Trinity of Existence, Consciousness and Bliss knowing, loving and enjoying Itself from a local perspective, outside of the infinite immediacy of the non-local Divine Nature. This is the fuller meaning of *Dasein* reinterpreted through a more comprehensive ontology of human existence. God's *Dasein* might be thought of analogously as the Demiurge of the Gnostics, Universal Mind, or an intermediary and local form between non-local Existence and all the individual things that exist.

The notion of the Demiurge attempts to describe how the infinite or near infinite can act upon finitude. In the same way that a browser translates source code into a graphical user interface on a computer, the Demiurge translates the eternal thoughts of God into dimensional formatting.[25] Attempting to link an eternal and unchanging God to the creation, via the Demiurge, Overmind or some other earlier conceptual framework, such as essence and Existence is an attempt to understand how the process of creation might work. Ultimately, the Demiurge is a result, so to speak, of the Reality Dysfunction. An eternal observer, observing Himself, outside Himself, is the metaphysical analog to the collapse of the quantum wave through observation that results in the phenomenon of decoherence and the world that we know.

When Jesus claims, for example, that we are God's children, He means it quite literally. We are be-ings of the Being or the *dasein* of Existence, which makes all things be. God or Being, as He is in eternity, paradoxically **is and is not** the same God who knows Himself *locally, as other than Himself,* in space and time, except in the abstract sense of the word. Jesus claimed that when we did good to others, in terms of feeding the hungry or visiting prisoners that *we did it to him.* There is simply no way of understanding this unless God is not somehow subject to his creation in a derivative and participated manner.

The "Big Bang Theory" of science, in the light of a derivative reality for Existence, is in accordance with metaphysics: a vast explosion out of nothingness that the creation of time, space and energy would necessitate. A Being of infinite power, consciousness and ecstasy transforms Himself [26] (almost like a transformer stepping down

---

25 Gnosis: (http://montalk.net/gnosis/171/corruption-of-the-demiurge)
26 This is where language and analogy limp. God doesn't transform Himself per se; His knowledge of Himself includes all the ways in which He might be imitated, derivatively, by creation.

current into something more useable) into a local, virtual or derivative form (be-ing) possessing nearly infinite energy in the form of matter. He does this to know Himself in a new and different way—as being finite but given that He cannot increase in self-knowledge, this is simply a virtual convention to help us understand the dynamics of Divine Consciousness.

There are those who will argue that there is no need for God to do this, as all perfections are already possessed by Him pre-eminently and that his consciousness is entirely equivalent to His Nature. But to be what you are not and to share what you are with what you create—even briefly in time—now that is an adventure for an infinite and eternal Being. One can almost imagine that the act of creation led to humor, with the very first words out of the mouth of the God, who, while He knows Himself to be the eternal and immutable God, yet also, suddenly, knows Himself in a new way, through the mirror of space and time, as an entity *once removed* from the stupendous Act of His own self-existence in the Reality Dysfunction to be—"oh my." God would, of course, know this eternally but in reference to time, it might be thought of as a specific instance within the Reality Dysfunction.

Aquinas captures the flavor of what the Reality Dysfunction may be pointing to, as a round-the-corner analogy, when he says:

> *"Hence, although God wills things apart from Himself only for the sake of the end, which is His own goodness, it does not follow that anything else moves His will, except His goodness.* **So, as He understands things apart from Himself** *by understanding His own essence, so He wills things apart from Himself by willing His own goodness." [27]*

If we were to translate this, superimposing the language of locality and non-locality, by way of metaphor, we would get the following:

---

27 Thomas Aquinas, *Summa Theologica*, God and the Divine Attributes, Q. 19, Art. 3, Pt. 1

"Hence, although God [non-locally][28] wills things apart from Himself [in the Reality Dysfunction] only for the sake of the end, which is His own goodness, it does not follow that anything else [local] moves His will, except His [non-local] goodness. So, as He understands things apart from Himself [locally in the Reality Dysfunction] by understanding His own [non-local] essence, so He wills things [locally] apart from Himself by willing His own goodness."

Note that the virtual differentiation occurs in time, not in God. Given that there cannot be a "before and after" in God, we can only predicate this "willing apart from Himself" analogously and locally in the Reality Dysfunction. God differentiates everything just by being what He Is. All things are ordered in and by His presence. This is *superordination*, which is manifested, analogically, in terms of locality and non-locality. We keep trying to understand this as a subject-object relationship but it can't be done. The light that creates is infinitely and non-locally orthogonal to our own.

THE CULTURE WAR AND EXISTENCE

This time war caused by the Reality Dysfunction, whereby the end of things may be at variance with the present, is also reflected in the enormous variety of human opinion and belief at any given moment in time; it is a reflection of a multiplicity of viewpoints generated by an original act of self-knowledge in space and time. This is also why it is terribly important to understand causality. In order to grasp the calculus of causality, all of the parts must be in hand. What we call the culture war is, in its deepest expression, an extended argument between those who want to believe in a personal God and those who want to believe in either no God or an impersonal God. Ultimately,

---

28 It must be stated categorically that the use of non-locality as a metaphor is, like the word "existence", a way of describing that which ultimately cannot be described.

it is not possible, in my opinion, to have transcendental moral values without understanding the non-local origin of those values

Once we understand that our natures, and to some extent our circumstances, are given to us by the act of God's own self-knowledge, then we can grasp that in order to orient ourselves in time and space, in accordance with this knowledge, that moral and intellectual excellence is required. Moral and intellectual virtue (acting in accordance with right reason) are, in this respect, a recovery operation for an original goodness that has been given to each one of us as a gift but which tends to be obscured by our biology and the Reality Dysfunction. Virtue mysteriously connects us to the hidden dimensions of causality, time and divinity.

> *Virtue is our connection to the reality function. It is an algorithm for good habits and a compass that points to goodness as its true north.*

Vice limits our behavior to the biological immediacy of the present moment in which desire is king. Having a moral compass and a series of steps (an algorithm) to deal with bad appetites enables us to navigate the pitfalls of evolutionary biology and the siren call of desire. Virtue, in this respect, represents the *domestication* of appetite and desire. Even the *tactical virtues* espoused by Jack Donovan, in his book, *The Way of Men*: strength, courage, mastery and honor would be a welcome change from our culture's endless, subjective celebration of feeling and non-causal links to purely emotional dispositions.

American's fourth President, John Adams, set the standard for the relationship of virtue to the public order.

> *"I go on this great Republican principle, that the people will have virtue and intelligence to select men of virtue and wisdom. Is there no virtue among us? If there be not, we are in a wretched situation. No theoretical checks, no form of government can render us secure. To suppose that any form of government will*

secure liberty or happiness without any virtue in the people is a
chimerical idea. "[29]

The current disposition of science and society towards a non-causal explanation of the universe simply erodes the consciousness of moral
virtue as it might be applied to society and the public order. It also
indicates how strongly mega concepts, both rational and irrational, can
have on the public imagination. The purported *stochastic aggregation*[30]
of reality, as described by atheistic science, with no implicit intelligence
behind it, is so contrived as not to be easily believed by most thoughtful individuals. This view is often confabulated with religion but the
religious and the scientific understanding of the meaning of existence
can be relatively separated and examined for useful information. Is Existence related to a divine reality or is it simply a discontinuous process
that is merely reflective of the meanings we impose on it? Our current
culture wars are primarily based on which view of Existence is inadvertently or directly subscribed to.

The power behind the notion of a randomly formed universe lies,
conceptually, in not having to utilize any explanation that is not directly
related to the material order. It is Occam's razor meets Alice in Wonderland and moral issues are, relatively speaking, just a matter of social
contract and subjectivity. In other words, in an atheistic universe, whether you manufacture sex toys for a living or launch spaceships—it is a
morally irrelevant question in the objective sense—because there is no
objective or causal order to refer to. For those who believe in a universe
without ontological meaning, words like honor and truth mean very little. They mean what we want them to mean. This is why Nietzsche says
that when we ask the "last men" what truth means, they will "blink."

The poet Ernst Meister captures the confusion that has come
about from the claim that the world is not really "out there"—that it
is a fabrication of our sensory apparatus based on a cascade of causally

---

29 Diggins, John, *The Lost Soul of American Politics*, from the works of John Adams
30 "Randomly determined groupings; having a random probability distribution or pattern (s) that may be analyzed statistically but may not be predicted precisely."

disconnected processes. He says, "The paradox is this: If the world may not exist, why do we think it does, and what sense can be made of it? How do we navigate space, the world and the complexity of embodied existence [without rationally compelling] causal pathways?"

How we understand the formative presence of something that is more than time, simultaneously *within time and outside time*, could lead to a scientific and moral enterprise of astounding dimensions. We find what we look for. Evidence for the activity of an Unmoved Mover such as the quest for the so-called God particle, the Higgs-Boson, is indicative of the potential. In addition to the possibility of a change in our collective approach to moral discourse and moral education, new and different ways of understanding matter and the universe around us may also be at hand.

INFORMATION AND ENERGY

Science tells us that there are only two types of fundamental particles in the universe: fermions and bosons. Simply stated: fermions are all the local particles that make up matter. Fermions include electrons, neutrons, quarks, protons, and atoms consisting of various combinations of some or all elementary particles. Bosons are, and represent so to speak, all the local particles that carry force/mass (for example, photons). A third fundamental particle will, likely, be discovered—something akin to the Higgs-Boson[31]—but so different that the Higgs-Boson will only serve as an analog to what this other particle might do.

---

31 "Here's the gist of the standard model, which was developed in the early 1970s: Our entire universe is made of 12 different matter particles and four forces [source: European Organization for Nuclear Research]. Among those 12 particles, you'll encounter six quarks and six leptons. Quarks make up protons and neutrons, while members of the lepton family include the electron and the electron neutrino, its neutrally charged counterpart. Scientists think that leptons and quarks are indivisible; that you can't break them apart into smaller particles. Along with all those particles, the standard model also acknowledges four forces: gravity, electromagnetic, strong and weak. As theories go, the standard model has been very effective, aside from its failure to fit in gravity. Armed with it, physicists have predicted the existence of certain particles years before they were verified empirically. Unfortunately, the model still has another missing piece — the Higgs boson." http://science.howstuffworks.com/higgs-boson1.htm

The basic idea behind the Higgs Field, as it is called, is that all particles (that have mass) have to interact with the Higgs Field to acquire the necessary mass *in order to incorporate gravity into the Standard Model.* The Higgs Boson transfers mass to bosons based on some set of (as of yet) not completely known algorithms, which will, likely, be based on and mediated by yet another particle. This would represent a Fifth and as of yet unidentified Force of nature in addition to gravity, electromagnetism and the strong and weak forces.[32]

If we think about the fundamental nature of physical reality as a kind of trinity consisting of fermions, bosons and Higgs particles what we are likely to find is that the Higgs Boson (or an as of yet unnamed fourth particle) will also carry or mediate additional information, non-locally, across all particles, in a similar causal manner as alluded to by the ancient idea of form or essence. If information is exchanged between the implicate and explicate order, the notion of signal[33] comes into play. Information, when exchanged between the implicate and explicate orders, seems to be transformed into energy. This transformation of information into energy may mirror the process whereby Existence or the Uncreated communicates Itself, by way of causality in the Reality Dysfunction, with what is created. Dimensionally Interactive Cyber Kinesis is multi-dimensional kinetic energy bound to both energy and information. The ancients understood this energy as "form" or essence. This is, more than likely, the way that Divine intelligence propagates itself, derivatively, throughout the universe. It is in this way that atoms and subatomic particles might be said to be "conscious." This is, in fact, a metaphysical hypothesis for the existence of a Fifth Force.

Martin Gardner, who wrote Scientific American's Mathematical Games column for 25 years, noted in a book review that "David Chalmers, an Australian philosopher, has called the problem of explaining

---

32 This was written before the 2015 discovery of evidence of a Fifth Force, found initially by Hungarian scientists and confirmed in 2016 by others. http://www.sciencealert. com/new-study-confirms-physicists-might-have-spotted-a-fifth-force-of-nature
33 Signal: an event or act that shows that something exists or gives information about something.

consciousness the "hard problem". The easy problem is understanding unconscious behavior, such as breathing, digestion, walking, perceiving, and a thousand other things. Grappling with the hard problem has become one of the hottest topics[34] facing philosophers, psychologists, and neuroscientists." According to philosopher John Searle, reviewing Nicholas Humphrey's *Red: A Study of Consciousness* (New York Review of Books), Amazon listed 3,865 books on consciousness in 1985. Douglas Hofstadter's, *I Am a Strange Loop,* published in 1987 was yet another attempt by a very good scientist and writer to reduce self-identity to the status of an accident.[35]

Gardner goes on to say that "like his friend Dennet, who wrote a book brazenly titled, *Consciousness Explained,* Hofstadter believes that he too has explained it. Alas, like Dennet, he has merely described it. It is easy to describe a rainbow. It is not so easy to explain a rainbow. It is easy to describe consciousness. It is not so easy to explain the magic by which a batch of molecules produce it."[36] To quote a quip by Alfred North Whitehead, "Hofstadter and Dennet "leave the darkness of the subject unobscured."[37]

"Let me spread my cards on the table. I belong to a small group of thinkers called the "mysterians". It includes such philosophers as Searle (he is the scoundrel of Hofstadter's book), Thomas Nagel, Colin McGinn, Jerry Fodor, also Noam Chomsky, Roger Penrose, and a few others. We share a conviction that no philosopher or scientist living today has the foggiest notion of how consciousness, and its inseparable companion free will, emerge, as they surely do, from a material brain. It is impossible to imagine being aware we exist without having some free will, if only the ability to blink or to decide what to think about next. It is equally impossible to imagine having free will without being at least partly conscious."[38]

34 Book Reviews: http://www.ams.org/notices/200707/tx070700852p.pdf
35 Ibid
36 The American Mathematical Society, Book Reviews: http://www.ams.org/notices/200707/tx070700852p.pdf
37 Ibid
38 Ibid

Contrary to the reductionist point of view espoused by Dennett, Hofstader and many others, there is considerable evidence, provided by superstring theory[39] that multiple dimensions (as many as 10 or more) known collectively as *hyperspace* may be involved in the implicate transmission of information and causality that the ancients tried to accomplish with the idea of form and that science has tried to portray with various and ever more complex configurations of subatomic particles. Imagining forms as vibrating superstrings in multiple dimensions or as a kind of bridge between the implicate (non-local) and explicate (local) order of reality can do much to bridge the gap between ancient and modern thinking. Even noting that such a bridge between locality and non-locality might exist could put science on the track of whatever system of dimensionally interactive signals might be exchanged between these different orders of reality.

How is information exchanged between non-local and local time and space? The exploration of possible and, as of yet, unknown structures in this area may yield valuable clues about the nature of the universe and its relation to Existence. What is now becoming more apparent is that particle theory may have to give way to string theory as a more complete explanation of physical reality. It may be that the search for the so-called "God Particle" in the Higgs-Boson is the dying spasm (at least in the popular imagination) of a quasi-mechanistic view of quantum mechanics. This view was never entirely satisfactory—even to many physicists.

Physicist, Michio Kaku, notes that "In fact, in one swoop, this 10 dimensional string theory gives us a simple, compelling unification of all forces. Like a violin string, these tiny strings can vibrate [at the speed of light] and create resonances or "notes" [also at the speed of light]. That explains why there are so many sub-atomic particles (collectively known as hadrons): they are just notes on a superstring. (This seems so simple, but in the 1950s, physicists were drowning in an av-

---

39 *Hyperspace: A Scientific Odyssey Through Parallel Universes, Time Warps, and the Tenth Dimension*, Michio Kaku, Oxford University Press, NY

alanche of sub-atomic particles. J.R. Oppenheimer, who helped build the atomic bomb, even said, out of sheer frustration, that the Nobel Prize should go to the physicist who does NOT discover a new particle that year!) Similarly, when the string moves in space and time, it warps the space around it just as Einstein predicted. Thus, in a remarkably simple picture, we can unify gravity (as the bending of space caused by moving strings) with the other quantum forces (now viewed as vibrations of the string.)"[40]

The notion of superstrings has met with some resistance from the scientific community as the ultimate conclusion of Existence, as something other than energy, looms in the distance. Superstring theory almost begs the question: what is organizing the strings or who or what might be playing the "notes"? The theory increases, at the very least, the need for a principle of coordination at odds with the notion of a stochastic universe. Even now some scientists are arguing for an 11th dimension to account for how the other 10 dimensions work together!

Artificial Intelligence, in all likelihood, will not be produced by our current scientific mindset but by a science looking for evidence of the activity of Einstein's "Old One" or a greater concept of existence than afforded by the First Law of Thermodynamics. Utilizing a different starting point than stochastic aggregation may lead to the discovery of undreamed of treasures that could initiate startling new inventions related to artificial intelligence through quantum computing, anti-gravity, teleportation and a return to a John Adams-like public understanding of virtue and vice. This would create a new anchoring for concepts that the Founding Fathers used to create the Declaration of Independence and the Constitution.

Is it possible to have a more rational accounting of the universe that we find ourselves in without recourse to the sterile pronouncements of atheistic science or the overly structured vision of religion? The current rise of Islam, for example, is almost in direct proportion to the modern insistence that God has no part in the organization of the

---

40 http://mkaku.org/home/articles/hyperspace-and-a-theory-of-everything/

universe. Fundamentalism, in all its forms, simply mirrors the enthusiastic banishment of God that atheistic fundamentalism has established. A more balanced approach that assumes an intelligence behind evolution might do much to bring about a more cosmopolitan and tolerant view of both science and religion.

God does not need our protection; it is man who needs protection from a host of bad ideas that the power we have been given can generate. It should be clear that the power to believe, for example, enables a tremendous amount of good and yet also makes possible a great deal of evil. Suicide bombers, Christian martyrs, heroes, scientists, philosophers and dictators all sup from the same infinite source of freedom. If we do not learn to understand our relationship to the Source that is Existence, we will, collectively, continue to grind out errors of belief and action.

If we understand time as simply an empty bucket in which random things occur, then perhaps there is no need to reason further but if you find yourself wondering "why?" more often than not, then *God Has Skin in The Game* may be your ticket to a profound and new way of looking at our country and its place in the world.

Chapter 4

POLITICS AND THE SOUL

"For I do nothing but go about persuading you all, old and young alike, not to take thought for your persons and your properties, but first and chiefly to care about the greatest improvement of the soul. I tell you that virtue is not given by money, but that from virtue come money and every other good of man, public as well as private."

—Plato,
The Apology of Socrates

Nearly twenty-five centuries have passed since Socrates pronounced these words before the men of Athens. The power of his words, as passed on to us by Plato, foreshadows a philosophical concern that has occupied the thoughts of political and philosophical thinkers for generations. American culture, in general, has yet to fully

103

reflect on the meaning of virtue or to transmit the moral values associated with the idea of the soul, in any religiously neutral form through educational or political institutions.

The concept of the soul predates Socrates and the Greeks and yet, with the exception of Aristotle, Jesus Christ and Aquinas few in the Western philosophical and theological tradition have ever stated more clearly the importance of the soul and the relation of virtue or excellence to both private and public good. How is it then that the soul and virtue are not discussed publicly as relevant issues in the twentieth century? [1]

There are two reasons: Christianity, Islam and Judaism, in a centuries-long assimilation of Greek philosophy, preserved and inadvertently obscured these concepts for Western civilization by relating them dogmatically to religious ideas, which changed their original non-sectarian meaning. This created a climate whereby superstition, the old shadow of religion, was able to flourish. Under these circumstances and during the Catholic Middle Ages in particular, the deity's favors were bought and sold on a daily basis through a peculiar calculus of prayer, money and ritual. Secondly, the development of the scientific method beginning in the sixteenth and seventeenth centuries created an atmosphere of skepticism regarding traditional ethics, metaphysics and religion. The often brash methodologies of the new sciences offered little in place of concepts like the soul, which were gutted, as the apparent importance of empirical data shouldered aside all other concerns as irrelevant.

Additionally, the spiritual weakness of the new disciples of progress was augmented by Christianity's general failure to maintain a non-religious understanding of virtue as it degenerated into a multiplicity of competing sects. The great chasm in our understanding of the soul in the twentieth century is partially attributable to the splintering effect of the Protestant Reformation. Despite the cultural innovations of the Renaissance, which brought Greek philosophy into the European

---

1   What is known as "virtue ethics" has enjoyed an academic revival over the past 50
      years but has never become culturally mainstream.

mainstream, the tendency to dismiss the association of Catholic teachings with the wisdom of the past set the stage for the abandonment of a very rich and deep intellectual history. This combination of the failure to transmit a cohesive non-religious teaching on virtue and the soul, and the shattering cultural effect of the Reformation produced a psychic disaster, which may well be the historic epicenter of the past millennium.

Philosophically speaking, it is a notion of no little import that for about four thousand years the idea of the soul was a major issue for the civilizations of Egypt, Greece, India and Western Europe. Regrettably, the concept is infrequently discussed in the twentieth century—outside of religious circles. In our day, the soul might be considered the least addressed political and moral issue, while it should be the most important.

There can be little successful discussion of human and moral values without some understanding of both the common ground and the differences between subjectivity and objectivity. Subjectivity and objectivity are starkly illustrated when biology meets intellectual judgment for the imposition of delayed gratification to achieve certain results. Commonly known as virtue, or acting in accordance with right reason, virtue is always, and to some extent, at war with subjective norms of behavior.

Another way of understanding the dimensions of subjectivity and objectivity is to make a comparison with time. There were two kinds of time postulated by the ancient Greeks: *Chronos* and *Kairos*. *Chronos* corresponds to objective time or what we might call clock time. *Kairos* refers to subjective time or what we might call quality or emotional time. Chronological time and Kaironic time commonly overlap in human experience. However, there is a third kind of time, *hidden time*, which intersects chronological and subjective time and which is the locus of an almost endless set of discussions and controversy.

Hidden time is a matrix for past, present and future. It is time, present to itself, through a complex causal chain that begins in the identity of a kind of intelligence that we can barely begin to measure but which seems to have ordered time and space for its own purposes. Hidden time attests to a structure in the universe that has not yet been scientifically measured or fully understood.

Making an inferential leap, which can be substantiated as we move forward, we can state that hidden time is *Divine Time*; it is the Eternal knowing Itself as it might be imitated in time. The magic of Divine time lies precisely in its unmeasured potential. It permeates and flavors chronological and *kaironic* time by seeding buds of awareness and being that we can register and act upon but not always fully comprehend.

MAPPING GOODNESS

The ultimate meaning of human subjectivity cannot be fathomed without reaching for the highest aspirations of the human heart. The desire for a better world, made up of energetic, wise, heroic, and thoughtful individuals is the dream of Western culture. Yet where is the analog to what we desire? How could we even know that goodness exists, unless we had some sure and hidden knowledge of it? This desire for goodness may be understood as a testament to the hidden, temporal structure of the soul as it is known by the Divine Mind. The soul itself, likewise, can only be understood as an artifact of a kind of time that is neither objective nor subjective but rather is something entirely different. Time is a temporal manifestation of eternity, a derivative of a unity that expresses time as a function of knowledge understood across an infinite number of possible universes.

The relationship between goodness and happiness becomes apparent, if happiness is understood as both the highest subjective good attainable and as a state of the soul which is dependent on moral actions. The association of goodness, happiness and moral actions, relating to a higher understanding of time, constitutes a moral paradigm that the West is rapidly forgetting. Additionally, and when the soul is understood as a manifestation of a far greater intellectual and moral consciousness than its own, then moral and intellectual perfection tends to mirror and acknowledge its origin in the consciousness of the Divine.

The soul and its relationship to hidden or divine time is the missing link between the idea of the good, objective concepts, the notions of character and virtue, and the vague clearing house of ideas we call God and religion. Such issues as the right to work, adequate wages, industrial development, family values, ecology, racism, feminism, same-sex attraction, abortion and the morality of war cannot be adequately addressed without some understanding of the soul. If what is good for either the individual or society cannot be tied to a standard, then truly no person's ideas are better than any other.

The subjectivity of values born of an inadequate concept of soul has contributed to the social chaos of the twentieth century. Individuals and nations are no longer able to enforce standards of any kind. We see for example, a return to the most primitive barbarism and banditry in Africa, America and the Ukraine. Meanwhile, the American political process has degenerated into an exchange of slogans, and all manner of lies and distortions, instead of ideas. These conditions are not merely the result of economic or social difficulties but stem from ideas or, more precisely the lack of ideas connected to an objective moral order. The social disorder and violence on the rise throughout Western civilization, appears to be directly attributable to a specific intellectual and moral failure.

We have failed to properly understand the meaning, structure and social consequences of unmodified human desire and will, the power of soul some philosophers have called "appetite".

The butchering of five million Jews, twenty million ethnic Russians, three million Cambodians and possibly as many as sixty million Chinese,[2] in the name of various twentieth century ideologies mas-

---

2   Richard Lewis Walker, *China Under Communism: The First Five Years,* Yale University Press; First edition (1955)

querading as rational activity can only be understood from a perspective that understands how human appetites are rooted in the enormous powers of the soul. The powers of the soul, when cultivated improperly, can create the potential for titanic social and personal disorder.

The power of appetite, or what Freud called the *cathection of the Id*,[3] is an overall component of psychic energy. Death on the colossal scale, which we have seen in the past century, is not only evil but is activity that results when values that support life are not cultivated. Under such circumstances, those appetites relating to death and destruction will prevail. Like a huge crocodile that just wants to eat, everything from young children to beautiful maidens is grist for the mill of unregulated appetites. One has only to think of the appalling Chairman Mao, commenting out loud from the security of his sealed train, during a famine he caused: "Death has become quite commonplace."

The reptilian instincts of the crocodile provide us with a metaphor for what can lurk beneath the calm waters of everyday existence. Without an understanding of biology and appetite, human beings can fall prey to biological hungers that prowl the waters of the soul like crocodiles of an uncertain origin. Chairman Mao, like many other dictators of the twentieth century, was for all intents and purposes, a reptile in human form. Likewise, take a moment to visualize Hugh Hefner, members of the Rolling Stones and other long-time rock and roll band members. Note that there is, often, a similar reptilian cast to their visages. They have become, simply, creatures of appetite. Some of these reptilian characters may have more violent appetites than others but that is only an accident of circumstance. Sigmund Freud stated that:

"We are without a term analogous to 'libido' for describing the energy of the destructive instinct." [4]

---

3   Freud, Sigmund, An *Outline of Psychoanalysis*, The Norton Library, NY, 1960, pg.7
4   Freud, Sigmund, An *Outline of Psychoanalysis*, The Norton Library, NY, 1960

Freud was without this "adequate term" for the destructive instincts of biology because he had no comprehensive metaphysical or psychic analog to describe energy that might come, not only from inside the body, but from outside the body. Where does psychic energy in general come from? What relationship does human consciousness have with external energy sources? The ancient idea of the soul provides us with a far more complex model for describing the energy input and output of consciousness than does any current psychological or sociological model. The concept of the soul is a historical and intellectual artifact that represents an attempt to describe in various ways, the juncture between consciousness and existence.

Unless the Second Law of Thermodynamics (which states that energy will automatically seek the lowest and most stable state) is opposed by the positive and developmental energies of the soul, as expressed in moral and intellectual excellence, then social decline and savagery is inevitable—it is the easiest state to be in. Is it not easier to kill those who disagree with you, than attempt to lead them to an appreciation of your point of view? Isn't rape easier than cultivating the affections of a strong woman? Just shoot them or violate them, no thinking or self-restraint required. Don't we see this going on all over the world? The dictionary defines incontinence as:

> *"Incontinence: Lack of self-control, from incontinens, not containing, intemperate...1. lack of restraint of the passions or appetites; free or uncontrolled indulgence of the passions or appetites; especially, lack of restraint of the sexual appetite; lewdness. 2. incapable of containing, keeping or holding..."* [5]

Every culture has to deal with the issue of bad desires or bad appetites. The failure to deal with this issue is the fulcrum upon which cultures rise and fall. Scientists have long been puzzled by the rapid collapse of the Mayan civilization of Central America. The Mayas seemed

---

5   *Webster's New Twentieth Century Dictionary Unabridged*

to have had most of the characteristics of an advanced culture. They were sophisticated astronomers, architects, builders and farmers, yet the civilization almost disappeared, leaving only empty cities and temples. Current theories about excessive population growth related to climate change do not adequately account for the demise of the Mayas.

The most advanced hypothesis, now emerging, is that this already bloodthirsty but hitherto well-regulated culture perished in an unbelievably savage social decline, in which vicious tribal and personal vendettas created a social chaos from which the society never emerged. In short, the Mayan society perished due to its inability to limit the growth of both personal and social vices. Just go to any American high school that has problems with gang warfare and imagine it on a larger scale, somewhat like a *Mad Max* movie, and you get some idea of what can happen to a society when the baser, reptilian instincts of its members go unchecked. This may be what happened to the Mayas. They, who believed that the world was carried on the back of a huge crocodile, ended up embracing the inner reptile to their utter ruin.

Looking at the cycle of civilizations as a whole, a pattern emerges. What we see is that whole societies can unwittingly embrace vice by allowing the Second Law of Thermodynamics to operate without opposition. A society that allows impulsive sexual activity and other forms of excessive appetitive engagement can open itself up to a downward energy spiral. Energy, under the Second Law of Thermodynamics, simply seeks release to a lower and more stable state unless opposed by something other than itself. Murder and rape can lead to lower energy states. In the absence of principle, much as we see today, murder and rape become commonplace. A society that embraces the Laws of Thermodynamics, even if it is unaware of those laws, is generally speaking, unable to oppose the culturally negative influence of lower energy states. The essence of moral principle is to understand that a higher energy state, rather than a lower energy state, is required to build a society. Natural tendencies are not always good or even socially desirable.

Historically speaking, it might be said that there is an age-old political and social struggle between those who believe in the existence of objective, moral values, or an objective notion of human nature (even if those terms are not fully understood) and those who, for all practical purposes believe that morality is whatever you can make, legislate, or force it to be. Fundamentally the conflict has been between those who believed that God, Natural Law (or some kind of cosmic, moral order) was needed as a *referent* for the regulation of human desires and those who believed there were no referents.

VALUES AND THE CONCEPT OF SELF-INTEREST

Today, the two camps could be very generally classified as consisting of the logical positivists, moral relativists and extreme liberals on the side of a do-your-own-thing kind of morality, and the neo-Aristotelians, conservatives, and the spiritually inclined, who argue for a conformity of actions with an objective moral order or natural set of laws that exists independently of contractual consensus. This is why viewing energy as being neither created nor destroyed or understanding that Existence is what causes energy to exist is an important distinction. The atheistic position that energy is neither created nor destroyed has no fixed moral consensus outside of what can be legislated.

What is interesting, from this perspective, is that these two groups reflect positions held in the most general way by the Democrats and the Republicans in the United States. There is indeed a philosophy behind both parties that neither party articulates and consequently, they fail to understand the origin of their differences. All the controversy surrounding the notion of family and moral values shows quite clearly the basic inability of both parties to articulate either their origins or their positions.

Values make little or no sense without an order or a philosophy which relates them to life as a whole. Values are a product of a systematic categorizing of what is judged good and what is better or worse. This systematic categorizing or prioritizing of what is good, when discussed in relation to the notion of good and bad appetites (or desire), is the essential stuff out of which morality and the algorithms of common sense are made. To speak about values without talking about ethics and morality (which is a branch of philosophy) is a form of cultural amnesia.

For example, in American folklore, the stereotypical notion of the "good guys" and the "bad guys" shows us how values become popularized and also obscured. During colonial times, the "good guys" were the colonists and the "bad guys" were the British. The Civil War pitted the 'just' North against the 'evil' South. The great westward expansion had as its heroes, the colonists and the cowboys who fought the Indian enemy. The "good guys" are the lawmen or heroes, and the "bad guys" are the rotten outlaws. We know that many of these stereotypes are just that, and that the real story behind some of these images may be different from the popular conception. The "good guys" somewhere along the way, stepped off the stage of morality and are now only identified by cultural symbols that have replaced moral introspection.

The problem we have today is not in identifying the "bad guys"— there are plenty of them: Industrial polluters, dictators, human rights violators, greedy corporations, drug dealers, sex traders and a host of other readily identifiable public enemies. The difficulty we have is in articulating why the "good guys" are in fact good and why the "bad guys" are really bad.

All people distinguish between what they term 'good' and what they term 'bad'. The difficulty comes when individuals disagree on what is actually good and what is actually bad, and then are unable to decide how humanity as a whole should behave. Americans have side-stepped the problem in a unique way, by allowing each man and woman, the freedom to determine what he or she thinks is good.

The pursuit of personally chosen 'goods' is what constitutes self-determination or self-interest.

The problem we face today as a nation is that the abstract notion of the "good" which was based on moral ideas associated with the soul and religion, has been displaced by the morally neutral idea of self-interest. A current example of self-interest replacing moral introspection is the issue regarding the televising of violent or salacious material during prime-time viewing. The problem is not cast as one of appetitive indulgence, or right and wrong, it is cast merely as a rights issue. Are the rights of adults to watch whatever they feel, violated by the time constraints that might be put on them by moral concerns for children? In other words, the self-interest of adults is at conflict with other self-interests that happen to have the label moral but are just another form of self-interest, no better or no worse than any other.

The operative idea behind the legitimacy and the ascendancy of the notion of self-interest is that different groups, who are actively pursuing self-interest will tend to balance each other out, and this in turn will 'level the playing field' for all participants. This is true, but there is an additional requirement for self-interest to really work in a community. That requirement is the virtue of honesty. There will always be differences between men and women of good will that may be resolved by compromise and the balancing of various self-interests. However, self-interest politics are radically compromised by the vice of dishonesty, which allows various groups to monopolize the process.

We believe in the right to bear arms as an expression of freedom and self-interest, but what kind of arms? Clearly, we ought to be able to keep a weapon in the home for self-defense, but an automatic weapon capable of one hundred rounds a minute? Why not a flame thrower or a surface-to-air missile; better yet, a tank for getting through bad traffic! Should the right to bear arms allow us to purchase twenty or thirty automatic rifles at a time? Common sense would indicate that only gun collectors or small armies need such weaponry. Our insistence on observing constitutional rights from an absolutely literal-minded perspective is indicative of the problems that occur when self-restraint or continence is not cultivated.

Another illustration of self-interest run amok are the economic concerns of heavy industry, versus proponents of ecological and health issues. The two groups tend to balance each other out through healthy compromise—even though there is always a struggle in defining the ground rules of what constitutes reasonable or necessary. The process is radically disrupted however, when both sides engage in untruthful propaganda about the issues, or submit pseudo-scientific evidence to support wishful thinking. No one should doubt, for example, the healthy social balance that has been obtained in the struggle between the smoking and anti-smoking lobbies. Everyone has been better served by the idea that smoking is not healthy but it is a far cry to move from moderation, to attempts to sue tobacco companies for the vices, stupidity and failing health of those who refuse to quit, or limit their intake of tobacco. No one should require an education beyond the elementary school level to realize that inhaling burning leaves could not possibly be healthy.

False advertising is endemic to American industry and is a result of the point of view that all self-interest is legitimate and that few limits may be placed on self-determination. Everyone from child molesters to drug users have used the notion of self-interest or absolute freedom of self-determination to defend their right to harm both themselves and others. The tobacco executive who repeatedly denies knowing anything about the harmful effects of smoking, the educator who defensively claims that public education is doing a good job but could do better, and the gun lobbyist who invokes self-defense as a mantra against thinking about the consequences of selling automatic weapons to violent young men are all using the notion of self-interest (supported by a huge legal industry) to their advantage and to the disadvantage of the general public. None of these individuals will publicly discuss what might be true because legally and professionally it would be tantamount to career suicide.

Lying at all levels of society and governance absolutely cripples the effectiveness of any social order or corporation. The correction of any system cannot be made without properly identifying causes. This was noted in the mid 1700's by American patriot Thomas Paine:

"It is impossible to calculate the moral mischief that mental lying has produced in society. When man has so far corrupted and prostituted the chastity of his mind, as to subscribe his profession-al belief to things he does not believe, he has prepared himself for the commission of every other crime."

Lying in politics, government and in the media, in general, has reached a point whereby no issue can be discussed clearly without partisans accusing the other side of some sort of grotesque bias. The question emerges: how do we make truth profitable or congruent with Existence—not as we want it to be but as it Is? Self-interest is based on a philosophy that is morally flawed because it is, ultimately, too rooted in desire to be anything but morally neutral. What we need is a new philosophy that will enable us to take advantage of the power of self-interest and put it in the context of moral and intellectual excellence. Truth, unfortunately, can seldom assault entrenched appetites head-on. Once aroused and empowered, unrestrained appetites are a formidable opponent. Truth has a certain delicacy about it and much like a beautiful and respected woman who commands, not by brute force but by the power of her character, truth has to move with a certain grace and timing. Politically speaking this is like a dance between a crocodile and a maiden.

There is a fundamental presupposition at work in the American psyche that says all people will behave in accordance with the rules of fair play provided they have a decent job, are reasonably well-educated, housed and fed. This is a kind of middle class belief in basic human goodness. There is in this idea of the well-adjusted and well-intentioned American the same kind of image at work as we see in the notion of the "good guys" versus the "bad guys." The average sometimes struggling American is the 'good guy', and all those who would infringe upon his or her freedom and right to self-determination (no matter what kind) are the 'bad guys'.

This image has a certain hollowness—not that it is by itself totally incorrect—but that it inadequately explains how people become law-abiding and hard-working citizens, who vote and care for their fellow man. The basic question is this: if all human beings were allowed to do as they desired and had the means to do so, would they be happy and would society as a whole prosper? The answer is apparently, no, as the satisfaction of desire and self-interest, without reference to morality, does not appear to have contributed to the longevity or stability of any society.

Why did the Roman Empire in the West collapse? I submit (as other historians have done) that the uncontrolled indulgence of the appetites, which is a frequent result of morally unmodified self-interest, reached the point where it exceeded any limitations that might have required the wealthy to subject their own interests, to the better or greater interest of society. This is commonly known as civic virtue or excellence. Indeed, the notion of the Polis (City) had reached such a nadir that men and women could no longer think beyond the location of their genitals. The debauchery of the later Roman Empire is well-documented in this regard.

Human beings have struggled from time immemorial with desire and reason; i.e., what is experienced as good from the standpoint of desire or biological immediacy, and what is understood to be a better good from the high ground of reasoned judgment and a consideration of both time and consequence. There has always been a kind of tension between the intellect and the emotions (or as the Greeks called them—the passions). We all do things that we know we should not do but do anyway, because they are desirable.

Anyone who has struggled with giving up smoking or trying to exercise on a regular basis can attest to the struggle between feeling and intellect. There is, as it were, two concepts of the good that wage war in every human breast; the good from the perspective of desire and subjectivity, and the good as judged and prioritized by the intellect and will from the perspective of a more complex sense of time.

These different concepts of the good indicate a temporal hierarchy of values and are the basis for speculation on the structure of what has been called Natural Law. The notion that 'goods' exist outside of the parameters of our immediate, biologically driven desires suggests that there is, at the very least, an objective structure of goodness based on our perception of future goods to be acquired.

This struggle is glossed over in our culture with the use of concepts like self-discipline and hard work as "catch-alls" to cover the difficulties of actually thinking through the consequences and ramifications of the daily war in the human heart. Self-discipline is simply a tool of the will, used by the virtuous, to achieve certain ends. Saying 'no' to a desire is simultaneously saying 'yes' to a prioritized good.

Every morning, when most people rise, there is a struggle that we all take for granted. Yet the struggle to get out of bed is a perfect example of everyday virtue and the establishing of various habitual algorithms to assist in the process. The body wishes to continue sleeping and to enjoy this obvious good; the mind says there is greater good to be pursued, namely, making a living and providing food and shelter for dependents, or tending to the needs of family, home and state. We do this every day and fail to note the ramifications of this simple act of prioritizing the good. Suppose a lot of other things in life were just like this; i.e., various desires having to be temporarily or permanently suppressed for the sake of a greater good? Most responsible people do this without ever really giving it a great deal of thought. They have been trained to behave in this manner and delayed gratification is accepted as commonplace.

Our culture and education train people to behave in a certain way but never really explains to them the reasons why such behavior might be necessary. This is one reason why many individuals have fallen prey to the lure of the easy money of the drug and sex trades. Why shouldn't they sell drugs or sex? They enjoy both; they make good money and they support families and friends. The fact that it is illegal is of little emotional relevance in the face of potential for gratification. Desire is King.

Note the incredible subjectivism that has crept into our culture. Everything is related to how we *feel* about a subject. We don't relate appetite to emotion but rather lump both our reasoning processes and our emotions into a grab-bag called *feeling*. The obvious corollary to a decline in the use of reason and an increase in the use of *feelings* is an increase in appetite related crime. If we *feel* like stealing, robbing, beating or wearing the clothing of the opposite sex, then we do so, with no reference to any moral code whatsoever because there is no code—only the code of our appetites or feelings. This is purely atavistic, or pre-rational thinking. It is no accident that gang membership and violence are on the upswing world-wide. Emotional and appetitive subjectivism ultimately degenerates into amorality, violence, narrow-mindedness and intolerance.

CRITICAL THEORY AND THE FRANKFURT SCHOOL

The current violence in our inner cities and the present dysfunctionality of American family life, with a fifty percent divorce rate, is completely understandable given that large sections of academia subscribe to a derivative form of Critical Theory known as *emotivism*. According to this aspect of Critical Theory, which is defined below, all moral preferences are based on feeling and given that feelings are entirely subjective, all moral arguments are therefore subjective and ultimately circular. Under these circumstances all moral codes are equivalent. Critical Theory has spread like a cancer from post-Marxist European and academic circles to American universities.

"Critical Theory has a narrow and a broad meaning in philosophy and in the history of the social sciences. "Critical Theory" in the narrow sense designates several generations of German philosophers and social theorists in the Western European Marxist tradition known as the Frankfurt School. According to these theorists, a "critical" theory may be distinguished from a "traditional" theory according to a specific practical purpose: a theory is critical to the extent that it seeks human "emancipation from slavery", acts as a "liberating...influence", and works "to create a world which satisfies the needs and powers" of human beings (Horkheimer 1972, 246). "[6] Clearly, the idea is that traditional moral theories contribute to human servitude and must be considered outmoded.

We see echoes of this notion at work in the black community where the shooting of almost any black individual by police is viewed as an act of racism. The notion that the victim might have been misbehaving or committing criminal acts is shoved aside in an emotional and tribal rush to judgment. The Black Lives Matter Movement, in this context, functions as a "critical" activity in that it liberates blacks from the ostensible oppression of white society and the police. This is why the black community can get up in arms about the shooting of a black criminal by police but not voice the same level of objection to black-on-black crime. Critical principles, then, supplant the standard understanding that rioting over perceived wrongs has to be in proportion to real and not imagined offenses. Michael Walsh notes in his book, *The Devil's Pleasure Palace: The Cult of Critical Theory and the Subversion of the West,* that the current narrative of leftist academia, which has its origins in the Frankfurt School[7] has released "a horde of demons into the American psyche."

---

6   http://plato.stanford.edu/entries/critical-theory/
7   "What came to be informally known as "The Frankfurt School" of Critical Social Theory was originally established in Germany in 1923 as the Frankfurt Institute for Social Research. Initially funded by Felix Weil, a young and financially well-off Marxist thinker, the goal of the institute was to bring together different strands of Marxist thinking into one interdisciplinary research center. Over the course of the 1920s and 1930s, the institute attracted some of most important Marxist scholars of the time (see the "Notable Theorists" section below).
The thinking of the Frankfurt School was heavily shaped by three key historical events: (1) the failure of the working-class revolution that Marx had predicted in Western Europe, (2) the rise of Nazism and (3) the expansion of capitalism into a new, "mass" form of production and consumption, often referred to as "Fordism" after the assembly line production practices of Henry Ford's automotive company. Confronted with modern historical events that Marx himself did not predict, the theorists of the Frankfurt School began to redevelop Marxist thought to help them make sense of these new cultural conditions. In addition Marx, members of the Frankfurt School were influenced by the ideas of other major social theorists and philosophers such as Georg Hegel, Sigmund Freud, Max Weber, Friedrich Nietzsche and Immanuel Kant." http://routledgesoc.com/profile/frankfurt-school

"The crucial importance of narrative to the leftist project cannot be overstated. Storytelling—or a form of it in which old themes are mined and twisted—sits at the center of everything the Left does. Leftists are fueled by a belief that in the modern world, it does not so much matter what the facts are, as long as the story is well told. Living in a malevolent upside-down fantasy world, they would rather heed their hearts than their minds, their impulses than their senses; the gulf between empirical reality and their ideology-infused daydreams regularly shocks and surprises them, even as it discomforts or kills millions who suffer the consequences of their delusions." [8]

Now to be sure, the Right suffers a similar dysfunction in that the narrative is sometimes more important than the facts but the goal of rational discourse is to constantly evaluate the facts and not to ideologically push for anything, unless it is good or truly beneficial, based on a standard of what works for the greatest good of the many. What usually doesn't work are ideas that are not truly related to cause and effect. Approximately 35 million people have died from AIDS, for example, and yet the left is not calling for a ban on promiscuous sex. Our health institutions and doctors only caution the public on risky sex with few, if any, references to moral codes. After all, if guns kill people, why not penises? And of course it is nonsense: guns no more kill people than penises do. People with a poorly developed moral sense kill other people with guns, penises, knives, clubs, feet and fists.

The idea that the presence of guns can lead to additional violence is sometimes valid but so is the notion that women wearing skimpy clothing and men consuming porn leads to sexual misconduct. Why the concern for the former and little or no concern over the latter? The source of confusion for the left is that, collectively speaking, it does not understand that goodness without a referent to eternal principles is not

8   Walsh, Michael, *The Devil's, Pleasure Palace: The Cult of Critical Theory and the Subversion of the West*, pg. 33, Encounter Books, New York and London, 2015

goodness but merely self-interest. Morality is like Kryptonite to the Left—just wave a conservative slogan in front of them and watch the looks of horror—you can't talk about "that" but abortion, gay sex and men who want to become women or vice versa—that is all acceptable and should be spoken about with respect.

Critical Theory is also complementary to aggressive multi-culturalism. There is nothing wrong with many cultures feeding unique values and ideas into the collective consciousness of a country or what is now referred to as inter-subjectivity.[9] That is healthy. What is unhealthy is the notion that all cultures are equal or equivalent, or that shared ideas are simply a form of inter-subjectivity based on "co-operation agreements" [10]that have nothing to do with the influence of an objective or independent moral order. Some cultures have bad habits and some cultures are, simply, inferior to others despite particular gifts that may be of benefit to all. In other words, inter-subjectivity only explains how we can hold common ideas or beliefs. It does not explain why inter-subjectivity exists or why some forms of inter-subjectivity are better than others.

Even those holding the most relativistic beliefs might agree that consistency of inter-subjectivity, by way of co-operation agreements, is essential for inter-subjectivity to have any stability. How is it possible to have consistency in co-operation agreements without adverting to principles? The answer is that it isn't possible for long and Critical Theory is a prime example of moral thinking disconnected from the idea of virtue. Critical Theory, on the face of it, makes a certain kind of sense. It is, so to speak, the right idea with the wrong set of principles. Virtue, in all its forms, is "critical" in order to release human beings from the servitude of unrelenting and chaotic appetites. Traditional thinking becomes "non-critical" and irrelevant when it does not properly connect causes to effects or gets caught up in the ritualistic and largely ceremonial parrot-

---

9   Yuval Noah Harari in his recent book *Sapiens: A Brief History of Humankind, Harper Collins, NY* is a recent expositor of the notion that inter-subjectivity and imagination are the sole source of belief and what we call truth.

10 Ibid

ing of ideas that we often see on the right or in large organizations that pay lip service to the original principles that made them great.

The notion, for example, that we "are" our feelings runs counter to the teachings of the ancients, who taught us to be suspicious of an over-reliance on feelings. Buddhism, for example, teaches that the identification of "feelings" with ourselves leads, ultimately to unhappiness.[11] We are not simply our emotional states. We have emotions, we have feelings, we have thoughts and we are free to choose or not choose among them. The great Zen masters used to refer to thoughts and feelings as birds flying across the sky of the mind. The idea was to observe thoughts in a detached manner so as not to become attached to any one of them.

The recent Supreme Court ruling on gay marriage is simply an argument based on emotivism. How is it possible that a hitherto undiscovered right to same-sex marriage was discovered by the present court? The answer is that it wasn't discovered—it was invented or pulled out of the thin air by judges who seem incapable of arguing from the principles upon which the Declaration of Independence and the Constitution were founded. The five judges who voted for same-sex marriage appear to have been motivated on the basis of how they felt about the matter— not on how they judged the matter to be related to the intent of the Constitution and the Declaration of Independence.

> *"Only in America, did a nation's founders recognize that rights, though endowed by the Creator as unalienable prerogatives, would not be sustained in society unless they were protected under a code of law which was itself in harmony with a higher law. They called it "natural law," or" Nature's law." Such law is the ultimate source and established limit for all of man's laws and is intended to protect each of these natural rights for all of mankind. The Declaration of Independence of 1776 established the premise that in America a people might assume the*

---

11 Ibid

station "to which the laws of Nature and Nature's God entitle them." [12]

Clearly, "life, liberty and the pursuit of happiness" must have some boundaries. Same-sex attraction has never been considered consonant with the laws of nature; although it is in accord with sexual indulgence. Homosexuality used to be called a "crime against nature." [13] When there is no concept of human nature within a society, then it is logical that what might have been considered previously contrary to human nature would come into question. There is no moral boundary from which to consider the question of homosexuality if there is no moral standard against which such behavior can be measured.

The notion that "love is love"—irrespective of gender—is true enough but the notion of what is lawful in love cannot even begin to be answered without the notion that some distancing of ourselves from our appetites may be necessary. What do we say, for example to the man or woman for whom theft or cruelty brings happiness? What can we say to the mutual consent between sadist and masochist—unless there is a moral code that might look with suspicion upon unregulated appetites? The notion that consent is all that is required for an action to be moral simply doesn't follow any pattern of cause and effect that might be attributed to abiding by principles. What is legal or illegal should track, to some degree, what is moral, otherwise it is not in accord with either nature or the best interests of human society.

The use of feeling as the ultimate referent for behavior leads to a peculiar emotional slavery. My two favorites anecdotes in this regard are one: the man who raped a woman and offered as his explanation that she smelled good, and two: the story of the young man who, when asked why he killed the other youth gave the answer, "because he was

---

12 http://www.nccs.net/natural-law-the-ultimate-source-of-constitutional-law.php
13 "The crime against nature or unnatural act has been a legal term in English-speaking states for forms of sexual behavior not considered natural and seen as punishable offenses. Sexual practices that have historically been considered to be "crimes against nature" include anal sex and bestiality." [WP]

'dissing (disrespecting) me." [14] This kind of emotional enslavement is the enthronement of appetitive or emotional subjectivity over rational, long-term thinking. The problem necessarily invites an explanation as to how this dismal state of affairs might be remedied. This problem is not unrelated to other society-wide problems of declining productivity and an obsession with making a fast dollar, whether through drug-dealing or bank-related real estate swindles.

THE VIRTUES AND THE WAR AGAINST BIOLOGY

The concept of virtue as portrayed by Aristotle provides a useful tonic to our current intellectual failure to properly identify the reason the 'bad guys' are really bad and why the 'good guys' are really better. Aristotle and the early Greeks defined virtue as "an activity of soul in accordance with right reason." Aristotle portrays this concept of virtue in the *Nichomachean Ethics* as follows:

> *"We must, however, not only describe virtue as a state of character, but also say what sort of state it is. We may remark then, that every virtue or excellence both brings into good condition the thing of which it is the excellence and makes the work of that thing be done well... What affirmation and negation are in thinking, pursuit and avoidance are in desire; so that since moral virtue is a state of character concerned with choice, and choice is deliberate desire, therefore both the reasoning must be true and the desire right, if the choice is to be good, and the latter must pursue what the former asserts. "* [15]

The emotions and the appetites or desires have as their "object" either the pursuit of some perceived good or the avoidance of some perceived evil. What feelings do, is tell us what is good but only as pre-

---

14 Citation from the Washington Post, date and source unknown
15 Aristotle, *Nichomachean Ethics, Bk. 1, Ch. 1*

sented under the aspect of *desirability*. Unfortunately, *desirability*, as one aspect of what is good, does not tell us about the long-term results of that which is desired. Over-eating is a prime example of this. Food frequently looks so good that we eat more of it than is healthy. This disjunction between desirability and goodness is extremely common. The pleasure of over-eating is a 'good' but it is a limited good in relation to health and well-being as a whole.

Goodness always focuses on a larger view of time, action and consequence as opposed to biology and vice, which gravitates towards the immediate and thoughtless satisfaction of any desire. This is a consequence of the time war; the instincts of biology, which are almost always immediate, are at war with the long-term understanding of intellect and the higher sensibilities of the will, which participate in the larger intentionality of existence, as it is known by the supreme intellect of the Divine.

The excellent or virtuous use of the intellect and will represses nothing but that which should be suppressed, i.e., our biological nature. Suppression or the practice of self-restraint, as opposed to repression, creates a certain kind of space or option of choice for the emotions, freeing a person from the narrow temporality of desire and emotion. This is generally known as delayed gratification. The repressed person should be carefully distinguished from an individual who practices self-restraint and delayed gratification.

A repressed person is unable to engage the will in appropriate actions—when desired. The person who exercises self-restraint over animal instincts in favor of long-term goals, carefully keeps a lid on what should not be let out or channels the phenomenally creative and destructive power of the Freudian Id (what the ancients called appetite) in a constructive manner.

There should be an unresolved tension between the subjective power of appetitive feeling and the abstract, objective power of intellection. This tension is best lived-out in moral excellence, whereby intellect and will are relatively separated from the emotional fusion of desire, by freely willing what is a better good—relative to the prudent knowledge of what it is that makes a person good. Virtue in this respect is simply a way of establishing an effective algorithm or series of steps for dealing with the problems presented by biological impulses.

This is one practical application of Natural Law, a way of getting us from the "here" of nature as it is, to the "there" of a reformed nature connected to some ordering and refining principle within a larger context of time than absolute immediacy. We have often heard about the domestication of fire as an indication of civilization but seldom hear about the domestication of appetite, via the notion of virtue, as a pre-requisite for lasting cultural development.

The virtues of wisdom and prudence, which allow us to have a greater knowledge of causality, are rooted in the powers of the soul. The will which is part of the appetitive power of the soul gives us the ability to choose and potentially, the inclination to do what is really good. The soul's possession of that which is good develops potential, by actualizing a thing to be more of what it is, and not less (as in defect or vice). This is why the faces of the wise and brave are often radiant and the faces of the morally corrupt are often cold and hard, or vacant. As my father, Dr. Sean O'Reilly MD., noted many years ago:

> *"Moral values have a primacy among all other personal values;*
> *it is a greater good for the person to be endowed with them than*
> *with any other. Thus Socrates could say, "It is better for man to*
> *suffer injustice than to commit it."* [16]

The soul has been described in many ways, by different cultures and religions. The underlying reality of the concept indicates that it is something more than either we or it appear to be. The very idea of the soul resonates with a force of origin, beyond our present capability to fully grasp. The soul, like the full sails of a clipper ship, reveals the force of an outside power. The soul in the most abstract sense is an idea about the power and structure of *life* and its relation to matter, morality, time and eternity that has been developing for millennia. This cosmology of the soul, which may antedate written human history, can

---

16 Sean O'Reilly, MD, *Bioethics and the Limits of Science*, Christendom Press, 1980

be better understood, if examined in relation to the history of the idea of *being*. The structure of the soul, when analyzed in relation to the idea of being, yields a treasure trove of wisdom.

There is no issue which so reveals the role of reason and virtue in history as the question: what is being? An examination of the philosophical history of the question of being reveals a set of closely related questions. Is there a relationship between the philosophers' notions of being and essence and modern physics' understanding of energy and hyperspace (hidden spaces of greater than four dimensions)? What are the differences, what are the similarities? Is it possible that the ideas of being and essence describe non-Euclidean space in a way that modern physics is still groping for? Furthermore, what is the relationship between existence, being and the soul and how do these relations affect our understanding of politics and virtue?

Our daily experience and understanding of what might be termed, intuitive events, is critical to understanding ancient concepts such as essence and virtue. Any investigation into the role of reason in history will come across these ideas, as men and women attempt to integrate their understanding of being, in terms of their relations with society. Ultimately, the question of being and its relationship to such concepts as God and the soul will become pivotal political questions as the frontiers of moral and political change start to converge.

VICE AND THE HIDDEN HAND OF BIOLOGY

There has been much talk in recent years of excellence and character building. How can this be properly discussed without some understanding of virtue or its dark twin, vice? The five Intellectual virtues (good habits of mind) for Aristotle were:

Science
Wisdom
Understanding

Prudence
Art (understood in the sense of craftsmanship or sport)

We cultivate the acquired intellectual virtues in this country and look at the tremendous results! Science and technology, which are a result of an assiduous cultivation of intellectual excellence in the arts and sciences have improved the living conditions for millions of people. The Moral virtues, or those "good" habits which help us to control the appetites are seldom discussed with the exception of Justice. Most people think of appetite as only the appetite for food. This robs us of a really useful index for evaluating our desires. There at least eleven good moral habits that govern desire:

Courage
Continence (self-restraint in regards to bodily functions)
Liberality
Magnificence
Magnanimity (giving without regard for gain)
Honor (a state of character which is a result of the practice of moral virtue)
Gentleness
Friendship
Temperance (self-restraint in regards to pleasure)
Truthfulness
Justice

No discussion of virtue would be complete without a cataloging of the bad acts or vices. Vice, for many of the ancient Greek philosophers, was simply a defect of behavior in regards to the regulation of the appetites. The fourteen traditional vices are:

Gluttony
Greed

Laziness
Intemperance
Lack of self-restraint (incontinence)
Cowardice
Injustice
Lying
Parsimony
Rudeness
Ill-temper
Impatience
Violence
Hatred.

The vices are bad habits that take away from the perfection of the individual by allowing the appetites to rule instead of being ruled. A bad neighborhood for example is where habitual incontinence in the form of vice and brutishness rules. Have you ever wondered why we instinctively shy away from people with crooked eyes or bad vibes? Have we forgotten that the original meaning of the word, *'vicious'* is vice-ridden? Vice is the hidden hand of biology, when it is neither monitored or regulated.

There is a rich history and use of the concepts of virtue and vice in both Greek philosophy, as functional derivatives of *states* of the soul, and later in the Judeo Christian moral tradition as part of the structure of Natural Law. The concept of virtue itself is however, religiously neutral. Intellectual and moral excellence is not religion. Self-restraint, good manners and a sound education, for example, are as useful to the atheist as they are for the religious. Who can disagree with the habitual cultivation of excellence? Benjamin Franklin noted the following moral and intellectual virtues: [17]Note that they constitute algorithms or effective procedures in opposition to biology and the immediacy of desire and impulse.

17 Benjamin Franklin, *Autobiography*, New York: Derby & Jackson, 1859

1. TEMPERANCE— Eat not to dullness; drink not to elevation.

2. SILENCE—Speak not but what may benefit others or yourself; avoid trifling conversation.

3. ORDER— Let all your things have their places; let each part of your business have its time.

4. RESOLUTION— Resolve to perform what you ought; perform without fail what you resolve.

5. FRUGALITY— Make no expense but to do good to others or yourself; that is, waste nothing.

6. INDUSTRY—Lose no time; be always employed in something useful; cut off all unnecessary actions.

7. SINCERITY— Use no hurtful deceit; think innocently and justly; and, if you speak, speak accordingly.

8. JUSTICE— Wrong none by doing injuries, or omitting the benefits that are your duty.

9. MODERATION—Avoid extremes; forbear resenting injuries so much as you think they deserve.

10. CLEANLINESS—Tolerate no uncleanliness in body, clothes, or habitation.

11. TRANQUILITY—Be not disturbed at trifles, or at accidents common or unavoidable.

12. CHASTITY—[Franklin does not define this. In his day it would have been obvious what it was, i.e., sexual purity in regards to act, thought and intention.]

13. HUMILITY— Imitate Jesus and Socrates.

Unless we bring the concepts of virtue and vice into the public arena for discussion and attempt to understand the various interpenetrations of objective and personal time with the much larger sense of time that the Divine brings to life, we simply will never have the tools to adequately raise the standard of ethical consciousness in America. No one will really know who the 'good guys' are and the 'bad guys' will win.

Chapter 5

LOOKING AT AMERICA

"Bad men cannot make good citizens. It is when a people forget God that tyrants forge their chains. A vitiated state of morals, a corrupted public conscience, is incompatible with freedom. No free government or the blessing of liberty, can be preserved to any people but by a firm adherence to justice, moderation, temperance, frugality and virtue; and by a frequent recurrence to fundamental principles."

—Patrick Henry

THE FIVE INSTITUTIONS

A strange concept has slowly taken hold of the public mind in America. This is the idea that jobs and public services are rights that exist independently of what we do as a culture. There is about this idea something that reminds me of a headless monster. For example, we have frequently heard about the need to invest more in our poorer communities, as if *investment* were something that existed independently of individuals, business, education, families, government and religion. What person in his or her right mind would want to start a business in a community where theft, violence and drugs are the norm? Investment in this context becomes, solely, a well-meaning abstraction with no reference to reality.

The notion that government should serve as an intermediary between the public and the private sector seems somehow lost in the labyrinth of our desires and wishes for a better life. We tend to forget that society is composed of five great institutions[1] (listed in alphabetical order): Business, Education, Family, Government and Religion. The orderly development of society would seem to involve balance, cooperation and respect between these five orders of social reality.

History teaches us that if any one of these five institutions becomes unbalanced or has influence out of proportion to its proper function, the entire social order will suffer. Two historical examples that come to mind are the Inquisition, whereby religious authority ruled through the political order, and the social hardships imposed by Communist regimes that allowed government to usurp the functions of the other social institutions.

Jobs and public services are created out of a matrix that involves the five institutions each doing their respective tasks well. Aristotle's definition of virtue as "an activity of soul in accordance with right reason" applies no less to individuals as it does to public institutions. It is simply impossible to have problems in one institution of society that do not affect the others. Government can no more create all the productive jobs and services required by a modern society, than can families or private business. Families and businesses cannot survive without the protection of government, nor can government survive without successful businesses and families. Many problems that the

---

1   I am indebted to Patrick Fagan for bringing this idea to my attention.

Third World faces are a direct result of the failure of one or more of the five institutions.

The current economic and fiscal swamp in which we find ourselves can be directly attributed to a failure of both liberals and conservatives to fully grasp the interrelated nature of the institutions of Business, Education, Family, Government and Religion. The greatest thing a government and statesmen can do is to encourage cooperation between all the institutions that make up a society. Government serves best when there is a recognition that good governance exists to serve and to facilitate the dynamic between short-term business needs and long-term economic interests that benefit the maximum number of citizens.

The interrelated nature of the five institutions is complemented by The Principle of Subsidiarity. "One of the key principles of Catholic social thought is known as the *principle of subsidiarity*. This tenet holds that nothing should be done by a larger and more complex organization which can be done as well by a smaller and simpler organization. In other words, any activity which can be performed by a more decentralized entity should be. This principle is a bulwark of limited government and personal freedom. It conflicts with the passion for centralization and bureaucracy characteristic of the Welfare State."[2]

"This is why Pope John Paul II took the 'social assistance state' to task in his 1991 encyclical *Centesimus Annus*. The Pontiff wrote that the Welfare State was contradicting the principle of subsidiarity by intervening directly and depriving society of its responsibility. This [according to the Pontiff] leads to a loss of human energies and an inordinate increase of public agencies which are dominated more by bureaucratic ways of thinking than by concern for serving their clients and which are accompanied by an enormous increase in spending."[3] One of the ways in which bureaucratic thinking allows for the growth of parasitical financial activity is by not paying attention to what is

---

2 Bosnitch, David A: http://www.acton.org/pub/religion-liberty/volume-6-number-4/principle-subsidiarity
3 Ibid

actually happening in the marketplace. The huge losses that occurred in the real estate market due to the subprime mortgage crash of 2005-2008 were a direct result of the failure of agencies such as the Securities and Exchange Commission (SEC), which are specifically tasked with regulating financial instruments.

Did any member of the SEC or any other Federal organization go to jail for the failure to rein in the major institutional players in the subprime mortgage crisis? The answer is, sadly, no. The excuse provided congressional investigators was that they (the members of the SEC) were not given the tools to jail or otherwise discipline bad players. What the members of the SEC should have been doing was beating the drum about the problem of creating securities that were inadequately backed by sound mortgages. Unfortunately, these kinds of corrections do not happen in the clubby atmosphere between bureaucratic regulators and very clever but unethical institutional players.

Dr. Paul Craig Roberts, Chairman of the Institute for a Political Economy notes that the *re-enserfment* of Americans is occurring on three levels. "One...comes from the off-shoring of jobs. Americans, for example, have a shrinking participation in the production of the goods and services that are marketed to them. On another level we are experiencing the *financialization* of the Western economy about which Michael Hudson is the leading expert (*Killing The Host*). "Financialization" is the process of removing any public presence in the economy and converting the economic surplus into interest payments to the financial sector. These two developments deprive people of economic prospects. A third development deprives them of political rights. The Trans-Pacific and Trans-Atlantic Partnerships [for example] eliminate political sovereignty and turn governance over to global corporations.

These so called "trade partnerships" have nothing to do with trade. These agreements, negotiated in secrecy, grant immunity to corporations from the laws of the countries in which they do business. This is achieved by declaring any interference by existing and prospective laws and regulations on corporate profits as restraints on trade for which corporations can sue and fine "sovereign" governments. For example, the ban in France and other countries on GMO products would be negated by the Trans-Atlantic Partnership. Democracy is simply replaced by corporate rule."[4]

There is a myth in America that this country was built on private enterprise. This is a corporate fairy tale. America was built by the five basic institutions all working together—sometimes well and sometimes poorly. A classic example of five institution cooperation was American government sponsorship of the western territories in the 1800's. This partnership between the public and the private sector was a means of opening up undeveloped areas, with the implicit idea that business, education, family and church would establish the Nation beyond its present boundaries and make for a more prosperous America. The same might be said for our national system of highways.

What government can do to create jobs and services is to sponsor and create conditions that encourage the growth of the other institutions. Aristotle described the moral virtue of *magnificence* as the ability to make large expenditures on a scale appropriate to needs, particularly in regards to building. Modern examples of magnificence are America's system of highways, the space program and even social security. What government can do best is leverage the power of numbers or what is today referred to as crowd sourcing in order to achieve complex and expensive projects. What is taxation, when you think about it, but crowd-sourcing of a very simple and ancient type?

Creating political algorithms that capitalize on the benefits of long-term planning versus the raucous demands of the present moment mirrors the personal struggle that every human being must wage: the sacrificing of immediate gratification for long-term gain. This is the most fundamental of all algorithms and is characteristic of all virtue or what is considered moral and intellectual excellence: the intellectual management of and, if necessary, suppression of impulse and the guiding of emotion towards long-term goals.

---

4   Paul Craig Roberts, http://www.paulcraigroberts.org/pages/about-paul-craig-roberts/

We urgently need magnificent enterprises for the present generation. An example of this might be government sponsorship of high speed bullet trains or Elon Musk's Hyperloop's[5] to facilitate a business exchange between rural and urban America. Families need reasonably priced homes to live in and the only way to get that is by acquiring and developing cheaper land that can be commuted to. As it is, in many states, some individuals drive upwards of 100 miles a day just to have a decent home and be able to work in an urban environment.

The Chinese and Japanese governments tend to exercise civic virtue and magnificence on a large scale. Some Japanese companies, for example, have 200 to 500-year business plans. The success of Japanese industry is directly related to the cultivation of both intellectual and moral excellence. Despite business, sex and other scandals, self-restraint in other areas of appetitive diversion is accepted as a natural requirement for success in Japan and tends to be practiced as a matter of common sense. Most Japanese view the American lack of emotional self-discipline and our current economic problems as both incomprehensible and related. The legendary orderliness of Japanese society represents a social structure that *embodies* appetitive management, even if sexual continence is not practiced as well as it might be.

American society needs to move towards understanding the complex interrelationship between the five institutions and virtue, and seek ways to promote reasonable growth in an environmentally sound manner. Ultimately, as a species, we may be able to leave this planet and seek other areas for growth and expansion but unless we perfect the process of social growth and development here on earth, we may devolve into a new dark age, where the politics of scarcity will assume the ancient visage of war.

---

5   "The Hyperloop is a conceptual high-speed transportation system incorporating reduced-pressure tubes in which pressurized capsules ride on an air cushion driven by linear induction motors and air compressors." [WP]

THE UNRAVELING OF AMERICA

The Democratic and Republican conventions over the past forty years have given us a marvelous insight into the current destitution of American Democracy. Some viewers have found various comedy shows' reporting of the Conventions far more interesting than the real thing. Comedians have addressed issues that have been on all of our minds like "he is lying" or "what is she smoking?" As Donald Soper cleverly noted, in England, on the similar quality of debate in the English House of Lords, "It is, I think, good evidence for life after death."

There has certainly been tremendous style and enthusiasm shown by many speakers at these conventions but practical ideas seem to evaporate in the heat of slogan-driven public relations. Three of the more common slogans for example, when interpreted have a different meaning. *Pro-Choice means*: whatever I choose is good and *marriage equality* means that no one should challenge the gender involved in marriage. *Family Values* means: I have values and you don't. Unfortunately, the exchange of slogans or hearsay does not constitute a serious engagement of issues unless employed as a rhetorical adjunct to a larger discourse. Thucydides noted the problem as far back as the Peloponnesian War: "So little pains do the vulgar take in the investigation of the truth, accepting readily the first story that comes to hand."

The incredible lack of educated or philosophical argument regarding any of the major issues that affect our nation today is one of the major causes of our declining economy, rising crime rates, pathetic system of education and the general lack of optimism that has accompanied our social decline. Some of the solutions for a variety of our social ills may be found in the great river of Western classical thought that comes to us from Socrates, Plato, Aristotle, Cicero, Duns Scotus and Aquinas. Unfortunately, the works of these philosophers are generally not read as texts with solutions for modern day problems but as exercises in torture for college students. Aristotle and Plato, for example, are read with the aid of abbreviated texts and material is promptly forgotten after the obligatory testing is finished.

Cicero, the great Roman philosopher who served as a moral and political beacon for centuries after his death, even until the 1800s, is seldom read today. Thomas Aquinas, whose philosophical thinking has yet to be fully understood, is passed off as a clone of Aristotle by academic boneheads who have given us such legacies as values clarification and students who are unable to read. Learning disabilities (despite the truly learning disabled) are in fashion now due to an educational system that never taught students to read properly in the first place. Do you remember, "See spot run" or "Oh, oh Jane, oh, oh Jane?" My father started to read Latin and Greek in a one-room schoolhouse in Ireland *before* he was six. What kind of nonsense prevents many Americans from learning to read English, properly, until they are nearly teens?

WPA Image provided courtesy of the American taxpayer in the 1930's

Education, almost more than any other discipline, must have a clear set of principles in order to transmit the values of the past so that they might be improved upon and kept by future generations. Basic phonics served educators well since the beginning of the 19th century of but now we have large numbers of pupils at the elementary school level that are not even properly taught phonics for fear of offending those who might prefer to speak in the variants of English commonly known as slang or even more absurdly—jive.[6]

This has led to the challenging of elementary school testing on the basis of students not being able to understand the language. This is what happens when common methods of understanding cause and effect are not employed by educators. And how could they when academia churns out a constant downplaying of moral cause and effect on almost every level of human understanding?

How is it possible that America, which until the 1970's out produced the world in all areas of manufacturing and invented the automobile, is now a declining industrial power? Did it happen because everyone else caught up? Hardly. The industrialization of countries that had previously been unindustrialized prior to the 1960's only made the competition more intense. Our industrial decline has occurred for many reasons but primarily it is due to political and labor groups who have forgotten that production of goods and services is not a natural resource like air or wood.

The production of useful goods and services is directly related to the intelligent actualization of human potential through sound education and principles of human development and growth. It doesn't take a wizard to figure out that opposition to human growth and sensible expansion, coupled with the environmental view that humanity is spreading like a cancer on the planet will sooner or later result in stagnation rather than responsible growth. The well-known opposition of liberals to the development of *capital goods* here in the US, i.e., dams, factories, power plants, both nuclear and conventional, and the

---

6   Jive: commonly known as black English

increase in a multitude of environmental rules that impede the development of business has resulted in a view of human activity profoundly opposed to the injunction of Genesis, which is to go forth and subdue the earth and everything on it.

Look around you; does a day go by that you don't hear about some horrible crime or some terrible violence that one man or woman, or one nation or tribe has done to another? Look at the endless fighting in North Africa and the Middle East, the dismemberment of the Ukraine by Russian 'volunteers' and vacationers, and the mass-starvation facing many countries. Civic order, national unity and the ability to speak without lying or spinning the facts are direct by-products of not having a moral schematic that values truth and reality over a subjective or tribal interpretation of reality.

Wilfred M. McClay, the G.T. and Libby Blankenship Professor of the History of Liberty at the University of Oklahoma, describes the problem that current historical revisionism on campus is creating. This revisionism goes hand-in-hand with the failure of the environmental movement to understand the need for capital goods production. The environmental view of sexuality is similarly distorted by unrealistic fears of population growth, unrelated to the dynamics of economic development, which can change not only expected outcomes but increase the means of productivity to accommodate population growth.

"The change is very clear: the new framework represents a shift from national identity to sub-cultural identity. Indeed, the new framework is so populated with examples of American history as the conflict between social groups, and so inattentive to the sources of national cohesion, that it is hard to see how students will gain any coherent idea of what those sources might be. This does them and all Americans an immense disservice. Instead of combating fracture, it embraces it." [7]

7   Imprimis, a publication of Hillsdale College, July/August 2015, Volume 44, Number 7/8, pages 6-7

Wherever you see the tribe or ethnicity being used as a substitute for principle, you can be sure that reason is taking the back seat. An example of this sort of political irrationality (based solely on self-interest) is the movement for DC. Statehood in America. How intellectually retrograde can you get? According this kind of thinking, every major city in the United States could or should be a state. Come to think of it why don't we divide each of the new city states into tribes? Cool, then we could have real wars again...

HEDONISM IN BALTIMORE

By now, the images of the Ferguson, Baltimore and other riots have started to recede from the public consciousness like a bad dream. What is left in the public mind is a kind of cognitive dissonance[8] that has yet to be unpacked and articulated by the political pygmies of both the left and the right. What was missing from all commentary was a clear analysis of why violence for pleasure's sake is on the rise in America. Make no mistake about it, the police in many communities suffer from this psycho-pathological form of incontinence no less than the rioters who beat unfortunate bystanders. Why is it that we never seem to discuss the pleasure that human beings seem to take in hurting each other? Obviously there must be some enjoyment involved or we wouldn't have such grotesquely inflated violent crime statistics. Most of us seem to be satisfied with the response of, "oh people like that are sick." Possibly they are not sick, perhaps they are merely hedonists.

It is a terrible thing to say but there appears to be some correlation between violence and pleasure. Most of us seem to enjoy violent movies. Why don't we prefer *Lassie*? There is in each one of us—at our evolutionary core, the remnant of something that is brutally conscious of only the most elementary pleasures. Call it the Id of Freud, the dark

---

8 "In psychology, cognitive dissonance is the mental stress or discomfort experienced by an individual who holds two or more contradictory beliefs, ideas, or values at the same time, or is confronted by new information that conflicts with existing beliefs, ideas, or values." [WP]

side, the beast, the limbic system, the vital, our biological nature or Satan's little helper—it is all the same system of impulses that resists regulation. There is something of it in the lion stalking and killing a baby elephant or a newborn doe. It lives only to devour and to smack its lips rudely in the collective face of the living. Those who live in the pleasure of the immediate moment only, without reference to regulative standards, have unwittingly allowed this evolutionary holdover to be their moral guide.

The moral difficulty of living in the moment, without guidelines, may be described as follows: if an individual's sole yardstick of what is good is based solely on feeling and not on how they reason using standards, then surely pleasure will be the ultimate determinant of their behavior. The difficulty with feeling-based moral systems is that some individuals may take pleasure in things that are not good for others or themselves. The Roman, Seneca (4 BC–65 AD) noted in his book, *Tranquility of Mind:*

> *"There are certain bodily sores which welcome the hands that will hurt them, and long to be touched, and a foul itch loves to be scratched: in the same way I would say that those minds on which desires have broken out like horrid sores take delight in toil and aggravation."* [9]

This is all very obvious in one sense but in another, not obvious at all. What Seneca indicates is that not only pleasure but some kinds of mental disturbances and disorders are on a continuum with subjectivity, and for this reason, pleasure and even what we assign our attention to—without an objective moral framework—cannot be the only standard for action. Sadism, for example, is simply another pleasure and if there is no reason not to indulge, then there are those who obviously will indulge.

---

9   Kyle Eschenroeder, from The Art of Manliness http://www.artofmanliness.com/2016/08/15/what-do-you-want-to-want/?

Videotapes of the devolved, sucker-punching their victims, or rioters throwing bricks at police show human beings engaging in sadistic activity with gusto. What is needed is a philosophical analysis of sadism to help clear the air of the sophomoric comments of psychologists who talk about the frustration of the poor or racism as if it were an irresistible force. There are numerous countries where there are poor and frustrated people who do not behave like animals.

The correlation of crime solely with poverty, if not also understood as being linked to moral devolution, as part of a set of interrelated conditions, does not allow the establishment of a visible, causal chain that can be ameliorated by policies that might improve such behavior. What we frequently see among liberals on the left is an improper correlation of bad behavior with conditions that should be but are not linked to the real causes of moral devolution, which begins with the failure to restrain sexual and other appetites. Poor impulse management, in other words, must be linked (as one of multiple causes) to social problems involving crime and poverty.

"The age-old problem of correlation versus causation illustrates the dangers of ignorance in all its many forms. When the ancients were able to predict solar eclipses and other astronomical phenomena with regularity this "foretelling" became a sign of authenticity in regards not just to these pronouncements but all prophecies made by the priests. This was a correlation of one true thing with other pronouncements that may or may not have been true. This is known in logic as a *post hoc* fallacy—meaning "after this, therefore caused by this". If an [ancient] priest, to use another example, was offering human sacrifice and at the moment the still-beating heart was pulled from the victim's chest, lightening appeared in the sky, the appearance of the lightening, which may have been entirely accidental, might be correlated positively with the sacrifice, by the priest, as a sign of approval from the gods. This is, clearly, correlation being used inappropriately, in lieu of a proper understanding of causation."[10]

---

10 O'Reilly, Sean, *Authority, Creativity and the Third Imperium: Why God's Knowing Him-*

Likewise, understanding that the relationship between feeling good and moral excellence is causally related and not just improperly correlated with civic duty or religion was noted by the Greeks. Epicurus (341-270 B.C.) believed that the greatest pleasure came from self-restraint and that there was a moral hierarchy in the choosing of various pleasures. He has been misunderstood as a promoter of unbridled hedonism but this was not the case. His understanding of morality was much closer to that of Aristotle's, in that moral excellence and the pursuit of legitimate pleasure are not understood as mutually exclusive terms. There is indeed a pleasure to be had in acting reasonably and exercising some control over our baser instincts. Traditionally, this has been known collectively as the moral excellence (or virtue) of honor. The shamefulness of sadistic or unkind acts, by contrast, consists of disregarding the well-being of our fellow human beings in favor of whatever biological impulses happen to infest our consciousness. A sadist might be thought of as lacking any self-control over primitive urges.

Looking backwards, in more recent times, for prominent examples of non-impulse management, the O.J. Simpson legal circus and Lorena Bobbit's impromptu surgical removal of her husband's penis, remind us that feelings are a powerful factor in the way we choose to act and that if we live solely in our feelings, then we may behave in non-rational ways. Humankind frequently walks the no-man's land between the rational and the irrational. It is, however, the mark of an honorable man or woman to balance the irrational and the rational by choosing those actions which channel their more hurtful instincts into creative action. The mark of the beast is aptly that of fire, destruction and snapping jaws.

EVOLUTION AND DEVOLUTION

The extraordinary level of recent youthful violence in our inner cities and elsewhere has been much commented upon lately but seldom do we see an analysis that addresses the root causes. We are familiar with the usual—almost polite and obvious explanations that poverty, homelessness, drugs and lack of education are all to blame, but nowhere is the real reason for violence addressed; nor is a solution offered. I set up a program, many years ago, to teach philosophy to hard-core inmates at Lorton Penitentiary in Virginia, in order to evaluate their response to moral philosophy. After a morning session, one of the inmates said to me: "You know, no one has ever told some of these guys that they have to exercise self-restraint." Why are we surprised then that young people are behaving like animals, when no one has ever told them or showed them good reasons for exercising self-control?

There is a very basic formulation of the problem which goes something like this: Devolution is as much a possibility for human beings as is evolution. More succinctly stated, men and women have the capacity to behave like animals. One of the purposes of education and culture in general is to keep people from behaving as if they belonged to another species. It must be stressed that the obviousness of this answer should not be used to brush off what is being implied—for the implications are extraordinary.

Evolution, as it is commonly understood, involves lower species evolving into higher species, through both mutation and natural selection. Natural selection simply means that the strongest and healthiest members of a species are the most likely to successfully reproduce. Humankind is the only species which is capable of altering the process of natural selection by extensively modifying its environment. The failure to modify our environment culturally, through education and family life, results in a return to societal natural selection and animal behavior, whereby the strong rule the weak. Additionally, we are inverting the process of natural selection, by making the strong and successful the least likely to reproduce more than one or two young.

Animals for the most part behave like animals. They eat when they want to and have sex when they feel like it—particularly, when the female is fertile. They also sleep for as long or as little as they like.

The majority defecate in public and generally don't tidy up after themselves. An animal lives in the immediacy of its feelings. For this reason, I am not the least surprised when a young human killer responds to queries about a senseless murder with, "I felt like it" or some other similar response. Devolving human beings do such things routinely, unless trained or schooled otherwise.

> *"For man, when perfected, is the best of animals, but, when separated from the law and justice, he is the worst of all; since armed injustice is the more dangerous, and he is equipped at birth with arms, meant to be used by intelligence and virtue, which he may use for the worst ends. Wherefore, if he have not virtue, he is the most unholy and most savage of animals, and the most full of lust and gluttony."*

> —Aristotle,
> Politics, Bk.2, Ch.2

The possibility that men and women have the option in a free society of behaving like animals is an issue that has not been adequately addressed in America. Our cultural understanding of human nature assumes development, as opposed to entropy and stagnation. Even though religion discusses fallen nature and sin, and the moral philosophers, virtue and vice, we still must reflect on our basic biology and the possibility that a culture and a people can devolve, as well as evolve.

We must develop the concept of devolution as it applies to human beings, so that we might better understand what it is we have to do to behave like human beings. Aristotle, who lived over 350 years before Christ focused on the soul and made it central to both his political and philosophical treatises. Aristotle did not do this because he was particularly religious, but as a philosopher and biologist, he clearly saw that there had to be a principle of organization that simultaneously transcended and embraced nature.

We need to get back to the notion that man can be considered as a whole and not merely as a sum of parts. How do men and women become degraded or how do they become like Gods? Aristotle's understanding of virtue and vice is most helpful here. The definitions might be paraphrased as follows:

Acting in accordance with right reason is that set of considered actions and habits that make us more rational and vice is that action or set of unconsidered actions and habits that make us less rational.

Humanity has always had to strike a social balance between its animal side and its human side. Let us not pretend that our primitive side does not exist or that there is no way to be better. All decent human beings must struggle day in and day out, not to indulge their biological nature with acts of petty or major violence and irrationality. Don't we experience this every day with our loved ones? Have you ever caught yourself arguing wildly with a loved one and wondered if it might not be better just to bark at them? (Imagine yourself and the other person as two dogs, both growling and barking at each other.) Come to think of it, barking might be more constructive, as our words are often just a substitute for savaging the identity/hide of the other person.

Five days a week I have to get out of bed at a time that does not correspond to my feelings of having slept enough. I have to get up and go to work, whether I feel like it or not. If I need to go to the bathroom during the course of the day, I restrain my urge to relieve myself immediately and head for the nearest restroom. The same applies to sexual urges. There is a time and a place for everything for the civilized person. I did not, however, come to be this way without training and long personal effort. What happens when the lines get blurred with some people and they never learn that they have to exercise even the simplest forms of self-restraint? Someone insults me, so I do what I feel like doing; if that includes murder and mayhem, so be it. Suppose I feel like having sex—why not do it with whomever is handy—whether they want to do it with you or not?

Our civilization is rapidly approaching this parody of human behavior that I have been outlining. ISIS burns and drowns people alive in metal cages due to ideologies that are not even remotely rational. Even the simplest moral conventions are being challenged. Human beings coming into emergency rooms, due to bizarre sexual practices, signals wholesale abandonment of sexual common sense—regardless of sexual orientation. "Fisting" or sticking a fist into someone's rectum is not an urban myth but it is part of a disturbing and emerging pattern. On the most basic level, almost anything can feel good, whether it is sexual depravity or murder but the fundamental issue is: should we allow ourselves these liberties? Cicero, (106-43 BC) the great Roman moral philosopher chastised the intelligentsia of his day by saying:

> *"It is scandalous that the philosophers entertain opinions that any common farm laborer would not hesitate to dismiss."*

We might say the same today about some of our mental health professionals and lawmakers. Anyone who watched the late Senator, Edward Kennedy, speak about some moral issue was surely inclined to feel queasy. If Kennedy had been black and had drowned a white woman, he would have been languishing in jail for thirty years. When Kennedy even used the word moral, I had to laugh. He had no more a clue as to what moral meant than does the appalling Hillary Clinton or Nancy Pelosi in the present day.

The solutions to violence, crime and political stupidity in this country will begin to emerge when we start frankly discussing the dangers of acting like animals and what it is we must do to improve ourselves. A philosophy of virtue ethics or psychology of self-restraint and delayed gratification is sorely needed. We must also seek to better understand the possibilities for cultural and personal devolution in a society that may ultimately be able to gratify every basic human desire and need. Our future as a civilization depends on it.

CICERO'S THREE CATEGORIES OF MORAL GOODNESS

Cicero held that moral goodness fell into **three** basic categories. The **first** was the ability to distinguish truth from falsity and to understand the relationships between one phenomenon and another, and the causes and consequences of each one. The **second** was the ability to restrain the emotions and to make appetite or desire amenable to reason. The **third** was the capacity to behave with consideration and understanding towards other people. These virtues of honesty, self-restraint, consideration and understanding are basic to the formation of any culture. We simply cannot afford *not* to teach our young people how to cultivate these aspects of good character.

How many months has it been since someone yelled or screamed obscenities at you for some innocuous driving infraction or an assumed slight to their integrity? How often do you park your car and look around because you need to make sure you will safely be able to get back into your vehicle? How many school children have lives of quiet desperation because of the young criminals who inhabit their schools and the teachers who are incapable of helping them due to regulations made by administrators who only care about their next paycheck? How tired are you of having always to watch where you are going and what you are doing, so as to keep yourself and your family safe from criminals and deviates?

If any of these questions remind you of how angry you are at the present state of American culture and make you wonder if there was something that could be done to improve the moral literacy of the Nation, then let's try to find out what we are doing wrong and how we got there in the first place.

Chapter 6

POLITICS, THE FOUNDING FATHERS AND VIRTUE

"Since happiness is an activity of soul in accordance with perfect virtue, we must consider the nature of virtue; for perhaps we shall thus see better the nature of happiness. The true student of politics, too is thought to have studied virtue above all things; for he wishes to makes his fellow citizens good and obedient to the laws."

—Aristotle,
Nichomachean Ethics, Bk. 1: Ch. 12

POLITICS AS THE SCIENCE OF THE GOOD

Consider the foregoing quotation. Can the reader imagine an American politician discussing the soul and happiness in conjunction with the notion of politics? You probably find it difficult to imagine because

153

the majority of American politicians do not really know what virtue is, let alone the proper definition of the word soul or even politics. There is a connection between the idea of the 'good', the soul and excellence (virtue) that is simply not on the moral map of most politicians.

Aristotle defines politics as the *"science of the good for the many"*. He might as well have said that it is for the establishing of algorithms of efficiency for human behavior. If this is so, how is it that politics has become a science of the good for the special interest group? How is it that the soul or the 'good' as concepts are seldom utilized in either modern politics or education? Do we say that these are old ideas that only applied to the Greeks, or do we assert that these are timeless ideas? We must categorically state that if the original meaning of politics is not linked to an understanding of the 'good', excellence and the soul, this deviation will result in an impoverishment of politics.

Aristotle gives us, perhaps, the most comprehensive and penetrating inquiry, regarding the meaning of politics and its relation to the good, excellence and the soul, in both the *Nichomachean Ethics* and the *Politics*.

> *"Every art and every inquiry and similarly every action and pursuit is thought to aim at some good; and for this reason the good has rightly been declared to be that at which all things aim... Now there are many actions, arts and sciences, their ends also are many; the end of the medical art is health, that of shipbuilding a vessel, that of strategy, victory, that of economics, wealth...If, then, there is some end of the things we do, which we desire for its own sake...clearly this must be the good and the chief good. Will not the knowledge of it, then have a great influence on life? Shall we not, like archers who have a mark to aim at, be more likely to hit upon what is right? If so, we must try, in outline at least to determine what it is and of which of the sciences or capacities it is the object. It would seem to belong to the most authoritative art and that which is most truly the master art. And politics appears*

to be of this nature; for it is this that ordains which of the sciences which should be studied in a state...it legislates what we are to do and what we are to abstain from, the end of this science must include those of the others, so that this end must be the good for man."

How interesting! Politics is a science that legislates what we are to do and what we are to abstain from. Obviously, those people who insist upon their right to be free of government interference in all moral matters must be unaware of this. How many times have you heard, "What you do in your bedroom has nothing to do with your job, and the government has no right to legislate morality." Both of these statements are so obviously vague and untrue, one can wonder why they are entertained by so many, apparently, intelligent individuals.

A sexually challenged politician or educator who likes to dress like a poodle and be whipped in the privacy of his or her bedroom is hardly a candidate for an overall, rational behavior award. The difficulty in evaluating such behavior in individuals, who are otherwise functionally productive, stems from confusing the intellectual with the moral virtues. They are not absolutely related, i.e., a deficiency in the moral virtues does not prevent the acquisition of intellectual excellence. A man could theoretically be a good dentist and engage in bestiality. Immorality is a problem because the moral virtue of self-restraint or continence is required as a practical matter for *superior* intellectual and moral development. Perhaps it seems too obvious, but incontinence and its more developed cousin, vice cause moral habits to devolve. Try to be a good student on a daily diet of sex, beer, marijuana and violence and you may understand the difficulty.

Unfortunately, there are those whose intelligence is so great that no matter how they abuse themselves, they are able to excel intellectually. This only confuses those who are less gifted. They point to the bright ones who are corrupt and think that they too ought to be able to get away with the same excesses and do well at their studies. What is overlooked is that the corrupt geniuses would be able to do far greater things if they exercised moral discipline.

For the majority of mankind, the energy required for advanced intellectual development is directly tied to overall psychic energy usage. *Sublimation*[1] is the missing link between moral and intellectual development, and excellence. The discipline required to govern sexual appetites is useful in all walks of life for achieving ends that require substantial effort. However, if you do not believe that there are any appetites to regulate, then what you do, or don't do, won't necessarily appear to make any difference to you—other than contribute to your personal confusion and disorder. However, don't tell me that you would visit or trust a doctor who, in his spare time, puts small rodents up his rectum for sexual satisfaction or elect to public office, a pederast whose preference is for boys four years and under.

Obviously, the government does legislate morality. Murder is prohibited, as is the taking of harmful narcotics. If you don't think that you have an appetite for murder, think about your last encounter with someone who was extremely rude to you, or your lover or spouse. Clearly, we do have an appetite for murder, most of us just don't indulge it. Unfortunately, some of our citizens are now in the unhappy position of being so uninhibited that murder is no longer an unthinkable option. "*What, he insulted you; let me blow him away.*" Does this kind of activity produce happiness? I think it rather produces a stupefying satisfaction, which allows the appetites to increase both their range and hold over an individual.

The wild irrationality of Idi Amin, Stalin, Caligula and movements like ISIS come to mind here. The appetites are a harsh ruler;

---

1   "Sublimation is the transformation of unwanted impulses [this includes sexual impulses] into something less harmful. This can simply be a distracting release or may be a constructive and valuable piece of work. When we are faced with the dissonance of uncomfortable thoughts, [including but not limited to anger, jealousy, envy and lust] we create psychic energy. This has to go somewhere. Sublimation channels this energy away from destructive acts and into something that is socially acceptable and/or creatively effective. Many sports and games are sublimations of aggressive urges, as we sublimate the desire to fight into the ritualistic activities of formal competition." http://changingminds.org/explanations/behaviors/coping/sublimation.htm

every whim must be gratified. "I feel like cutting his head off—no problem and while you are at it, execute the foreign minister, I don't like his shoes." Think about it, how many of us are that close to the craziness of unregulated appetites?

> "Perhaps, however, it seems a truth which is generally admitted, that happiness is the supreme good; what is wanted is to define its nature a little more clearly. The best way of arriving at such a definition will probably be to ascertain the function of Man. For as with a flute-player, a statuary, or any artisan, or in fact anybody who has a definite function and action, his goodness, or excellence seems to lie in his function, so it would seem to be with Man, if indeed he has a definite function. Can it be said that, while a carpenter and a cobbler have definite functions and actions, Man, unlike them is naturally functionless?" [2]

The primary function of man, according to Aristotle is the rational ordering of the appetites in conjunction with intellectual development. These are the most elementary algorithms or steps to be established in order to live a reasonable and ordered life. Happiness comes to the man or woman who is able to fulfill their primary function. If we were to put a more global label on this rational ordering of the appetites, we would say that the development of personal potential—both intellectual and moral is the foundation upon which a life of excellence and consequently, happiness is built.

Happiness, like sunshine, is a product of fusion. Likewise, the fusion of intellect and appetite in the production of virtuous or worthwhile activity produces or can produce happiness. No such fusion can take place where either intellect or appetite is unbalanced. Conversely, the lack of worthwhile activity produces unhappiness, as the intellect is unable to carry out its function of ordering the appetites and developing the intellect. (This is why Aristotle's philosophy is a philosophy

---

2   Aristotle, *Nichomachean Ethics*

that is intellectually and morally pro-growth.)

Aristotle links the notions of soul and virtue. Virtue is an *activity of soul in accordance with reason.* It is precisely for this reason that much of the meaning of Aristotle is lost on college students. 'Soul', 'virtue'— blank stares from the sexually jaded student body…There can be little understanding of Aristotelian politics and the notion of the good, or even happiness, without an understanding of the structure of the soul and its relation to the development of virtue. This is disturbing because moral ideas, based on Greek philosophy, were of considerable interest to some of America's Founding Fathers and part of the foundation of their thinking. In order to better understand the history of moral development or the lack thereof in American culture, the opinions of John Adams and James Madison are worth examining.

THE FOUNDING FATHERS AND VIRTUE

Today, American politics has divorced itself from any moral code, based on the bizarre equating of morality with religion. Nothing could be further from the truth. Washington, Jefferson, Adams, Madison and Hamilton were just a few of the founding fathers who were conversant with the notion of virtue and its utility with regard to political issues and human nature.

The wisdom of the founding fathers was that they understood that men and women were motivated primarily by self-interest, and that virtue or benevolence in general could not be counted on to regulate political affairs. The influence of self-interest and the subsequent factionalization of groups, with interests in common, was uppermost on their minds in designing the political structure of American government. The very structure of House, Senate, Judiciary and Presidency enhances the possibility for balance and dialogue between opposing groups.

Nonetheless, the founding fathers were of a mixed mind when contemplating the role of virtue in society. Self-interest, while seen as the supreme regulator of the affairs of men could not wholly be relied upon for the regulation of the affairs of the commonwealth, any more than could virtue. There is, then, a tension between virtue and self-interest which was never fully resolved by the founding fathers. Indeed, it might be argued that the very structure of a system of checks and balances was designed to accommodate this problem.

John Adams, of all the Founding Fathers, while he thoroughly supported the concept of virtue, seems to have been skeptical of the overall practical effect that reason and virtue might have on a society.

> "If Socrates and Plato, Cicero and Seneca, Hutchinson and But-ler are to be credited, reason is rightfully supreme in man, and therefore it would be most suitable to the reason of mankind to have no civil or political government at all. The moral government of God and his vice-regent Conscience, ought to be sufficient to restrain men to obedience, to justice and benevolence, at all times and in all places; we must therefore descend from the dignity of our nature, when we think of civil government at all. But the nature of mankind is one thing, and the reason of mankind another; and the first has the same relation to the last as the whole to the part: the passions and appetites are parts of human nature as well as reason and the moral sense. In the institution of government, it must be remembered, that although reason ought always to govern individuals, it certainly never did since the Fall, and never will till the Millennium; and human nature must be taken as it is, as it has been, and will be." [3]

John Adams, although a pessimist in regards to the ultimate utility of virtue, clearly saw that Government might be required for the regulation of the appetites, as individuals alone appear to be incapable of self-regulation. The question of a balance between the regulation of the appetites by the individual and those regulations imposed by law suggests that the matter has not been fully resolved. There is, we can

---

3   John Diggins, *The Lost Soul of American Politics*, from the works of John Adams

say, an *equilibrium point* between the self-regulation of the appetites and the external regulation imposed by law but how that point might be determined relates more to art than to law.

For example, murder is prohibited by law as a protection against individuals who are unable to control their appetite for vengeance. The regulation of murder should be by self-administration, i.e., murder should be a moral prohibition exercised by the will of the individual. In the majority of rational societies, this is the case. Murder is restrained, by the virtue of the general public, and in those instances, where the occasional individual fails in the exercising of his or her moral duty, to restrain themselves from the pleasure of murder, society exercises a permanent form of self-restraint in the form of imprisonment or capital punishment.

What happens, however, when a significant segment of a population, such as in Chicago, engages in murder as part of gang warfare or even as form of hedonism or recreation? The equilibrium between the rule of self-regulation and the public order of law is distorted. The general virtue of the public is required for the law to work effectively, otherwise martial law is required. Madison noted in Federalist Paper 51 that government alone could not maintain the conditions for either liberty or happiness:

> "But what is government itself, but the greatest of all reflections on human nature? If men were angels, no government would be necessary. If angels were to govern men, neither external nor internal controls on government would be necessary. In framing a government which is to be administered by men over men, the great difficulty lies in this: you must first enable the government to control the governed; and in the next place oblige it to control itself. A dependence on the people is, no doubt, the primary control on the government; but experience has taught mankind the necessity of auxiliary precautions.

Adams and Madison are looking at the problem of human appetites from two different perspectives that are complementary. Adams sees that the appetites of mankind are as much a part of human nature as is reason and need to be held in check by political structures. Madison emphasizes that the regulation of appetites by reason, in and through both moral and intellectual virtue, is as essential for the well-being of government, as it is for the perfection of the individual.

What is lacking in both positions is a philosophy of the will that integrates both the idea of unruly appetites and the notions of the good, virtue (excellence), politics and time in one comprehensive perspective. It might be said that Adams and Madison both came close to articulating the need for a public philosophy but due to the presence and influence of religion, this distinction and utility, outside of religion, was overlooked or not seen as necessary. In other words, during colonial times, religion in the form of Protestant Christianity, functioned as the public philosophy and bedrock upon which any discussion of virtue would have taken place.

Both Adams and Madison had a familiarity with the general principles of classical philosophy, but neither developed an integrated perspective based on a fully articulated metaphysics of the soul. The lack of this fully integrated philosophy of the soul, as it might be coupled to a public philosophy has haunted America since its founding and indeed, in my opinion, has haunted western European culture since both the rise of Catholicism and the Protestant Reformation.

VIRTUE AND SELF-INTEREST

In his book, *The Lost Soul of American Politics,* John Diggins argues that:

> *"The classical idea of virtue as resistance to political corruption and a patriotic subordination of private interests to the public good was an idea whose time had come and gone by 1787, when the Constitution was framed."*

Diggins may in fact be correct that the notion of virtue was not in vogue in 1787 and that self-interest and property acquisition were the prime motivations in all political considerations but his definition of virtue is inadequate. The subordination of private interests to the public good is an *effect* of virtue and not a definition. Indeed, Diggins' passive definition of virtue is characteristic of many peoples' understanding of virtue and represents a serious misunderstanding of the nature of virtue and divorces virtue from its primary object which is the "good".

American politics does not consider the notion of the "good" but rather, the notion of self-interest. Self-interest is a way of allowing everyone to choose what he or she thinks is good *without a third party taking an objective position as to whether or not it actually is good.* The substitution meaning here—of the good by self-interest constitutes an incredible failure not just of linguistic discrimination but a failure to deal with over 2,000 years of moral discourse.

Neither Diggins nor anyone else could argue persuasively that self-interest is the same as the good but the practical effect of making self-interest the predominant political good of a society relegates all discussion of what is really good to a relativistic framework, which may be dismissed, based solely on personal preference, i.e., your good may not be my good. Even though human beings disagree about what is good and bad, this should not be considered a sufficient reason to totally dismiss objective standards of right and wrong.

THE DIFFERENCE BETWEEN GOOD AND EVIL

The notion of the "good" can sometimes be better understood by contrasting it with its opposite, evil. One of the best definitions of evil that I've ever heard was presented in a college class that I attended in Rome, in the early 1970s, by Father William Cain:

"Evil is the absence of a 'good' which could and should be present."

If a company lies about the performance of its own products or sells products based on false advertising, they are in fact engaging in "evil" actions. The public is being deprived of a good or better product which could and should be available. If I have a hammer and someone asks me, "is that a good hammer?" I will respond by saying, "yes" or "no" or "it's okay." If it is good, what makes it good? It might fit my hand well, be of the right weight for hitting nails properly and have a cushioned handle to absorb blows. If I say, "it is good," my judgment is based on my experiential understanding of what constitutes a good hammer. The 'goodness' of the hammer lies in its excellence of function. If someone says, "I have a good car," we all know what that means. Conversely, if I say that I have a bad car or bad hammer we also know exactly what that means—even if the particulars vary.

Individual preferences may make what is good for one person, not as good for another but the principle is the same. The good is relative to the nature of the thing that goodness is spoken of, in conjunction with the nature of the being who is using it. There is a proportion between what is good for the individual and the 'goodness' spoken of. Given that human nature is the same—most of us have two arms and two legs, skin, a mouth, eyes, ears and so forth, we can expect that many of the things that are considered 'good' will be considered good, in varying degrees, by all. This is why most of us get annoyed when we encounter something that is poorly made or poorly done. *We know that it is defective in relation to its proper function.* Nothing makes us angrier than poorly designed tools. Defective products indicate a thoughtlessness or lack of intellectual and moral virtue that went into their making. The absence of a "good" which could and should be present is an "evil" relative to what should be there and isn't.

THE MORAL NARRATIVE

The lack of something that *could and should be present* is almost always offensive to our sense of justice and fair play. We recognize a proportionality between the way things are and the way they should be. This would be impossible to know without some subtle knowledge of proportionality and goodness. The observation or perception that some 'good' which could and should be present, and is not, is at the root of the moral imperative: *Ought to Be*. This also the essence of almost every moral narrative. The notion of what 'ought to be' suggests that there is a model or paradigm for the excellence which is missing. Just as we might visualize the perfect hammer or perfect car, we can envision a model for moral goodness.

Aristotle notes that moral virtue is "a habit of choosing the rational mean." What he means by this is that the will, which is part of the appetite must choose to engage rationality as opposed to choosing or embracing irrational behavior. This might be thought of as just an abstraction but it is also an activity, as moral goodness is not found anywhere but in actions, or as a result of actions. Choice is the critical component of all moral action. Choice presumes that there are appetites that need to be filtered and good intellectual habits to be cultivated in lieu of doing whatever you might feel like doing.

The perfect actions of moral goodness that would be required to fit our ideal image are such that they exceed our ability to quite grasp them. This is why the soul appears to be such a nebulous concept—it too is based on an *act* that we cannot quite mentally grasp. This is due to the nature of the soul which is oriented towards a future and an end that we do not yet understand.

> *The notion of moral goodness participates in the mysterious future orientation of the soul and is on a continuum with Divine intentionality, which is non-local in terms of **affect** but local in terms of **effect**.*

'Goods' apprehended by desire are usually immediate such as food, sex, money, clothing, anger, love, etc. Moral 'goods' usually involve the element of future time as opposed to immediacy. The payoff may be later—not right now. Think of almost any moral good and you will realize that it usually involves saying no to lesser 'good', in favor of affirming a higher 'good'. Plato went so far as to say in *The Republic* that the intellect understands its objects only insofar as it sees in what way they are good.

> *"You have often heard that the idea of the Good is the greatest object of learning, by recourse to which just things and other things become useful and beneficial...If we do not know it, without this, however well we may know other things, you know that it is no advantage to us...If it is not known in what just and beautiful things are good, [how they are good] they will not have acquired a guardian worth much for them if he does not know this; and I divine that until then he will not know any of these sufficiently."*

The concept of a higher good or moral hierarchy leading to ever higher 'goods' lends itself to speculation on the nature of the highest good. Theologians and philosophers have speculated for centuries on just such concerns and their wisdom remains a treasure trove of unexploited ideas for a modern rethinking of the meaning of the 'good' and the development of a new moral narrative.

THE ULTIMATE GOOD

Aristotle and Plato's exemplar of the good is found in God, something echoed by St. Augustine.

> *"All limited goods are good by participation in the Ultimate Good. This effectively established a transcendent paradigm of the Good."* [4]

---

4   Hibbs, Thomas, *The Hierarchy of Moral Discourses in Aquinas*, pg. 201, American Catholic Philosophical Quarterly, Spring 1990

The notion of divine things permeates much of Aristotle and Plato, not only in concept but as moral and religious pedagogy. The ancients were not so worried about the separation of philosophy and theology as scholars are today. Plato is emphatic, in the Timaeus, about the connection between the ultimate good and all good things:

> *"Let us state, then, the cause for which he who established it established becoming and this All: He was good, and to the good there never comes jealousy about anything. And being free from this, he wished that all things become as far as possible like himself...God wished all things to be good and nothing bad as far as possible."*

The notion of a proportionality between limited goods and the ultimate good suggests a causal link much meditated upon by Plato and suggested by Aristotle. The larger causality of the ultimate good indicates that temporal considerations of what is good must yield to the larger notion of excellence in the mind of God. God has a far greater sense of what is good for us than we are able to determine for ourselves. Thomas Aquinas's definition of virtue, drawn from Peter Lombard's *Sentences,* is quite interesting in this regard.[5]

> *"Virtue is a good quality of the mind, by which we live righteously, of which no one can make bad use, which God works in us, without us."*

Aquinas is referring to what is called "infused"[6] virtue, i.e., moral and spiritual virtue infused by a participation in God's Life, which is grace. The acquired virtues, produced by good habits, and demonstrated by Aristotle in the *Nicomachean Ethics* are only the beginning of a

5   Pinsent, Andrew, *The Second Person Perspective in Aquinas's Ethics*, Routledge Books, an imprint of Taylor and Francis, 2012, New York, NY, pg. 13

6   Pinsent, Andrew, *The Second Person Perspective in Aquinas's Ethics*, Routledge Books, an imprint of Taylor and Francis, 2012, New York, NY, pgs. 31-39

truly ethical and moral life. The infused virtues, typically, can be said to build upon the acquired virtues, although what can be infused by God is not, as Aquinas notes, limited by human circumstance.

Clearly, the intellectual virtues can be misused when scientists create weapons of mass destruction or equipment that can be used for immoral purposes. When the intellectual virtues are cultivated, without the counterbalancing effect of the moral and spiritual virtues, human beings can become one-sided and intolerant of goodness. Michael Walsh notes that "Andrew Gopnik, an otherwise fine writer for the *New Yorker*, has called abortion "one of the greatest moral achievements in human history—the full emancipation of women."[7] A moral achievement built upon the death of the young and women who have unprotected sex with men who, as Ann Coulter notes, that they don't like is truly a mind-boggling inversion of traditional values. One is reminded of Humpty Dumpty in Lewis Carroll's, *Alice in Wonderland.*

> *"When I use a word, "Humpty Dumpty said, in rather a scornful tone, "It means just what I choose it to mean—neither more nor less." "The question is," said Alice, "whether you can make words mean so many different things." "The question is," said Humpty Dumpty, "which is to be master—that is all."* [8]

The notion of all "goods" being related to the ultimate good is what constitutes the basis of Natural Law. This relation between the ultimate good and all limited goods is precisely what is severed by self-interest politics. Self-interest politics takes the notions of chronological and eternal time and subordinates them to *kaironic* or subjective time.

---

7   Walsh, Michael, *The Devil's, Pleasure Palace: The Cult of Critical Theory and the Subversion of the West*, pg. 194, Encounter Books, New York and London, 2015
8   Ibid, pg. 58, which in turn, was taken from Lewis Carroll's *Alice in Wonderland*

Chapter 7

CONSERVATIVES, LIBERALS AND MORALITY

"When all is said and done, there are as many empty-headed conservatives as liberals who have not arrived at their beliefs through any deliberative process, but stumbled into a set of beliefs half-formed by experience and half-formed by a mediocre education and a culturally anemic society."

—James O'Reilly,
Commentary

SELF-INTEREST AND MORALITY

One of the fundamental intellectual conflicts at work in democracies today is the struggle between those who believe solely in the motive

169

power of self-interest, and those who think that objective moral values are more important than power and self-interest. The argument should not however, be cast as an either or proposition. Is it possible that power and self-interest could be tempered by morality without being diluted to the point of ineffectiveness? Is it possible that instead of the radical polarity that now exists between liberals and conservatives, we could redefine the ground rules, so that all parties know in fact what they are really doing? Indeed, the system of checks and balances that is the trademark of the American political system suggests that both self-interest and virtue are allowed for, and accounted for. They now must also be understood in relation to the social difficulties this nation now faces.

The failure of those on the Right to understand the social consequences of economic self-interest as promoted by purely market driven capitalism is compounded by the failure of those on the Left to understand that self-interest alone should never be allowed to be the sole arbitrator of either an individual's affairs or a nation's affairs.

The Vietnam War was a classic example of the intellectual and moral confusion that can occur when self-interest, without reference to morality, is allowed to determine political agendas. On the face of it, many Americans were morally opposed to Communist expansion because one of the central tenants of Communism is that immoral means justify ends. (Execution, torture and the curbing of individual liberty are the historically documented methodologies of choice among Communists.) On the other hand, we admired the Communists' bravery and dedication during the war, and sympathized with their nationalism and desire to "do their own thing." The radical failure of many Americans to condemn Communism on the basis of its immorality was directly due to their misunderstanding (and indeed sympathy with the notion) that self-interest in all forms, and the acquisition of power should be allowed, *if desired.*

The way the war was handled—the de facto non-declaration of war, a war that was not a war, the shameless posturing of politicians and the refusal to do whatever was necessary to win, all contributed to a public confusion as to what the war was about. Richard Marcinko, the founder of Seal Team Six, puts his finger on the problem, when he described the actions of visiting Congressmen in his book, *Rogue Warrior.*

> *"It was in Cambodia that I first learned about visiting legislators. It was an eye-opener, too. We received a fair number of codels in Phnom Penh during my posting. Codel is bureaucratese for Congressional Delegation. Allegedly, these trips—which are sponsored by various House and Senate committees, subcommittees, and working groups—are fact-finding missions that help our duly elected public servants make educated decisions when they vote on the nation's future. Most of the codels I spent time with, however were made up of congressmen and senators who wanted only to shop or get laid, or both...The question most asked by codels was, where can a congressman get an absolutely perfect blow-job, or some incredible fuckee-fuckee..."* [1]

The failure of many congressional intellectuals, to grasp the moral dimension of the war and to focus solely on their respective party ideologies or personal fulfillment, while brave men on both sides were dying, contributed to the shallow thinking that would allow what was a major war, not to be declared a war. The Vietnam War was described as immoral, only in terms of our killing of the Viet Cong. The immorality of Communism was seldom discussed, due to our overall cultural ignorance of the meaning of morality.

Collectivism is an evil that can only be understood by those who realize that freedom and responsibility are moral requirements of the human soul. Capitalism, likewise, is an evil when freedom is used as a cloak for a lack of moral and social responsibility. The respective ideologies of capitalism and communism need to be understood in a moral context before anyone can explain why Western democracy

---

1   Marcinko, Richard, *Rogue Warrior*, pgs., 194-195

is better in general than the ideology of Communism. What we have today is that there is no public context for the discussion of a hierarchy of values other than a kind of vague grab bag of things that we think are right and other things that may bother us. Without objective moral standards all discussions of value degenerate into emotional slug-fests.

JOHN LOCKE AND SELF-INTEREST

The most disturbing result of the Vietnam War is that most Americans still don't understand why we were there because the moral and philosophical reasons for our being there were never fully articulated, except in terms of factional sloganeering. Unfortunately, the basic issue which many of the proponents of self-interest and nationalism fail to address, is the underlying 'Lockean' assumption that self-interest and nationalism are always enlightened.

John Locke was an eighteenth century American thinker who was popular in Europe and America. He was concerned about the abuses of monarchy and sought to express in political terms some formula which would limit the power of government over individual self-worth and self-determination. His philosophy found a foothold in the American psyche and has remained part of our way of life.

> *"His teaching is one of the most powerful ideologies ever invented, if not the most powerful. It promised an unheard-of degree of individual freedom, an unlimited opportunity to compete for material well-being, and an unprecedented limitation on the arbitrary powers of government to interfere with individual initiative. In all these ways it expressed a modern liberal idea that contrasted with the hierarchical domination and exclusiveness of most of the human past...but by the mid-eighteenth century the secular aspects of his teaching had been detached from his overall vision. What his American followers emphasized was the right to life, liberty and the pursuit of happiness as exemplified*

by the solitary individuals' appropriation of property from the state of nature. Government is then instituted for the protection of that property. **All limits on the freedom and autonomy of the individual, other than those he freely consents to in entering the (quite limited) social contract, are rejected.**" [2]

Locke's philosophy is at the root of many of our social and political difficulties. We simply refuse to allow anything but individual preferences (the pursuit of self-interest) to rule in the social order. America is a collection of individuals all doing their own thing to such a degree that national unity on important issues is often compromised. Unfortunately, in the absence of a public moral code, market forces are allowed to determine both morality and law. The chaos on the streets of America is the ultimate expression of unbridled self-interest. No one is of course allowed to say whose self-interest is better or whose is worse. Therefore, we have such ridiculous scenarios as thieves successfully suing homeowners for cutting themselves on razor wire fences because they were not properly notified of the danger to their persons.

Locke's moral philosophy, although not necessarily adopted by American culture, was Locke's own counterweight to his political views. Locke would never have imagined that self-interest would be considered aside from some kind of moral norms.

"It is probable that Locke thought of his teaching primarily as a protest against the social and cultural constrictions of the past, and that he did not imagine any nation would put the whole conception into practice at one swoop, certainly not without the religious constraints that were basic to his thought." [3]

The failure to evaluate events in terms of what *ought* to have been, as opposed to what *actually happened* muddies our thinking. It is very

2   Bellah, Madsen, Sullivan, Swindler and Tipton, *The Good Society*, Borzoi Books, Published by Alfred Knopf, Inc., 1991, pg. 68
3   Ibid, pg. 67

odd that history as *what happened* is often cited as an authority for what should be. If Americans have in fact always acted on the basis of self-interest and power politics, we must ask the question: has it been morally right that they have done so or has it merely been advantageous?

Cicero noted over two thousand years ago that there was a distinction to be observed between what was merely advantageous and what was morally right. The fact that a course of action is in one's self-interest or is advantageous is obviously not necessarily the same as what is morally right. If a person finds a wallet containing a thousand dollars, it would be in his or her self-interest and to their advantage to keep it. However, it would be an injustice to the individual to whom the wallet belonged to retain it.

Now there is a deeper current here and it goes something like this: If I believe that there is an objective moral order and that bad action (s) will soil my honor or injure my relationship with the Supreme Being, then I will return the wallet out of self-interest. This is however, a higher form of self-interest than that of the amoral person who keeps the thousand dollars, and buys drugs with it and pays his or her mortgage. Whose self-interest is more admirable? Self-interest alone cannot justify actions, unless located within some kind of moral context. Parents for example, are not allowed to sell their children, despite the fact that it might be in their self-interest to do so. Freedom without responsibility is obviously worthless, although Locke's ideology might lead one to believe otherwise.

Proponents of Locke's economic philosophy seem to assume that self-interest and liberation are automatically ethical, as they see that impediments to freedom, such as existed in that era, imposed limitations on human creativity and productivity which in and of themselves were evils. I will suggest that there is a confusion of terms. The liberation that self-interest engenders is not necessarily good, unless put to good use. The self-interest of a con artist should not be thought of as having the same validity as that of an engineer who builds bridges in third world countries for minimal compensation.

Locke's philosophy would have been categorically rejected by Socrates and the majority of Greek thinkers who came after him. Most classical philosophers clearly realized that the unlimited acquisition of wealth, or even the right to such an acquisition, would in and of itself produce nothing valuable—unless counterbalanced by the notion of virtue. The medieval theologians were no less insistent that the acquisition of wealth, as a means, and not as an end, distinguished the rational from the irrational.

Aristotle clearly describes the acquisition of external goods as only one of the many means necessary for securing the good life:

"Certainly no one will dispute the propriety of that partition of goods which separates them into three classes, viz. external good, goods of the body, and goods of the soul, or deny that the happy man must have all three. For no one would maintain that he is happy who has not in him a particle of courage or temperance or justice or prudence, (or) who is afraid of every insect which flutters past him, and will commit any crime, however great, in order to gratify his lust of meat or drink, who would sacrifice his dearest friend for the sake of half-a-farthing,[4] and is as feeble and false in mind as a child or a madman. These propositions are almost universally acknowledged as soon as they are uttered, but men differ about the degree or relative superiority of this or that good. Some think that a very moderate amount of virtue is enough, but set no limit to their desires of wealth, property, reputation and the like. To whom we reply by an appeal to fact, which easily proves that mankind does not acquire or preserve virtue by the help of external goods, but external goods by the help of virtue, and that happiness, whether consisting in pleasure or virtue, or both, is more often found with those who are

---

4   This is, of course, a translation by an Englishman. The Greeks did not have farthings but you get the point.

*most highly cultivated in their mind and in their character, and
have only a moderate share of external goods, than among those
who possess external goods to a useless extent but are deficient in
higher qualities; and this is not only a matter of experience, but
if reflected upon, will easily appear in accordance with reason."* [5]

Everyone understands what the goods of the body are and external
goods, such as good government, but what of the goods of the soul?
The excellence of soul that is discerned in all applications of virtue is
ignored by all but the cultured who are usually neither conservative nor
liberal. What distinguishes hard-core liberals from conservatives more
than anything else is the conservative belief in the soul and virtue.

*Scratch a hard-core liberal and you will seldom find a clear con-
cept of moral virtue as it might relate to sexuality.*

Conservatives, in practice are nearly as bad because they articulate
all of their free market ideas, and notions of education and morality,
without understanding the origins of their assertions. They are thus
unable to adequately communicate the differences between their positions and those of liberals, in regards to key issues.

THE DISASSOCIATION OF SENSIBILITY

The inability of conservatives and liberals to adequately defend their
respective positions, is best described by a term invented by T.S. Eliot.
He stated that western culture suffered from what he called, *the disassociation of sensibility.*[6] The 'disassociation of sensibility' might be described,

---

5   Aristotle, *Politics*, Bk VI, Ch. 8
6   "A term used by T. S. Eliot to describe the disjunction of thought and feeling that
    he perceives in English literature from the seventeenth century onward. For writers
    such as John Donne, Eliot argues, a thought was an experience; it was integrated with
    emotional and bodily response. Since the time of John Milton, however, thought has
    been divorced from feeling, and as the former became more refined and subtle, the
    latter became cruder. According to Eliot, the dissociation of sensibility is a linguistic

generally speaking, as the product of a discontinuous view of Existence. When a culture or an individual loses sight of metaphysical or spiritual origins and yet continues to act according to standards which are no longer believed in, or explainable, the disassociation of sensibility becomes evident. It is a separation of thought from feeling and is a problem that has increased in direct proportion to the spread of empirical thinking. The rationalist, generally speaking, attempts to bring thought and feeling together in pleasing intellectual and moral harmonies. The empiricist separates thought from feeling.

How does the disassociation of sensibility affect Americans? The legal profession, for example, has become extremely adroit at separating thought and feeling through the co-operation agreements known as contracts. However, contracts made under financial duress, or developed simply to take advantage of one individual over another, have divorced thought from its emotional and moral components. This is not to say that contracts are not useful but that they can be misused without having moral or sensible oversight.

A classic example of the disassociation of sensibility in financial markets might be a second mortgage line of credit that calls for higher rates after the initial term of the contract is up. The contract might stipulate that the terms can be made more favorable by refinancing but also stipulates that in the event of non-refinancing, the contract defaults to the higher term. What can typically happen is that a consumer will be asked to submit paperwork to refinance the loan, and if not qualified, will be told the higher contractual rate will apply. In other words, the customer did not qualify for the lower rate on the refinance but no qualification whatsoever, other than the contract, is required to charge the consumer more. In other words, based on contract law and underwriting regulations, a customer may not qualify for a refinance but *no qualification,* other than a signature on a contract, is required to actually charge him or her more. This is, simply, a separation of common sense from thought.

---

and cultural malaise from which English literature and society have never recovered." *Glossary of Literary Theory* by Greig E. Henderson and Christopher Brown. http://www. library.utoronto.ca/utel/glossary/Dissociation_of_sensibility.html

The Constitution is also a kind of contract between government
and the people but the Constitution, without the emotional and moral component of the Declaration of Independence, is a document of
thought separated from emotion and morality. Many of those on the
left, for example, will say with a perfectly straight face that no mention of God is made in the Constitution and because the Constitution
is the law of the land, there should be no reference to God in public
affairs. The second line of the Declaration should shatter that point
of view for anyone not engaging in the active disassociation of moral
sensibility from reason.

> *"We hold these truths to be self-evident, that all men are creat-
> ed equal, that they are endowed by their Creator with certain
> unalienable Rights, that among these are Life, Liberty and the
> pursuit of Happiness."*

Abraham Lincoln believed that the Declaration of Independence
was a statement of principles through which the United States Constitution should be interpreted. Critics skilled in the art of separating
thought from moral emotion would of course disagree. The holding of
moral feelings apart from reason and thinking enables the left to engage in all manner of scurrilous activities. The notions of "homophobia" and "choice" are, literally, concoctions of the willful disassociation
of moral sensibility from reason. The natural revulsion of normal human beings to unnatural acts that have, in part, caused the deaths from
AIDS[7] of over thirty-five million people worldwide is not homophobia; it is moral and intellectual disgust.

---

7   In 2015, 36.7 million people were living with HIV. In 2015, 2.1 million people were
     newly infected with HIV. 150,000 were under the age of 15. Every day about 5,753
     people contract HIV—about 240 every hour. In 2015, 1.1 million people died from
     AIDS-related illnesses.
     Since the beginning of the pandemic, 78 million people have contracted HIV and 35
     million have died of AIDS-related causes.
     As of December 2015, 17 million people living with HIV (46% of the total) had access
     to   anti-retroviral therapy. http://www.amfar.org/worldwide-aids-stats/

The continual disassociation of thought and feeling engendered by a disingenuous legal empiricism (the law is "positive" that is to say self-referential) is responsible for the perpetration of the abortion movement. Women are encouraged to think about children in the womb as, "the products of conception" or as an embryo—anything but a child. This is an attempt to separate the mother from her natural moral reaction to being pregnant, which is usually, "I am going to have a baby" to "I have something foreign in me that I need to get rid of." America's current acceptance of abortion and homosexuality has had a chilling effect on moral and intellectual sensibilities to the point that the murder of a U.S. Ambassador in Libya and members of his security detail cannot be correlated with the inaction of an administration that was attempting not to disrupt the re-election of the incumbent. The disassociation of moral sensibility from thought is so complete in the political process that no lie is too outrageous to be presented as truth.

Within the rank and file of the average citizen there are many people who do not go to church or even believe in religion but when asked about the raising of their children, will stoutly say that their children will go to church regardless of their (the parents') personal beliefs. If pressed for an explanation, they will say that it has a 'good influence'. Another example might be our belief that people should act politely. But why, if there are no objective morals or any reason for being polite, should we behave well? Indeed, self-interest may dictate that we act otherwise—and who is to tell us what we should or should not do? Without a moral code that might exist independently of our subjective opinions, we are at the mercy of self-interest and self-interest, as we have seen, is not necessarily enlightened.

There are, for example, some absolutely ridiculous sociological analyses of why black children talk louder than white children. Black children are more uninhibited than white children, we are sagely told and therefore, speak more loudly and self-assuredly. What these sociological imbeciles fail to notice is that black children also commit more crimes and spend more time in jail, than white children. But this is a statistically taboo subject; it must be, the quasi-reasoning goes, because we live in a 'racist society'. Those who make these arguments fail to realize that uninhibited behavior is not necessarily good, and that with uninhibited speech comes uninhibited things, such as violence and drug taking, not to mention poor vocabularies and an uneducated and rude manner of speaking. Have you ever listened to rap songs about killing police and raping bitches?

African children in many parts of Africa do not speak this way. Why is it acceptable here in the United States? Again, freedom and self-interest are invoked and brandished like amulets to ward off any attack of rational thought. We are told that they want to speak that way and that we should not think one culture is better than another. "How dare you imagine that your culture is better than mine" is the prevailing attitude. Are all cultures equal? No. God forbid that some parents might be offended because the behavior of their children might be held to rational, objective standards. How dare you teach moral values that might offend someone's civil liberty to behave like an animal! These attitudes are all the more reason to formulate an objective, non-partisan, non-religious discipline of morality, based on the now radical but nonetheless ancient concepts of virtue, vice and soul.

THE DIFFERENCE BETWEEN CONSERVATIVES AND LIBERALS

How do we formulate these differences between conservatives and liberals, in terms of some kind of formula? I would like to advance a hypothesis that goes like this: conservatives are always more concerned about the rigid application of specific ideas, imposed on a society for the achievement of certain effects, whereas liberals are more concerned about the abolition of static values and more concerned about the free acquisition of such ideas, based on self-interest or the kind of personal autonomy that is called "agency". Conservatives tend to focus on a moral order derived from some understanding of Existence that is related to God. Liberals attempt to relate their understanding of morality to a discontinuous or disassociated view of Existence more closely related to empirical science's understanding of existence as undifferentiated energy.

The best example of these two approaches are liberal, versus traditional notions of education. The more conservative educational approach is to inculcate by repetition regardless of the self-interest of the students. Self-interest is held in abeyance by discipline and appetites are subjugated through delayed gratification. The liberal approach to education is more of a smorgasbord approach, whereby a variety of informational pathways are presented to students, so that choices might be made in accordance with each student's self-interest or self-understanding.

What do we say however, to those students who do not wish to learn or to choose rationally between disciplines? It is precisely for this reason that self-interest cannot be the sole operative principle of education or of politics for that matter. Obviously choice must take place but it must take place within a context. That context, common sense would argue, is the forum of morality.

If there is one thing that liberals and conservatives most disagree upon and least understand however, it is the notion of morality. Morality very simply described, involves making good choices regarding our appetites. Morality enables us to stand up to biology and inclination and act as independent or self-directed agents. Morality, in other words, better enables "agency" or sovereignty than appetitive indulgence. Without some understanding of the imputed relationship of Existence to goodness, there will be no effective moral code.

O'REILLY'S FIRST MORAL LAW

Litigation and lawlessness increase in direct proportion to our failure to understand and deal with the notion of bad appetites.

Stated more simply: Incontinence or appetitive excess causes social disorder when it is coupled with a decline in the understanding of objective values. Appetite is such a simple and yet complex concept. Understood as desire alone, it is a rootless concept. Understood as a power of the soul, it connects us to the history of philosophy and to countless generations of thinkers.

Following Augustine, Thomas Aquinas denies that any created good can count as the last end of human life. The reason is that the perfect good completely quiets the appetite, and since the object of the will is universal good, no particular or limited material "good" can sate the appetite.

The notion of God as Existence being the ultimate object of all human desire is at the very core of all spiritual values. After all, if God is believed in at all, then it would not be unreasonable to assume that He is the source of all good things. The notion of a hierarchy of 'goods' culminating in the supreme goodness of God appears to be completely lost on all those who do not believe in moral or spiritual values. Indeed, if there is no objective hierarchy of goods, then one might rightly argue that what is 'good' can only be subjectively determined. Aristotle clearly believed in a hierarchy of moral goods based on his understanding that there was a definable structure of both human nature and the soul.

For Aristotle, the appetite was one of *five powers* of the soul:

1. The *Vegetative power* (or Genetic power) which governs bodily functions and growth in general

2. *Locomotive power* which governs movement

3. *Appetitive power* which governs appetite, will and emotion

4. *Sensitive power* which governs taste, touch, sight, sound and smell

5. *Intellectual power* which governs the mind and soul in general

These powers are functions of the soul in Aristotle's metaphysics. Aristotle describes the soul in *De Anima*, as "the first act of a body having life potential" (we will discuss this notion of the soul and potentiality in greater detail, in later chapters). Aristotle defines virtue as a habitual state of character (or intellectual and moral excellence) which is cultivated by a rational directing of the appetitive power of the soul. Vice, on the other hand, is considered to be a lack of directive (or excellence of the will) where the appetites are concerned.

THOMAS HOBBES AND THE DISASSOCIATION OF SENSIBILITY

Thomas Hobbes, who personally knew Bacon and Galileo in the latter half of the 1600's is a pivotal character in the transitional period between the fall of the scholastic and Aristotelian tempered metaphysics and the rise of modern day science. The disassociation of sensibility, referred to by Eliot, may be seen in the political writing of Thomas Hobbes. Hobbs who was as disingenuous as a modern American liberal, sums up the temper of the times when he says:

> "*For there is no finis ultimus, utmost aim, nor summum bonum, greatest good, as is spoken of in the books of the old moral philosophers. Nor can a man any more live, whose desires are at an end, than he, whose senses and imaginations are at a stand. Felicity is a continual progress of the desire, from one object to another; the attaining of the former, being still but the way to the latter. The*

cause whereof is, that the object of man's desire, is not to enjoy once only, and for one instant of time; but to assure forever, the way of his future desires."[8]

Hobbes is entirely correct in advocating that desire in some shape, form or fashion motivates all mankind. He confuses the issue though, by assuming that the moral philosophers of old would disagree with him. The great moral philosophers simply qualify desire by placing it within a hierarchical structure of values that definitively considers some desires inferior to others. Hobbes portrays desire as a monolithic mass that is not to be differentiated by anything other than desire itself. This seems to be a critical muddying of the waters, historically speaking, giving rise to our current mass of undifferentiated assumptions.

What does Mr. Hobbes have to say about the classical definition of the will as being part of the appetite? Well, he doesn't like it and offers us a fine example of opaque reasoning to justify his position.

"The definition of the will, commonly given by the schools, that it is a rational appetite, is not good. For if it were, then there could be no voluntary act against reason. For a voluntary act is that, which proceedeth from the will, and no other. But if instead of a rational appetite, we shall say an appetite resulting from precedent deliberation, then the definition is the same that I have given here. Will, therefore, is the last appetite in deliberating."[9]

Hobbes attempts to show that there is no operative rational principle at work in deliberation. He does not *want* to believe that either the intellect or the will might be manifestations or powers of the soul. The notion that 'will' might be divided into will and free will apparently does not occur to him. Why is he dwelling on this issue? Hobbes is an early metaphysical liberal who is trying to have his cake and eat it

8   T.V. Smith, Marjorie Green, *From Descartes to Locke*, University of Chicago Press, 1940, pg. 186
9   Ibid

too. The definition of the will that he is objecting to, simply means that the will is guided by reason, inasmuch as reason (as part of its general workload) presents to the will, 'goods' for its inspection. If the reasoning is deficient, then the will which is part of the appetitive power, enacts choice, instead of the will being led as it were, like a recalcitrant child, along the proper pathway.

What Hobbes really wants to say is that appetite alone is determinative of morality and that the idea of free will and freedom of choice is an illusion of appetitive power. Hobbes' predilection for seeing appetite, without reason, as the root of all human motivation is a foreshadowing of our modern psychological penchant for explaining everything that might be considered higher, as a product of something lower, namely that totem of modern Western civilization, the Id.

FREUD'S CONCEPT OF APPETITE

> "We have arrived at our knowledge of this psychical apparatus by studying the individual development of human beings. To the oldest of these psychical provinces or agencies we give the name of Id. It contains everything that is inherited, that is present at birth, that is laid down in the constitution—above all, therefore, the instincts, which originate from the somatic organization and which find a first psychical expression here (in the Id) in forms unknown to us." [10]

The ego is, for Freud, merely an evolutionary apparatus developed from the Id over time. This apparatus has no connection with anything like a soul (this is to be considered an illusion generated by the instinctual transposition of the energies of the Id) and ceases to exist, when the organism dies. To talk about virtue or the soul to anyone infected by such a point of view is futile; it reminds me of Nietzsche's last men, who when asked what truth was would only blink.

---

10 Freud, Sigmund, An *Outline of Psychoanalysis*, The Norton Library, NY, 1960, pg.5

"The power of the Id expresses the true purpose of the individual organism's life. This consists in the satisfaction of its innate needs. No such purpose as that of keeping itself alive or of protecting itself from dangers by means of anxiety can be attributed to the Id. That is the task of the ego, whose business it also is to discover the most favorable and least perilous method of obtaining satisfaction, taking the external world into account. The super-ego may bring fresh needs to the fore, but its main function remains the limitation of satisfactions." [11]

Freud's theories are useful in articulating the relationship between the appetites and the will and have delineated an entire area unknown to classical antiquity. However, psychology, when presented as an all-embracing system of definition for all things human, ceases to be psychology and becomes philosophy. Sigmund Freud never engaged the great systems of Aristotle or Aquinas and it is more than likely that he knew very little about their work, except what he might have received second-hand from the historically and philosophically inept professors of the late 1800's, who kept insisting upon their right to reinvent the wheel.

The description of the super ego's function as the limitation of satisfactions is particularly corrosive of moral values. By ascribing to the super ego values that might be chosen by a man or woman, seeking what is morally superior, a pall is cast on the authenticity of such moral choices. The super ego functions as a convenient clutch bag in Freudian Psychology, which explains moral choices as an expression of parental or social restrictions, which have become internalized. The notion of free-will or choice is notably absent. What Freud neglected to describe was the 'dark ego', whereby bad choices and habits get internalized, as if they were good things.

Since the time of Aristotle, (amongst realistic philosophers) the will has generally been considered part of the appetitive power of the

11 Ibid

soul. How do we understand a bad 'will'? Furthermore, how do we understand bad desires or bad appetites? Is there a relationship between bad desires and bad character?

> *"If we think television has had a bad influence on us, wait for virtual reality! The possibilities for wasting lives are enormous. I see room after room of helmeted men and women humping phantoms, waving swords at shadows, dining on empty air."* [12]

Self-interest as the pursuit and satisfaction of appetites (which can be economically productive) may, if not tempered by virtue contain the seeds of our destruction as a culture. There can be no understanding of bad appetites inside a world view that sees all human actions as ultimately reducible to the pleasure seeking operations of the Id. This is why educators and politicians today have a terrible time trying to establish any kind of moral norms. For the true liberal, everyone's norms are to be considered equal in the light of self-interest or the pleasure principle. The notion of unalloyed self-interest, as possibly destructive, may be the key to re-evaluating many of our educational and political decisions and indeed, may be the key to understanding the course of our lives.

---

12 James O'Reilly, *Commentary*

II

THE MISSING LINK BETWEEN MORALITY, POLITICS AND THE SOUL

"A major symptom of a man's—or a culture's intellectual and moral disintegration is the shrinking of vision and goals to the concrete-bound range of the immediate moment. This means: The progressive disappearance of abstractions from a man's mental processes or from a society's concerns. The manifestation of a disintegrating consciousness is the inability to think and act in terms of principles."

—Ayn Rand,
The Anatomy of Compromise

Chapter 8

BEING AND THE GREEK ORIGINS OF WESTERN PHILOSOPHY

"Aristotle is a river of flowing gold."

—Cicero 50 BC

BEING, NATURE AND THE SOUL

Philosophical wisdom is a river that carries its own history. At any given time, a reader can step into this river and find himself or herself carried by currents that may be 200 or even 4,000 years old. Such is the power and universality of some ideas that time is no barrier to their discussion. *Being* is one such idea.

When organized Christianity appeared on the historical scene, in the first and second centuries after the birth of Christ, it did not step onto an empty stage. The path of Christianity was well-prepared in the ancient world by Jewish, Greek and Roman philosophers, who had described the differences between right and wrong, and had elaborated a complex moral code and sophisticated political structure which even by contemporary standards was remarkably detailed and well thought out in many instances.

The great Greek and Roman philosophers understood the uncertainties of the world around them and the difficulty with which a civilization was maintained. War was a constant threat and organized banditry a perennial problem. Plato and Aristotle clearly understood the need to have an organized understanding of the human person in order to develop the character of the individual so that he or she would be capable of the work for which they were best suited by nature and circumstance. The survival of Athenian Greek civilization depended on how well its citizenry could be molded so as to defend the democratic ideals and way of life for which it stood.

The Greek city-states, particularly Athens, traded extensively with their neighbors in the Mediterranean. Not only were exotic goods and spices available, ideas flowed freely between port cities. Philosophical and religious ideas from Egypt and what is now the Middle East poured readily into the coastal cities and were absorbed by the curious and those seeking a greater understanding of the world around them.

The idea of the soul was one such idea which, like the rare goods which poured into Athens, came in many forms. The 'Ka', 'Ba', 'Akh' and 'Ab' of Egypt, the Hebrew, 'Nefesh' and probably a variety of other soul concepts, were ideas that provided the seminal minds of the early Greek thinkers with rich material to ponder. However, the Greeks of the fifth century before Christ were not satisfied with many of the answers that the surrounding cultures had provided towards an explanation of the mysteries of life.

"When the early Greek thinkers initiated philosophical speculation, the very first question they asked themselves was: what stuff

*is reality made of? Taken in itself, this question was strikingly indicative of the most fundamental need of the human mind. To understand something is for us to conceive it as identical with something else that we already know...the early Greek thinkers successively attempted to reduce nature in general to water, then to air, then to fire, until one of them at last hit upon the right answer to the question, by saying that the primary stuff which reality is made of is **being**...it cannot be doubted that, whatever else they may be, water, air and fire have in common at least this property, **that they are.** Each of them is a being and, since the same can be said of everything else, we cannot avoid the conclusion that being is the only property certainly shared in common by all that which is. **Being**, then is the fundamental and ultimate element of reality."* [1]

This concept of *being*, which appears to have been formulated by Parmenides, represented a huge step forward for metaphysics, as metaphysics was given its unique subject matter. The Greeks, who also had sophisticated theories about the indivisible particles of matter called 'atomos' or atoms were able to go beyond matter, in their deepening inquiry into the meaning of reality. They argued that matter alone did not account for visible reality, that there was a higher principal at work, namely *being*.

Today, we might argue that being could be defined as energy but this needs to be clarified. Energy is defined as the capacity to do work and is therefore potential until actualized. Potential energy is similar to what Aristotle referred to as *prime matter*. Prime matter is matter that can become any other kind of matter. It is matter or energy that does not have a substantial form. Being, in the singular sense of the word, is energy that is being actualized to manifest in a particular way. An actualized potential is roughly equivalent to what Aristotle described

---

1   Gilson, Etienne, *Being and Some Philosophers*, Pontifical Institute of Medieval Studies, Toronto, Canada, 1952, second edition, pg. 6

as the *form*. The form makes any specific packet of matter to be what it is but where or what is the form? An analogy might be helpful here.

Science tells us that lightning travels faster from the ground up, than it does from the clouds down. Lightning is a two-stroke action with radical potential being structured in the ground prior to the upward stroke. This is why the air will feel charged prior to the return stroke. The upward stroke is what kills people struck by lightning, not the downward stroke. Neither stroke *by itself* constitutes what we call lightning but together they *are* lightning. What this means is that potential is deposited, as it were, by the actual energy of the lightning *before* it is actually seen as lightning. Potential and actual energy together make up what is called reality but potentiality and actuality themselves *appear to be structured* by a higher actuality that is apparently hidden by time.

Unfortunately, Parmenides obscured this kind of actuality in terms of his formulation of what *being* really was. Being was for Parmenides, the One, i.e., all being was a manifestation of one underlying reality. Parmenides took the rather simple position, which does not admit any sort of paradox, that the One was the fundamental reality. The One is the fundamental reality when considered as existence but existence is neither the one nor the many. It is something quite beyond both concepts. Parmenides concept of existence was similar to that of the Hindus, with their notion of *Maya* as the 'play' or the world as an illusion of the Godhead. If *being* does not exist on its own in some way, then it must necessarily be a manifestation of something else, i.e., the One.

If all things are made up of *being* (actual and potential energy combined in some quantum[2] manner) it is possible to ask a further question. Does *being* account for itself, i.e., does *being* make itself *be*? On the face of it, this may seem like a silly question, because one could just as easily ask the question: does matter account for itself? If matter or being accounts for itself, philosophy has no further purpose, as

---

2   Quantum is the Latin word for amount and, in modern understanding, means the smallest possible discrete unit of any physical property, such as energy or matter .

it would then be the province of science to determine what principles matter operated according to. This is essentially the position of the behavioral sciences today. They have usurped the position of Philosophy and we have such imperfect disciplines as Psychology and Sociology which purport to explain all human behavior in terms of a set of principles divorced from both metaphysics and morality. Aristotle's words are corrective in this regard:

"There is a science which investigates being as being and the attributes which belong to this in virtue of its own nature. Now this is not the same as any of the so-called special sciences; for none of these others treats universally of being as being. They cut off a part of being and investigate the attributes of this part; this is what the mathematical sciences do for instance. Now since we are seeking the first principles and the highest causes, clearly there must be something to which these belong in virtue of its own nature. If then those who sought the elements of existing things were seeking these same principles, it is necessary that the elements must be elements of being, not by accident but just because it is being. Therefore, it is of being as being that we must also grasp the first causes." [3]

What we can say from the perspective of the Reality Dysfunction and Dimensionally Interactive Cyber Kinesis is that the first creation is one in which God, as we might think of Him, creates both Himself and prime matter (potential being). Creation might be viewed as a hierarchical cascade consisting of three divine modalities:

- The Trinity as Existence, Consciousness and Bliss[4]
- God Knowing Himself, outside Himself, in the Reality Dysfunction

---

3   Aristotle, *Metaphysics*, Bk IV, Chapter 2, pg. 733
4   For the Christian this would be: Father, Son and Holy Ghost

• Dimensionally Interactive Cyber Kinesis or being as
the delta point between locality and non-locality

*Dimensionally Interactive Cyber Kinesis is a more complex way
of expressing the notion of matter and form that is commensurate
with both the discoveries of physics and the metaphysical notion
that God makes the entire creation be by knowing it, as He eternally knows Himself, outside Himself in the Reality Dysfunction.
Everything in this scenario from the smallest atomic particle to
the farthest star has some small degree of consciousness at work
in the heart of its be-ing. God's knowledge of Himself, outside
Himself, does not occur within the Eternal Godhead, as no new
knowledge or understanding can be added to His Nature, rather, this "knowing" occurs in the virtual reality or theophany of
God known as creation. What God Himself IS remains utterly
unknown except to the persons of the Godhead.*

The idea of being which interested the Greeks from the time of
Socrates until the rise of Christianity can be understood as Dimensionally Interactive Cyber Kinesis or as matter embedded with intelligence or information. In order to fully understand how revolutionary
this idea was and is, an examination of how the Greeks understood the
connection between being and the soul is worth reviewing.

If all things are made up of *being,* then the question can be posed:
what principles *differentiate* being? If a dog is different from a cat, and
a cat is different again from a horse or a stone, then what is the principle of individuation? Plato (427-347 BC) attempted to describe this
principle as an eternal pattern which he called *Form* or *Idea.* Ideas like
that of Plato's famous Horse exist independently of all separate horses,
with each individual horse somehow participating in the self-existing
pattern of *horseness,* which might be thought of as taking its existence
from God's eternal knowledge of the forms. Unfortunately, Plato's
forms don't explain how exactly individual horses participate in the

nature of "horseness".[5] Modern science has a parallel problem in explaining how or why subatomic particles would bother organizing themselves into extremely complex living organisms.

Aristotle's (382-322 BC) solution to the problem was to locate the Ideas, or Forms as principles of actuation of the specific being; i.e., a horse was a horse because both its matter and its form, when combined, enabled it *to be* a horse. This principal of its matter Aristotle designated as substance, (that which stands under) which was a combination of matter and form. The substance of non-living things was merely that—a nature or form, and matter. However, in living things, the principle of actuation and differentiation was called soul. For example, a man or woman is human and shares the characteristics of human nature but also has an additional principle of individuation and actuality called soul.

'Soul' can be thought of as a life-force but is, apparently, something more. The soul acts—it does something. All forms are organized and energized towards a *telos* (a future end) but the soul has its *telos* more deeply engraved, so to speak, in its be-ing. The soul organizes the potentially of matter according to the actuality which it is. This actuality seeks to transform matter into a mirror of itself. Aristotle understood form (or essence or nature—the terms are synonyms) and soul as principles of actuality. Together, matter (potentiality) and form make up the world as we know it. Aristotle didn't quite solve the problem, however, of differentiation. Claiming that the form or soul explains the structure of a living being is like a modern scientist pointing to DNA and claiming that questions regarding the origin of life are solved due to the presence of DNA. Clearly, a wider understanding of causality was and is required to explain the peculiar coherence, complexity and persistence of the universe that was readily apparent to the Greeks.

---

5   Samuel E. Stumpf, *Socrates to Sartre: A History of Philosophy*, Ch.4, pg. 97, McGraw-Hill Book Company, 1966

THE FOUR CAUSES

Aristotle's genius is most clearly shown in his articulation of causality according to the famous Four Causes. The Four Causes directly relate the notions of Being and Soul, to a metaphysical structure of change, which points in a direction beyond the soul.

> *"Although the word cause refers in modern use primarily to an event prior to an effect, for Aristotle, it meant an explanation. His four causes represent therefore a broad pattern or framework for the total explanation of anything and everything."* [6]

We have all heard the argument that matter as we know it: desks, trees, flesh and rain is really only made up of whirling electrons and sub-atomic particles organized into quanta or packets of energy. There is a popular assumption that is based on this idea and it goes like this:

> *Because reality is composed of quanta that can manifest as either particle or wave, the world is really only an illusion and therefore all moral rules are relative to that illusion and not to anything that is objectively real.*

The notion that all matter may be composed of elementary particles in motion doesn't mean that they are insubstantial or an illusion. If the particles in my body are moving at the same relative speed as the particles in the desk in front of me, then for all practical purposes, they are both solid. The idea that things are not real because they are made up of moving particles or that they are just discontinuous 'events' makes it extremely difficult to formulate theories of an objective reality or an objective standard of ethical or reasonable behavior.

Discoveries in science are, paradoxically, providing philosophers with additional verification that the discontinuous version of reality posited by scientific atheism may not be correct. Physicist David Bohm,

---

6   Ibid

for example, did some extraordinary work on plasma in the 1940's at the Berkeley Radiation Laboratory.[7] What he discovered was ground-breaking. A plasma is a gas containing a high density of electrons and positive ions, i.e., atoms that have a positive charge. To Bohm's amazement he found that once they were in plasma form electrons stopped behaving like individuals and started behaving as if they were part of a larger and interconnected whole.[8] He observed almost organic forms of cellular style organization within the plasma. He noted that the electron sea seemed alive.[9] Bohm called the collective movement of electrons within the electron sea *plasmons*. This is, perhaps, an early discovery of hidden forms of causality that appear to operate outside of the currently established laws of physics.

Quantum physicist Erwin Shrödinger, as early as 1944, theorized that DNA could function as a "quantum antenna" for non-local communication between cells and organisms.[10] Shrödinger was speculating that the DNA of living organisms had receptor or resonance potential for receiving and decoding information from non-local space.[11] Modern science has now confirmed that biological luminescence, (biophotons) which is about one hundred million times weaker than daylight, may be involved in intracellular communication.[12] These biophotons may be linked to each other, via quantum entanglement with other, as of yet, unknown non-local processes. The astonishing variety of living organisms is enhanced by an understanding that life itself may be a manifestation of the particle/wave duality of quanta with biology simply being the particulate manifestation of multi-dimensional processes. In this respect, Aristotle and Aquinas' teachings on the forms is not too far off the mark, if the forms are considered Divine artifacts, or representative of a multi-dimensional interface between local and non-local consciousness.

7   Talbot, Michael, *The Holographic Universe*, Harper Perennial, 1991, pg. 38
8   Ibid
9   Ibid
10 Pim van Lommel, M.D.,*Consciousness Beyond Life: The Science of the Near Death Experience,* pg. 271, Harper Collins, N.Y. 2011
11 Ibid
12 Ibid, pg. 272

Aristotle's concept of the *Four Causes* gives us an additional grip on what we see in the world around us. The Four Causes are: formal, material, efficient and final causality. An automobile, for example, is first of all being an automobile—that is the *formal* cause (keep reading, this will be explained). Secondly, it is made of various materials; that is the *material* cause. Third, it is conceived and made by man, who is the *efficient* cause. Finally, it has a purpose, an 'end' for which it was made; this is the *final* cause. These four causes are intimately related to each other, as they are all events that occur in the generation of what we call reality.

The formal cause is the most difficult cause of all to understand, when applied to living things. The formal cause of a tree is *"treeness"* but where does this idea of "treeness" come from? What is its efficient and final cause? Plato associated the forms with what he called the *Demiurge* which was a kind of intermediary between the One (God) and the visible universe. In other words, Plato's God is the ultimate source of being with the demiurge being the principle in between, a kind of translator between Being and being, much in the same way that a browser translates source code for a computer's graphical user interface.

Plato's metaphysics are highly visual. It is easy enough to see what he is getting at but then the question of what constitutes the form of the forms intrudes. All things exist but what is making the forms exist, and more importantly, why? Are they eternal, as Plato thought, having their origin in the mind of God, or are they something else? Plato's metaphysical system does not appear to go far enough in showing the both the essential relatedness and radical difference between *being* manifesting as the *Many* and *Being* as the One, or Existence.

Aristotle, as Plato's pupil, inherited both the idea of being and the concept of the *atomos* (the smallest particle which could not be further subdivided) from earlier Greek philosophers. There were those in Aristotle's time, such as Democritus, who believed that the entire universe was just a result of random movements of these atoms. Aristotle simply didn't buy this theory. He was an early biologist and observed that there were too many non-random events in nature. He saw purposeful action in nature and biological organisms were seen, even in his time, as demonstrably complex.

The notion of soul, as a formal cause, related to the Unmoved Mover, locates the nature of soul in a higher dimensionality than that of time. This was the essential intuition of Socrates, Plato and Aristotle. Aristotle, more than likely, simply assumed that this was the case and that those he spoke to were also familiar with the notion of the soul as being associated in some way with the Unmoved Mover in eternity. This was a period in history when there was no real distinction between theology and metaphysics; it was all philosophy to the Greeks, with perhaps the exception of the priestly caste, whose members may have viewed metaphysics with suspicion.

Aristotle was interested in the origin of all things and he realized that there had to be a principle that governed the order that he saw around him. The idea of the form provided him with this principle but the ultimate origin and genesis of the forms remained obscure. A critical concept seemed to be missing.

Chapter 9

EXISTENCE: THE ULTIMATE CAUSE OF BEING

*"...the ancients, who were our betters and nearer the gods
than we are, handed down the tradition, that whatever things
are said to be, are composed of one and many, and have
finite and infinite implanted in them...
this unity we shall find in everything."*

—Plato,
Philebus

ESSENCE AND EXISTENCE

The most curious thing about Aristotle is that he appears not to have fully investigated the metaphysical consequences of the relationship between Existence and essence as those ideas might apply to the concept of soul. This has been noted by many of Aristotle's Christian critics. We don't have all of Aristotle's original works and much of what we have would be closer to what might be called teaching notes, so the criticism may not be entirely justified.

The idea of the form as something that is *in act* tells us what the form or essence is doing but does not explain *how* that can be. For instance, I have before me my son's dog, Fabiola. Fabiola is a Welsh Springer Spaniel but, nonetheless, a dog. She has the animal soul and nature of a dog which makes her *be* a dog and not a horse. Her genetic material is a reflection of the specific composition of matter and form (substance) which makes her be what she is. **What is making that soul and dog nature be what they are?** Aristotle's philosophy appears to take for granted the existence of the forms—or does it?

> *"But if there is something which is capable of moving things or producing them but is not actually doing so, there will not necessarily be movement; for that which has a potency need not exercise it. Nothing, then is gained even if we suppose eternal Entities, as the proponents of the Forms do, unless there is to be in them some principle which can cause change; nay even this is not enough, nor is another Entity besides the Forms enough; for if it is not to act, there will be no movement. Further, even if it acts, this will not be enough, if its Entity is potency; for there will not be eternal movement, since that which is potentially may possibly not be. There must...be such a principle, whose very Entity is act."* [1]

What are we to make of this statement? Clearly, this principle whose "entity is act" cannot have any degree of potentiality, otherwise it would not be eternal. What is this entity? Is it God or is it the soul? Aristotle appears to be referring to God or a kind of Existence that

---

1   Aristotle, *Metaphysics*

is completely different from all other existences in that it is without potentiality. It does not participate in anything else for its Existence, it is pure Act. Aristotle never seems to fully capitalize on this insight, even though he does say that all things imitate this Unmoved Mover, in the same way that the lover is moved by the beloved. This is an extraordinary teaching but one from which Aristotle does not, apparently proceed. What is missing is an ontological reason why the rest of the universe should even want or have to imitate the Unmoved Mover.

Aristotle may have perceived that attributing creation to the Unmoved Mover might have suggested a before and after in God—in short, potentiality, which he correctly saw as impossible. Aristotle believed that the Universe was eternal, neither being created nor destroyed. (This is similar to our modern definition of energy which is seen to be neither created nor destroyed.) Aristotle did not fall into the metaphysical trap of a before and after in God, but then neither did he advance much further, in terms of his speculation about the nature of the Unmoved Mover.

What is the relation of the Unmoved Mover, this Act, to the other mini acts that constitute the natures or essences of all specifically existing things? More directly, what is the relationship between the entity who *is* act and the soul? Is the soul some kind of independent entity made possible by the big 'Kahuna'[2] upstairs? What are the characteristics of this independent entity? What kind of relationship does it have with God? Is it immortal? Aristotle is strangely reticent. It is possible that Aristotle may have articulated some doctrine of participation, in this act of Existence, which is not attested to in the existing works that have been handed down to posterity.

Nonetheless, the stage was set for Thomas Aquinas (1225-1274 AD) who, like some of the early Church Fathers before him, immediately grasped that Aristotle's Unmoved Mover was no less than the *I Am Who Am* of the Old Testament and ultimately, a foreshadowing

---

2   Kahuna was the old Hawaiian title for a shaman, and the term is still used in that context by some native Hawaiians. It is also used in modern culture to indicate anyone who is an expert at something.

of the New Testament revelation of the Holy Trinity. The Trinity *being* three persons with one paradoxical nature in pure Act with no admixture of potentiality. Aquinas neatly sidesteps the problem of a before and after, in the creation, by advocating that God creates without movement i.e., without the interval of time.

> *"Since therefore God is outside the whole order of creation, and all creatures are ordered to Him, and not conversely, it is manifest that creatures are really related to God Himself; whereas in God there is no real relation to creatures but a relation only in idea, inasmuch as creatures are referred to Him. Thus there is nothing to prevent these names which import relation to the creature from being predicated of God temporally, not by reason of any change in Him, but by reason of the change in the creature; as a column is on the right of an animal, without change in itself, but by change in the animal."[3]*

Furthermore, Aquinas states:

> *"Creation places something in the thing created according to relation only because what is created, is not made by movement, or by change. For what is made by movement or by change is made by something pre-existing...Hence creation in the creature is only a certain relation to the Creator as to the principle of its being... But in God, relation to the creature is not a real relation, but only a relation of reason; whereas the relation of the creature to God is a real relation...[4]*

It is precisely this relation of reason or relation of idea that constitutes the virtual reality of time and space (commonly thought of as the creation) that is required for God to know Himself *as other than*

---

3 Aquinas, Thomas, *Summa Theologica*, Q. 13, Article 7
4 Ibid, Q. 45, Art 3, Pt. 1

Himself. Put another way, the real relation of the creature to God is a dependency but it is a dependency created by God's eternal nature. Aquinas would argue that God has no need to know Himself, outside Himself, as all perfections are already present to Him and in His being but the problem of time remains. How does the God of the Bible, who appears to engage humanity in time, not change unless that change occurs within the framework of a virtual or derivative kind of reality? If you imagine yourself sitting in a chair, your act of sitting does not make the potted plant over to your right be there but it is, relationally speaking, to your right by virtue of your sitting where you are. In the same way, by analogy, God's existence causes things to be in a virtual manner in reference to His Eternal Knowledge, which is one with His Existence.

God's Existence works in a way that is, analogously speaking, at right angles, or orthogonally infinite to the way we think of and perceive reality. While it is clear that the univocal nature of God's consciousness precludes temporal relations between the Divine Ideas within the Divine Nature, it is by no means clear that the Divine Ideas can be considered entirely univocal, as their expression in time requires equivocal meaning. In the same way that a cause leaves its imprint on an effect, the contingent existence of all things is the mark of that which is no-thing, making something exist. The relations between that which is no-thing and those things that have existence is not a reciprocal relation, except in time. The equivocal meaning of the Divine Ideas is what Plato and Aristotle both struggled with. Understanding that change cannot occur in God, they needed a way of accounting for change in the external world. The concept of eternal Ideas, somehow outside of time but influencing time and space might be thought of as an early attempt at describing what is defined in this work as the Reality Dysfunction.

What both Aristotle and Aquinas grasped was that the enormous power of God's Existence was translated in some way, by God's knowledge, into form or essence. God is, in this sense, the elephant in the room. Grasping the notion that an infinite power, ultimately, generates everything that we see about us by virtue of its own infinite existence and without changing is a staggering concept. The notion that energy is neither created nor destroyed might be thought of as the shadow cast by the Reality Dysfunction. Peering around the corner of existing things, we get a hint of marvelous treasures—if only we could stick our necks out a little bit further.

How can Existence, which cannot change, make anything be without changing and if it does not change, how do other things participate in its existence? The only explanation that makes any sense is that what God knows comes to exist in time (as essence or form) even though what God knows is, ultimately, co-eternal with His own being. Aquinas postulated that this was *creation by approbation* or that God's knowledge, itself, made things be. Aquinas also claimed that *relation* to God was only a real relation for what was created but not a real relation to God.

The metaphysics of *relation* might be thought of as a way of attempting to understand how Existence analogously *superordinates*[5] all things proportionately to itself. Given that we are dealing with a way of being that transcends our ability to adequately describe, we can only point our fingers in directions that might give us additional purchase on understanding God's celestial mechanics. What we can say with assurance is that the God of 100,000,000 BC is the same God the Father that Jesus refers to and Augustine centuries later, as a "Beauty so ancient and so new..."

The notion of *superordination,* which is a kind of ratio, enables the metaphysician consider how God's Existence orders the universe without any change occurring in Himself. Rather than thinking about

---

5   Definition: of or being the relation of a broader category to a narrower category that it encompasses, such as metal in relation to iron

cause and effect in a linear manner, when dealing with God, cause and effect has to be radically interrogated and re-interpreted using specialized language. Every cause has a point of origin; Existence has no such point of origin, so the way we approach Existence as the ultimate cause is truly groping in the dark.

The only logical distinction that the mind can make, in this regard, is that the *possession* of knowledge is a secondary activity from the Act that *is* that knowledge. God does not possess knowledge, He is His own knowledge, except by way of derivation, in the mysterious intermediary act known as essence or form. Superordination might be thought of as continuous creation, without effort on the part of God, within the Reality Dysfunction.

One way of considering superordination might be to think of *creation by approbation* as a consequence of an eternal superordination, which is really a kind of transcendental algorithm. The first approbation is the creation of something like a Demiurge or that which eternally adjudicates the distinctions between matter and form based on relations known by the Divine Mind—much like a browser interpreting and formatting original source code. The second "approbation" might be thought of as being the creation of angelic beings. The third "approbation" might be considered the creation of mankind. Superordination might also be considered as nothing at all—as in a no-thingness that makes everything be according to an infinite, transcendental logic that cannot be penetrated by the human mind.

Clearly, if God has thoughts, they are not thoughts as we know them but a set of complex variables that function analogous to subatomic particles being part of a larger molecular whole. God's thoughts are part of a continuous whole in the Act of Existence that can be broken-out in terms of granular locality and unbroken non-locality depending on which side of Existence you are looking at.

In the same way that the ancient Egyptians would have gone mad had they been able to visit the Grand Canyon and seen more rock to carve than would have been humanly possible in any one lifetime, so too the paradoxes of existence make philosophers want to tear their hair out by the roots. One comes back again and again to Existence, which presents Itself as an unscalable wall at the edge of time and mind.

The philosophical story of Existence and its relationship to the concept of soul may be become clearer by examining God and His Ideas from the perspective of Islamic theology. The rise of Islam, in approximately 610 AD, and its subsequent conflict with Christianity produced an intellectual windfall that western scholars seldom reflect upon today. Islam not only tried to conquer Christianity by force but sought to intellectually defeat the proponents of Christ by utilizing Aristotle to promote the Islamic theological agenda.

AVICENNA'S VERSION OF THE REALITY DYSFUNCTION

Avicenna (980 AD) was the son of a Persian money changer. He was extremely bright as a child and received a first-class education. He later studied medicine and philosophy in North Africa and it is said that he read Aristotle's *Metaphysics* forty times before he understood it.[6] He was one of the most famous of the medieval Islamic philosophers and theologians. He was also known for his book, *Canon of Medicine,* which was used in Europe for four hundred years after his death.

Avicenna's great claim to philosophical distinction came with his advocating that existence was an accident. His argument went something like this: God knows all things from all eternity, therefore, their essences, forms and souls already exist in His mind; when they are actually created, their subsequent existence in this world is an accident. In order to understand the significance of this argument, let's review Aristotle's ten accidents. The accidents or categories were things that needed an already existing entity to exist themselves. For example, color is an accident of *relation;* it requires something to inhere in, a medium like air, water or living matter and then it requires an observer. We do not see colors in the infra-red part of the spectrum because we are

---

6   *Encyclopedia of Religion,* old version, pg. 272

physically not configured to do so.

A chair may have colors that I cannot see but it is still a chair. Strip off the accidents of any object, until you have the thing itself. Chair, as a concept, has a certain meaning regardless of *shape, size, color* or *location*, etc. Similarly, *quantity, quality, relation, place, time, position, state, action, affection* and *substance* are all accidents, or categories, i.e., they are things that are predicated of something more fundamental. Another example would be 'eating'; eating by itself means nothing, unless someone or some creature is eating. **Even the composite of matter and form, *substance,* is an accident in relation to the existence of the form**. The substance of a chair does not exhaust the species 'chair'; i.e., a million chairs or one chair does not exhaust the potentiality of the species.

Avicenna's argument that existence was an accident raised the hackles of all those philosophers who grasped the implications of what he was saying. If existence was an accident, then the freedom of God would be dissolved.

"What occurs metaphysically when God creates the world? Existence and essence are identically one in Him. God is the necessary being. God knows the pure natures (natures as possibilities) from all eternity; and when he creates, He confers upon them the accident of being or existence. In this fashion, the world of things truly does hold its being on suffrage. Avicenna clearly believed that he had safeguarded metaphysically the truth of Revelation. But had he done so really? The God of Scripture and of Revelation is truly the Lord and He brooks no competitors. But Avicenna's God is the Lord only of the existential order, and that order is merely accidental to boot! God is not the Lord of the essential or natural order. He is rather constrained to know that order from all eternity because it is there before His mind, not as existent but as intelligibility given as possibility...God cannot do much about the possibles except create them, and even then, He is constrained

to create them in the intelligible order in which they are given to Him. The freedom of the God of Revelation thus dissolves within the metaphysics of Avicenna...Avicenna's God might be compared to the Queen of England, to a figurehead monarch. No law in England has validity, unless it bears the Queens signature." [7]

Nonetheless, Avicenna's contribution to metaphysics should not be overlooked, because for the first time, a clear cut distinction is advocated between the being of something and the principle which makes it be, namely, Existence. (Avicenna is also pointing in the direction of what scientists today would describe as the possibility of a virtual and derivative universe.) Avicenna's formulation, however, is in part due to the perennial temptation of the human mind to imagine something as existing before it actually exists—as if it were a ghost in the mind of God. This was noted, as we discussed earlier, by Duns Scotus many centuries later.[8] God however, can be composed of no potentiality whatsoever. The problem of formulating an adequate concept of Existence without using the language and implication of potentiality and consequently time is extremely difficult.

"This structure, as Aristotle demonstrated, is rooted in the form. But "is" cannot be conceived or defined in any sense at all; "is" is neither structure nor form. But how can we understand a principle which cannot be fitted into an idea or concept? The metaphysics of Aquinas is one long attempt to answer that question. The road is so difficult that the philosopher is forced to recall what Heidegger says of Parmenides: he discovered being for the West then lost it in the very act of finding it. How can we retain the "is" of Parmenides without freezing it into a conceptual being...the mind tends to reduce to nothing that which it cannot conceptualize." [9]

---

7   Wilhelmsen, Frederick, *The Paradoxical Structure of Existence*, University of Dallas Press, 1970, pg. 30
8   This book, page 85
9   Wilhelmsen, Frederick, *The Paradoxical Structure of Existence*, University of Dallas

The only way really to attempt to understand the problem of existence and change is to accept Avicenna's distinction as an attempt to move in the right direction. God's knowledge of Himself, *outside Himself,* might be thought of as the fundamental act of differentiation. God, it would seem, cannot simultaneously be the giver of existence and have no relation to that secondary form of existence, or theophany,[10] based on a theological or metaphysical attempt to insulate the authority of God from any logical or abstract constriction. The only constriction that can be placed on God is the constriction that God voluntarily makes in knowing Himself, outside Himself, or knowing Himself as He might be imitated. God does not change in this scenario, only the scenario changes. As theologian Karl Rahner notes:

"When God wants to be what is not God, man comes to be." [11]

To say that God could *not* become that which he is not in a virtual realm, or in the realm of what Aquinas would call relations of reason, would be an impossibility. There is a certain kind of jump that is required in love that involves self-abnegation and in one sense that this is what God seems to have done with the entire created order. Creation is an act of love and it must, perforce, involve limitation and suffering in the virtual entity created. God's perfection would otherwise inflict a kind of virtual Docetism[12] on God's involvement with mankind. In other words, God's loving of the human soul is based in part, on a knowledge that is other than that of Himself in all of His perfection. It involves imperfection and time in a virtual construct that the ancients referred to as a theophany[13] and which is described in this book as

Press, 1970, pg. 30

10 "Theophany (from the Ancient Greek meaning "appearance of a god") refers to the appearance of a deity to a human or other being."

11 *Does God Change?* by Thomas Weinandy, OFM Cap., St. Bede's Publications, pg. 164, 1984, Still River, MA

12 The Docetists were a heretical group within early Christianity that believed that Jesus only took on the appearance of a man and didn't really have a human body.

13 A manifestation of God in time

Dimensionally Interactive Cyber Kinesis, or the infinite consciousness and energy of God, as it might be understood in the Reality Dysfunction. It does not involve a change in God but in the set of relations, intrinsic to the eternal knowledge of the unchangeable Divine Mind, extrinsically expressed as a virtual reality. Rahner expresses this succinctly in the following way:

"If we face squarely and uncompromising the fact of the Incarnation which our faith in the fundamental dogma of Christianity testifies to, then we have to say plainly: God can become something. He who is not subject to change in Himself can himself be subject to change in something else." [14]

God's loving of the human soul is also beautifully illustrated in a poem by Amos Alcott Bronson in the 19th century. What is described is how God subjects Himself to Love.

> *"For souls that of His own good life partake*
> *He loves as His own self; dear as His eye*
> *They are to Him. He'll never them forsake.*
> *When they shall die, then God Himself shall die.*
> *They live, they live in blest eternity."* [15]

The beauty of Aristotle's original notion of form and actuality, much like Bronson's poem, is that it is not tied to a specifically religious agenda. Despite the enormous utility of subsequent metaphysical deliberation on the notion of Existence, there is something particularly pristine about Aristotle's Concept of Existence as the Unmoved Mover. It is perhaps to Aristotle's everlasting credit that some of his greatest defenders have been Islamic and Christian theologians.

---

14 Karl Rahner as quoted in: *Does God Change?* by Thomas Weinandy, OFM Cap., St. Bede's Publications, pg. 168, 1984, Still River, MA

15 *Orphic Sayings and Table Talk*, Amos Bronson Alcott from *A Treasury of Philosophy*, Dagobert. D. Runes, Philosophical Library, New York, NY., pg. 25

AVERROES

Another great Islamic, Aristotelian commentator and theologian was Averroes, which is a corruption of the Arabic name Ibn Rushd. "Ibn Rushd was born in Cordova, Spain, to a family with a long and well-respected tradition of legal and public service. His grandfather, the influential Abdul-Walid Muhammad (d. 1126), was the chief judge of Cordova, under the Almoravid dynasty, establishing himself as a specialist in legal methodology and in the teachings of the various legal schools."[16] Averroes, likewise, studied medicine and law in Cordova, Spain and was initially requested to translate Aristotle, by an Amir, who complained about the obscurity of the Greek philosophers. His works enjoyed a great influence, initially, in North Africa and Spain but he fell into disrepute around 1165 AD when his texts were thought to be heretical and influenced by Jewish thought. His works did in fact have a significant influence on Jewish and Christian philosophy in the 13th and 14th centuries and might serve as the basis for a new understanding of Islam—within Islam itself.

"His influential commentaries and unique interpretations on Aristotle revived Western scholarly interest in ancient Greek philosophy, whose works for the most part had been neglected since the sixth century AD. He critically examined the alleged tension between philosophy and religion in the Decisive Treatise, and he challenged the anti-philosophical sentiments within the Sunni tradition sparked by al-Ghazzali [a Muslim theologian of Persian descent]. This critique ignited a similar re-examination within the Christian tradition, influencing a line of scholars who would come to be identified as the "Averroists." [17]

---

16 http://www.iep.utm.edu/ibnrushd/
17 http://www.iep.utm.edu/ibnrushd/

Averroes launched a devastating critique of Avicenna with his polemic entitled, *The Destruction*. This book in particular attacks Avicenna's assertion that existence is an accident. Averroes correctly intuited that if existence was an accident, then all accidental forms of being could rightly be said not to exist.[18] Note that an accident has no formal, independent existence on its own. Aristotle never said for example, that *quantity or action* were not beings; but that any being they had was in conjunction with something that *was already existing*. For example, a strong man walking or a beautiful woman listening are descriptions of accidental qualities and actions, predicated of an existing man or woman. If Avicenna's formulation is correct, then we could say that *strong* and *walking* do not exist—even if they are in a subject. We would have to say that nothing exists except Being or the One, which would put us once again in Parmenides' camp. Parmenides if you recall, held that nothing existed except the One or God and that everything was just a limited manifestation of this entity (similar to the Hindu Maya or illusion).

Why is this even important as a point of argument? Surely this is just some obscure metaphysical hair splitting? What is at stake here is the very nature of reality. Things either really exist or they are an illusion, and only Existence exists. The whole basis of what is called realistic metaphysics is that things do really exist through the power of something that exists in Itself, viz., God. The question, which distinguishes which metaphysical camp you belong to, is *how* they exist. Do beings (and by that is meant substances, which are composites of matter and form) really exist on their own—or have they been given existence, in some way that is not cheapened or excluded, by the overwhelming power of their origin in ultimate causality? In other words, is everything made up of God, as opposed to being something distinct from and participating in God's Essence? The viewpoint of pantheism says that all things are really manifestations of God and of God only. There is no participation only the illusion of separateness.

---

18 Frederick Wilhelmsen, *The Paradoxical Structure of Existence*, University of Dallas Press, 1970, pg. 36

Some of the difficulty tends to be overcome by understanding that subsistent existence might be considered accidental only when viewed from Existence's (God's) perspective. Fr. Joseph Owens,[19] who was a student of Etienne Gilson, was famous for saying that God is the pencil but the pencil isn't God. This illustrates the first paradox of metaphysics: *God Is and He is not.* Existence shares itself in some mysterious way that does not subtract or add to itself in any way. Things *have* existence; God *is* Existence.

The fundamental question is not how God is bound by His Ideas but how His Ideas can be expressed at all without a derivative reality in which relations between ideas are real and not merely a product of the One. What is the calculus between the univocal reality of the Divine Essence and equivocal realities, which depend on that univocal reality to exist? Causes exist in their effects, pre-eminently. but only derivatively so. If a man makes a tool, he is the efficient cause of the tool and the function of the tool will reveal the intention of the maker. In the same way, the Reality Dysfunction is simply an eternal tool of the Divine intelligence to achieve an end.

Our job is to uncover the meaning of the Reality Dysfunction and overcome the appalling way that the notion of the fall of mankind has been intellectually hijacked to create unnecessary religious polarity and conflict. Whether or not there was ever a fall of man or an original sin is irrelevant to the notion that we need the assistance of Existence, regardless, in order to improve our lives and move forward. Politically speaking, this makes the recovery of a political philosophy that prioritizes the significance of Existence, the fulcrum for a complete reordering of the world's religious and political sensibilities and priorities.

---

19 "Owens received his PhD in 1951 from the Pontifical Institute of Mediaeval Studies, an affiliate of the University of Toronto, and remained at the Institute as a teacher and distinguished researcher for the rest of his career. He authored nine books and almost 150 academic papers. He was a Fellow of the Royal Society of Canada and served as president of the Metaphysical Society of America (1972), the Canadian Philosophical Association, the Society for Ancient Greek Philosophy, and the American Catholic Philosophical Association." [WP]

UNDERSTANDING CONTINGENCY AND DEVOLUTION

The distinction between having existence and Be-ing Existence is central to the notion of *contingency*. Contingency is the notion that all being depends on Existence for its existence. It was no accident that Aristotle suggested that the perfection of the Unmoved Mover attracted humanity to moral rectitude and perfection.

> *If the notion of contingency is jettisoned the linkage between being, morality and Existence dissolves. The Reality Dysfunction both creates the possibility of viewing the universe as without purpose, or as Shakespeare indicated, "A tale told by an idiot, signifying nothing..." or the possibility of viewing it as a hierarchy of meaning rooted in a transcendental source that is not bound in any way by time or relation.*

The difference is crucial for any reality-based metaphysics and ethics. If things don't really exist or are not hierarchically connected to a higher cause, then philosophy has no place to take a stand. Without being and Existence, politics is divorced from the notion of the "good" and precludes a consideration of the improvement of soul as part of the moral and political process. It is no exaggeration to say that this is the present state of philosophy and ethics in our western culture. There is no set morality or metaphysical structure because all relations are not related to anything at all—they are merely that—relations to relations and like sand castles, there is nothing holding them together but moist attractions that have no meaning.

> *"Ever since Kant divorced reason from reality, his intellectual descendants have been diligently widening the breach. In the name of reason, Pragmatism established a range-of-the-moment view as an enlightened perspective on life, context-dropping as a rule of epistemology, expediency as a principal of morality,*

and collective subjectivism as a substitute for metaphysics. Logical Positivism carried it farther and, in the name of reason, elevated the immemorial psycho-epistemology of shyster-lawyers to the status of scientific epistemological system-by proclaiming that knowledge consists of linguistic manipulations. Taking this seriously, Linguistic Analysis declared that the task of philosophy is, not to identify universal principles, but to tell people what they mean when they speak, which they are otherwise unable to know (which...by that time, was true—in philosophical circles). This was the final stroke of philosophy breaking its moorings and floating off, like a lighter than-air balloon, losing any semblance of connection to reality, any relevance to the problems of man's existence." [20]

Note that the following Wikipedia definition of essence and existence is entirely incorrect in that the 'traditional view' of realist philosophy is exactly the opposite of the definition given here.

"Existence precedes essence (French: l'existence précède l'essence) is a central claim of existentialism, which reverses the traditional philosophical view that the essence (the nature) of a thing is more fundamental and immutable than its existence (the mere fact of its Being). To existentialists, humans, through their consciousness, create their own values and determine a meaning for their life because the human being does not possess any inherent identity or value. That identity or value must be created by the individual. By posing the acts that constitute him or her, he or she makes his or her existence more significant."

Existence in the Catholic sense and because it was related directly to God's own Existence made essence or the nature of a thing easily

20 Gilson, Etienne, *Being and Some Philosophers*, Pontifical Institute of Medieval Studies, Toronto, Canada, 1952, second edition, pgs. 8 and 9

seen as being secondary or contingent. It was only with the banishment of essential existence, as a participation in God's Existence, after the rise of the Protestant Reformation and the subsequent adoption of empiricism as a kind of neo-theology that 'form' became part of the "tradition" that essence was viewed as being more fundamental than Existence (form and essence being, essentially, convertible terms). While the older traditional view of existence put forth by Aristotle and the later scholastics featured the predominance of Existence over essence, the later empirical leaning 'tradition' of Descartes and Kant was incoherent or mute in its understanding of the meaning of existence. Existence, stripped down to a kind of ghost in the machine, only functions within the marginalized rationalism of many forms of modern philosophy as an adjunct to psychological authenticity. As noted by Charles Péguy: "Kantian ethics has clean hands but, in a manner of speaking, actually no hands."

WICKED PROBLEMS

Sociologists today engage in a variety of linguistic shenanigans with terms like "wicked problem," which does not mean 'evil' as the *absence of a good that could and should be present* but "a problem that that is difficult or impossible to solve because of incomplete, contradictory, or changing requirements that are often difficult to recognize."[21] The use of term "wicked" has come to denote resistance to resolution, rather than evil. Moreover, because of complex interdependencies, the effort to solve one aspect of a wicked problem may reveal or create other problems." [22]

While this term can be useful when used in the right context, it

---

21 "The phrase, *wicked problem* was originally used in social planning. Its modern sense was introduced in 1967 by C. West Churchman in a guest editorial he wrote in the journal *Management Science*, responding to a previous use of the term by Horst Rittel. Churchman discussed the moral responsibility of operations research "to inform the manager in what respect our 'solutions' have failed to tame his wicked problems" [WP]

22 Ibid

can be argued that many "wicked problems" can be ameliorated or solved by the use of universal and clear definitions regarding good and evil. Wicked problems are much more likely to originate in non-casual systems that are self-referential. One has only to think of the recent idiocy in San Francisco where an illegal immigrant who should have been shipped out of the country five times killed a young woman but slipped through the cracks based on the notion of "sanctuary". For the conservative, the idea of a sanctuary city for illegal aliens is absurd. (A sanctuary city does not use local funding to implement federal law). For the wealthy in San Francisco, using a different example, cheap labor is needed to maintain the standard of living but housing is too expensive for low wage foreign workers so they have to live in crowded group housing. Group housing is a tenable solution to cheap labor but tends to create its own set of wicked social problems.

Same-sex attraction, for example, might be considered a "wicked problem" from the perspective of a moral system like virtue and vice. If virtue is defined as "acting in accordance with right reason" then it could certainly be argued that many authentic homosexuals (this excludes the morally confused bi-sexual) would be acting in accordance with right reason in choosing a life partner. One could also argue that a gay individual choosing to get "married" might be acting more in accordance with right reason by choosing to be "married" than engaging in a series of one-night stands. So there is a "wicked problem" here for the traditional moralist.

The wicked problem can, however, be clarified through interrogation. What, for example, might be the impediments to right reason? The impediments to right reason could be simply psychological, they might be genetic, social, based on bad habits, etc., so from the traditional point of view a homosexual may be morally disabled (sexually) in respect to right reason. Most of those suffering from same-sex attraction, for example, have little or no internal prohibition in regards to masturbation and the consumption of gay porn—both of which only increase the difficulty of curing bad habits. Additionally, the moralist can argue that natural virtue, which the morally leaning homosexual might choose, is not enough. The supernatural virtues of faith, hope and love must also be sought after and those virtues supersede the natural order.

Now most liberals can't stand this kind of thinking because it assumes an objective moral and spiritual order that to them is like "Kryptonite". But there really is no way out of the dilemma posed by "wicked problems" in the moral order. A moral system has to, ultimately, rely on something outside itself. A subjective moral order isn't a moral order at all—no matter how artful the practitioner(s). The woman who has an abortion, for example, can come up with all sorts of reasons for killing her baby but at the heart of the matter is something beyond mind or even analysis. There is something real that cannot be reduced via justification and the troubling question of moral honor in relation to human suffering remains. The difficulty remains because inter-subjectivity, without considering Existence's role in the nature of inter-subjectivity, can be a form of moral and intellectual poverty.

REFLEXIVITY

One of the essential differences between philosophers who believe that reality really exists and those who don't is the notion of Natural Law; i.e., that reality operates on the basis of certain rules that are outside of subjective consciousness. Most philosophers and individuals who do not believe in natural law will almost always argue that personal preference and culture determines morality. They will also argue that most forms of ethical causality are *reflexive*.[23] Reflexivity translated means that all rules have consequences but because they are simply made up through various co-operation agreements, the consequences of those rules are caused by the rules themselves and not due to any condition rooted in reality. Causes that are really only linked by effect

---

23 "Reflexivity refers to circular relationships between cause and effect. A reflexive relationship is bi-directional with both the cause and the effect affecting one another in a relationship in which neither can be assigned as causes or effects." [WP]

to other effects are insubstantial or merely relational. Reflexivity is, then, a modern and improved variation of the *post hoc* fallacy, which means, "after this, therefore caused by this."

Reflexivity is an important and useful concept as every assumption should be interrogated and not simply accepted because it has been made by a wise man or some other authority. One of the most violent religious divisions, for example, is between Sunni and Shiite Muslims over which group represents the succession of authority intended by Mohammed. Mohammed, like Jesus, had no intention of founding anything but one organization to propagate his message. The current division within Islam is, consequently, un-Islamic and might be thought of as being analogous to the scandalous mainline division within Christianity between Catholic and Protestant.

If any prophet or religious founder was not actually inspired by God, then the teachings of whatever religion he or she may have founded may be void on objective and not merely reflexive grounds. One has only to think of the appalling Henry VIII in this regard. How anyone could possibly take as their religious founder a man who simply wanted a new wife is beyond the limits of a normal moral and spiritual imagination. Apologists for Anglicanism will argue that Henry was simply trying to separate Church and State, which did not exist at the time. The relative separation of Church and State—had it existed in the time of Henry VIII—would have enabled him to have gotten divorced in a civil court and many good men might have lived. However, anyone who looks closely at English history will see that Henry's "Great Matter" (his pending divorce from Catherine of Aragon) was his primary concern and the separation of Church and State, by making him the titular head of the Church of England, was simply an opportunity to seize the wealth of the Catholic Church.

Henry executed many good men, including former Chancellor and friend Thomas More (1478-1535 AD) and Bishop John Fisher (1469-1535 AD) in order to grant his sexuality free rein. Henry the VIII died of syphilis or a heart attack, or both, in January of 1547 AD.

What sort of legitimate spiritual leader dies from syphilis and degrades the religion of an entire nation in the process? Regardless of Henry's mixed and suspect motivations, the "intransigence" of Thomas More was based on his fidelity to the notion that there could not be an ultimate separation of Church and State without doing violation to Christendom. Had he been able to enlarge upon the subject in terms of a relative separation of Church and State, a compromise might have been reached that would have preserved the Catholic Church in England.

Similarly, and going backwards in time, when the Pharisees accused Jesus of blasphemy, it was because of a system that could not admit new information about God. The same inability of the Jews of Jesus's time to imagine that anything new might be received outside their tradition made it impossible for them to hear his message. Reflexive conclusions and a limited moral imagination made it difficult for them to consider that they might have been receiving new information. What we often think of as causes are not causes at all but effects and this is the value of certain forms of historical deconstruction. However, it cannot be used to make the claim that all causes are merely a result of inter-subjective co-operation agreements,[24] or the effects of other effects, without an over-riding form of final causality.

Some academics, who practice linguistic deconstruction, are attracted to the Hindu notion of reality as an illusion or *Maya*. Consequently, if all rules are purely subjective or culturally determined (this is not to say that they would argue that culturally subjective rules, such as traffic regulations are not useful) there really is no place for moral guidebooks that might lay claim to be operating manuals for the inhabitants of reality. For the deconstructionist, much like Henry VIII, morality is and was, ultimately, whatever conforms to the landscape of desire. Moral codes make little sense unless there is a linking of behavior to an authority which is transcendent. The fundamental question of who gets to speak for God has been a source of enormous conflict within and between religious groups. The persecution of Jesus and the

---

24 Yuval Noah Harari, *Sapiens: A Brief History of Humankind*, Harper Collins, NY

subsequent persecution of the Catholic Church by Henry VIII, although separated by centuries, have a loose commonality in that the cultural expression of religion at the time was inadequate to deal with new information and changing circumstances.

A deeper question can be asked in this context. Does God only speak to mankind in one instance, or just several times at some point in the distant past, or is God, as New Age spiritual writer Neale Donald Walsche indicates, "speaking to all of us, all of the time"? If the latter is the case, a corollary or derivative question can also be posed. If God is speaking to all of us, all of the time, how do we know if it is God who is speaking? Is it possible that there is another entity that seeks to displace God? Are false revelations possible? Without casting direct aspersions upon the Mormons or other religions, the notion that Joseph Smith, who supported polygamy and received tablets of gold from an angel is highly suspicious—particularly when those tablets are nowhere to be found. What would be the purpose of an adversary such as Satan in the world of the Reality Dysfunction? Is it possible that we ourselves are the adversary by accepting and holding to ideas about God that are inauthentic?

The fundamental issue might be stated as follows: is there such a thing as one Divine revelation given at only specific times in human history or is revelation a continuous process? The former is easier to "fix" in terms of hard and fast rules but the latter is more fluid and open to various interpretations that may be at odds with one another. Certitude always seeks a fixed point from which to proceed but love doesn't care so much about origins; it just listens and feels its way through to a sense of authenticity. How can we augment the process of discovering what is authentic about God and what is not?

Given that these are very difficult questions to answer using the scientific method, a metaphysical investigation of the nature of God and an examination of the claims made by man about God should have a high priority on any rational agenda. *God Has Skin in the Game: How a New Understanding of Politics and the Soul* is an attempt to lay the groundwork for an even-handed examination of how modern man might approach the problem that beliefs about God, via the plurality and divisiveness of religious belief systems, present for western civilization. It is one thing to have separation of Church from the State; it is entirely something else to separate God from the State. The former is a merely a relative separation of Church and religious modality from the State, the latter is a political divorce between God and politics that also severs the metaphysical and ethical link between body and soul.

HOW PHILOSOPHY GETS TRANSLATED SOCIALLY

Small intellectual detours have a way of derailing consciousness. This is why philosophers have argued like cats and dogs over what might appear to be minor issues. There is no room for error in algebra. The equation is either correct or it is false. The same may be said of philosophy; there are some things that are true and others that have to be false, for there to be any meaning whatsoever. Aristotle's famous principle of non-contradiction needs to be invoked. If A is A it cannot be true that A is B. A dog is a dog and not a cat. Substance (any combination of matter and form) cannot simultaneously be an accident and not exist at the same time. Things really do exist, even if their particular modalities are accidental, and if this is so, then there should be a set of laws or rules governing these modalities of being.

The confusion of general semantics for example, is based on a failure of classical metaphysics to present the notion of accidental being in a way that would make it apparent that all contingent being, within the Reality Dysfunction, is in a state of flux. A dog is in fact a dog but metaphysically speaking, that dog is different from the dog it was two minutes ago due to the unfolding of potential that the "ising" of that dog nature is engaged in. The "ising" of the dog is in flux (just as we are) because it is participating in the actualizing of what might be termed "dog potency." This does not mean that the unfolding of dog potency is unrelated to any physical or natural laws that might govern the operations of dog nature but it does mean that reality is more fluid and even more interrelated than the traditional model of Existence and contingent essences might have indicated if understood superficially.

The O.J. Simpson trial, in the 1990's, was an example of a complete breakdown of natural law based on a concept of existence that would allow it to be anything that it was desired to be. The sliminess of attorneys in raising legal issues solely for the purpose of discrediting evidence without reference to either facts or intentions is rooted in the view that reality is not what is actually out there but is whatever is made to be by the consciousness of the participants. Therefore, if it was felt that the LAPD was racist then that was sufficient reason for there to be a conspiracy of evidence planting—whether or not such a thing happened or not. Feelings are divorced from moral principles and become their own principles. The principle of *what I feel* becomes absolutely primary.

Newscasters, for example, almost always ask anyone they are interviewing: "How do you feel about this issue?" What they should ask is: "what do you think about it?" Our cultural bias in favor of feeling is most evident here. Note that the Webster dictionary definition of the intellect is: "The mind, the power to reason as distinguished from the power to feel."

Our society's inability to articulate sensible solutions for criminal and racial violence is the ultimate consequence of not believing in either reason or natural law. Racism in all forms is the ultimate banner of all those who have forgotten that culture is based on principles and that ultimately, principles are based on being. Racism is a feeling, seldom a principle. The color of someone's skin will only be a problem for those who have no metaphysical understanding of human nature and the rational principles that go into the making or unmaking of a culture. Moral illiteracy is the greatest obstacle that many of our poorer communities face. Being unable to "read" the appetites or not to have some understanding of biological impulses is a very dangerous form of poverty.

Physicists sometimes refer to "particle excitations" of the quantum field to describe molecular phenomena. This opaque language masks any potential causal processes that might be underlying or unifying the "particle excitations". Referring to particle excitations, as a substitute for causality, is like referring to a computer and all of its supporting code as a completely accidental occurrence. We know, of course, that this is not the case with manufactured objects.

The consequences of attributing complete flux and unknowability to being and existence, likewise, can be truly misleading and ultimately, frightening. When being becomes unknowable, the appetites become the only palpable reality, and unfortunately, where the appetites rule, there is chaos. Being, without reason and natural law, can become monstrous. The Socratic notion, of a soul being perfected and improved by noble actions and corrupted by bad actions is completely lost in modern society. A perfect example of the rational dysfunction engendered by false philosophy, which ignores the soul, is given to us courtesy of former 'rapper' (and now actor) Ice-T. Speaking at Stanford University about the 1992 Los Angeles riots, he said:

> *"That was the happiest day of my entire life. During the riot, I rolled into the neighborhood. I was chilling out, signing autographs. It was the most peaceful time I ever had being in South Central Los Angeles. Brothers were dancing. Music was playing. It was a very great thing."* [25]

The 'very great thing' that Ice-T referred to cost one billion dollars in property damage and resulted in 2,400 injuries and 53 deaths.[26] We may thank the positivist philosophers for their disciples amongst the black population, who are only acting out the consequences of the irrationality of their instructors. America's black cultural problems are a direct consequence of the actions of white social engineers and philosophers, who don't have the guts to see the ultimate consequences of the

---

25 *Focus on the Family*, a newsletter, June 1993
26 Ibid

metaphysical positions that they gather around like penned animals.

Dr. Andrew Pinsent notes that America is suffering from a "spiritual autism" caused by the failure of our culture to transmit a complete teaching on virtue as it was understood by both Aristotle and Aquinas.[27] If the notion of soul is de-linked from Existence or not even postulated as an operative principle in human affairs, demonic appetites will slowly overturn any constitutional system that assumes and requires virtue in its citizens to function.

27 Pinsent, Andrew, *The Second Person Perspective in Aquinas's Ethics*, Routledge Books, an imprint of Taylor and Francis, 2012, New York, NY, pg. 5

Chapter 10

HOW NOT UNDERSTANDING CAUSALITY HAS CONSEQUENCES

"Just as the term chariot is nothing but an expression for an axle, wheels, a body, a pole and other constituent parts combined in a particular manner, but when we analyze the various parts one by one we find that in the absolute sense there is no chariot...In that same way, the terms living being and soul are nothing but expressions for the combination of the five skandhas, (the physical body, sensation, perception, habitual tendencies and consciousness) but when we analyze those aggregates of being one by one, we find that in the absolute sense there is no living being or soul with which to form such assumptions as I am or I."

—Buddhaghosa,
Visuddhimagga

THE DISCONTINUITY OF BEING

If it could be said that Aristotelian realism believed in being and the "real" as being composed or ordered in terms of potency and act as did the medieval realists, Aquinas and Duns Scotus, many centuries later, then it should be forcibly stated that many of the philosophers of the past 500 years have not believed in such a view of reality. The deliberations of Berkeley, Hume and Kant have led western philosophy down the perilous road of nihilism, by cutting off the human mind and spirit from the font of being (or quantum reality) to which the mind and heart so naturally turn.

Buddhaghosa (India 400 AD) has succinctly expressed modern philosophical conceptions of existence and essence in the foregoing chapter quote. What is missing from his insight is the notion that the potential for the various parts of the chariot to be assembled, intentionally, is already posited in being, as potential, by a greater agency than human thought. In other words, without this greater agency or Act there would be no potential for even the parts of the chariot to exist, let alone their assembly. What is potential only exists because there is something that already knows all potentiality and all the permutations that potency and act might take. We, as humans, are the second tier of "knowers" in a system, so to speak, that is completely known by a Being or beings that are Existence itself.

The message from modern philosophy (i.e., the past 400 years), much like Buddhaghosa, is that causality is either an illusion or a mental abstraction of a larger whole and that reality is merely a series of discontinuous events, with no relation to each other—other than proximity. David Hume (1711-1776 AD) was, along with John Locke and Bishop Berkeley, one of the early promoters of the notion that our senses simply provided data that was either true or false relative to circumstance. He stated, for example, that it is "by means of some impression...that we are able to mark the difference betwixt [vice and virtue]." "Where do these impressions come from? They are "derived from a *moral sense*" which provides us with impressions of moral approval and disapproval in evaluating the character traits of human beings, and the actions which these traits give rise to." [1]

> "*Moral sentiments, according to Hume, are basic units of sense-experience, and as such, they can be neither true nor false.*" [2]

The linguistic and semantic analyses of Wittgenstein, Korzybski, Rorty and a plague of other deconstructionists in this century are only a continuing symptom of the separation of human sensibilities from Existence and Divine things that began shortly after the Protestant Reformation. Once separated from the authentic source of Catholic metaphysics and theology, Protestantism, despite its intentions to the contrary, began a long decline into symbolism and moral confusion.

More recently, self-professed atheist, Yuval N. Harari, author of *Sapiens: A Brief History of Humankind*, for example, argues that all of the abstract moral and legal structures of mankind are simply "cooperation agreements" to facilitate activity among large groups of people. They have no other significance. Some logical positivists have made asinine statements to the effect that Aristotle and Plato are irrelevant to modern man. The notion that the ideas of "dead white men"[3] are irrelevant because they have some sort of racial bias is so obviously a concoction of morally and politically juvenile thinking that it can't be taken seriously.

Martin Heidegger (1889-1976 AD), who understood the failure of philosophy in the West and its religious antecedents, blasted the empty-headed scholars of the twentieth century in his opus, *Being And*

---

1   Sveinbjorn Thordarson, *Hume's Moral Sense Theory and the Spectre of Relativism* http://sveinbjorn.org/hume_sense_theory_relativism

2   Ibid

3   "Traditional literature has been found to have been written by "dead white males" to serve the ideological aims of a conservative and repressive Anglo hegemony...In an array of reactions against the race, gender, and class biases found to be woven into the tradition of Anglo literature, multicultural writers and political literary theorists have sought to expose, resist, and redress injustices and prejudices. These prejudices are often covert – disguised in literature and other discourses as positive ideals and objective truths – but they slant our sense of reality in favor of power and privilege." [WP]

Time for their refusal to consider anew the question of being.

> *"On the basis of the Greeks' initial contributions towards an interpretation of Being, a dogma has been developed which not only declares the question about the meaning of Being to be superfluous, but sanctions its complete neglect. It is said that 'Being' is the most universal and emptiest of concepts. As such it resists every attempt at definition. Nor does this most universal and hence indefinable concept require any definition, for everyone uses it constantly and already understands what he means by it. In this way, that which the ancient philosophers found continually disturbing, as something obscure and hidden has taken on a clarity and self-evidence such that if anyone continues to ask about it is charged with an error of method."* [4]

JOHN LOCKE

Thomas Hobbes (1588-1679), John Locke (1632-1704), Bishop George Berkeley (1685-1753) and David Hume (1711-1776) did much to set the stage for the present situation of modern philosophy which Heidegger points to with great clarity. Hobbes, Locke, Berkeley and Hume believed that reality or being was ultimately unknowable. For Locke, sensation gave us a probable picture of reality and no more. There are no epistemological details for Locke, there is only the *tabula rasa* (blank slate) of the mind which receives sensations and determines thereby, what is being sensed.

> *"I see no reason, therefore, to believe that the soul thinks before the senses have furnished it with ideas to think on...If it shall be demanded, then, when a man begins to have any ideas? I think that the true answer is, when he first has any sensation."* [5]

---

4   Heidegger, Martin, *Being and Time*, pg. 2

5   T.V. Smith, Marjorie Green, *From Descartes to Locke*, University of Chicago Press, 1940, pgs. 356 & 357

Locke's reduction of thinking to sensation is almost juvenile in the light of several thousand years of metaphysical speculation on the subject. As composite beings (composed of matter and form), humankind receives information through sensation but that is only the beginning of knowledge. Aristotle's notion of the intellect, as having the power to become the form of any existing thing, bridges the gap between ourselves and the existing, outside world. Locke's understanding of how the mind knows or grasps reality is truly inadequate.

> "Nor indeed can we rank and sort things, and consequently (which is the end of sorting) denominate them by their real essences, *because we know them not*. Our faculties carry us no farther toward the knowledge and distinction of substances, than a collection of those sensible ideas which we observe in them; which, however, made with the greatest diligence and exactness we are capable of, yet it is more remote from the true internal constitution from which those qualities flow, than, as I said, a countryman's idea is from the inward contrivance of that famous clock at Strasbourg, whereof he only sees the outward figure and motions." [6]

The intellectual pessimism that is the cause of this kind of thinking has more anti-clerical and anti-religious roots than might first seem to be the case. What is the real reason for this denial of any knowledge of the substance? There are clues scattered throughout the writings of this new age of intellectuals possessed of a superficial knowledge of metaphysics that spanned a time period from the 1500s through the 19th century. There are repeated derogatory references to the 'schools' and the 'schoolmen'. Locke complains at length about the schoolmen and their lack of clarity in the notion of substance.

> "But as to our ideas of substances, we have few or no abstract names at all. For though the schools have introduced animalitas,

---

6   Ibid., pg. 413

corporietas, and some others; yet they hold no proportion with
that infinite number of names of substances, to which they never
were ridiculous enough to attempt the coining of abstract ones;
and those few that the schools forged, and put into the mouths of
their scholars, could never yet get admittance into common use,
or obtain the license of public approbation. Which seems to me at
least to intimate the confession of all mankind, that they have no
ideas of the real essences of substances, since they have not names
for such ideas..." [7]

More than likely, it was Locke and not the schoolmen who had
no idea of the meaning of substance nor did Locke understand that the
meaning of the 'real essences' is not disclosed by the essences themselves but by that which makes those essences or substances be what
they are. Locke did not understand existence, nor did he bother to
inquire further into the meaning of scholastic distinctions. Locke's failure to understand the position of classical philosophy, as advocated by
the 'schoolmen' is, in part, due to the inflexibility of scholastic thinking
in the sixteenth century. Their obsession with obscurity, as evidenced
by their use of 'Latin only' texts, (as if Latin, a metaphysically useful
language, was the only language that one could philosophize with) did
little to promote the superiority of their ideas.

The invention of the printing press in 1439 set in motion a flow
of ideas and information that enabled people, who were not officially
scholars, to engage in free thinking unencumbered by religious ideology. Unfortunately, much of the wisdom of the scholastics would not
become available until much later when the Latin texts were translated
into English. In the meantime, metaphysically speaking, many thinkers were, so to speak, busy reinventing the wheel. Ideas long-discredit-
ed began to make their way back into the public view as the scholastics
failed to keep up with the trend towards more open-minded thinking.

---

7   Ibid., pg. 415

THE DEMISE OF THE SCHOLASTICS

The Catholic priests and scholars who followed and defended the teachings of Thomas Aquinas (1225-1274) were known as scholastics or schoolmen. Aquinas synthesized the insights of Classical Greek Philosophy with the Revelation of Christianity, in his mammoth, *Summa Theologica*. The Church, while initially hesitant to endorse Aquinas, finally recognized the enormous value of his work by granting him the title of Doctor of the Church.

The casuistry (science or doctrine of settling matters of conscience) that followed in later centuries, as practiced by some scholars, had developed to such a point that they engaged in an over-classification of all aspects of human moral activity from a theological and philosophical perspective. The intellect had usurped the other powers of soul, to such a degree that philosophy lent itself to a one-sided development of human character. By the sixteenth and seventeenth centuries, they had become unimpeachable in their arrogance and encrusted with tradition to the point of being hide-bound. We see much of this same kind of insufferable certitude in Moslem apologists. They simply cannot ever be wrong. The Reformation was in part, a direct response to the rigidity of Catholic theologians and apologists.

Nonetheless, the scholastics preserved the wisdom of the Greeks and the early Church Fathers and added their own priceless contributions to the collective wisdom of the Catholic Church and mankind. No one can doubt their good intentions, hard work, and general holiness or their desire to save mankind from the darkness of immorality. The question is: despite their shortcomings, how could they have lost a cultural battle that they had fought and won for centuries? With the fall of the scholastics, the splintering of Christianity into multiple competing sects was like a second fall of Rome. The high culture of more than a thousand years, despite its obvious faults, was fragmented and further darkened.

The scholastics failed, in part, due to their inability to change and expand the formulation of their ideas, which was necessitated by the revolution that was beginning to take place in both religion and the sciences. Additionally, their understanding of the soul as a static entity, albeit supported by grace, didn't match the actual dynamism of the soul, which is rooted in the astonishing freedom of God's own Existence. God's Existence is not static or something that is complete. Rather it is so dynamic that it is pure actuality unconstrained by anything but itself. The scholastics confused their own interpretive systems with the reality of God's consciousness. Even though they would have denied this characterization, they ended up equating their abstractions with a kind of pietistic simulacrum that has very little to do with the dynamism of God's Existence except by way of analogy. It is simply not enough to say that "analogy limps" when you are describing a reality that has an infinite and exponential rate of *unchangeable change* as its Existence.

The scholastics, by not having the tools to adequately describe what we now understand as the non-local nature of Divine Consciousness, operating locally in the visible universe, opened themselves up to the charges of the Protestants that they did not believe in the saving attributes of the Personhood of God, as found in Jesus Christ. This was, of course, not entirely true but the overriding emphasis on the sacramental system,[8] instead of a transcendent and transforming personal contact with Christ, opened the Catholic doctrine up to the criticism reserved for ideological manipulation and retention of political and religious power at the expense of direct contact.

Islam as a reaction to the Christian formulation, in the person of Mohammed, was able to capitalize on the notion of God's unity at the expense of His personhood by focusing on His Oneness much like Judaism or the old monotheism of ancient Egypt. What seems to emerge

---

8   What many of the Protestant critics of Catholicism have, likewise, failed to understand is that the sacramental system was designed by Jesus to assist mankind in receiving the benefits of grace. Think of it as a kind of spiritual intranet and not merely a symbolic gesture of solidarity.

from a historical study of middle east religions is that an emphasis on either God's unity or his Personhood, at the expense of understanding (in hindsight), the dual nature of His Existence in the Reality Dysfunction creates an imbalance in the natural forces of belief. The Christian formulation that God is both Three and One is correct but in practical terms, God's unity is overshadowed in Christianity by an over-emphasis on the Three Persons. Using the particle-wave analogy of modern physics it is, perhaps, more correct to say that God is One if described non-locally and three Persons using the notion of locality to express what is fundamentally One manifesting as three Persons.

The polarity and plurality of religious beliefs generated by the Protestant Reformation was only indicative of the burning need to reformulate both metaphysics and religion into a responsive body of knowledge, accessible and understandable by all mankind. The Protestant Reformation not only failed to do this, it created an insufferable cloud of ignorance about metaphysics that still affects western culture.

The Rise of the Protestant Reformation allowed philosophy to be overtaken by the ignorance of opinion that Plato had despised. The Reformers in their zeal despised all things Catholic, including but not limited to, scholasticism and metaphysics. They began in spirit, to re-embody the dichotomy between faith and reason that had been healed for over a thousand years. The early Christian Church Father, Tertullian, felt that faith and reason could have no reciprocal relation. His famous, *"What has faith to do with reason"* might well have been the motto of the Protestants, as they slid further down the path of moral and intellectual incoherence.

THE PROTESTANTS AND THE HERESIES OF THE PAST

In order to understand why the Protestants of Locke's era were so dead set against the Catholic metaphysical formulation that was the bedrock of traditional Catholicism, we need to go back to earlier heresies that arose regarding the nature of Jesus. Many of these early heresies revolved around different interpretations of how Jesus was related to Mary, and the unchangeable nature of God. Protestantism, while not directly engaging the old heresies, embraced older notions of religion as being merely symbolic with the idea that no intermediary was required or needed between man and God.

If no intermediary was required; is there really much difference between God, conceived of as Apollo, and God described as the Holy Trinity? Other than the assertion that one God is "truer" than the other, the subjective claim of receiving benefits from Apollo could not be dismissed on the basis of another equally subjective claim pertaining to the benefits obtained from believing in Jesus Christ. Without an understanding of the non-local nature and effect of the Catholic sacraments, they simply devolve, in the Protestant world view, into mere symbolism.

One of the first major heresies was *Arianism*, first proposed early in the 4th century by the Alexandrian presbyter Arius, in Egypt. It affirmed that Christ was not truly divine but only a created being. Arius' basic premise was that the uniqueness of God, who alone is self-existent and immutable, would preclude the notion of a man who shared in this divine self-existence. Many modern day Protestants act as if Jesus had no power to invest the "keys of the kingdom" in one institution. The idea that Jesus came to found multiple versions of Christianity is repugnant to both reason and common sense.

The Nestorians[9] in approximately 386 AD proclaimed that Mary was only the mother of Jesus the man and not mother of the Son of God. This essentially reduced Jesus to a kind of prophet or figurehead. The Docetists,[10] beginning in 190 AD, claimed that the physical presence of Jesus was just a projection or manifestation of the Second Person of the Trinity and that Jesus was not, therefore, a real man. The

---

9 Nestorianism is a Christological doctrine that emphasizes the disunion between the human and divine natures of Jesus. It was advanced by Nestorius (386–450), Patriarch of Constantinople from 428–431. [WP]

10 A heretical sect dating back to Apostolic times. Their name is derived from dokesis, "appearance" or "semblance", because they taught that Christ only "appeared" or "seemed to be a man, to have been born, to have lived and suffered. [WP]

common thread running through these three heresies was what we would refer to today as symbolism. Jesus, according to these early heresies, would only have been a symbol of some sort of divine action. This is a teaching that many Protestant denominations have adopted over the years despite paying lip service to the divinity of Christ. If the Protestant Eucharist is merely a symbol, for example, it is a hop, skip and jump to reducing all of Christianity to symbolism—if not in theory then in practice.

JESUS AND THE THEOLOGIANS

Jesus presented a profound problem to both philosophers and theologians. How do you metaphysically account for a man who claims to be the Son of God? It took the Catholic Church no less than three Ecumenical Councils to hammer out a complete understanding of how Jesus could be both God and man without falling into metaphysical and theological error in terms of the formulation. The Council of Nicea in 325 AD, the Council of Ephesus in 431 AD and the Council of Chalcedon in 451 AD finally concluded with the teaching that Jesus Christ was a divine person with two natures in a hypostatic[11] union. Intellectually this formulation makes sense as it preserves both the unchanging nature of God and his human nature. Nonetheless, given that God's nature is impassible or unchanging, the Incarnation presents a unique challenge to this point of view. How, exactly does an unchanging God become a man by assuming a human nature?

The solution of the Councils was that the Second Person of the Trinity "assumes" a human nature in time. This formulation also presents a unique set of difficulties. Did Jesus, as God and Man, not exist prior to the Incarnation except as a kind of abstract excellence within the Divine Essence? This is logically problematic for a number of reasons even though Jesus, as a man, does not add anything to God

---

11 Hypostatic Union (from the Greek meaning sediment, foundation, substance, or subsistence) is a term in Christian theology employs to describe the union of two natures: Christ's humanity and divinity in one hypostasis, or individual existence.

that God does not already have. The problem revolves around *how* the eternal Second Person of the Trinity *engages the change in time* that is required for His Person to Incarnate. Either the change is integral to eternity in some way or Jesus the man, as both God and man, only comes to exist in the virtual reality that is created by the Reality Dysfunction.

The Gospel of John, Chapter 7, reveals an extraordinary dynamic between God and humanity, and between Jesus and the Father. Jesus tells them that they will be taught by God. The larger message is that God has a "system" for transmitting His life to humanity. One of these systemic instruments is the institution of the Eucharist. This is not just a symbol but a real means of transmitting the life of grace between God the Father and humanity. (Keep this question in the back of your mind: does grace work by magic or is it a real effect that might be measured scientifically, albeit, indirectly?)

"Stop grumbling among yourselves," Jesus answered. "No one can come to me unless the Father who sent me draws them, and I will raise them up at the last day. It is written in the Prophets: 'They will all be taught by God.' Everyone who has heard the Father and learned from him comes to me. No one has seen the Father except the one who is from God; only he has seen the Father. Very truly I tell you, the one who believes has eternal life. I am the bread of life. Your ancestors ate the manna in the wilderness, yet they died. But here is the bread that comes down from heaven, which anyone may eat and not die. I am the living bread that came down from heaven. Whoever eats this bread will live forever. This bread is my flesh, which I will give for the life of the world."[12]

"Then the Jews began to argue sharply among themselves, "How can this man give us his flesh to eat?" Jesus said to them, "Very truly I tell you, unless you eat the flesh of the Son of Man and drink his blood, you have no life in you. Whoever eats my flesh and drinks my blood has eternal life, and I will raise them up at the last day. For my

---

12 The Gospel of John 6:43-53

flesh is real food and my blood is real drink. Whoever eats my flesh and drinks my blood remains in me, and I in them. Just as the living Father sent me and I live because of the Father, so the one who feeds on me will live because of me. This is the bread that came down from heaven. Your ancestors ate manna and died, but whoever feeds on this bread will live forever." [13]

He said this while teaching in the synagogue in Capernaum. On hearing it, many of his disciples said, "This is a hard teaching. Who can accept it?" Aware that his disciples were grumbling about this, Jesus said to them, "Does this offend you? *Then what if you see the Son of Man ascend to where he was before!* The Spirit gives life; the flesh counts for nothing [because it is the manifestation of a deeper reality]. The words I have spoken to you—they are full of the Spirit and life. Yet there are some of you who do not believe." For Jesus had known from the beginning which of them did not believe and who would betray him. He went on to say, "This is why I told you that no one can come to me unless the Father has enabled them."[14]

The notion of God as a "consumable" leading to eternal life has no antecedent of any significance in antiquity. The relationship between God and man, as portrayed in the Old Testament, has come full circle. Not only does God the Father "enable" men, his Son is now going to enter further into human existence as a form of spiritual nourishment. Those listening to Jesus think he may have gone off the deep end. The metaphysical implications are profound for anyone who is willing to think about it. Is this really and truly God who will feed us or is it a derivation of God—an intermediary form whereby human beings have a new, participated relationship with the Infinite One? The answer that bridges all poles of the question is one that says that God is really and truly feeding us but He is doing it through a derivative or physical manifestation[15] of Himself in time.

---

13 Ibid

14 Ibid

15 Transmogrification or the changing of one form into another is a kind of spiritual al-
chemy that would be the prerogative of Existence. In the case of the bread and wine in

The Jews said, "this is a hard teaching" and many of them left him. We have to ask ourselves what this might mean in terms of the Reality Dysfunction. The Jews rightfully felt that the Eternal One could not possibly interact with them in this way. What they were missing is that there is a third alternative, a third way of considering God's presence in the world. The Eucharist is a creation in time and, as such, is a non-local bridge between time and eternity. It is not un-created, it is created and it is, much like the rest of creation, is a kind of virtual reality in relation to God. This third alternative is that God's presence in the world is a derivative or local presence of a nature that is fundamentally non-local.

Despite hundreds of books written on the subject of God's presence in the world, the answer as to how God's non-local nature might be manifested locally, given the eternal and unchangeable nature of God, has never been entirely clear. The Catholic notion of the Mystical Body of Christ fingers the reality but the Mystical Body can only be understood as an extension or modality of Christ's presence in the world. What that presence is or how it can be, when an unchangeable God is involved, is the million-dollar question. The Reality Dysfunction, whereby God knows Himself, outside himself or locally, is an attempt to get some traction on a very difficult set of ideas that relate to God's Existence within and outside of time.

God's knowing Himself, outside Himself, results in the body of humanity united to the Divine Person as part of our collective and divine heritage. What Jesus does with the institution of the Eucharist is make what was previously un-manifest now manifest. What the New Age movement refers to as blended personalities[16] is an apt metaphor for Christians in a "state of grace". They are blended personalities, exhibiting both their own personal qualities and those of Christ. The

---

Catholic Theology, the form of the bread is changed into the form of Existence, which is, by its nature invisible. How such a change can be mediated between the Eternal and the temporal is an algorithmic mystery.

16 A blended personality is one in which a human being, through contact with disembodied entities, becomes "blended" in that where one begins and where the other leaves off starts to become blurred.

difference between Protestants and Catholics, in this regard, is one of degree. There is nothing to prevent God from being available to all men without the intermediary function of Church but Jesus specifically states that He came to found a Church upon the "rock of Peter"— meaning the rock of human weakness—as it might be transformed by grace in participation with His Divine Nature. The fundamental difference between Protestantism and Catholicism, in this regard, is not merely doctrinal but existential. Jesus either had the power to set up an institution for the purpose of dispensing grace through a new medium or He did not.

This new medium is, I will suggest, a multi-dimensional access to, or non-local participation in Divine Life that is real. In other words, grace cannot be concocted merely by human imagination but is, in fact, the operation of Divine Intelligence, manifested locally within human affairs. When Catholics say that they feel better in a state of grace than they do outside of that state, what they mean is that they have a real experience of the indwelling presence of Spirit, which makes them feel whole or complete. This is a local experience of the affect and effect of a non-local reality.

Conflicting statements provided by Jesus Himself in regards to what he meant by "Church" suggests that he may not have fully understood how his followers might interpret His words.[17] Stating that the Father desires "worshippers in Spirit and Truth" rather than those who just "rattle off prayers like the pagans do" lends itself to the Protestant interpretation of diffused Church authority. What we can read into this is that Jesus was for a lighter and more effective ministry than what we currently see in Church hierarchies, which have only replicated the appalling focus on legalism that He condemned the Pharisees for.

---

17 A more correct interpretation would be that His words were never properly recorded and the bits that we have, based on second-hand accounts outside of the Gospel of John, may be suspect to some degree.

JESUS AND THE REALITY DYSFUNCTION

"And He is the image of the invisible God, the first-born of all creation. For by Him all things were created, both in the heavens and on earth, visible and invisible, whether thrones or dominions or rulers or authorities—all things have been created by Him and for Him. And He is before all things, and in Him all things hold together. "

—Colossians 1:15-21

One interpretation of the Reality Dysfunction is to assert that God's self-knowledge of Himself, outside Himself, finds its full expression in Jesus Christ and the creation. An understanding of how Jesus is linked to the entire universe tends to shed light on His suffering and persecution. A Divine Person cannot be said to suffer, except within the context of a virtual or derivative reality. Does the eternal Father experience the suffering of the eternal Son? Does the eternal Holy Spirit suffer? How then can Jesus Christ suffer without a relative separation between the Person of God as Christ and the Person of God as the blended entity of Jesus Christ? It may be that both God the Father and the Third Person of the Trinity function as a kind of higher self within the human consciousness of Jesus. This would mean that Jesus might not have been fully conscious of His divine nature, *as a man would understand it.* Indeed, how could flesh hold the non-local knowledge that only a discarnate being could fully have?

This notion would be brushed off by adherents of the *hypostatic union*,[18] as being explained by the perfection of God not changing, except as a manifestation within time. The Incarnation would be thought of as adding nothing new to God that He does not already possess. The hypostatic union is a formulation of how One Person can be joined to

---

18 A theological term used with reference to the Incarnation to express the revealed truth that in Christ, one person subsists in two natures, the Divine and the human. Hypostasis means that which lies beneath as basis or foundation.

both human and Divine Natures without change occurring in God. It is still not a full accounting of why God would chose to operate in this way or how it really might work. If anything, the notion of the hypostatic union tends to confirm that the Incarnation only occurs within the virtual reality we have described as the Reality Dysfunction. In other words, we can confirm that the union of the Divine Person with two natures occurs without change in God but how this might be interpreted in the light of the Reality Dysfunction may be at odds with the traditional understanding of creation. The Reality Dysfunction does, however, enable us to better understand what creation is in relation to the Divine Mind.

All of creation is analogous to the hypostatic union when it is considered from the perspective of the Reality Dysfunction. Creation is a local function of a non-local entity.

"Our Father, who art in Heaven, hallowed be thy name, thy kingdom come, thy will be done on earth as it is in Heaven." These words of Jesus, expressed in prayer, perfectly express the derivative consciousness of God in the Reality Dysfunction. The kingdom, which is to come, is already known. God is not waiting for the kingdom to come. It is here now according to Jesus, waiting only for us to acknowledge that it exists. This is why faith is so important to Him: it is an acknowledgement of the invisible power of God the Father in the here and now. The Father's Existence for Jesus is a metaphysical constant that He refers to many times. The notion that He is "the Son of Man" captures his reluctance to say that He is God. He does not say "I am God." What He does is attempt to express, in the language of his time, the limitation of his relationship to the Father, as the Son of Man. Christians interpret this to mean that Jesus, as the second person of the Trinity, assumed a human nature in time without the change occurring in eternity but we do have to ask ourselves what this might mean in practical metaphysical terms.

The notions of God's Nature and God's kingdom can be expressed as follows. An infinity of energy, consciousness and love knows each thing at one instant, in a created moment, outside of eternity that produces space, time and matter in the transcendental Act of God knowing Himself, outside Himself that is limited only by His own Nature. This limitation is necessitated by the immutable fact that God cannot change. What changes is reality in relation to God, not the other way around and this is why Jesus was reluctant to talk about Himself, except in relatively vague language. He is God but He isn't God in the Reality Dysfunction, which allows God to assume a human nature in time. God cannot change, so God does not assume a human nature in eternity but in time, and this can only be in a derivative or virtual reality. There can be no change in God, otherwise the Incarnation would represent something new to God. This is a fundamental paradox that Jesus indicates by word and deed.

There are certain peculiar sayings attributed to Jesus that indicate some incongruities in terms of His Divine knowledge that are in conformity with the limiting dynamics of the Reality Dysfunction. When He says, for example, that only the Father "knows the day and the hour" of the end of the world, Jesus appears not to know what a fully equal and conscious member of Godhead would know with certainty. Likewise, when he cries out on the cross, "my God, my God why have you abandoned me," there is the sense that Jesus *the man* did not fully understand what Jesus the Second Person of the Trinity surely would have known. And how could He have known? Any divine person that manifests locally, is "part" of a non-local Existence that is infinitely greater but the hypostatic link between locality and non-locality, in this instance, may be subject to the dynamics of the Reality Dysfunction.

There is room within these two, perhaps, overly-commented upon instances, for a theological investigation into the psychological consequences[19] of one Person having two natures. Indeed, the Incarnation of Christ may be a metaphor for our own existence. We are God

19 This is one of the subjects of Kenotic Theology.

"locally" knowing Himself as Jesus, in all of His humanity, and that includes us—in a derivative way. Jesus was, in a very real sense, the "firstborn of all creation" as St. Paul noted, at the beginning of this section, in Colossians 1:15-21.

The rest of humanity follows His lead and are linked to Him due to his transformation of human nature *before* and after the Incarnation in terms of a non-local spiritual and evolutionary pressure that manifests locally in time. If a Divine and non-local person truly assumed human nature, then humanity can never be the same. This is one of the reasons that Christians divide history into B.C. and A.D. (before Christ and in the year of our Lord or Anno Domini). It is pure historical revisionism to refer to A.D. as the Common Era. What made it "common" was the commonly held belief that Jesus Christ was the Son of God and that one Church alone represented this commonality.

The reduction of a personal God to the idea of Existence or radical extra-mentality is metaphysically useful but cannot be used to describe the larger reality of His Existence both non-locally and locally. Philosophical principles do not exist solely in the abstract. God's Existence is a living reality that can only be understood in terms of what might be described as a phenomenology of Divine subjectivity. The *Reality Dysfunction*, in which the Infinite considers Itself infinitely and locally in time, assures us that there will always be more to understand about God, not less.

HOBBES' CRUSADE AGAINST METAPHYSICS

Thomas Hobbes' (1588-1679) book, *Leviathan*, has elements of an old-fashioned Protestant disdain for metaphysical intellection that has, ultimately, resulted in our modern disdain for the linking of time to eternity. Note that Hobbes, who would have lived in the shadow of Henry VIII's Anglican Church, is already on the path of religious deconstruction that is so common to the present age. The Anglicans will insist that they are not Protestants but the reality is that they were, ultimately, part of the movement of "New Men" that the Reformation produced and that the Church of England concurred with, albeit in a more limited way.

> *"Now to descend to the particular tenets of vain philosophy, derived to the Universities, and thence into the Church, partly from Aristotle, partly from blindness of understanding...From these metaphysics, which are mingled with the Scripture to make school divinity, we are told, there be in the world certain essences separated from bodies, which they call abstract essences and substantial forms. For the interpreting of which jargon, there is need of somewhat more than ordinary attention in this place. Also I ask pardon of those that are not used to this kind of discourse, for applying myself to those that are...And if it were so, that there were a language without any verb answerable to est, or is, or be: yet the men that used it would be not a jot the less capable of inferring, concluding, and of all kinds of reasoning, than were the Greeks and Latins. But what would become of these terms entity, essence, essential, essentiality that are derived from it and of many more on these, applied as they most commonly are? They are therefore no names of things; but signs, by which we make known, that we conceive the consequences of one name or attribute to another."* [20]

All this would be laughable but Hobbes is dead serious. He manages to mix a serious ignorance of philosophy with a shameless insinuation of sectarian un-patriotism in the following:

> *"But to what purpose, may some man say, is such subtlety in a work of this nature, where I pretend to nothing but what is necessary to the doctrine of government and obedience? It is to this*

20 T.V. Smith, Marjorie Green, *From Descartes to Locke*, University of Chicago Press, 1940, pgs. 120-122.

purpose, that men may no longer suffer themselves to be abused, by them, (i.e., the Catholic clerics) that by this doctrine of separated essences, built on the vain philosophy of Aristotle, would fright them from obeying the laws of their country, with empty names; as men fright birds from the corn with an empty doublet, a hat, and a crooked stick...Upon the same ground they say, that the figure, and color and taste of a piece of bread (i.e., the Eucharist) has a being, there where they say there is no bread. And upon this same ground they say, that faith and wisdom, and other virtues, are sometimes poured into a man, sometimes blown into him from Heaven, as if the virtuous and their virtues could be asunder; and a great many other things that serve to lessen the dependence of subjects on the sovereign power of their country." [21]

Hobbes is a classic example of a man who does not understand the difference between intellectual, moral and spiritual values. Think of him as a more educated version of TV host, Bill Maher. He is typical of his time in that he supposes that intellectual excellence in the form of science will very soon dispense with the need for the Catholic metaphysics and spirituality that he mocks. His attack on Aristotle and the Eucharist is, however, curiously appropriate from his point of view. The notion of *transubstantiation* or the transformation of the *form* of the bread, into the form of God is a Thomistic metaphysical formulation that is based on both Aristotle and Aquinas' teaching on matter and form. Hobbes correctly assaults this notion as irrelevant blather because if he didn't, he might have to take it seriously. The dismissal of metaphysics by intellectually retrograde thinkers is typical of all shallow thinking. Dismiss what is not understood as nonsense—then no thinking about it is required. Hobbes, like many of the liberals of our time, have their own version of transubstantiation: they transform truth into irrelevancy and clarity into intellectual gibberish.

---

21 Ibid

BERKELEY AND PARMENIDES

George Berkeley (1685-1753) attempted to bridge the gap created by the demise of scholasticism and the ascent of the metaphysically crippled reasoning evidenced in the writings of Thomas Hobbes and John Locke. Berkeley was an English Anglican Bishop who attempted to link God back to metaphysics:

> *"The observing mind of God makes possible the continued apparent existence of material objects. God arouses sensations in us on a regular, coherent order. Selves and God make up the universe."* [22]

Unfortunately, Berkeley obscures the essential distinction between essence and Existence (the 'real distinction') with his idea that God causes any sensations that we might have. The first part of what he says is correct, if we understand quantum decoherence to be the result of an eternal observer, but it does not follow that God is both the doer and the doing without making some critical distinctions.

What is clear in Berkeley's formulation is the Parmenidean idea of all things really only being manifestations of the One. If God does not grant reality its own separate existence, by way of participation, then He Himself is the manifestation of the Many, i.e., all the existing things that we see and experience. This sort of pantheistic thinking, which has become common in the twenty-first century, puts us into bed with the Hindus and the notion of Maya—the illusion created by the thinking of the One. Ultimately, the notion of Maya, in the popular imagination, becomes a reason to deny objective notions of morality. If everything is an illusion, then causality and my responsibility for causality is also an illusion. On the other hand, understanding Maya as the quantum decoherence of an original unity, caused by an eternal observer, keeps the moral link between locality and non-locality open.

---

22 Ibid

O'REILLY'S SECOND MORAL LAW

Many years ago, the following incredible statement was printed in an editorial in the Washington Post:

> *"The urge to rape is like the physical craving for food or sleep, some experts say. And despite increasing penalties for committing the crime, there is no way to cure that hunger."* [23]

The moral cluelessness of this statement by so-called experts ought to be enough to disgust any normal person. There is no doubt that individuals with powerful sex drives may feel this way but to assert this position as if there were no way of resisting it borders on moral absurdity. This kind of thinking is a direct consequence of a causeless view of reality, where desires dominate rationality, and human beings are helpless to control them. Man is the efficient cause of his own actions. The kinds of actions we have to resist can increase our moral strength. The failure to make some attempt to resist what may be reasonably construed as "bad desires" is moral cowardice. Perhaps the urge to murder will next be included in the experts' list of incurable human problems.

There are dreadful consequences that await those who abdicate reality to the causeless muck of reality as envisioned by Jean Paul Sartre in 1905.

> *"I lean my hand on the seat but pull it back hurriedly: it exists. This thing I'm sitting on, leaning my hand on, is called a seat. They make it purposely for people to sit on, they took leather, springs and cloth, they went to work with the idea of making a seat and when they finished, that was what they had made...I murmur: It's a seat, a little like an exorcism. But the word stays on my lips: it refuses to go and put itself on the thing. It stays*

---

23 Keller, Marjorie, *The Washington Post*, date unknown

what is, with its red plush, thousands of little red paws in the air,
all still, little dead paws. This enormous belly turned upward,
bleeding, inflated...it is not a seat. It could just as well be a dead
donkey...It seems ridiculous to call them seats or to say anything
at all about them; I am in the midst of things, nameless things.
Alone, without words, defenseless, they surround me, are beneath
me, behind me, above me. They demand nothing, they don't
impose themselves: they are there." [24]

I read these lines and I ask myself, how is it possible that anyone could agree with this perception of reality? The answer is painfully clear. Many individuals experience reality, on occasion, just as Sartre did. The ultimate, and awful conclusion is that perceptions get translated according to the rules and principles laid down by the mind and enforced by the will. If the mind is so unstructured, as to allow negative ideas and appetites to pass, morally unfiltered by the will into its processes, then the mind's eye can become full of lurid and depraved images. When feelings are not interrogated for moral significance or are, a-priori, deemed ontologically meaningless, then acts of violence become intelligible. Why not stick a knife in someone's eye, or kill, or rape? These are things with no moral significance; only the heavy honey of pleasure creates a glue of meaning for these acts. The growth in meaninglessness and hopelessness is a result of not observing the consequences of denying O'Reilly's Second Moral Law:

When moral ideas are not linked to non-local values, there is
little or no accountability or meaning.

Recently, a young man was attacked and killed by Hispanic and black degenerates wielding machetes. One pair of these clueless individuals decided that they couldn't wait to have sex so they copulated

---

24 John Paul Sartre, Nausea, from *A History of Western Philosophy: Kant to Wittgenstein and Sartre,* W. T. Jones, pg. 421

next to the dead body.[25] During another, unrelated crime, there was a heterosexual couple (this time two Caucasians) who had sex on top of the two men they had just murdered but "couldn't get off" because it was "weird".[26] Now if anyone thinks that this kind of cross-racial behavior is not the result of the moral sterility that results from a kind of practical atheism or is not directly or indirectly caused by the uncritical consumption of illicit sex and porn, then please consult your nearest witch doctor. There are, unfortunately, serious consequences when reality, indeed the world, is perceived as part of a mindless universe without connection to moral and spiritual values, or even a way of knowing or connecting to any set of values that might reside in a higher reality than brute matter.

KANT'S DANCE ON THE GRAVEYARD OF SCHOLASTICISM

Aristotle and Thomas Aquinas' concept of reality is bracing when compared to the obscure epistemological deliberations of Immanuel Kant or the later, vague assertions of modern psychologists in regards to how the mind processes knowledge. The notion, for example, that the mind works like a camera is so superficial as not to be worthy of serious consideration. When was the last time your camera expressed an interest in your photographs? Likewise, theories of "constructive interaction" are all addenda to the notion that learning and knowledge are just the aggregation of one set of electrons, by association, with another. There is no hierarchy of objective values that the mind engages in atheistic or politically correct derivatives of process philosophy. There are only "associations" that are organized based on various cooperation agreements or natural forces that themselves are entirely relative.

---

25 Hacked to Death: http://www.nydailynews.com/news/crime/florida-students-hack-boy-17-machete-bury-alive-article-1.2331701

26 http://www.huffingtonpost.com/2014/09/26/joshua-miner-alisa-massa-ro-sex-dead-bodies_n_5889822.html

Aristotle, on the other hand, relates thinking directly to the soul:

*"If thinking is like perceiving, it must be either a process in which the soul is acted upon by what is capable of being thought, or a process different from but analogous to that. **The thinking part of the soul must therefore be, while impassable, capable of receiving the form of the object; that it, must be potentially identical in character with its object without being the object.** Mind must be related to what is thinkable, as sense is to what is sensible...It was a good idea to call the soul the 'place of forms'; though this description holds only of the intellective soul, and even this is the forms only potentially, not actually...**Actual knowledge is identical with its object**...It follows that the soul is analogous to the hand; for as the hand is a tool of tools, so the mind is the form of forms..."* [27]

Aristotle's epistemology, with its precise algorithms between body and soul, was forcefully reiterated in the work of St. Thomas Aquinas and applied to many of the problems that were involved in explaining how spiritual and moral truths could be reliably known. For Thomas Aquinas, there was no contradiction between faith, truth and reason—only logical difficulties that could be overcome through the careful wielding of distinctions. There was, in fact, no stated division between the Rationalist and the Empirical mindset until both the Renaissance and The Reformation had effectively wrecked the carefully constructed world of the medieval philosophers and theologians. Philosophy, from the time of Plato and Aristotle and up through the Middle Ages, was profoundly rationalist and only empirical insofar as facts could be observed. The soul, for example, cannot, at present, be the subject of empirical inquiry but for the rationalist it is an obvious hypothetical and theoretical construct.

Kant's intention was to move beyond the burgeoning dichotomy between Rationalism and Empiricism, which had been generated by

27 Mckeon, *The Basic Works of Aristotle*, On the Soul (De Anima), Bk 111, Ch. 7

the fall of the scholastic world view that saw the world as being pro-foundly knowable. "The rationalists had tried to show that we can understand the world by careful use of reason; this guarantees the [fac-ticity] of our knowledge but leaves serious questions about its practical content. The empiricists, on the other hand, had argued that all of our knowledge must be firmly grounded in experience; practical content is thus secured, but it turns out that we can be certain of very little. Both approaches have failed, Kant supposed, because both are premised on the same mistaken assumption."[28]

"Progress in philosophy, according to Kant, requires that we frame the epistemological problem in an entirely different way. The crucial question is not *how we can bring ourselves to understand the world, but how the world comes to be understood by us.* Instead of trying, by reason or experience, to make our concepts match the nature of objects, Kant held, we must allow the structure of our concepts shape our experience of objects. This is the purpose of Kant's Critique of Pure Reason (1781, 1787): to show how reason determines the con-ditions under which experience and knowledge are possible."[29] This represents a radically different algorithm of knowledge and judgement than was entertained by the ancient world, which saw careful judge-ments as being reliable to the extent that the data provided was reli-able. (The notion of epistemological uncertainty was later taken up by Korzybski in his work on General Semantics, which we will examine in later a later chapter.)

What we can see at work in Kant is the assumption that mental structures, in addition to what is "out there" are together deter-mining what it is we can actually know reliably. This is not a problem for the rationalist at all, as knowledge of the outside world is assumed to be reliable and why wouldn't it be so?

---

28 http://www.philosophypages.com/hy/5f.htm
29 Ibid: http://www.philosophypages.com/hy/5f.htm

What was a problem for Kant and the emerging empirical mentality was an imagined or contrived problem, which was based on the fundamental and hidden desire to render the entire metaphysical enterprise of the scholastics a matter of theological artifice. If religious truths could be subject to metaphysical uncertainly, then they could be dismissed. It is the opinion of this author that the split between Rationalism, as it was represented by the ancients, and Empiricism as represented by metaphysical juveniles like Descartes, was driven by the will to disbelieve old truths. In other words, the power of religion was broken by empiricism by subjecting the data of religion to a standard that denied the reality of the soul and its metaphysical powers.

"In the *Prolegomena to any Future Metaphysic* (1783) Kant presented the central themes of the first Critique in a somewhat different manner, starting from instances in which we do appear to have achieved knowledge and asking under what conditions each case becomes possible. So he began by carefully drawing a pair of crucial distinctions among the judgments we do actually make. The first distinction separates *a priori* from *a posteriori* judgments by reference to the origin of our knowledge of them. A priori judgments are based upon reason alone, independently of all sensory experience, and therefore apply with strict universality.

A posteriori judgments, on the other hand, must be grounded upon experience and are consequently limited and uncertain in their application to specific cases. Thus, this distinction also marks the difference traditionally noted in logic between necessary and contingent truths."[30] This is a distinction that Aristotelian epistemology, which is fundamentally based on knowing by *becoming the form of the thing known*, does not require. Judgement, for the Aristotelian, comes after knowing the form, it does not construct the form out of an algorithmic hodgepodge of sensory data. The sensory data simply confirms the existence of the form in the same way that heat confirms the existence of a heat source. The source itself exists independently of our senses.

---

30 Ibid: http://www.philosophypages.com/hy/5f.htm

"But Kant also made a less familiar distinction between analytic and synthetic judgments, according to the information conveyed as their content. Analytic judgments are those whose predicates are wholly contained in their subjects; since they add nothing to our concept of the subject, such judgments are purely explicative and can be deduced from the principle of non-contradiction. Synthetic judgments, on the other hand, are those whose predicates are wholly distinct from their subjects, to which they must be shown to relate because of some real connection external to the concepts themselves. Hence, synthetic judgments are genuinely informative but require justification by reference to some outside principle."[31]

Kant supposed that previous philosophers had failed to differentiate properly between these two distinctions. However, Kant's vague description of judgment, as his fundamental concept, leaves much to be desired.

> "*A movement of thought in which two items are brought together and combined. We judge whenever we say, that house is large, that dog is a Sealyham, or the interior angles of a triangle equal two right angles. The mind brings the items together in judgment because it detects a connection between them.*" [32]

"A movement of thought?" Could Kant be more opaque? What sort of dance was he doing on the graveyard of scholasticism? We might as well argue that a dog or a cat could analyze and compare thoughts in the same way. Comparison, as a concept, does not correctly or algorithmically describe what actually happens in thought and judgment. Comparison is the end result of a deeper epistemological process than comparison of camera-like images. For Aristotle and Thomas Aquinas, in judgment, the *agent intellect* affirms or denies based on what the

---

31 Ibid
32 W.T. Jones, *A History of Western Philosophy: Kant to Wittgenstein and Sartre*, Harcourt Brace and World Inc., Atlanta, pg. 63

possible intellect has become on the *plane of the act of knowing.*[33]   If we translate this in terms of local and non-local interaction, we can say that both the intellect and the will have non-local access to information. Ultimately, this is what distinguishes the rationalist from the empiricist. The rationalist takes the information provided by empirical science and says look here! What do you think this means if you add X, as in some sort of synthetic a-priori information, to it?

EPISTEMOLOGICAL ALGORITHMS

Aristotelian and Thomistic epistemology involves a non-local conversion of information that is first grasped, locally, through the senses. This is known as *conversio ad phantasm* in Latin or simply, "the conversion to the phantasm". This dialog between local sensory data and the non-local processes of the soul is what might be called an *epistemological algorithm*. Step 1: the *possible intellect* is that part of the intellectual power that like a piece of soft wax, enables our souls to receive the impression of any form processed via sensory data. Step 2: the agent intellect, as a different manifestation of the same power, enables us to receive and to categorize the sense impressions and phantasms generated by forms impacting the possible intellect. What this means concretely is that we know things by *becoming* them in a non-local manner. We really know the thing itself with the same certainty that we know ourselves. We can compare because we know that there are differences between ourselves and things that exist outside of our individual consciousness.

> *"For Thomas Aquinas, the human intellect's understanding of essences depends on "phantasms," or likenesses of particulars, which are formed by the imagination from sensory experience of particulars. From such phantasms, the agent intellect abstracts the "intelligible species" that are likenesses of universals, and which inform the possible intellect, making possible acts of cognizing*

---

33 Wilhelmsen, Frederick, College Lectures, University of Dallas, 1970-1974

'man' or 'horse' universally. But Aquinas also insists on another, more puzzling role for the phantasms in intellectual cognition: In the moment of cognizing 'man' or 'horse', the intellect "turns toward the phantasms in order to behold the universal nature in the individual of which it is the essence." The authority for this view comes from Aristotle's statement in De Anima that "the soul in no way understands without phantasms," and that "it understands the species of intellectives in the phantasms." [34]

Kant, on the other hand, argued that we could never know the thing itself *(the noumenon)* [35] as the inmost reality of things remained inaccessible to the human intellect. Without a scientific understanding of the notions of locality and non-locality, which was several hundred years in the future, it was simply easier to dismiss the *conversio ad phantasm* as an Aristotelian and scholastic invention unrelated to reality. Kant was an early espouser of the notion that we only grasp effects or processes. What Kant called *synthetic a-priori judgements* [36] leaves a rationalist loophole, if you will, in his epistemology. What is even the basis for the possibility of synthetic a-priori judgements if not Existence itself? If the mind cannot know anything with certainty, or with so many filters that it can be interrogated for authenticity and deemed unreliable, then moral relativism[37] will not be an illogical consequence.

---

34 Cory Scarpelli, Therese, What Is an Intellectual "Turn"? The Liber de Causis, Avicenna, and Aquinas's Turn to Phantasms http://www.scielo.org.mx/scielo.php?script=sci_arttext&pid=S0188-66492013000200004

35 Ibid

36 "Analytic a-posteriori judgments cannot arise, since there is never any need to appeal to experience in support of a purely explicative assertion. Synthetic a-posteriori judgments are the relatively uncontroversial matters of fact we come to know by means of our sensory experience (though Wolff had tried to derive even these from the principle of contradiction).Analytic a-priori judgments, everyone agrees, include all merely logical truths and straightforward matters of definition; they are necessarily true. *Synthetic a priori judgments are the crucial case,* since only they could provide new information that is necessarily true. But neither Leibniz nor Hume considered the possibility of any such case. http://www.philosophypages.com/hy/5f.htm

37 Moral relativism is the view that moral judgments are true or false only relative to some particular standpoint (for instance, that of a culture or a historical period) and that no standpoint is uniquely privileged over all others.

Kant tried to climb back up the ladder of realism but never quite made it back to the top. What he did was make a-priori synthetic judgments, the peephole onto being and Existence. If he had simply been able to look around the metaphysical corner that was blocking his view, he would have seen the wide avenues of epistemological knowledge that Aristotle and Aquinas had already bequeathed to the modern world. Unfortunately, the Catholic Church had wrapped the magnificent epistemology of Aristotle and Aquinas in so many layers of pietism that no one could see the beauty of the mechanics underneath all the dross. The legacy of Kant and the subsequent school of German idealism,[38] (best espoused by Fichte, Schelling and Hegel) despite Kant's substantial moral philosophy and his intention to the contrary was, ultimately, to result in greater metaphysical uncertainty and not less.

We do, however, have to ask ourselves—again—what Kant was trying to recover or what were the gaps in metaphysics that prompted his investigations and those of many of his contemporaries? A morally sober reflection on history indicates that once the scholastics were banished from the academic scene in Protestant Europe, a metaphysical desolation set in. The metaphysics of being, and the rational and cleanly constructed epistemology, so well-articulated by Aristotle, Aquinas and many others, once discarded, left a huge hole in the collective intelligence of the West. It was this philosophical "hole" regarding basic epistemology that Thomas Hobbes (1588-1677), John Locke (1632-1704), Spinoza, (1632-1677) Leibniz (1646-1716), Kant (1724-1804) and the German school of idealism, along with the Masons and even the Illuminati tried to fill after Descartes attempted to deconstruct and reconstruct metaphysics on what we would now call an empirical basis.

Descartes (1596-1650) superficial, "I think therefore I am" is metaphysically backwards. "I am; therefore, I think" would be the better understanding. The consequences of understanding *being*, as a discontinuous process, without reference to Existence, leads to many

---

38 German idealism is the name of a movement in German philosophy that began in the 1780's and lasted until the 1840's.

intellectual difficulties. The problems caused by this view of being and reality were noted early on, by the famous 16th century poet John Donne.

> *"And new philosophy calls all in doubt,*
> *The element of fire is quiet put out;*
> *The sun is lost, and the earth, and no man's wit*
> *Can well direct him where to look for it.*
> *And freely men confess that this world's spent,*
> *When in the planets, and firmament*
> *They seek so many new, then see that this*
> *Is crumbled out again to atomies.*
> *Tis all in pieces, all coherence gone;*
> *All just supply, and all relation:*
> *Prince, subject, Father Son, are things forgot. "* [39]

DESCARTES AND THE SUBJECT-OBJECT DICHOTOMY

> *"Since Descartes' time the problem of the subject object relation*
> *has bedeviled philosophy's attempts to understand the world. The*
> *framework it has left us with has been one in which we picture*
> *the subject as something 'here' and the object as another thing*
> *'there,' and their relations as describable according to the laws*
> *of causality... This is the notion of the Cartesian grid as somehow*
> *prior to and determinative of being...Aristotle, in relativising*
> *both space and time, systematically undermines the possibility of*
> *such a grid and, thus cuts off from the start the modern problem-*
> *atic of the subject-object relation. "* [40]

---

39 Donne, John, *An Anatomy of the World, Bartlett's Familiar Quotations*, pg. 254
40 James R. Mensch, *Aristotle and the Overcoming of the Subject Object Dichotomy*, ACPA
    Quarterly, Autumn 1991, pg. 465

The mechanical conception of cause and effect, in vogue in the seventeenth century had much to do with Descartes' inaccurate understanding of causality. The notion of time as a linear sequence with past, present and future as completely exclusive terms has contributed to our present misunderstanding of causality. Being is no more caused by time than it is by sunshine. Both being and time are consequences of the transcendental algorithms of the Reality Dysfunction.

> *"Admitting that being must be capable of temporal presence, two different paths seem open to us. Either we can assert that being is an ultimate ground or we can ask after the ground of being in the sense of seeking the ground of this presence. The modern period has pursued the second alternative. It takes time as the ground of being insofar as it sees time as that which makes being temporally present—this through its flow from now to successive now."* [41]

There has been a radical failure on the part of modern philosophy to fully examine both its own presuppositions and the social consequences of metaphysical positions. Time, used as a way of explaining *being* turns out not to be an explanation at all. Rather it is an obfuscation that allows being to be reduced to nothing and to further prevent any real questioning of the meaning of being. This turns out (as Heidegger so forcefully decried) to be a rather slimy way of avoiding the issue of being altogether. Any consideration of the idea of *being* necessarily involves the idea of causality and consequently, the responsibility that might be associated with moral action. Time, seen as the origin of *being* obfuscates both causality and responsibility, by turning *being* into a radical discontinuity of discrete non-related moments, which in turn have only the meanings that we give them. Welcome to the universe of moral relativism.

The critical difference between the origins of modern philosophy as found in the thinking of Descartes and the best of Greek philosophy was that process or act was never seen by the ancients as being something that

---

41 Ibid

occurred in isolation. Process was always part of some other process or action—causality was linked. The insistence of modern science on causeless scenarios is based on scientific fairy tales rooted in the bizarre notion that somehow things just happen—you know the academic version of the 'stuff just happens' routine. Psychology and Sociology are products of this discontinuous view of being, which is a direct outgrowth of philosophical positions taken during the time period from the Reformation, to the present day. These disciplines study mental and physical phenomena with no reference to being. Ask a psychologist what being means and you will more than likely get a blank stare.

THE CONVERGENCE OF PHYSICS AND METAPHYSICS

Two thousand years of philosophical history has been largely discarded by the advocates of hard-core empirical science and scientific variants of psychology such as Behaviorism, which treats philosophy as mere speculation unrelated to science. The proper subjects of metaphysics, however, are being and Existence, which are oddly paralleled by science's understanding of both being and Existence as various forms of energy that are neither created nor destroyed. Physics takes the existence of things as a given but never distinguishes between what a thing is and what, ultimately, might make it be beyond its components. Hiding within a kind of infinite regression, physics obscures causality by delaying its analysis as something that is yet to be discovered from within the complex relations of all hadrons across time and dimension. The common interpretation of Schrödinger's equation,[42] for example, assumes that the Hamiltonian, or the overall sum of energy in a closed system is

---

42 "In quantum mechanics, the Schrödinger equation is a partial differential equation that describes how wave functions decohere in time. It was formulated in late 1925, and published in 1926, by the Austrian physicist Erwin Schrödinger." [WP]
Where i is the imaginary unit, ħ is the Planck constant divided by 2π, the symbol $\partial/\partial t$ indicates a partial derivative with respect to time t, Ψ (the Greek letter psi) is the wave function of the quantum system, and $\hat{H}$ is the Hamiltonian operator (which characterizes the total energy of any given wave function and takes different forms depending on the situation). [WP] https://en.wikipedia.org/wiki/Schrodinger_equation.

completely understood. This is an assumption that the dynamics of life would seem to challenge. According to Mae-Wan Ho of the Bioelectro-dynamics Laboratory in the UK, Schrödinger believed that negentropy was free energy *not* entirely associated with a closed system or harvested, as many scientists alternatively suggest, from the sun.[43]

Looking at Schrödinger's equation from a metaphysical perspective, it might be said that the Hamiltonian should be considered as being not fully expressible, if Existence is involved in the energetic relations between hadrons as an unknown variable. In other words, what science is assuming is a closed system may not be closed at all if the Fifth Law of Thermodynamics is invoked. "The overall form of Schrödinger's equation is not unusual or unexpected as it uses the principle of the conservation of energy. The terms of the non-relativistic Schrödinger equation can be interpreted as total energy of the system, equal to the system kinetic energy plus the system potential energy. In this respect, it is just the same as in classical physics."[44]

The many worlds interpretation (MWI), which views all possibilities as branching universes; Schrödinger's pilot waves,[45] which are caused by complex interactions between hadrons; "handshakes" from different futures acting as guiding quantum waves, etc., are all derivations of the stochastic point of view embraced by most physicists. They seek to discover the order of the universe in the random aggregation of possibilities that interact—in other words, there is no real order in the

---

43 http://www.i-sis.org.uk/negentr.php
44 [Ibid]
45 "Bohmian mechanics, which is also called the de Broglie-Bohm theory, the pilot-wave model, and the causal interpretation of quantum mechanics, is a version of quantum theory discovered by Louis de Broglie in 1927 and rediscovered by David Bohm in 1952. It is the simplest example of what is often called a hidden variables interpretation of quantum mechanics. In Bohmian mechanics a system of particles is described in part by its wave function, evolving, as usual, according to Schrödinger's equation. However, the wave function provides only a partial description of the system. This description is completed by the specification of the actual positions of the particles. The latter evolve according to the "guiding equation," which expresses the velocities of the particles in terms of the wave function. Thus, in Bohmian mechanics the configuration of a system of particles evolves via a deterministic motion choreographed by the wave function." http://plato.stanford.edu/entries/qm-bohm/

universe—only the appearance of order caused by multiple and separate levels of reality. This is why many atheistic scientists react hysterically to the notion of Intelligent Design. They cannot abide the thought that there might be a Universal Observer or Lawgiver in the universe. If this were so, moral and spiritual laws (heaven forbid) might have to be entertained. Physics, from a philosophical perspective, might be critiqued as merely a science of being that should be qualified or informed by metaphysics, which studies both being and Existence.

As Stephen Barr, professor of Physics at the University of Delaware notes, "thus, the traditional view is that the probabilities in quantum mechanics—and hence the "wave-function" that encodes them— refer to the state of knowledge of some "observer". (In the words of the famous physicist Sir James Jeans, **wave-functions are "knowledge waves."**)[46] An observer's knowledge—and hence the wave-function that encodes it—makes a discontinuous jump when he/she comes to know the outcome of a measurement (the famous "quantum jump", traditionally called the "collapse of the wave function") [AKA Decoherence]. But the Schrödinger equations that describe any physical process do not give such jumps! So something must be involved when knowledge changes besides physical processes"..."The upshot is this: If the mathematics of quantum mechanics is right (as most fundamental physicists believe), and if materialism is right, one is forced to accept the Many Worlds Interpretation of quantum mechanics. And that is awfully heavy baggage for materialism to carry."[47]

"If, on the other hand, we accept the more traditional understanding of quantum mechanics that goes back to von Neumann, one is led by its logic (as physicists Wigner and Peierls were) to the conclusion that not everything is just matter in motion, and that in particular there is something about the human mind that transcends matter and its laws. It then becomes possible to take seriously certain questions

---

46 This is what we are referring to as Dimensionally Interactive Cyber Kinesis in this book.

47 https://www.bigquestionsonline.com/2012/07/10/does-quantum-physics-make-easier-believe-god/

that materialism had ruled out of court: If the human mind transcends matter to some extent, could there not exist minds that transcend the physical universe altogether? And might there not even exist an ultimate Mind?"[48] These are the kinds of questions that a rationalist can and will ask but a materialist won't. Materialists often resist even moving in the direction of such thinking because they intuitively know where it is going.

Barr goes on to say that "another way to frame the argument is in terms of the "ontological status" of wave-functions. The most obvious thing is to think of a wave-function as simply a straightforward description of "the world as it is". But that is equivalent to the MWI, because generally speaking the wave-function of a system contains a large number of branches in which the system behaves in different ways. The alternative view (adopted in the Copenhagen interpretation) is that a wave-function is not an account of the world as it is, but of some observer's state of knowledge of the world. That interpretation brings knowledge (and therefore mind) into the discussion as something that is as fundamental as matter, because wave-functions themselves are fundamental to our understanding of the world."[49]

HYPERSPACE AND THE FORMS

There is a further consideration, however, science and metaphysics in general have been lacking a critical unifying concept. The notion of *hyperspace* or a continuum of dimensions greater than four (length, width, height and time) gives us access to an exciting new world of critical thinking that both science and metaphysics can relate to with confidence. Physicist Michio Kaku, in his book *Hyperspace* gives the following example, which was taken from an earlier book entitled, *Flatland: A Romance of Many Dimensions* published in 1888 by Edwin A. Abbott. He says that if you imagine a two-dimensional creature sitting in

---

48 Ibid
49 Ibid

a two-dimensional jail and then visualize a three-dimensional creature plucking him out of his cell that you can get some idea of the utility of hyperspace. For the two-dimensional creature the word *up* has no meaning and so when the three-dimensional creature plucks him from his cell, he *appears* to have disappeared. So too, a creature from the fifth or sixth dimension might pluck us out of our normal four dimensions of space-time and we would think it magic.

The notion of *Transcendental* or non-local *acts* manifesting in the Reality Dysfunction, which create and sustain entities that we describe as essences and souls, (or for that matter, the superstrings of physics) as being on a continuum with the non-local cyber-kinetic self-knowledge of the Divine, which inhabits time and eternity, gives us a working tool that can help bridge the gap between metaphysics and science. Superstrings vibrating in 11, or even more dimensions, can function as a modern analog to the idea of "form" if science is able to take the notion of existence up to the next level. Rising above the First Law of Thermodynamics, which states that energy is neither created nor destroyed, would enable science to take a radically different approach to problem solving.

Cyber-Kinesis[50] can be thought of as a metaphor for the action of superstrings, or transcendental algorithms moving at the speed of light, in relation to the derivative processes of the Divine Mind; it is the action of the Demiurge written in florescent ink. Cyber-Kinesis is the activity of the Divine Mind outside of Eternity. Cyber-Kinesis, is in this regard, Divine "thinking" in multiple dimensions commensurate with the algorithmic insight provided by the notion of a proportionality between Existence and being.

The famous "forms" or essences of Aristotle, Aquinas and scholasticism, in general, are the non-local manifestation or unseen

---

50 Sean J. O'Reilly, *How to Manage Your Destructive Impulses with Cyber-Kinetics: Redirect Sexual Energy and Discover Your More Spiritually Enlightened, Evolved Self,* 10 Speed Press, 2001. Dimensionally interactive cyber-kinesis might be thought of as a metaphysical interpretation of how the superstrings of physics work in terms of affecting mind, spirit and soul within the limits of the Reality Dysfunction. Kinetic energy is the energy of motion.

*hylomorphic component of the Reality Dysfunction. In this respect, the forms are simply God's Ideas as he understands Himself outside Himself. These forms are proportionally linked to the Divine Essence but are limited in their expression not only by their final causality, which is perfect by way of Divine intention but imperfectly in respect to the fundamental non-proportionality that exists between Existence and all that exists contingently. The "forms" or essences are a result of "Acts" or dimensionally interactive cyber kinesis that science now understands in terms of Superstring Theory. The "forms" constitute the **exchange** between what is non-local and that which is local. They are a representation of an already derivative reality outside the Divine Mind. The notion of form sits like a jewel in the middle of 21st century science and no one has noticed it.*

It might be said that all of us inhabit a Dimensionally Interactive Cyber Kinetic sea because God creates and enters local time with enormous non-local kinetic energy in the Reality Dysfunction. As an effect participates in its cause, so too do we have multi-dimensional kinetic energy (which is localized) from an original non-local Source. It is this extraordinary force, which enables human beings to invest such power in both privately held and in publicly professed belief systems.

This force can be explained sideways by looking again at $E=mc2$ and the way that light behaves, which we examined in Chapter 1, The Metaphysics of Light. The following two questions were asked: "Why would you have to multiply the mass by the speed of light to determine how much energy is bound up inside it? The reason is that whenever you convert part of a walnut or any other piece of matter to pure energy, the resulting energy is by definition moving at the speed of light. Pure energy is electromagnetic radiation—whether light or X-rays or whatever—and electromagnetic radiation travels at a constant speed of 300,000 km/sec (186,000 miles/sec)."[51]

---

51 http://www.pbs.org/wgbh/nova/einstein/lrk-hand-emc2expl.html

"Why, then, do you have to square the speed of light? It has to do with the nature of energy. When something is moving four times as fast as something else, *it doesn't have four times the energy but rather 16 times the energy*—in other words, that figure is squared. So the speed of light squared is the conversion factor that decides just how much energy lies within a walnut or any other chunk of matter. And because the speed of light squared is a huge number—90,000,000,000 (km/sec)2—the amount of energy bound up into even the smallest mass is truly mind-boggling."[52]

"Here's an example. If you could turn every one of the atoms in a paper clip into pure energy—leaving no mass whatsoever—the paper clip would yield 18 kilotons of TNT. That's roughly the size of the bomb that destroyed Hiroshima in 1945. On Earth, however, there is no practical way to convert a paper clip or any other object entirely to energy. It would require temperatures and pressures greater than those at the core of our sun."[53]

The 11th dimension, as mentioned earlier and according to Kaku, is a characteristic of space-time that has been proposed as a possible answer to questions that arise in Superstring Theory. The [hypothesis behind] superstrings involves the existence of nine dimensions of space and one dimension of time (a total of 10). According to this notion, we observe only three spatial dimensions and one time dimension because the other six spatial dimensions are "curled up" or "compactified." According to Superstring Theory, all of the elementary particles in the universe are composed of vibrating, one-dimensional mathematical objects known as strings. The theory does not explicitly state what the strings are made of or where they come from; rather, they are proposed as geometric ideals. Each string has a length of 1035 meters, many times smaller than the diameter of the nucleus of an atom. Kaku's definition of a Superstring is worth looking at again; it is a concept of astonishing power and clarity.

---

52 Ibid
53 http://www.pbs.org/wgbh/nova/einstein/lrk-hand-emc2expl.html

"[Any given subatomic particle (or hadron)[54] is made of a string that vibrates and rotates at the speed of light.]" This is a transcendental set of algorithms possessing extraordinary power. And who knows; they may actually be vibrating at 4 times the speed of light.

A particular hadron gets its unique identity from the manner in which the string rotates and vibrates according to the dynamics of Einstein's theory of general relativity. The frequency of vibration corresponds [algorithmically] to the mass of the particle."[55] The hadrons known as Higgs Bosons are another way of theoretically approaching the problem of mass and how it is algorithmically assigned. The difference between the so-called Standard Model[56] of physics and the emerging paradigm of String Theory couldn't be clearer. Within the superstring model, it is the *frequency of vibration* that algorithmically apportions particle mass and not simply a specific or even random interaction between hadrons.

String Theory indicates composition of notes and this is why many physicists have resisted even the idea of superstrings: they can see where it is going and it is not in the direction of stochastic relations between hadrons. Where there might be an imputed composition, there may be a composer and that would be anathema to those who might

---

54 In particle physics, a hadron (Greek: ἁδρός, hadrós, "stout, thick") is a composite particle made of quarks held together by the strong force (in a similar way as molecules are held together by the electromagnetic force). [WP]

55 http://whatis.techtarget.com/definition/11th-dimension

56 "Here's the gist of the Standard Model, which was developed in the early 1970s: The entire universe is made of 12 different matter particles and four forces. [source: European Organization for Nuclear Research]. Among those 12 particles, you'll encounter six quarks and six leptons. Quarks make up protons and neutrons, while members of the lepton family include the electron and the electron neutrino, its neutrally charged counterpart. Scientists think that leptons and quarks are indivisible; that you can't break them apart into smaller particles. Along with all those particles, the standard model also acknowledges four forces: gravity, electromagnetic, strong and weak. As theories go, the standard model has been very effective, aside from its failure to fit in gravity. Armed with it, physicists have predicted the existence of certain particles years before they were verified." empiricallyhttp://science.howstuffworks.com/higgs-boson1.htm

prefer to see the universe as simply the product of random forces or "excitations" of quantum foam.

BRANES AS A MODERN UNDERSTANDING OF FORM

Branes are mathematical objects created by superstrings. "In string theory and related theories such as supergravity theories, a *brane* is a physical object that generalizes the notion of a point particle to higher dimensions. For example, a point particle can be viewed as a brane of dimension zero, while a string can be viewed as a brane of dimension one."[57] Note that a superstring could also be viewed as a series of dimensions depending on the "note" played. What is a brane at a dimension of zero but something that is more non-local than existent? If you think about it, "mathematical objects created by superstrings" sounds like a potentially modern definition of the ancient idea of *form*, which is essentially, (no pun intended) a self-limited act of the Divine intelligence operating in and across time and dimension. Geometry, trigonometry, physics and general mathematics are functions and descriptions of relations between objects or the abstractions of objects projected onto spatial coordinates. Why would any of these functions operate, as they do, unless they were not previously known outside of human consciousness?

"The nagging question remains, "Where do the strings come from?" There are five different versions of superstring theory that explain the way subatomic particles behave. Are all five versions correct, or are some correct and others wrong? In an attempt to answer these questions, some physicists have suggested that there exists an 11th dimension, which is "compactified" like the other six spatial dimensions we do not directly observe. Superstring theory with the inclusion of the 11th dimension is sometimes called M Theory or the Theory of Everything (TOE)." [58]

---

57 Ibid
58 http://whatis.techtarget.com/definition/11th-dimension

There is, of course, another Theory of Everything that has been around for a very long time and that is the metaphysical notion of an ordered universe in relation to a principle that is and of itself both order and Existence. This older Theory of Everything touches upon every aspect of the human condition. The TOE of physics is simply a further extrapolation of the First Law of Thermodynamics and while very useful, lacks a certain transformative power for the human condition. If the older Theory of Everything is to have any relevance it must touch and transform all of our sacred cows. One such "cow" is the discipline of Psychology. Psychology, which means, in the original sense of the word, "soul study" cannot be understood without referring it to Existence as the source of everything that relates to the development of a good soul. Psychology, when it only studies discontinuous phenomena, has very little moral relevance to the human condition.

Chapter 11

BEING, PSYCHOLOGY AND VIRTUE

"It is true that...there is psychology which...claims to be the universal fundamental science of spirit. Still our hope for real rationality i.e., for real insight, is disappointed here as elsewhere. The psychologists simply fail to see that they too study neither themselves nor the scientists who are doing the investigating nor their own vital environing world...By the same token, they do not see that in pursuing their aims they are seeking a truth in itself, universally valid for everyone. By its objectivism, psychology simply cannot make a study of the soul in its properly essential sense, which is to say, the ego that acts and is acted upon. Though by determining the bodily function involved in an experience of evaluation or willing, it may objectify the experience and handle it inductively, can it do the same for purposes, values and norms?...Completely ignored is the fact that objectivism, as the genuine work of the investigator intent upon finding true norms, presupposes just such norms...More and more perceptible becomes the overall need for a reform of modern psychology in its entirety...In our time we everywhere

meet the burning need for an understanding of spirit, while the
un-clarity of the methodological and factual connection between
the natural sciences and the sciences of the spirit has become
almost unbearable." [1]

—Husserl

EPOCHE

Husserl, the founder of phenomenology was not arguing for a study
of the soul, as an objective science in the foregoing quote but was
rather, insisting that science could not properly investigate spirit, as
science presupposed its own norms, in such a way that the relationship
between those norms and any phenomenon obscures the actual, lived
experience. He saw the need for an investigative methodology utilizing
an initial suspension of judgment and intellection which he called *epoche* or the *phenomenological reduction*. Epoche consisted of bracketing the
logical mind's inferences and presuppositions, in order to apprehend
the primordial phenomenon of experience.

Let's say that two scientists, a man and woman, who have worked
with each other for a long time are gazing at a sunset. The woman is
enjoying the potential romance created by the soft winds and beautiful
light of the setting sun. Let's also assume that they both secretly like
each other but that the man feels uncomfortable with any feelings of
romance. He finds that by attempting to analyze the spectrographic
composition of the colors, he feels more secure or less at odds with his
own feelings, which are surfacing.

We might assume that the woman is closer to the primordial experience of the sunset because she is allowing it to speak to her. The
male may be preoccupied with some scientific irrelevancy, which in-
hibits his experience of the *sunset woman* beside him. He may be out
of touch with his feelings, while she is side-stepping her scientific dis-

---

1   Husserl quoted from James R. Mensch's, *Aristotle and the Overcoming of the Subject
     Object Dichotomy,* ACPA Quarterly, Autumn 1991, pg. 465

position and slipping into the flow of reality. He has not bracketed his experience at all but has imposed a structure on the natural flow of his affections due to some personal difficulties. The female scientist on the other hand, who may be no less scientifically capable than her friend, brackets the chatter of the analytic mind and allows herself to experience the sunset, without the superfluous noise of interpretative structures.

Another more common example of bracketing or epoche would be the experience many of us have had of wanting to say something in a conversation and then, suddenly, stopping because of something we sensed that seemed out of order. That *something* sensed might be a larger intuitive understanding of the conversation and the parties involved, which makes us correctly hesitate in expressing what we may feel like saying. The conscious mind might see nothing wrong with what we wanted to say but the unconscious or perhaps supra-conscious mind may have already made its own calculations of propriety based on a non-local access to information about the present or the future which we may not be consciously aware of.

The thrust of phenomenology, which deals with phenomena, represents an attempt to get back to some original apprehension of the 'thing itself.' Since modern philosophy has told mankind that it cannot know anything with certainty, sooner or later it was inevitable that a discipline would arise which would attempt to apprehend a greater, rather than a lesser degree of the primordial reality of things.

Husserl's lament cannot be understood without understanding the intellectual decline that had accompanied the waning of Christian moral influence in the Europe of the late 1800s. This decline was precipitated by the earlier Protestant Reformation and the later ascent of the scientific method, as it was applied to both the development of the sciences and the human mind. Aristotle, if you will recall, insisted that the intellect had two functions: Moral and Intellectual. The moral function of the intellect was to control the appetites and this in fact is the basis of all moral virtue. What happened during the Protestant

Reformation was an increasing distrust of reason in the discussion of spiritual or moral matters. Something was either sinful or it wasn't, you were either saved or damned—everything was cast in black and white. This ghastly lack of rationality in moral matters set the stage for those who would simply disregard the Christian heritage and substitute it with something else, viz., humanistic psychology.

FREUD AND THE RULE OF THE APPETITES

Sigmund Freud (1856-1939) merely picked up the pieces of a culture that was already in intellectual disarray and repackaged them for an increasingly credulous public. This is not to say that Freud's ideas were met with universal acclaim; they were not but his subsequent influence has been great. Freud's greatest idea and also his very worst was the notion that the appetites rule the psychic constitution.

> "It is easy to see that the [ego is that part of the Id] which has been modified by the direct influence of the external world through the medium of the perceptual consciousness; in a sense it is an extension of the surface-differentiation. Moreover, the ego seeks to bring the influence of the external world to bear upon the Id and its tendencies and endeavors to substitute the reality principle for the pleasure principle which reigns unrestrictedly in the Id. For the ego, perception plays the part which in the Id falls to instinct...
>
> The ego represents what may be called reason and common sense, in contrast to the Id, which contains the passions. All this falls into line with popular distinctions which we are all familiar with...The functional importance of the ego is manifested in the fact that normally control over the approaches to motility devolves upon it. Thus is its relation to the Id it is like a man on horseback, who has to hold in check the superior strength of the horse; with this difference, that the rider tries to do so with his

own strength while the ego uses borrowed forces. This analogy may be carried a little further. Often a rider, if he is not to be parted from his horse, is obliged to guide it where he wants it to go, so in the same way the ego is in the habit of transforming the Id's will into action as if it were its own." [2]

This extraordinarily clear statement of Freud's understanding of what he means by the activity of the ego and the Id is relatively shallow in the light of Greek moral philosophy. Plato, who also used the analogy of horse and rider but with vastly different intentions, might have found Freud's interpretation fascinating but would also, in all likelihood, have found it depersonalizing. Freud's brilliant but incomplete descriptions of our mental apparatus, unfortunately, reduces all human impulses to modifications of the intentionality of the Id. Freud attempts to substitute the Id for the soul and reduces the person to an accretion of similar energetic impulses in the ego.

This attempt to reduce human beings to an expression of appetitive resolve results in a depersonalization of the individual that is common in our culture today. This is why we find it very difficult to define what is moral or what is immoral. From the psychological perspective, human beings do not have either good intentions or bad intentions; they simply have different modifications of desire and energy that are all ultimately equivalent. Biology doesn't make the distinction between right and wrong, biology only *wants and acts*. Freud's understanding of the human mind, then, is based on his particular interpretation of biology and the human mind, which leans heavily on materialism rather than on the kind of rationalism that came from Jung and later, more enlightened schools of psychology.

Freud's contribution to the collective wisdom of mankind should not be too down-played by critics, however, as it is useful to understand the structure of the appetitive power of the soul in relation to the oth-

---

2   Freud, Sigmund, *The Ego and the Id*, Norton Library, NY, 1960, pg.15

er powers. Unconscious appetites affect our thinking—often without our being fully aware of them. Therefore, it is of supreme importance to scrutinize our intentions for the subtle activities of the unconscious appetites that affect us all. This is, however, not exactly what Freud had in mind.

The Freudian structure of ego, super ego and unconscious Id tied together by the all-embracing glue of the pleasure principal has, unfortunately, done much to undermine the concept of virtue and the notion of the intellect as a power of the soul. The idea that the human person might be thought of as merely an ego or a derived expression of the energy of the Id is depersonalizing and misleading. For Freud, one of the primary functions of mind seems to be repression—hardly an uplifting concept.

> "*The historical accident that psycho-analysis had its origin in connection with the study of hysteria led at once to the hypothesis of repression (or more generally, of defense) as a mental function, and this in turn to a topographical hypothesis—to a picture of the mind as including two portions, one repressed and the other repressing. The quality of 'consciousness' was evidently closely involved in these hypotheses; and it was easy to equate the repressed part of the mind with what was 'unconscious' opposed by an ego.*"[3]

Indeed, it could be argued that the very notion of a static, repressive operation of the mind could be transposed on the idea of virtue. Such a conclusion would, in fact, erode even the belief in rational control of the appetites. This is true to the extent that culturally and imaginatively as a people, we assume that many of our problems are the result of an unhealthy repression. The best example is sexual desire. If an individual exercises sexual self-control, or as Aristotle would have said, sexual continence, he or she may be perceived as being self-repressed and unhealthy. Comments such as, "You're a virgin, I didn't

---

3   Ibid, pg. 10

know there were any virgins left" or "no reason you shouldn't mastur-bate, it's unhealthy not to" are commonplace. Unfortunately, this is the popular legacy of Freud's thinking, even though he himself clearly saw the importance of the sublimation of sexual desire. This is not to suggest that there is not such a thing as unhealthy repression but there is a big difference between thoughtful self-restraint and uninhibited self-indulgence masquerading as health.

FREUD AND THE DISEASE-BASED MODEL OF PSYCHOLOGY

There seems to be an assumption of disease in the operations of the mind that Freud never quite gets away from. Did Freud ever study healthy individuals? Why would anyone use a disease-based model for an analysis of human mental health? Perhaps Freud betrays his own intellectual origins here. He is convinced that there is something fun-damentally wrong with our understanding of the human mind and that this issue cannot be addressed without recourse to psychoanalysis. Freud is right in one sense. The moral and intellectual vacuum created by the mathematical and machine models of human consciousness, in vogue in the late 1800's, created a public hunger for reality.

Freud's mental explorations represent the initial re-discovery of a continent already banished by those who could not stand the language of spirituality or the thought that there might be things unseen in the human psyche beyond bowel movements, eating, sleeping, ejaculat-ing and conversing. The notion of the unconscious provides us with a glimpse of what was once the power of the concept of soul. Freud would of course be horrified by this analysis, as he had no intention of showing that there was any such thing as the soul. His discovery of vast areas of unconscious activity in the human psyche, nonetheless shows us that there are things unseen at work in the human mind.

This unconscious is the ocean that Carl Jung sets sail upon. Jung with his notion of archetypes in the human consciousness joins com-pany with Plato, and psychology is once again looking at philosophy.

The difficulty, however, is that psychology does not look to the primary tool of philosophy, the intellect, for its inspiration, nor does psychology look to the metaphysical history of the idea of being for insight. Many schools of psychology look for truth in psychological structures created by experience, with the assumption being that the interaction of mind and experience creates mental structures which ultimately explain all human behavior.

The notion of a trans-temporal entity like the soul is seldom used (with the exception of Jung and a few others) to explain how human beings can rise above the limitations created by abnormal mental artifacts. Indeed, classical Freudianism would seem to indicate that salvation is accomplished by allowing the appetites to transcend conscious structures and thus become fully operative and free from the suppression created by the ego. The assumption being of course that the appetites are naturally good and ordered, which is patent lunacy.

MODERN PSYCHOLOGY AND CULTURAL DELUSIONS

Modern psychology has created a large scale, psychotic cultural delusion. Perhaps we could call it *psycho-delusion*. Psychosis is defined generally as living and believing in a mental world that does not correspond to reality. If this is the case, then modern psychology might be said to be preoccupied with unreality. The source of an individual's psychological difficulty cannot be simply located in deficient mental structures, rather it must be located in a disproportionate response or activity, as understood in relation to the soul's engagement or disengagement with God and reality. One of the best examples of this, 'Being out of touch with reality', that I have ever seen is a description in the Washington Post, describing a visit to a youth detention center:

> *"I was at Oak Hill, the District's juvenile detention center in Laurel, to hear WRC-TV anchorman Jim Vance tell the boys how much he loved them and how they could make it if they tried. I*

also was asked to give an inspirational talk at a later date, but after sitting in a gymnasium full of these sullen, hunched-back, baggy-pants wearing teenage inmates, I began to wonder: Why? Channel 4's Vance gave a fine speech about going from a youth gang in Philadelphia to becoming a well-paid newscaster. But these kids had their own routes from gangland to glory. They made television news the old-fashioned way: they killed people. Despite all of the pain and suffering you have caused, your neighbors voted against the death penalty, Terry Shelton, a detention center treatment specialist told the boys. It was the day after the election. The staff clapped. **The boys, including a 15-year-old charged with killing five people, looked at Shelton like he was from Mars...***How ironic though, that Oak Hill sits next door to the National Security Agency in Laurel, its high tech antennas and satellite dishes combing the skies for intelligence about international threats. And yet they can't even see the kids who cut through the razor wire-topped fence and escape through their yard."* [4]

The victims of the young men at that detention center were as surely killed by the morally bankrupt, social gospels of psychology and sociology, as they were by guns. Our society has abandoned young men and particularly young black men to the savagery of unexamined and uncontrolled appetites. How can we expect anyone to act in a rational manner when they have never been given the moral tools that they need to understand either themselves or others?

Philip Gold has a humorous description of his interpretation of the same phenomenon which I have been attempting to describe. He calls it *Psycho-bondage.*

"America as a civilization, lives in psycho-bondage. By this I mean a civilization whose dominant value system is psychological (How does this make me feel, especially about myself?) rather

4   Courtland Milloy, *The Washington Post*, Nov. 8, 1992

than overtly theological, ideological, scientific-rational, or even crudely materialistic. Feelings are of course universal. They are also powerful determinants of behavior. But in a civilization living in psycho-bondage, inner states act as more than motivation. They also provide the payoff, the goal; they become ends in themselves...

A civilization living in psycho-bondage cannot have a rational political life—the coming together of men and women to determine the structure and content of the common world. Electoral politics has long been degraded to the frantic pushing of various 'hot buttons' by therapeutic candidates and their handlers...

Nor can a civilization in psycho-bondage maintain its social relationships—the latticework of mediating and nurturing institutions standing between the individual and the state. When dealings between people are valued primarily because of their psychological payoffs, and discarded when those payoffs become inadequate or boring, horrendous behaviors and conditions result. What are spousal and child abuse save the adult inability to control emotions?" [5]

PSYCHOLOGY AS VOODOO

Psychology as a discipline studies one aspect of being and that is the aspect of our mental lives as affected by both the biological structure of the mind and the interrelationship that the mind has with actually existing reality. Psychology in this regard is as much a part of the study of being as is medicine and mathematics. There must be a line drawn, however, as to what constitutes the boundaries of psychology. Psychology is at its best a study of the relationship between the soul, the mind, God and the world. At its worst, Psychology ignores the other aspects of philosophy of which it is a part. A metaphysically and morally in-

---

5   Philip Gold, *The Washington Post*, November 8, 1992

formed Psychology utilizing the concepts of virtue and vice would be a great boon to mankind, but as an apparatus which ends up justifying the basest of human appetites, it must be rooted up, ridiculed and defrocked of scientific respectability. Psychology without metaphysics is voodoo.

Karl Jaspers,[6] who was a psychologist and friend of Martin Heidegger and who became a philosopher noted that "Man is always more than whatever can be known about him."[7] Psychology, as a discipline without metaphysics, is like the law without morality. It is a discipline that does not convince the average man that it is rooted in eternal or morally useful truths. It has, in fact, become a tool of the legal profession and has been used to further disconnect moral truths from political realities.

The very worst use of voodoo psychology is in the courtroom. How on earth did psychologists become any more approved to reach a conclusion about the genesis of an individual's character, than the philosophers or the religious? What process of certification was submitted to the general public? Was the matter voted on? Why is a psychologist any more objective in his attitude than a rabbi or priest?[8] Is anyone aware that Psychology is not a unified discipline but is in fact composed of hundreds of conflicting schools of thought and opinion?

---

6   "He died in 1969, at age 86, famous in his native Germany. But for the rest of the world, Karl Jaspers remains only partly known: he was that friend of Heidegger's, who fell out with him over Nazism, or perhaps that teacher of Arendt, who encouraged her liberalism. He is, in the world of the intelligentsia, of academic philosophy, a vague figure; but there is another place where he is an equally ambiguous presence. It is an unusual place; not the clean auditoria of academic lecture halls; rather, the old and worn hallways of psychiatric hospitals. Jaspers is likely better known among psychiatrists than among philosophers. Here is the paradox: perhaps the greatest existential philosopher of our age was not really a philosopher at all, but a physician, a psychiatrist, a man who, fully trained, turned his back on his profession so he could understand the nature of Being. He is the last existentialist, the other existentialist—not Heidegger or Sartre or their reflections —dead for a generation, and more unknown than ever." http://metapsychology.mentalhelp.net/poc/view_doc.php?type=book&id=2541&cn=396

7   *Jaspers, Karl: The Shipwreck of Existence, pg. 194*

8   Hagan, Margaret A, *Whores of the Court: The Fraud of Psychiatric Testimony and the Rape of American Justice*, Regan Books, an Imprint of Harper Collins

Which members of what schools of psychology are approved to testify in court, and on what basis have they been approved? The answer is that they are all equally approved, as long as they have the proper self-serving credentials. We have been duped by quasi-professionals who have hoodwinked everyone into thinking that they are objective and impartial analysts of human behavior.

III

EXISTENCE AND THE SOUL

*"There was Aristotle, a very distinguished writer, of whom you
have heard,—a philosopher, in short, whom it took centuries to
learn, centuries to unlearn, and is now going to take a generation or more to learn again."* [1]

—Oliver Wendell Holmes

---

1   Holmes, Oliver Wendell, *The Autocrat of the Breakfast Table* (London; New York, 1906),
    249 as cited by Etienne Gilson in *Three Quests in Philosophy*, PIMS, 2008

Chapter 12

METAPHYSICS AND THE FRONTIERS OF SCIENCE

"The empiricist...thinks he believes only what he sees, but he is much better at believing than at seeing."

—George Santayana,
Skepticism and Animal Faith

SEARCHING FOR ANSWERS TO A PERENNIAL QUESTION

We might think of early philosophical speculation on the nature of the universe as a primitive form of physics, although Aristotle thought that metaphysics was a higher intellectual discipline than understanding the mathematical relationships of the physical order that later became modern physics. Over the centuries, many different philosophers, mathematicians and theologians have attempted to understand the relationship between the One and the Many. I will try to summarize them, briefly, by focusing on the different ways it is possible to understand what the ancients primarily understood as essence and Existence in relation to the perennial question of the One and the Many.

The Gnostics,[2] who grew out of first and second century Christianity, attempted to understand the relationship between the finite and the infinite as mediated by Plato's Demiurge.[3] The word "demiurge" is an English word from a Latinized form of the Greek, *which means* literally "public worker", and which was originally a common noun meaning "craftsman" or "artisan", but gradually it came to mean "producer" and eventually "creator". The philosophical usage and the proper noun derive from Plato's *Timaeus*, written c. 360 BC, in which the demiurge is presented as the creator of the universe." [4]

"It is said that the Demiurge converts abstract metaphysical archetypes (higher thoughts/ideas) into physically manifest forms, akin to your browser turning source code into a displayed web page. Just as a browser obediently displays what it's given, the Demiurge projects, shapes, and perpetuates physicality in accordance with the archetypal[5]

---

2   "Gnosticism (from Ancient Greek: meaning "learned" is a modern term categorizing a collection of ancient religions from the second century AD whose adherents shunned the material world–which they viewed as created by the demiurge–and embraced the spiritual world. Gnostic ideas influenced many ancient religions that teach that *gnosis* (variously interpreted as knowledge- enlightenment, salvation, emancipation or 'oneness with God') may be reached by practicing philanthropy to the point of personal poverty, sexual abstinence (as far as possible for *hearers*, entirely for initiates) and diligently searching for wisdom by helping others." (WP)

3   "Why is the concept of a Demiurge even necessary? Well, we know from the "reality creation" phenomenon that our own minds can shape reality by directly altering the probability of events. Due to the dependence of reality on mind, it would seem that reality is being projected by our minds. And yet, reality continues to exist even in our absence. When we stop paying attention to something physical, it does not wink out of existence. Obviously there must be something other than our own consciousness at work, something that is always there, that functions as the default generator and perpetuator of physicality. This would be the Demiurge." (http://montalk.net/gnosis/171/corruption-of-the-demiurge)

4   (Ibid)

5   Archetypes are the building blocks of meaning, the fundamental alphabet of existence, the abstract thoughts of the divine, of which all things are but particular expressions.

thoughts fed into it by the Creator." [6]The ancients, of course, had nothing quite like computer code and servers, or the benefit of modern physics to describe the relationship between the One and the Many but they did the best they could with the intellectual tools that were at hand. Their ideas all have value and are worth considering when confronting the still colossal enterprise of understanding the relationship of Existence to the rest of the universe.

The medieval philosophers, who came many centuries after the Gnostics, sought to understand the relationship between the One and the Many using the earlier Greek language of essence and Existence. Leibnitz (1646-1716) following the medieval theologians, and one of the creators of calculus, attempted to use the Greek notion of monad[7] in lieu of 'essence' to describe the reality behind individually existing things. Leibniz, to his credit, was attempting to recover some of the dynamism that he perceived must exist between Existence and all the different things that have or participate in Existence. Like Plato, he identified monads as the repository of Divine Ideas inserted, as it were, into time and being and linked to infinity through an unknown mechanism, which this book identifies as the Reality Dysfunction.

Leibnitz, more than likely, never fully understood that the dynamism between essence and Existence had already been well-developed by Aquinas due to the academically degraded position of scholastic knowledge after the Reformation (1517-1648 AD). This can be indirectly confirmed by the lack of inclusion of St. Thomas's thinking, by way of general reference, in Leibnitz and almost all of his contemporaries' thinking. This cannot be chalked-up to an intellectual deficiency in the teaching of St. Thomas. The existence of Aquinas's texts in Latin

---

(http://montalk.net/gnosis/171/corruption-of-the-demiurge)

6   Ibid

7   Monad, in the sense of "ultimate, indivisible unit," appears very early in the history of Greek philosophy. In the ancient accounts of the doctrines of Pythagoras, it occurs as the name of the unity from which, as from a principle (arche), all number and multiplicity are derived. In the Platonic "Dialogues" it is used in the plural (monades) as a synonym for the Ideas. In Aristotle's "Metaphysics" it occurs as the principle (arche) of number, itself being devoid of quantity, indivisible and unchangeable. (http://www.newadvent.org/cathen/10447b.htm)

only did nothing to ameliorate the ignorance of his work among forward thinking and brilliant individuals such as Leibnitz and Spinoza. One suspects that if Leibnitz could have fully understood the nature of Aquinas' superb insight into Existence as not existing that he might have moved in the direction of understanding the creation as a derivative action of the Eternal's self-knowledge.

Spinoza (1632-1677 AD) who influenced the romantic poet Novalis and the German philosopher Hegel, was on a very modern track with his notion of the effects of reason as being different from reason.[8] However, failing to understand the effects of reason, viz., the effects of mental structures on our perception of reality, without tying those effects to real things, helped precipitate the radical separation of being from Being that is characteristic of almost all forms of materialism. If all we know are processes that appear to be real things, then reality has no existential ground for metaphysics to stand on. This leads to the notion that metaphysics is a dead-end for human reason and that all processes of life are simply the province of science. They should be the focus of both metaphysics and science—not one or the other.

Spinoza's understanding of death, described as: "I understand the body to die when its parts are so disposed that they acquire a different proportion of motion and rest to one another."[9] is classic separation of cause from effect—at least at first pass. "A different proportion of rest and motion relative to each other," without an underlying and binding process that supports those proportions, is rich fodder for those who want to see reality as the production of the particle interactions produced by an "excitation" of quantum foam. What can be seen in Spinoza is a kind of celebration of discontinuity as principle of organization, which characterizes many aspects of modern cosmology. When energy is seen as being neither created nor destroyed, and is not the product of intelligence or eternal observation, then the logical next step is to postulate that the universe is an accident of perception.

---

8 Yitzhak Y. Melamed and Oded Shecter, *Spinoza on Death, "Our Present Life and Imagination,"* pgs. 1, 11 and 15, Academia Edu

9 Ibid, pg. 11

As a metaphysician, I look at Spinoza's ideas as being simultaneously reductionist and also forward looking. They are reductionist in that they tend, at first glance, to support the discontinuity of causality, which was not the understanding of the ancients but forward looking in that the idea of "rest and motion" is critical to understanding how, in fact, the essential order of forms must work to be intelligible. If we postulate that Dimensionally Interactive Cyber Kinesis is our access to Universal Mind, then various kinds of motion and rest must be understood in relation to that which is pure motion—the Actus Essendi or the Act of Existence. This might be understood as a kind of realist panpsychism[10] and this was an idea that Spinoza supported. His articulation and understanding of motion appears to lie somewhere between the ancient and modern understanding of time and motion.[11] Panpsychism, as a term, is an attempt to recover what the realist philosophy of Aristotle and the great medievalists simply assumed and qualified with the distinctions of matter and form.

More recent philosophers continued to try to understand the nature of Existence without, in my opinion, a substantial reference to, or understanding of either the work of Aristotle or Aquinas. The German philosopher Hegel (1770-1831 AD) attempted to describe a dialectic between Existence and existing things that involved the Absolute in a process of progressive incarnations, in time, through the conflict and resolution of opposite ideas. Hegel attempted to understand God and His relation to the universe in a more pantheistic manner than most of his contemporaries but he suffered from the same lack of knowledge that his predecessors endured: an ignorance of well-developed ideas from the scholastic period that might have, had he been aware of them, taken his philosophy in a different direction. Had decent translations been available, (and of course they weren't) Hegel would likely

---

10 "In philosophy, panpsychism is the view that consciousness, mind or soul (psyche) is a universal feature of all things, and the primordial feature from which all others are derived." [WP]

11 I cannot claim to be as familiar with the work of Baruch Spinoza as I should be but this analysis is in the ballpark of attribution.

have been intrigued by the metaphysical formulations of Scottus Eriugena. Who knows, had such texts been available, Hegel might have pre-empted Whitehead in the development of Process Philosophy.

> *"In opposition to the classical model of change as accidental (as argued by Aristotle) or illusory, process philosophy regards change as the cornerstone of reality—the cornerstone of the Being thought as Becoming. Modern philosophers who appeal to process rather than substance include Nietzsche, Heidegger, Charles Peirce, Alfred North Whitehead, Alan Watts, [Richard Rorty, Wittgenstein] Robert M. Pirsig, Charles Hartshorne, [Korzybski], Arran Gare, Nicholas Rescher, Colin Wilson, Gilles Deleuze [and others]. In physics Ilya Prigogine distinguishes between the "physics of being" and the "physics of becoming". Process philosophy covers not just scientific intuitions and experiences, but can be used as a conceptual bridge to facilitate discussions among religion, philosophy, and science."* [12]

Philosopher Alfred North Whitehead developed a more detailed offshoot of Hegel's dialectic that is known, more commonly, as Process Philosophy. The concept of *prehension*, [13] which might be thought of as an amoeba-like process between essence and Existence, involves conceiving of the relationship between essence and Existence as a process between a concrete and an eternal pole of God's Existence. While this may not be a fair characterization, given the full range of Whitehead's comprehensive and detailed thinking, what is true is that process philosophy tends to obscure the dynamic that occurs when a Person or Persons, and not simply a process, is involved in creation.

Even a relatively modern poet, William Butler Yeats, attempted to formulate the relationship between the finite and the infinite with

---

12 Process Philosophy: https://en.wikipedia.org/wiki/Process_philosophy
13 Prehension, similarly, allows for "existential occasions," which are causally connected to all of Existence, to take other existential occasions into themselves. This is what I would call the amoeba approach to existence.

the concept of *gyres* or vortexes between space and time.[14] These gyres were a way of poetically accounting for the relationship between what we experience in three and four dimensions and what seems to be another universe rich with possibility and meaning that overlaps or intersects our own. The poet, at the intersection of worlds, draws his or her inspiration from these higher spaces by stepping into the gyre.

Philosophy and poetry have one thing in common: they both seek to understand what appears to be a higher source of meaning in life. This higher source of meaning can be thought of as Existence in all its manifestations. However, attempting to understand the multi-dimensional relationship between Existence and existing things without a clear understanding of the works of Plato, Aristotle or Aquinas, while often useful and productive of new thinking, is also an enterprise that is akin to reinventing the wheel.[15]

The philosophies of what might be termed the Protestant period of Christianity, from the time of the Reformation until the present, must be understood as being qualitatively different in terms of all available knowledge *adverted to* than in the prior scholastic period. The 20th century has seen a renewed academic interest in medieval philosophy as new discoveries lead back beyond religious bias to what is true, good and beautiful. Consequently, the notions of decoherence and dimensionally interactive cyber kinesis, which relate the consciousness of God to space, time and matter in the Reality Dysfunction, bridge the old world of Aristotle and the scholastics, and the modern world of Process Philosophy. How time and eternity are conceived and how moral derivatives, in terms of principle, are expressed in belief and religion, are the constituent elements of the Time War.

Physicists are late-comers to this conflict and some of them tend to philosophize without reference to several thousand years of meta-

---

14 Georban, Kevin, *Everything Forever: Learning to See Timelessness* http://everythingforever.com/einstein.htm

15 By taking only a small slice from their thinking I am probably doing these philosophers a disservice but the reality is that by not engaging the thinking of those that went before them, the more modern philosophers tend to be at a metaphysical disadvantage.

physical speculation on subjects that overlap the enterprise of science. One has only to think of the philosophical drivel posed by the late Carl Sagan regarding the origins of life and the universe to understand how shallow the thinking of some scientists can be. On the other side of the coin, Ilya Prigogine's book, *From Being to Becoming: Time and Complexity in the Physical Sciences,* published in 1980 indicates that Prigogine was well on the path to recovering some of the insights of Aristotle.

Prigogine's argument is that the physical representation of systems as linear, reversible and deterministic states never change their identities through time, therefore they can never become anything radically new. All these systems can do is rearrange the parts already within the systems. In other words, a pile of tires cannot become a work of art without an outside agent enacting change. Prigogine noticed that there were natural systems that exhibited radical novelty—from simple crystallization to the continual becoming of living organisms and the cosmos itself. He suggested that the novelty exhibited in nature may require a new foundation for physics, one whose relationship to time, identity, chance and dynamism is different from that indicated by either quantum mechanics or stochastic aggregation. Prigogine does this using dense scientific language but the essence of what he is saying is that there appears to be a negentropic principle (such as is described by the proposed Fifth Law of Thermodynamics) at work in the universe.

IMPLICATE AND EXPLICATE

David Bohm (1917-1992) however, was one physicist, who having a general grasp of ancient philosophy, was able to theoretically express the hidden relationship between the finite and the infinite using almost metaphysical terms. His notion of *implicate* and *explicate orders*[16] with the implicate order being that of non-locality[17] and the explicate or local

---

16 (http://www.scienceandnonduality.com/david-bohm-implicate-order-and-holomovement/#sthash.2uW3y7cg.dpuf)

17 This was first described in the "EPR papers" of Einstein, Boris Podolsky and Nathan

order (what we see around us) as the product of hidden, multi-dimensional, implicate processes was almost more metaphysical than it was scientific. The more accepted scientific notion of non-locality or "spooky action at a distance" is, however, a critical concept for both physics and metaphysics because for the first time what philosophers have attempted to describe for centuries, in terms of essence and existence, now has a scientific basis. The definition of non-locality is worth revisiting as it tends to clarify Whitehead's notion of prehension or a dynamic between the concrete and the eternal poles of Existence.

"Non-locality describes the apparent ability of objects/particles to instantaneously know about each other's state, even when separated by large distances (potentially even billions of light years), almost as if the universe at large instantaneously arranges its particles in anticipation of future events." [18]

"Bohm believed that the "hiddeness" of non-locality may be reflective of a deeper dimension of reality. He maintains that space and time might actually be derived from an even deeper level of objective reality. This reality he calls the Implicate Order. Within the Implicate Order everything is connected; and, in theory, any individual element could reveal information about every other element in the universe."[19]

Richard Feynman, another prominent physicist, described the relationship between the One and the Many in terms of multiple universes, in which other worlds are just other directions in space, some less probable, some as equally probable as the one direction we might experience.[20] Feynman's summing of all possible histories could be de-

Rosen in 1935, and it is sometimes referred to as the EPR (Einstein-Podolsky-Rosen) paradox. It was even more starkly illustrated by Bell's Theorem, published by John Bell in 1964, and the subsequent practical experiments by John Clauser and Stuart Freedman in 1972 and by Alain Aspect in 1982. (http://www.physicsoftheuniverse. com/topics_quantum_nonlocality.html)

18 (http://www.physicsoftheuniverse.com/topics_quantum_nonlocality.html)
19 Talbot, Michael, *The Holographic Universe*, Harper Perennial 1991
20 Georban, Kevin, *Everything Forever: Learning to See Timelessness* (http://everythingforever.com/einstein.htm)

scribed as the first timeless description of a multitude of space-time worlds all existing simultaneously.[21] Professor Stephen Hawking of Cambridge, in a paper entitled *Cosmology from the Top Down*, wrote, "Some people make a great mystery of the multi-universe, or the Many-Worlds interpretation of quantum theory, but to me, these are just different expressions of the *Feynman path integral.*"[22]An integral is a mathematical object that can be interpreted as an area or a generalization of area. Integrals, together with derivatives,[23] are the fundamental objects of calculus. Calculus, itself, trembles at the border of the infinite and the finite. Anything that is manifest in time and space can be related to number. Between geometry, calculus and physics the mathematics of space and time can be outlined. What might be said about the mathematics of decoherence, when considered in reference to an eternal observer?

The Feynman Path Integral might be understood, metaphysically, as Existence knowing all the possible pathways that any form of existence (e/E) that it knows may take. Each possibility, each variation in a multitude of dimensional permutations is already known and matched in the instant of the Reality Dysfunction without in any way determining those pathways in a manner equivalent to pre-destination.

> *The Feynman Path Integral is, ultimately, a representation of the decoherence and organization of quantum reality by an eternal observer. The Feynman Path Integral might be thought of as one of the signatures of the Reality Dysfunction.*

Divine consciousness is not bound by the limitations of time; it is the master of time in the instant of the Reality Dysfunction and the *reditus*, (the return of the all to the All) which to Divine conscious-

---

21 Ibid

22 Ibid. Note that the integral is an important concept in mathematics. Integration is one of the two main operations in calculus, with its inverse, differentiation, being the other.

23 The derivative of a function represents an infinitesimal change in the function with respect to one of its variables.

ness is present in an eternal now. Time is ordered by something that is greater than time but in time it—whatever It Is—operates like the derivative of a function as it images an integral.

Aquinas described God's knowledge as being conjoined eternally to His will. *God understands Himself through Himself.*[24] The profundity of the mystery must be understood in the light of the non-existence in time and space of Existence except in derivative forms. It is but what it Is—being not a "what" but an Act without any kind of edges in time and space—making it extremely difficult to understand. We might as well say that God understands things through nothing at all. The only way to get a small handle on this is to say that God's Existence is at right angles to or infinitely orthogonal to our own. This is why we say that our existence, in the Reality Dysfunction, is analogous to a kind of virtual reality for God in the derived forms of His consciousness that He allows to exist, locally, outside Himself.

> *"The knowledge of God, joined to His will, is the cause of things. Hence it is not necessary that whatever God knows, is, was, or will be; but only is this necessary as regards what He wills to be, or permits to be. Further, it is in the knowledge of God not that they be but that they be possible."* [25] *This constitutes a calculus of sorts in that what "might be" can be distinguished, a-priori, from some perspective, from what is not to be. There is in God, however, no real distinction between what He wills and what He knows. The distinction can only occur within the Reality Dysfunction.*

Scottus Eriugena's insistence along with that of many Neo-Platonists that God would never be fully known, not even in the Beatific Vision,[26] is a reminder that God's Nature is a mystery that cannot be

---

24 Aquinas, Thomas, *Summa Theologica*, Pt. 1 Q. 14, Art 2
25 Ibid, Article 9, Reply Objection 3
26 "This is the ultimate direct self-communication of God to the individual person. A person possessing the beatific vision reaches, as a member of redeemed humanity in

penetrated by the human intellect or will unaided and even aided by the Divine Itself, remains vast, free and never fully disclosed.[27] The metaphysical notion of the vision of God is an idea that goes back a very long time. Plato, quoting Socrates, notes that:

> *"My opinion is that in the world of knowledge the idea of good (the Good) appears last of all, and is seen only with an effort; and, when seen, is also inferred to be the universal author of all things beautiful and right, parent of light and of the lord of light in this visible world, and the immediate source of reason and truth in the intellectual [realm]."* [28]

This presentation is consistent with the following New Testament statement in 1 Timothy, 6:16 and with the metaphysics of Thomas Aquinas: "God dwells in unapproachable light, whom no one has even seen or can see."

---

the *communion of saints*, perfect salvation in its entirety, i.e. heaven. The notion of vision stresses the intellectual component of salvation, though it encompasses the whole of human experience of joy, happiness coming from seeing God finally *face to face* and not imperfectly through faith. " [WP]

27 *John Scottus Eriugena*, Diedre Carabine, Professor and Director of the Institute of Ethics and Development Studies, Uganda Martyrs University; Oxford University Press, copyright 2000, page 103

28 Plato's Allegory of the Cave, which appears in *The Republic*, Book 7 (514a –520a)

Artist Gustave Dore's (1832-1883 AD) painting of the Beatific Vision
based on Dante's *Divine Comedy*. [Courtesy WP]

The vision of God is not a static idea. "According to Eriugena, even in the return of all diversity to the unity of God, the quest for God will be endless, for although God is "found" in theophany to a certain extent, God is not found as to what God is in God's self (P.V 919 A-D). But since that which is seeks and towards which it tends... is infinite and not to be comprehended by any creature, it necessarily follows that its quest is infinite."[29] What might be better understood and developed as a useful hypothesis is the dynamic involved in

29 *John Scottus Eriugena*, Carabine, Diedre, Professor and Director of the Institute of Ethics and Development Studies, Uganda Martyrs University; Oxford University Press, copyright 2000, page 103

the mysterious transition from Existence to specifically existing things. That transition must also be related to the return of being to Existence. What is the metaphysical calculus between Being and be-ing in both directions?

If we were to analogically describe form or essence as an integral what sort of process of differentiation between Being and be-ing might be mathematically described? We might say that there is a kind of predicate calculus[30] that could be used to postulate the relationship. If we say that all things have existence and that this particular thing—let's say a sock—exists, then from the point of view of a predicate calculus or predicate logic,[31] we would assert that the sock exists because it has existence. If we are to say that all things exist because of something that doesn't exist, then we would conclude that the sock belongs to the set of "things" that exist because of something that does not exist, which tends to be a predicated non sequitur

At some point in time be-ing, whether in the form of sub-atomic particles or some other manifestation, either appears magically out of nothing or there is some sort of process that can be uncovered, whereby what does not previously exist, comes to exist through something that does not appear to exist. We call this Existence but only by way of indicating that Existence Itself does not exist. What is indicated is that the activity of Existence, as the Unmoved Mover, can only be revealed, indirectly, through its effects, which when scrutinized both metaphysically and scientifically, will reveal inexhaustible riches. The existence of the atom was postulated by Democritus over 2,000 years before the present time. It took 2,000 years for science to acknowledge what

---

30 I am indebted to David Berlinski for this butchered insight and hope that he might, someday, express it far more elegantly. This comes from his magnificent book, *The Advent of the Algorithm, The Idea that Rules the World.*

31 "This formal system is distinguished from other systems in that its formulae contain variables which can be quantified. Two common quantifiers are the existential ⊠ ("there exists") and universal ⊠ ("for all") quantifiers. The variables could be elements in the universe under discussion, or perhaps relations or functions over that universe. For instance, an existential quantifier over a function symbol would be interpreted as modifier "there is a function". The foundations of predicate logic were developed independently by Gottlob Frege and Charles Sanders Peirce." [WP]

metaphysics had discovered centuries earlier. Let's hope that Existence, which can be inferred by any rational human being, does not have to wait the same length of time before being acknowledged by science.

Dimensionally Interactive Cyber Kinesis, being initiated in the Big Bang of the *Reality Dysfunction,* is just one of many attempts to articulate the peculiar relationship between being and Existence. The relationship between Being as non-local Existence and being as *being* in terms of contingent matter and form, the Theophanies or even monads, has as we have seen, a very long metaphysical history, which is being continued today, indirectly, by science.

Physicists have been engaged for the past one hundred years in the long process of mathematically describing reality, and the relationship between the finite and the infinite through various equations. Some theorists like John Witten and others are attempting to describe reality in terms of superstrings vibrating in multiple dimensions. This schema is also recreating many of the ideas found in metaphysics. A superstring vibrating at the speed of light in multiple dimensions, within a derivative form of the Divine Mind, is a quasi-scientific analog to what the philosophers referred to as an Idea in the mind of God. If the Divine Mind, as Demiurge, comprehends reality, locally, within time, it is likely through the medium of a fantastic orchestra of light and vibration on a cosmic scale.

Existence, reduced simply to energy that is neither created nor destroyed, as a consequence of an atheistic interpretation of the First law of Thermodynamics, is subject to the manipulations of political sophistry, which sees no connection between the contingent values that might flow from a Divine Being and the political order.

No matter what language or terms are used, the attempt to understand how the infinite or the unchangeable can operate within time and finitude, whether considered from the perspective of the Unmoved Mover, or energy that is neither created or destroyed is a first-class mystery—even if we understand many aspects of the process in outline. The idea that there is something to be investigated between non-local

Existence and "local" be-ing, such as Dimensionally Interactive Cyber Kinesis, or some other intermediary form, is the very essence of philosophical discourse and is now what tends to unite metaphysics and physics in a common enterprise.

Chapter 13

CULTURAL, MORAL AND RELIGIOUS IDEAS ABOUT THE SOUL AS A PREAMBLE TO THE PRESENT

"The laws of nature become simpler and more elegant when expressed in higher dimensions."

—Michio Kaku,
Hyperspace

THE SOUL AS AN INTELLECTUAL ARTIFACT

The idea that the soul even exists had its distant origins in the perceivable difference between the living and the non-living. A culture, no matter how remote in time, will always distinguish between the living and the dead. The soul represents one of the earliest abstractions, in that it attempts to show that there is an operative principle at work that distinguishes the living from the dead.

The most obvious and puzzling difference between the living and the dead is that a human or animal, when freshly killed, still has the same body that it had when it was alive. Decay sets in quickly but at least for a period of about twelve hours or more, the body looks largely the same as it did when it was alive. All this is very obvious in one sense but worth examining for its common sense value. Quite clearly the dead are missing some negentropic principle that they had when they were alive. The idea of the soul or spirit of the dead then, appears begin with this puzzlement over what has departed and what characteristics that it might have.

Many ancient cultures appear to have had burial rituals or ways of marking the demarcation between life and death and ascribing some meaning to it. All cultures and individuals appear to have some trepidation in the face of death; it is generally speaking, not something desirable. The majority of us cling to life and those who willingly risk death are considered brave or courageous. Indeed, it might be said that a number of our ideas about what morality is originate or are considered in the light of death. Because we fear death, we create social and moral structures to give us some guidance in the face of this fear. Many of our cultural ideas about God arise due to our fear of death, and what might or might not be, in the hereafter.

There has, apparently, been a long association with the idea of death and the idea of a God who is more clearly revealed after death than in the present. The uncritical acceptance of the terms of this association may lead to some difficulties. After all, if Existence doesn't reveal Itself completely now, then why should there be a complete, as opposed to partial revelation, after death? Nonetheless, an historical, trans-cultural connection exists between the idea of death and the idea of seeing God or the gods more clearly. The notion of the soul, life-force or spirit, as what we might describe as a negentropic principle, appears intimately connected with the notion of the Divine. The soul appears in the earliest cultures as a spiritual link with the Deity and as such, may be considered an ancient, intellectual artifact. Such an artifact, like all artifacts, yields valuable clues as to the characteristics and condition of a culture.

Early Neanderthal graves (80,000 B.C.) reveal funerary deposits and bodily orientations in graves that suggest at least a simple association of death with an afterlife. Considering the possibility that human beings may have walked the earth as long ago as two million years, the link between death and the notion of a soul or spirit may be very old indeed. In the late Bronze Age, specifically in Carnac, France, Stonehenge in England, and in Egypt and Mesopotamia, cremation was used as a way of freeing the spirit from the body.[1] The association of fire, breath, energy and spirit is a recurring theme that appears in many ancient cultures and religions.

The references to the soul in world literature and traditions that have been preserved over the past three thousand or so years are too numerous to be compiled in this chapter. The literature is so large that a book could be written on the history of the soul alone. There are however, a number of cultures in which the references to the idea of soul are so specific and have had such an influence on the culture, that they bear a closer examination for the purpose of understanding the relation between politics and the soul.

ANCESTRAL CULTURE AND MORALITY IN AFRICA AND THE AMERICAS

An examination of the multiplicity of beliefs, in ancient and present African culture, reveals the notion of two kinds of time: *mythical time* which is a kind of eternal time and *real time*, in which the life and death of the individual occurs. Between these two kinds of time, ritual is the mediating link.[2] The individual spirit moves between real time and

---

1   Ibid
2   Eliade, Mircea, *Encyclopedia of Religion*, pg. 133

mythical time at death in a variety of ways depending on the particular culture you examine.

African cultures, in general, appear to have had several key concepts of soul that appear regardless of tribal affiliation. The notion of an immortal double or life force that leaves the body at death is an almost universal theme. The idea of reincarnation or an afterlife for the spirits of the dead is almost a secondary consideration, as the living and the dead are on a continuum with the present, in most African cultures. The Bantu for example, distinguish between the 'vidye', who take an active part in the community and the 'fu' who are just the ordinary dead. [3]

> "The ancestors provide more than a personal and ethnic immortality, however. The hierarchical ancestral community is the repository of the accumulated knowledge of successive generations, and in this sense it is the memory of the ethnic group, the product of its origins and its past. It represents the law of the fathers, and it exercises a permanent regulatory function over the life of the group. This explains the importance of cult and ritual in African society." [4]

The dead represent a form of continuity with the past that allows those in the present to participate in their collective wisdom. The association of the soul with the continuity of culture emerges as an important consideration in African culture. Indeed, the notion of the soul or spirit of the dead as the link between past, present and future emerges quite clearly in any overview of African culture.

> "The study of immortality among American Indian and Eurasiatic peoples has revealed the existence of the **Road of the Dead**. Study of these routes of the deceased is of value for our knowledge

---

3   Ibid
4   Ibid

of these peoples' beliefs in immortality. They are of two principal kinds. The first is the heavenly road, reserved for chiefs, initiates, and those among the moral elite. The second is underground, or horizontal; it is the normal road leading to the world of the dead, or quite simply to the deceased familiar haunts. In the discovery of the roads of the dead, a major role has been played by shamanism, for it is through the shamans' journeys to the transcendental world that the living have been informed about the paths to the beyond." [5]

The notion of a moral elite, which takes the high road as opposed to the low road, is a common concept, emerging from studies of both African and American Indian cultures. The Bambara, for example, are a tribe in Mali whose members believe that the most perfect of the ancestors are allowed to gaze upon God.

In the Americas, the superiority of the moral pathway is most beautifully attested to in a 15th century poem attributed to Nezahualcoyotl, the philosopher king of Texcoco, who ruled in the Valley of Mexico. Nezahualcoyotl had a vision of the "unknown, unknowable Lord of everywhere" and had built a temple where no blood sacrifice of any kind was allowed.[6]

"the riches of this world are only lent to us
the things that are so good to enjoy we do not own
the sun pours down gold
fountains pour out green water
colors touch us like fingers
of green quetzal wings
none of this can we own for more than a day
none of these beautiful things can we keep for more than an hour
one thing alone can we own forever

---

5   Ibid pg. 135
6   [WP] https://en.wikipedia.org/wiki/Nezahualcoyotl

the memory of the just
the remembrance of a good act
the good remembrance of a just man
this one thing alone will never be taken away from us
will never die" [7]

EGYPT

The ancient Egyptians had a complex set of spiritual beliefs that differentiated the soul into three different components. There was the *Akh,* which was divine energy, the *Ba* which was the faculty of movement and the *Ka* which was the divine breath which supports all life.[8] The Ka was what we would think of today as an immortal soul. The complexity of Egyptian burial practices and the elaborate preparations for death, as exemplified by mummification and the pyramids, revolved around an understanding of the nature of the Ka and its place in the cosmos. The importance of mummification was based on the belief that at death, the *Ka* became separated from the body and then required a substitute to continue in existence.[9]

Those who died without leaving a mummy could nonetheless enjoy a blessed existence, in the boat of the Sun, if they had lived their lives in accordance with *Maat* (justice).[10] The connection between the ethical life and eternal reward is clearly present in Egyptian culture. What is even more interesting is that in ancient Egypt, the entire culture revolved around the futurity of the soul. It is believed that the worship of Osiris, which began in the Fifth Dynasty (2498–2345 B.C) initiated the Egyptian belief in the resurrection and an afterlife. This belief was, in all likelihood, common in the Middle East as a result of the long Egyptian influence in the area. As ruler of the dead, Osiris was sometimes called the "king of the living." Ancient Egyptians also

---

7   Eliade, Mircea, *Encyclopedia of Religion*
8   Ibid
9   Ibid
10   Ibid

considered the blessed dead, "the living ones." The vast expenditures on the Pyramids gives some indication how important the soul was in Egyptian society and how public policy was utilized for religious purposes. It has often been said that the monotheism of Egypt was the inspiration for the religion of the Jews and certainly elements of this ancient religion resurfaced in Islam as part of a long desert tradition in the Middle East.

INDIA

India has been and is a land obsessed with God and the soul. The Vedas, which were produced by the Aryans who invaded northwest India approximately 1500 B.C., are the oldest scriptures of Hinduism.[11] The word 'Veda' comes from the root word meaning 'know'. The Rigveda which is the earliest of the Vedas (1,000 B.C.) distinguishes between the body and the 'asu' which is the life force or breath and 'manas' which is the source of the intellect and feelings which is located in the heart.[12] The Upanishads, which were later Veda texts, describe the 'atman' as the undying personal self or soul which undergoes the cycle of rebirth, until united with the divine principal of the universe, Brahman. Indian thought has a vast metaphysical literature on the soul which is highly detailed. There are many schools of Indian spirituality which show the connection between a moral life and the attainment of enlightenment. Asceticism and self-denial are considered to be part of *bhakti*, or loving devotion to God.

Later Yogic thought (the word yoga means yoke) developed an elaborate theory of soul structure which is quite helpful in describing or providing a schematic for the soul. According to Yogic thought there are seven centers of consciousness which are located in the body but are not *of* the body. These seven centers or 'chakras' are manifestations of the activity of the atman or soul. A schematic of what the

---

11 Eliade, Mircea, *Encyclopedia of Religion*
12 Ibid

chakras[13] would look like is shown on the next page.

The relationship between the chakras and the body provides us with the first detailed metaphysical look at a possible body-soul relationship or analogical structure based on the ideas of locality and non-locality. The principle of chakra theory is that the *kundalini*, which is the non-local, primordial soul energy, lies coiled like a snake at the base of the spine. This *kundalini* rises through the chakras on its journey to the overhead centers of consciousness, through the virtuous practice of various disciplines, until enlightenment takes place. This soul energy can get side-tracked by excessive sexuality and immorality by bonding to the lower chakras in such a way that the energy cannot rise any further. The truth or falsity of this schema is not necessarily important but it provides a non-local model for a relationship between moral actions and the overall availability of psychic energy. (Energy rises, so to speak, based on moral excellence and the negentropic managing of natural instincts.)

---

13 Courtesy of free Google image search for Chakras

Seven Chakras

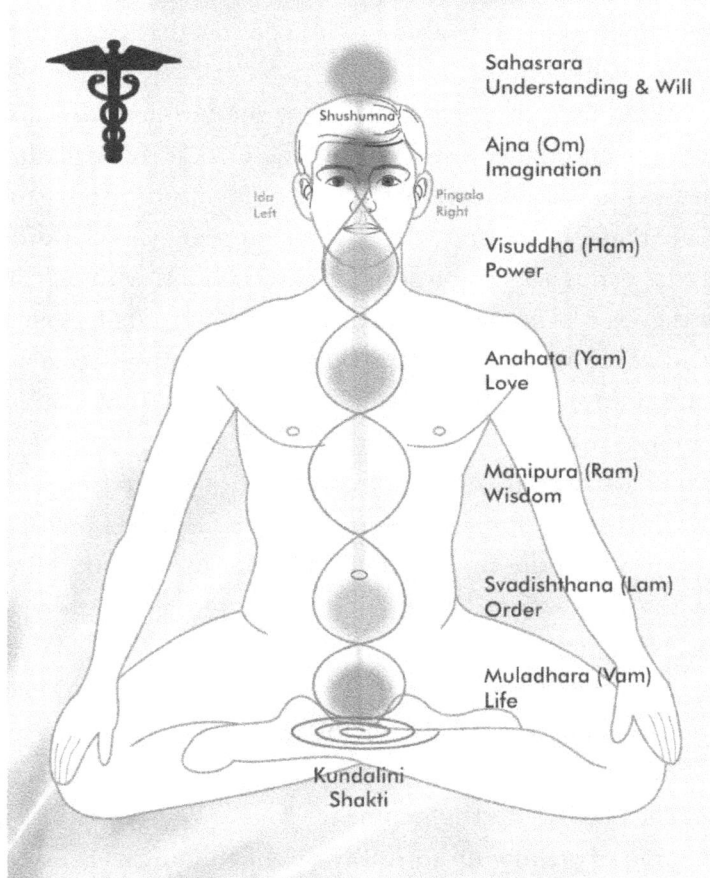

Sahasrara
Understanding & Will

Shushumna

Ajna (Om)
Imagination

Ida
Left

Pingala
Right

Visuddha (Ham)
Power

Anahata (Yam)
Love

Manipura (Ram)
Wisdom

Svadishthana (Lam)
Order

Muladhara (Vam)
Life

Kundalini
Shakti

BUDDHISM AND HINDUISM

The Buddhists, on the other hand, have generally maintained that there is no such thing as a distinct soul and that the illusion of soul is maintained by false identity with limited things. An identification through enlightenment with the divine reality is the only real identity of all things and this identity cannot be conceptualized. Nonetheless, moral purification is necessary to avoid the illicit identification of oneself with things that are not one's true self. The attainment of this non-soul identity is conditional upon the strictures of a moral existence, chiefly exemplified by an ignoring of the desires that create irrelevant structures of self-identity.

The Buddhists, in a sense, represent the ultimate conclusion of many aspects of Hindu thinking. If there is no formal difference between God and the individual atman or soul, ultimately, the only conclusion that can be drawn is that the appearance of a difference between the two is an illusion. The Hindu tradition with exception of some of the later Vedantic schools of thought (Vedanta means, literally, the end of the Vedas) is therefore diametrically opposed to the later Christian tradition that claims a radical distinction between God and His creation.

There have been many attempts in recent years to bridge the gap between Christianity and Hinduism, and many fruitful intellectual exchanges. However, the fundamental religious and cultural difference between the two cannot however be lightly glossed over by zealous syncretists. The later Greek and Christian concept of the soul as a dynamic, *existentially endowed* entity must be clearly distinguished from the somewhat passive character of the atman which appears only to need waking up, as opposed to being engaged by the will and intellect as part of the process of enlightenment. Walker Percy has a fascinating interpretation of waking up to reality or enlightenment as "rotation", i.e., there is a kind of stepping out of the mundane that occurs with a psychic rotation into a higher reality or higher awareness. What triggers this rotation is somewhat mysterious but the notion of the atman or higher self being able to "wake up" is an example and expression of how non-locality can erupt into and transform "local" conditions.

The wretched condition of India's poor is one example of how a non-dynamic concept of soul can affect political thinking. India's caste system, which in the past, assigned individuals to certain social categories based on birth and family was a direct consequence of considering the soul as a passive entity which must endure given conditions, as part of fate and karma. This later socialized and politicized concept of the soul, as a caste-bound entity is probably not at all what the authors of the Upanishads had in mind. There are some extremely pure and beautiful concepts of the soul in these writings. The Chandogya and Subala Upanishads, for example, show the soul to be a dynamic entity:

"This is my self (atman) within the heart, smaller than a grain of rice, or a corn of barley, or a mustard seed, or a grain of millet, or the kernel within a grain of millet. This is my self within the heart, greater than the earth, greater than the skies, greater than the heavens, greater than all the worlds...A wise person never sorrows, for he knows the soul (atman) to be vast, independent... without origin." [14]

A number of twentieth century Indian thinkers, notably Ghandi, Tagore, Sri Aurobindo and others came to understand that the passivity associated with the caste system had led to a stagnation of Indian society. They were, however, noticeably influenced by Christianity in this regard. One has only to read the biographical accounts of Sri Aurobindo, for example, to see the influence of his Episcopalian education in England. This is not to detract from the power and originality of his writings, which were rooted in both Vedantic philosophy (and therefore in the authority of the Vedas) and in his own unique faith and experience of the Divine.

Nonetheless, the failure of Indian society to overcome the caste system parallels the Christian inability to overcome slavery. The failure of religion to come to grips with moral deficiency is an indication that ideas regarding morality and spirituality can be at variance when the concept of Existence is not fully queried or adverted to. It is not possible to view Existence as being generous and good to all without rooting out ideas that can only be in opposition to the common perception of that goodness. It is interesting to note that the caste system today is

14 Eliade, Mircea, *Encyclopedia of Religion*

being overcome not by law but by economics, as lower caste members successfully compete against upper-caste businessmen by outbidding them on multi-national database accounts and services.

CHINESE PHILOSOPHY

The ancient Chinese concept of the soul utilizes a dual soul, which does not appear to be connected to a sense of individual immortality. There is the 'Po' which is the earthly aspect of the soul and the 'Hun' which is the heavenly aspect.[15] Both Po and Hun are nourished by Ch'i which is the binding force of the cosmos and are related to the Yin and Yang principles, which represent the creative and active aspects of the universe. The notion of creation is not part of Chinese cosmology or of their idea of soul. The world is taken as always becoming. This process is known as the great transformation or 'Ta-Hua', more commonly known to us today as the Tao. This is, from a modern perspective, an excellent articulation of the relationship between locality and non-locality.

> *"Ta-Hua makes every modality of being in the universe a dynamic change rather than a static structure. A piece of stone, a blade of grass, a horse, a human being, a spirit and Heaven all form a continuum. They are all integrated by the pervasive Ch'i (vital force and material force which constitutes both matter and energy) that penetrates every dimension of existence and functions as the constitutive element for each modality of being."* [16]

The notion of Heaven, being the exemplar of what is above and beyond man, in terms of both moral excellence and perfection in general, gives rise to the Confucian notion of *Li*. Li is a concept without a direct English translation but it essentially means "a binding way of

---

15 Ibid
16 Eliade, Mircea, *Encyclopedia of Religion*

honor" that is lived out by adhering to the social order of hierarchy and ritual, which is in turn, rooted in the *Tao*. The individual soul achieves an impersonal immortality through a participation in the excellence of both Heaven and earth.

The earlier Taoist tradition views Heaven as part of the Tao. The Tao exists before heaven and earth; it is a primordial wholeness, living and creative and also a paradisiacal state.[17]

> "*The attempts of Taoist adepts to re integrate this paradisiacal state constitutes their search for immortality, an exaltation of the primordial human condition. The attempt of Confucius (Kung-Tzu) was similar to that of Lao Tzu, in that both were based on ancient fundamental ideas—the Tao as the principal of macrocosm and microcosm to all levels of existence. Lao-tzu sought out the original unity within their own lives; Confucius looked for it in a balanced and just society. Lao-tzu was in search of the Tao, the ultimate, mysterious, unfathomable reality underlying all existence, seeking out the living wholeness through a reconciliation of opposites and a return to the beginnings. Confucius (551-479 BC) rejected neither the Tao, nor the god of Heaven, nor the veneration of ancestors. For him, the Tao was a decree from Heaven. He recommended a system of education that could transform the ordinary individual into a superior person, so that society might become an embodiment of the original cosmic harmony.*" [18]

As an aside, John Scottus Eriugena, was of the opinion that the fall of man occurred contemporary with creation and that paradise was simply the metaphor of what Divine Life holds for humanity at the long end of the *reditus* or the return of the all to the All.[19]

---

17 Ibid
18 Ibid
19 *John Scottus Eriugena, Diedre Carabine*, Professor and Director of the Institute of Ethics and Development Studies, Uganda Martyrs University; Oxford University Press, copyright 2000, pages 87-88

The proper ways of acting, so important in Confucian thinking, are a reflection of the natural order of things or the role of *Li*. The literal translation of "Li" means, among other things, markings in jade. "Jade means a precious stone with five virtues, benevolence (仁), righteousness (義), wisdom (智), bravery (勇), honesty and cleanliness (潔). Jade also has a religious meaning. Wizard (巫) in Chinese is from the symbol of two kinds of jade listed together as an offering to the gods and ancestors. Therefore, The meaning of jade to the Chinese is very important. A Chinese [bearing] jade means he is a man of virtue (君子) and respects the gods and [his] ancestors."[20] It later came to mean the treasure of a king. "Li" is not quite the same thing as the western notion of Natural Law but the basic concept or pattern is very similar. Human behavior is to be conditioned according to an unseen or hidden reality (the non-local Tao or true existence) which is a higher and more excellent reality than disclosed by common human perceptions but which is not wholly unrelated to human actions.

Confucius considered this kind of behavioral conditioning essential to realizing *wu-wei*—*right* action that comes naturally.[21] Edward Slingerland explains the process of its attainment in his book, Trying Not To Try: *Ancient China, Modern Science and the Power of Spontaneity.*[22]

"In the early stages of training, an aspiring Confucian gentleman needs to memorize entire shelves of archaic texts, learn the precise angle at which to bow, and learn the lengths of the steps with which he is to enter a room. His sitting mat must always be perfectly straight. All of this rigor and restraint, however, is ultimately aimed at producing a cultivated, but nonetheless genuine, form of spontaneity. Indeed, the process of training is

20 https://www.quora.com/What-is-the-significance-of-jade-in-Chinese-culture

21 Cited in Kyle Eschenroeder' excellent article in The Art of Manliness at: http://www. artofmanliness.com/2016/08/15/what-do-you-want-to-want/?

22 Ibid

not considered complete until the individual has passed completely beyond the need for thought or effort." [23]

"In other words, through deliberate training that at first feels tedious, *we eventually arrive at a point where we want what we want to want.*"[24] This is another way of describing moral and intellectual virtue. The more we do the right thing, the more it becomes naturally part of our behavior and disposition.

Confucius' predecessor, Lao Tzu, (571-531 BC) affirmed this kind of acquired virtue as the authentic way of the soul in one of the most marvelously succinct paragraphs ever written about the non-local characteristics of Existence.

"It is the Way and the Waygoer. It is the eternal road along which walk all beings, but no being made it, for itself is being. It is everything and nothing. From it all things spring, all things conform to it, and to it at last all things return. It is a square without angles, a sound which ears cannot hear, and an image without form. It is a vast net and though its meshes are as wide as the sea it lets nothing through. It is the sanctuary where all things find refuge. It is nowhere, but without looking out of the window you may see it. Desire not to desire, it teaches, and leave all things to take their course. He that humbles himself shall be preserved entire. He that bends shall be made straight. Failure is the foundation of success and success is the lurking-place of failure; but who can tell when the turning point will come? He who strives after tenderness can become even as a little child. Gentleness brings victory to him who attacks and safety to him who defends. Mighty is he who conquers himself." [25]

---

23 Slingerland, Edward, *Trying Not To Try*: Ancient China, Modern Science and the Power of Spontaneity, Broadway Books, 2015
24 Ibid
25 Lao Tzu, *The Way of Life*, translated by Witter Bynner, Capricorn Books, NY, 1944

There was no concept of personal freedom in ancient China that corresponds to our American concept of individual liberty. Freedom, however, seldom existed in a vacuum for the Chinese and always implied responsibility, and a connection to the culture at large. The very freedom that allows the individual American to achieve so much, also insulates him from a general responsibility to the culture at large. We need to return to the idea of responsibility and moral rectitude as being a collective responsibility and not a hindrance. Furthermore, those who are busy attempting to conquer themselves will have far less time on their hands to bother others. A great deal of physical and other forms of violence can be avoided when men and women are forced to look inwards for some measure of control over their appetites.

Li or a moral social order is absolutely necessary if we are to avoid the chaos that is slowly settling in some sections of the Third World. We are not at liberty to understand the world as simply as the ancient Africans, Chinese, Egyptians or the Indians did, but we do have the responsibility to see that their insights are preserved in a higher synthesis of philosophy, and not merely presented as examples of the relativism of all cultural beliefs. The work of Lao Tzu, in conjunction with the ethics of Aristotle, is an excellent place to begin such deliberations.

BELIEF

Belief might be seen as a reflection of an on-going synthesis of our understanding of God based on an infinite power that is our formal and final cause. Multiple belief systems are not merely an indication of cultural relativism but are on the contrary, indicative that culture and belief are relative to, and a product of, an on-going relationship with the infinity of the Divine Nature. The Reality Dysfunction makes all perceptions about God possible. The key is to understand how the relationship between God and man might be understood from an ontological, rather than a specifically religious point of view, in order to build a common and public understanding of both morality and virtue.

The idea of the soul is the concept in the middle and mediates in a sense, the extremes of the cultural, political and religious ideas that constitute the time war. As a conflict between various ideas about time, motion and existence, confabulated with religious precepts about the soul and behavior, the time war is often a confusing jumble of cross currents. The religious perspective always adds an additional dimension to cultural, philosophical or politicized ideas about the soul but without a working, secular concept of soul, both politics and religion founders. A clear concept of the soul is the ark that can weather every sea and preserves everything that is valuable in life.

Americans have difficulty considering a Public Philosophy, like that of the Confucians, because there are those who would say that such a philosophy would interfere with their freedom and must therefore not exist in the public sector. Those who would have no philosophy, or mention of God or the soul at all, in either their lives, or anyone else's should be heard, but their words should not drive all decisions. If an individual does not believe in either God or the soul, then surely they ought to be able to ignore those who do and perhaps laugh at them. The fear of both religion and the idea of the soul that many of these people evince is disturbing. So what if little Johnny, who can see naked women and watch all sorts of violence on his smart phone, hears about God, the soul or morality in school? Will he be worse off than if he had never heard of such concepts?

Understandably there are those who are afraid that certain Christian sects might predominate and exercise an excessive influence on the educational system should the soul be used and taught as a metaphysical construct to explain human actions and motivations. This problem, however, makes it all the more urgent to have a philosophy of soul that is broad and deep enough to encompass all schools of thought without either allowing any one faction to predominate, or watering down the material to the point of uselessness. This is the task of good philosophy and is in fact, a requirement of the real meaning of separation of Church and State.

A close reading of the Founding Fathers, for example, does not indicate that they wanted a separation of God and State but a relative separation of Church and State, which is an entirely different matter. Not wanting to have any one religion predominate in political affairs does not and should not translate into the complete removal of God from political affairs. The current separation of Church and State, as an atheistic separation of God and State, would not, generally speaking, be consonant with the intent of the Founding Fathers who were either solidly Christian or, at the very least, were Deists.

If more of our children were to become religious due to the influence of a public philosophy, would they be harmed? Let those who are afraid of religion be honest with themselves. Their fear and hatred of religion particularly, Christianity, are misplaced. The soul as a concept can be atheistic. There is much in Aristotle for example, to suggest that the soul does not exist beyond the life of the body but such a teaching does not abrogate the need for a teaching on virtue and public awareness of the hidden structure of dimensions adjacent to and beyond our own. Our bias towards not believing until seeing must be replaced by a mental gyroscopic correction in favor of listening to what the philosopher Heraclitus referred to as, *"the speaking togethering"* of reality.

This "speaking togethering" is rooted in God's causality and it is truly something that we can "hear" with non-local ears more than we can see. As effects residing in a Cause, we carry with us the force of something more ancient, powerful and wise than the entire universe. It is this force that we tap into whenever we say, "we believe". When we believe, we allow ourselves to open up to non-local forces greater than our own and attach both the force of will and this outside energy to a concept or idea—we say: "that is" and it can become a self-referential truth, regardless of whether or not it might be objectively described as true or false.

Jesus, for example, spoke many times about faith. His teaching indicated that faith allows the energy and power of the Father to flow to and through us. Faith, understood in modern terms, means that the relationship between God and man is on a continuum with one influencing the other. Think of it as a kind of intranet between God and the human soul. When Mary approaches Jesus, for example, during the wedding feast of Cana and tells him that the host has run out of wine, he indicates to her in no uncertain terms that "his time has not yet come." Nonetheless, she tells the chief steward, "to do as He says." The famous miracle of turning water into wine came about only because Mary had the kind of relationship of faith with the Father that Jesus often spoke about.

Faith, in this sense, involves a new kind of dynamism between God and man or a new form of blended consciousness between God and individual human beings. Christians typically refer to this blended state of consciousness as "being in a state of grace" when moral actions are in conformity with the will of God. This is not a static state but one of immense dynamism if it is understood correctly. God is not a fixed point that we have access to like filling up at the gas station. Loading up on God, so to speak, means being filled with the freedom and joy of the Spirit.

According to many ancient teachings, energy flows to thought and energy flows even more massively when thought is linked by belief or harnessed to a sure and powerful relationship with the Divine. We give a great deal of energy to belief, so be careful about what you believe in. The more we believe in something, the more energy flows in that direction. It is a self-reinforcing system and it can sometimes be extraordinarily dangerous unless it is tempered by a set of ideas that allow us to adjust the power button.

THE GREEKS AND THE IDEA OF THE SOUL

The ideas of the soul that we are most familiar with today originated with the Greeks. The earliest Greeks believed in a kind of animism called *hylozoism*, i.e., that all matter is animated by a life principle. Homer's Iliad and Odyssey (700-800 BC.) refer to the *psuche* which is a soul representing the individual personality. This soul is essentially inactive, other than that it is a prerequisite for life and it departs at death. *Psuche, thumos, menos* and the later nous were all words used to refer to various aspects of soul. *Thumos* (which may have originally meant smoke) appeared to be considered the center of the emotions, and *menos* appears to have indicated the activities of mind, as did nous.

There appears to have been an evolution in Greek thought regarding the soul. The loose constellation of ideas about what the soul was or does started to take greater shape and direction with Pythagoras (550 B.C.). Pythagoras introduced the idea of transmigration of souls, which added to increasingly sophisticated speculation on the meaning of the soul. Apparently, the idea of transmigration did not enter the mainstream of Greek religion without resistance and was the subject of some humor.

> *"A contemporary satirist relates that when Pythagoras saw a dog being beaten, he exclaimed: Stop! Do not beat him. It is the [soul] of a dead friend. I recognized him when I heard him whine."* [26]

The various Greek teachings on the soul seem to have coalesced in the teachings of Socrates. For Socrates, (479-379 BC.) the soul was *psuche* (psyche) and directly related to the deity. Plato, as the mouthpiece of Socrates, had many ideas about the soul which are still in use today. Socrates wrote nothing, so we must reconstruct Socrates' thoughts and ideas from Plato's *Dialogues*.

The dialogue with Euthyphro gives us an excellent example of Socrates' unique take on meaning as opposed to opinion. [27] Euthyphro is a young man who is bringing a charge against his own father for impiety. He meets Socrates at the Hall of King Archon where Socrates is himself waiting to see who brought charges against *him* for impiety. Socrates expresses great pleasure in meeting Euthyphro and then dis-

---

26 Stumpf, Samuel E., *Socrates to Sartre: A History of Philosophy*, McGraw-Hill Book Company, 1966, pg. 41

27 Ibid

covers what it is that the young man has come to the hall for. (Impiety is of course a charge of irreverence towards the Gods and as such, almost anything could be construed to be impious.)

Socrates inquires as to the meaning of impiety from Euthyphro and proceeds by way of questioning, to show the young man the fallacies of his thinking. Socrates asks him the question, *"Do the Gods love an act because it is pious or is it pious because the Gods love it?"* Euthyphro is unable to answer the question and instead talks in general about piety. Socrates suggests to him that if he really knew the meaning of impiety, then he might not be bringing charges against his father. He presses Euthyphro for a clearer definition of piety but the young man suddenly finds that he needs to leave for an appointment.

What clearly emerges from this dialogue is that Socrates is concerned about the real meaning of piety and that the definition of piety is important if one is to arrive at the truth. Socrates presupposes that there is an objective truth to be uncovered, otherwise there would be no meaning to either human actions or discourse. For Socrates, definition is an instrument of clear thinking because things are not what they are in themselves without the existential support of the Gods.[28]

"What impressed Socrates was that although particular events or things varied in some respects or passed away, there was something about them that was the same, that never varied and never passed away, and this was their definition or their essential nature. It was this permanent meaning that Socrates wanted Euthyphro to give him when he asked for that Idea of piety by which pious acts are pious. In a similar way, Socrates sought the Idea of Justice by which acts become just or the Idea of Beauty by which particular things are said to be beautiful, and the Idea of Goodness by which we recognize human acts to be good...In some way, the mind, he thought, thinks about two different kinds of objects whenever it thinks about anything. A beautiful flower is at once

---

28 Ibid

this particular flower and at the same time a single example or
partaker of the general or universal meaning of Beauty. The pro-
cess of definition was for Socrates the process whereby the mind
could distinguish or sort out these two objects of thought." [29]

The relationship between the universal idea and the particular expression of that idea is mirrored in the relationship of the One (God) and the Many (the multiple existing things in the universe). What God knows is somehow related to all universals.[30] Socrates' genius lay in recognizing that there was a relationship between the universal, the ideas of God and the soul. The soul, like God's Ideas endures beyond its particular bodily manifestations.

Socrates sought to discover a way in which the soul's qualities might be cultivated. He came to the conclusion that the soul recognizes truth and that by seeking truth, the soul is improved. His teaching on virtue or moral excellence is a recognition that the soul is affected by human actions. Plato took this one step further and taught that the soul was forgetful of its divine origin (the doctrine of *anamnesis*) and that all learning was a process of recollection. From the perspective afforded by this book, we would say that every effect carries with it some existential echo of its cause. The dimensionally interactive nature of cyber kinesis, caused by the Reality Dysfunction, makes it possible for us to not only "see the world in a grain of sand" but to be linked, existentially and dimensionally to the entire universe.

The idea of *psuche* or soul as possessing both a link with the deity and being subject to moral development was a unique development in Greek thinking. The sophists of Socrates' time, who believed in the relativity of all things were indirectly responsible for this doctrine. At the time, they were busily spreading the notion that there were no moral absolutes and no basis for moral rules, other than feelings or personal disposition. Socrates clearly saw that a society could not survive on

---

29 Ibid
30 This notion might be linked to the idea of *interference patterns* being used to generate holograms, which was pointed out in the Introduction to this book.

such standards and fought them tooth and nail.

> *"For Socrates, knowledge and virtue (acting in accordance with reason) were the same thing. If virtue has to do with making the soul as good as possible, it is therefore, closely related...When someone commits an evil act, said Socrates, he always does it thinking that it is good in some way...For him, virtue meant fulfilling one's function. As a rational human being, a man's function is to behave rationally. At the same time, every human being has the inescapable desire for happiness or the well-being of his soul. This inner well-being, this making the soul as good as possible, can only be achieved by certain appropriate modes of behavior...*
>
> *Socrates knew that some forms of behavior appear to produce happiness but in reality do not. For this reason, men frequently choose an act that may in itself be questionable but that they, nevertheless, think may bring them happiness. A thief may know that stealing as such is wrong, but he steals in the hope that it will bring him happiness. Similarly, men pursue power, physical pleasure and property, which are the symbols of success and happiness, confusing these with [real] happiness."* [31]

Vice was for Socrates simply ignorance, an inaccurate estimation of what would bring happiness. Think of it as what happens when the Reality Dysfunction is not acknowledged and compensated for by virtue. This extraordinary teaching on virtue and vice, in relation to human happiness and the concept of the undying reality of the soul had a powerful impact on Socrates' contemporary, Plato. Indeed, it might be

31 Stumpf, Samuel E., *Socrates to Sartre: A History of Philosophy*, McGraw-Hill Book Company, 1966, pg. 67

argued that if there is anything particularly distinctive about Western Civilization, it is that Socrates' notion of the soul, which was modified by Plato, Aristotle and Christianity set the stage for an understanding of the soul, society and politics which still reverberates today in the political and moral structures of Western Civilization.

Our modern amnesia of the relation between the soul of the good man and woman, and the good society is an expression of the Time War whereby the perception of atheistic, deconstructed time and spiritual time are at odds with one another. This is at the core of many of our social difficulties today.

The overcoming of the temporal splintering effect of the Reality Dysfunction begins with an acknowledgment that it is part of the human condition and that the opposite pole of the Reality Dysfunction, which consists of moral and intellectual excellence, in imitation of God's own sacrifice (in being and knowing Himself outside Himself), must be emphasized as part of the overcoming of all difficulties. Our being outside of ourselves to know ourselves, as other than who we really are, involves being tied to both our biology and something that is beyond biology. Virtue mirrors the excellence of soul that is necessary to recover from the various oppositions innate to the Reality Dysfunction. Virtue is truly the royal road between heaven and earth.

CHAPTER 14

SOME IDEAS ABOUT THE SOUL AND THE UNIVERSE

"To attain any assured knowledge about the soul is one of most difficult things in the world."

—Aristotle,
De Anima

THE SOUL AS A SPECIAL KIND OF FORM

Aristotle, as we saw in the opening chapters, synthesized the thinking of his time by refining the concept of *form* or what was later termed *essence* or *nature* by medieval theologians. The 'form' or 'nature' is the organizing principal, or as we might say today, the non-local *synergy*[1] of

---

1   The interaction of elements that when combined produce a total effect that is greater than the sum of the individual elements or contributing factors.

an object. Aristotle described the soul as a *living form* or the *first act of a body having life-potential* in his treatise on the soul, De Anima.

For Aristotle, the soul was simply the secondary principal of actuality and not a particularly religious concept. The form cannot be seen because it represents a futurity, part of which is only revealed in the now, as an unfolding of the potentiality of substance. *Substance* is the combination of potency and act with matter providing the potency and form providing the act. The form is in *act* and causes the given determinations that are disclosed by potentiality to unfold in time. A boy, given time will become a man. The potentiality of adulthood is a future actuality not yet manifested but potentially present.

Potentiality is deposited, as it were, by a greater actuality in the union of matter and form by the Unmoved Mover in the Reality Dysfunction.

"And on this account they were right who thought that the soul is neither apart from the body nor the same as the body; for it is not, indeed the body; yet it is something of the body. And therefore it is in a body, and a body of a definite kind; and not as some earlier thinkers made out, who related it to a body without defining at all the nature and quality of that body; despite the fact that it is apparent that **not any subject whatever can receive any form at random***. And that such is the case is confirmed by reason: the act of any one thing is of that which is in potency to it, and it occurs naturally and fittingly in matter appropriate to it. That the soul, then, is an actuality and formal principle of a thing in potency to exist accordingly, is evident from these considerations.*

Aristotle,
De Anima, Bk. 2, Ch. 2

Aristotle's teaching on the soul is not an easy one to grasp at first. The soul is not exactly in a thing inasmuch as it is the cause of a thing, and yet it is the thing, without being limited to the thing. Looking at Aristotle's teaching as a whole it is perhaps safe to say that *the soul is not inside the body but that the body is inside the soul*. This can be clarified if we think of anything that exists as being composed of potency and act. The potency cannot exist without a corresponding actuality. In other words, if there is potential, there must be something *that* potentiality exists in relation to. Potency exists because there is an actuality that represents the depositing agent of that potentiality. Now whether or not the form completely accounts for that depositing in potency within Aristotelianism is debatable. Aristotle seemed to think that the form might be "moved" in a manner, relative to its nature, by the Unmoved Mover on the basis of what it could be, potentially, in the future. Potential in Aristotle might be thought of as the present manifestation in time of something that has more of its existence in the future than it has in the present. The question can be asked, of course, why does the future or potential even exist unless it was known or decohered in some way by an outside agent? Modern science does not look in this direction because it has, a-priori, determined that causality is an illusion.

Metaphysically speaking, It makes more sense to think of the actuality of any form, *as being*, deposited by the supreme actuality of Existence itself. Things that are *in act* have a secondary form of existence that is based on participation in Existence itself. This was, in fact, the position of the later medieval philosophers on the relationship between the soul and God or Existence. The soul is, therefore, a form of causality, or more precisely, *formal causality*. Accordingly, plants have vegetative souls, animals have animal souls and man has a human soul. The soul of a man, for instance cannot simultaneously be the soul of a dolphin or a monkey. The form or soul of a thing is particular to that thing and that thing only.

*What is seen in all living things and material objects is potential-
ity being unfolded by an actuality which cannot be seen. According to Fr. Joseph Owens, "The notion of abstracting a universal
or 'essence' from singulars…does not occur in Aristotle. A sensible
thing may considered as universal or as singular. The difference
lies between potential and actual cognition. As known actually,
the sensible thing is singular. As known potentially, it is universal." ²What Aristotle does not do is ask if the Unmoved Mover's
eternal knowledge could make things both singular and universal. For Aristotle, this would have been a difficult undertaking,
as it would indicate change in God. By relating being to entity,
it might be thought that Aristotle was, even at this early stage of
metaphysics, attempting to understand that there was a distinction between the eternal knowledge of the Unmoved Mover as it
might be manifested in time and that knowledge as it might be
in eternity. This difficulty is overcome by the mediation of the
Reality Dysfunction or the virtual reality created by God's knowing Himself, outside Himself.*

Owens notes, quoting Aristotle, that "this form is the what-Is-Being, eternal, unchangeable [and] un-generated. As prior to the composite
[of matter and form as in substance] it is prior to the changeable singular,
and so prior to time, for time follows upon change."³ On the face of it,
this looks and sounds like Plato's notion of the eternal Ideas but it appears that Aristotle is attempting to articulate a peculiar relationship of
the Ideas to what is eternal and immovable. Owens goes on to say that
"a peculiarly Aristotelian word, *entelechy*, denotes act as extended beyond
movement."⁴ Aristotle indicates that every movement is "incomplete"
suggesting that something that does not move completes movement.

2   Owens, Joseph, *The Doctrine of Being in the Aristotelian Metaphysics*, pg. 389, Pontifical
    Institute of Mediaeval Studies, copyright 1951,Toronto, Ontario
3   Owens, Joseph, *The Doctrine of Being in the Aristotelian Metaphysics*, pgs. 394-397, Pon-
    tifical Institute of Mediaeval Studies, copyright 1951,Toronto, Ontario
4   Ibid, pages 404-405

The Aristotelian notion of *eidos*, which is both physical form and logical species[5] (something like the agent intellect's grasping of the species of the phantasm in scholastic metaphysics) cannot be fully understood, in my opinion, without resorting to the notion of the Reality Dysfunction or a kind of virtual reality whereby something that cannot change can cause change external to Itself. One senses, although it could be just my imagination, that Aristotle saw the problematic metaphysical consequences that Ideas generated by the Mind of the Unmoved Mover might produce but was unable to adequately formulate the necessary distinctions to correct those consequences due to the lack of analogical and other tools available to the thinkers of his time period.

The notion of soul then has complicated antecedents but from the perspective of metaphysics, we can pose the following question: does the actuality of the soul, regardless of its origin, have a structure? Aristotle taught that the soul's characteristics could be understood in terms of *powers* and that these powers were divided into *faculties*. For example, the will is a faculty of the appetitive power, digestion a faculty of the vegetative power and vision a faculty of the sensitive power.

The following might be helpful in understanding the structure of the human soul and its relation to the body. It is based on a later, more developed concept of the soul as it was described by medieval philosophers and Aquinas. (Note that the powers of the soul correspond, indirectly, to the Hindu concept of the chakras.)

THE POWERS OF THE SOUL

POWERS AND OPERATIONS

1. **Vegetative (Genetic) Power**
   The operations are generation, use of food (nutrition) and growth.

---

5   Ibid, page 293

2. **Sensitive Power**

ed into five interior senses and five exterior senses.

THE FIVE INTERIOR SENSES:

1. Common sense

2. Phantasy (images created with the passive intellect's apprehension of the form as in phantasm)

3. Imagination

4. Estimation (calculation)

5. Memory

THE FIVE EXTERIOR SENSES

1. Sight

2. Hearing

3. Touch

4. Smell

5. Taste

3. **The Appetitive Power**

The operations of the Appetitive Power are divided into **concupiscible** passions (emotions) and the **irascible** appetites, which are those that involve some level of difficulty. The concupiscible appetites are those that come to us more readily.

Examples: The passions of the irascible appetite are hope, despair, fear, daring and anger. The passions of the concupiscible appetite are love hatred, delight, sorrow or pain.

4. The Locomotive Power (movement)

5. Intellectual Power (divided into two faculties)

- Active intellect (sometimes referred to as the agent intellect)
- Possible intellect (sometimes referred to as the passive intellect)

From the point of view of Resolution Theory (discussed in the Introduction), which relates good and evil to the tendency toward or away from complexity, the structure of the soul might be thought of as a manifestation of the particular act, within the Divine Mind that constitutes the reality of the soul. This "act" is God knowing himself in a unique way both locally and non-locally in the Reality Dysfunction. The full actuality of the soul remains mysterious, and partially hidden, in the higher dimensions of hyperspace and non-locality as a whole. The potentiality of the body reveals the effects of the soul's manifestation. Potentiality reveals something profound about the dual nature of being. Being is either potential or it is actual; there is no in-between (except perhaps at the quantum level of reality). What we see in the world around us is actualized potentiality or *substantial being*. We do not see actuality at all. Things are what they are because they have the potential to be just what they are. A dog, being a dog, is exercising its potentiality to be a dog.

Another way of looking at this has been developed by Ken Wilber in his book, *A Brief History of Everything*. Wilber develops Arthur Koestler's notion of the *Holon*. A Holon is an entity (a being) that is a separate whole and simultaneously a part of some other whole. The world is composed of *holons* which simultaneously transcend themselves at the same time they are being themselves. They also englobe other *holons* in increasingly complex holonic structures. Note the causal disconnect of this concept with the notion of forms being supported by a transcendent Existence. When Existence is collapsed into the universe at large, a form of pantheism tends to be the result.

The concept of holons is not entirely dissimilar to the notion of *prehension* which is part of Whitehead's process philosophy. Prehension, similarly, allows for "existential occasions," which are causally connected to all of Existence, to take other existential occasions into themselves. In the end, concepts like the holon, prehension and Hegel's dialectic are attempts to understand how divine subjectivity can both support the universe and manifest in the present. Without an understanding of creation as a virtual reality and the existential dynamism of essence and Existence as the link between the eternal and the temporal, no understanding of "process" without a clear defining of the relevant elements can make satisfying intellectual sense.

ACTUALITY AND POTENTIALITY

"In book 9 of the Metaphysics, Aristotle is presenting 'being' as it is divided by actuality and potentiality. Now actuality cannot be defined, since it is primary, but after providing ways in which the intelligibility of actuality can be made manifest, Aristotle claims that actuality allows for a diversity of types, which are ultimately presented as 'actuality', 'operation,' and 'being imperfectly.' The first of these is like the very power of sight with regard to the organ, while the second is like the act of seeing with regard to the power of seeing. The third, finally, is like being moved. The first, accordingly, is like the root reality that is substance; the second is the activity that issues from something, its operation; and the third is that imperfect actuality that is motion."

*"Somewhat later on in the same book, Aristotle compares actu-
ality to potentiality, and in the course of that discussion, claims
that actuality is prior to potentiality in motion, time, and perfection. He also compares the two as to well and ill and shows that
actuality is better than potentiality. Finally, he also compares
the two as to knowledge of truth and falsity, and he shows that
actuality is the principle of understanding and that potentiality
is only understood by starting with actuality. Also, and this seems
important...the true and the noble is said to be found more in
being actually than in being potentially."* [6]

Aristotle understood the word "being" as meaning entity and frequently posed some of his thinking in terms of the *Entity of the entity*, meaning: what is the origin of the being of the being? My be-ing, who I
am, is related to my potentiality for being, which appears to be a given,
based on some mediating factor. This mediating factor is the form,
which when united with matter, is substance. The actuality of the form
is *prior to its possibility*, only in relation to the notion of Existence as a
transcendental whole; it is to form what the soul is to human nature.
Fr. Joseph Owens notes that the most "fundamental and fecund distinction" in Aristotelian thought is that the translation of the word
for 'individual' can mean undivided in form or undivided in number. [7]
What this means is that the cognition of the singular is cognition of
the form: for to know a thing is to know *what-Is-being*. To know the
form makes it possible to know both the singular and the universal
but the form, according to Owen's interpretation of Aristotle, makes
the form *prior* to both kinds of knowing. [8] How can this be without a
universal observer, as the metaphysics of Aquinas require? Aristotle,

---

6   American Catholic Philosophical Quarterly, *Religions and the Virtue of Religion*, Vol
    LXV, pg. 113, Mark F. Johnson, Why Five Ways?
7   Owens, Joseph, *The Doctrine of Being in the Aristotelian Metaphysics*, pg. 389, Pontifical
    Institute of Mediaeval Studies, copyright 1951,Toronto, Ontario, Canada
8   Ibid, pages, 389-391

in my opinion, cannot proceed further without invoking a derivative reality in which the Unmoved Mover can operate outside of Itself and this he does not appear to do.

What we can say from the perspective of Resolution Theory[9] is that the substance of human nature is englobed by the higher form that is the individual soul as known by the mind of God. This is analogous to more advanced kinds of brain tissue, englobing the more primitive brain parts, such as the hypothalamus. The soul unifies other forms in a synthetic activity that reflects its origin in the inexhaustible activity of the Unmoved Mover. The soul has not merely received actuality, it has been given actuality, some separate existence, its own motive power, and its own quasi-eternity.

Aristotle's concepts were so advanced that they never really took root in his own time. The relation of form, substance and soul to Existence remained unclear until the rise of the Islamic philosophers, nearly a thousand years later. Aristotle was rediscovered by Islam in the 6th or 7th century AD and was in turn reintroduced to Europe through the works of the Islamic philosophers and commentators, Averroes and Avicenna. Thomas Aquinas, in turn, reworked and expanded Aristotle and many other thinkers, in his great 13th century synthesis of philosophy and theology, the *Summa Theologica*.

ARISTOTLE, MODERN PHYSICS AND THE FOURIER TRANSFORMS

Modern science would do well to re-examine the Aristotelian concepts of 'form' or 'nature' and Aquinas's understanding of 'Existence' or 'Esse', as they would do much to explain (at least metaphorically) how trillions of sub-atomic particles behave, at any given moment, in a systematic and purposeful manner. The laws of physics and metaphysics are simplified by using the higher dimensions of hyperspace to account for the behavior of sub-atomic matter. Things both living and non-liv-

---

9   Resolution Theory relates good and evil to the tendency toward or away from complexity.

ing are no more a product of accidental molecular arrangements than is an automobile. The organizing principles of the Four Causes and specifically, the formal cause (or form) make the genetic material of a deer for example, different from that of a mountain lion and ultimately are what account for the differentiation and coherence of its matter.

A more modern interpretation of "essence" can be approached by understanding two concepts commonly used in physics: *The Hamiltonian* and the *Fourier Transforms*. In quantum mechanics, the Hamiltonian is the operator[10] corresponding to the total energy of a system and is usually denoted by the symbol *H*. If the Hamiltonian is only represented by observable energy, then it may or may not include hidden or unknown forms of energy. If we understand Aristotle's Unmoved Mover as exerting force on material existence, then it should be possible to pose this in quasi-mathematical language. Let's refer to this as the Hamiltonian plus or H+. (Hold that thought as we continue.)

Jean Fourier, an eighteenth century French mathematician developed a mathematical way of converting patterns into a language of simple wave forms. "The equations he developed to convert images into wave forms and back again are known as *Fourier Transforms*."[11] As a science instructor stated, by way of metaphor and analogy: "The Fourier Transforms can take a smoothie and show what the original ingredients were." [12]

Let's hypothesize that if you were able to take the Hamiltonian Plus and run it through the Fourier Transforms that you might be able to precipitate out, at least indirectly or inferentially, an X-factor that the + of the Hamiltonian might represent. This plus or X-factor may be the hidden hand of Existence or the Unmoved Mover. This hidden factor, much alluded to by philosophy and religion, has yet to be either fully uncovered or rigorously postulated by science. Indeed, the

---

10 In physics, an "operator" is a function over the space of physical states. As a result of its application on a physical state, another physical state is obtained, very often along with some extra relevant information. [WP]

11 Talbot, Michael, *The Holographic Universe*, Harper Perennial 1991, pg. 27

12 Kalid, Azad (http://science-society.com/the-latest-news/an-interactive-guide-to-the-fourier-transform)

opposite is true. Atheistic science, as a general rule, attempts at every turn to reduce the influence of intelligence and design in the universe to stochastic aggregation.

A further way of understanding the Fourier Transforms is to use them metaphorically, rather than scientifically, as a way of getting traction on the relationship between matter and form. If we refer to the form as the "noumenon" and the "phenomenon"[13] as the wave particle manifestation, then the Fourier Transforms might be used to postulate the existence of a kind of existential browser that helps transform non-locality, via the hidden wave functions of something like the Hamiltonian plus, into the visible world of locality. In other words, *decoherence* or the collapse of the quantum wave would always be associated with a Universal Observer that understands the entire universe in the single instant of time that we call creation.

The Fourier Transforms show how images can be converted to wavelength but they don't or can't clearly say why it happens or can occur to begin with. That is the province of metaphysics, although physics and metaphysics are, as indicated previously, on the border with a new semiotic[14] discipline related to the concepts of locality and non-locality that has yet to emerge or be accepted. The proposed Fifth Law of Thermodynamics suggests that the Fourier Transforms only work because they represent part of a computational intelligence that is so vast that all of human philosophical history may only amount to a minor scratching of the surface of what is yet to be discovered.

Aristotle's Unmoved Mover was not God, in the Christian sense of being the creator but rather that Being whom all things imitated and Who was, therefore, the source of all motion. Aristotle uses the example of a lover being moved by the beloved and describes the Unmoved Mover as: *a living being, eternal, most good.*[15] If such a being exists, it

13 Hockney, Mike, *The Last Man Who Knew Everything,* Hyperreality Books, July 2012
14 Semiotics: the study of signs and symbols and how they are used—usage, synonyms, more.
15 Owens, Joseph, *The Concept of Being in the Aristotelian Metaphysics*

would be non-rational not to assume that Its action upon the universe would not have physical analogs.

ARISTOTLE, RELIGION AND CAUSALITY

Moving from the Fourier Transforms to the Islamic commentators Avicenna and Averroes (whose philosophy we previously toured) might seem like an odd move but there are clues in metaphysics that may help us to understand, more completely, the direction physics now seems to be taking. Understanding how matter and energy are involved in change takes us back to many old questions raised over multiple centuries. The same questions have a habit of coming up over and over again but in different venues, ranging from philosophy to theology and to the forms of speculation that verge on being the stuff of science fiction.

Aristotle, for example, was not concerned in explaining how the 'One' could be the 'Many' but rather, was more interested in accounting for how the 'Many' could be 'One'. Islamic and Christian thinkers however had a completely different motivation and reason for wanting to account for the unity of the universe. Both Christianity and Islam claimed to be religions revealed to mankind, by God Himself. Therefore, the old Platonic speculations as to how the 'One' (God) could engender the 'Many' (the multiplicity of existing things) were revived with fervor.

The God of the Old Testament reveals himself to Moses in the burning bush as *"I am who am."* For early Christians and later Muslims, it was a small jump from the One of Plato and the Unmoved Mover of Aristotle, to an identification of the One, Unmoved Mover with the God of the Old Testament, who reveals Himself to be Existence itself. The concept of Existence, which was only one of Aristotle's innovations (he was interested in so many different things) becomes the key to understanding later Christian and Moslem Theology.

These ideas can be taken one step further, by saying that the 'forms' or 'natures' of things are evidence of the Unmoved Mover's eternal ideas, manifested in time. **These ideas are forms of Divine Consciousness** and are responsible for both purpose (final causality) and formal causality. We participate in this causality and our purposes and our standards can only be measured against the efficient and final causality of a God, whose consciousness transcends both science and religion.

> *Consciousness is defined by Webster's as: 1 a. the quality or state of being aware esp. of something within oneself; b. the state or fact of being conscious of an external object, state or fact; c. concern, awareness 2: the state of being characterized by sensation, emotion, volition and thought; mind 3: [the totality of conscious states of an individual], etc.*

The efficient causality, which we see in nature, and the final causality which is being generated by Existence or the Unmoved Mover must work together in a way that has not been completely articulated by traditional metaphysics. Surely, it makes no sense to think of efficient causality, without thinking of final causality as a kind of englobement of all forms of causality. Furthermore, causality makes little sense unless it is *related* to Divine Consciousness as a whole. This is why the human soul is generated through a partnership, as it were, between efficient and final causality. The Unmoved Mover who knows all possibility, inasmuch as He knows Himself, effortlessly bestows existence on all things. Time is an irrelevant consideration. Our temporality is before God as something already finished. He, She or It cannot be waiting around for us to pass away. All time is before the Unmoved Mover as part of the *Divine present*. Aquinas attests to this eloquently:

> *"Therefore, since the vision of divine knowledge is measured by eternity, which is all simultaneous and yet includes the whole of time without being absent from any part of it, it follows that God sees whatever happens in time, not as future, but as present. For*

what is seen by God is, indeed future to some other thing which it follows in time; to the divine vision, however, which is not in time but outside time, it is not future but present." [16]

Furthermore, it can be argued that God is His own *eternal present* or eternal now, otherwise there would be potentiality in God which is repugnant to reason. If this is the case, God's being *present* is not other than His own Consciousness and Nature.

FINAL CAUSALITY, TIME AND GENERAL SEMANTICS

Aristotle's notion of final causality involves the idea that the present and the past are determined by the future. Time is not merely explained as the unfolding of temporal 'nows' which absolutely determine the future but rather, time is understood as the manifestation of an entity that requires space to unfold. This is radically different from modern philosophy which holds that time determines being as a form of *presence*.[17] Nature, viewed in the Aristotelian manner, may be symbolically regarded as englobing all time and space with eternity/Existence.

Existence does not change in the Aristotelian view of time and space. What changes are all things in relation to something that does not and cannot change. Aquinas' doctrine of contingency is simply an extension of this argument, although Aquinas has to do some fancy footwork in order to accommodate the creation in relation to a being that does not change. This he accomplishes with the notion of relation. Relations between Existence and what is created are not real relations but the relation between what is created and Existence are very real indeed.

16 Owens, Joseph, *The Concept of Being in the Aristotelian Metaphysics,* citing Aquinas
17 Popik, Kristin M., *God's Knowledge: The Non Existent and the Future*; Faith and Reason, pg. 30 (1977) citing the Summa Theologica, D.V., 11, 12 F.
    Ibid

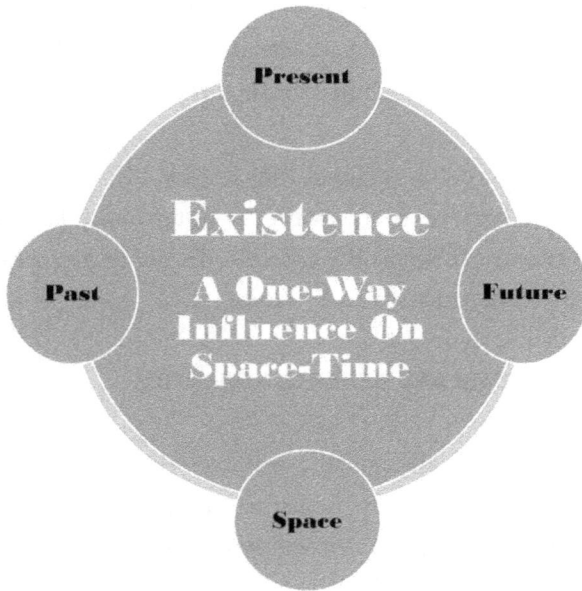

"*Here the future determines the past in its determination of the present. As determinative, the future stands as a goal, as a 'final cause' of the natural process. The goal makes the past into a resource, into 'material' as it were, for the process of its own realization. **The goal thus determines the past in the latter's determination of the present by structuring it as a potential** for some particular realization... What is common to all such processes is the notion of the completed reality which stands at their end as being not just the goal but also the cause of its own realization. As causally determinative, the goal gives us the movement of nature according to which time can be said to move from the future through the past to the present. This natural movement is what situates potentiality as a category of reality.*" [18]

---

18 Mensch, James R., *Aristotle and the Overcoming of the Subject Object Dichotomy*, ACPA Quarterly

Being, from this perspective, is a kind of *handshake* from eternity that determines time. Entities (or beings) are not caused by time, rather time is a manifestation of the movement of an entity, as potentiality is unfolded by the actuality of the entity. This actuality, which cannot be seen, is in fact the soul. The soul, either inanimate or animate, is the trans-temporal entity that manifests itself in time. This can be better understood, if we think of all of the Divine Ideas as participating in God's actuality in such a way that **there is an infinity of actuality behind each manifestation of a particular entity.** The Divine Essence limits each thing only to what it is, i.e., it cannot be other than what it is, but what it is in the absolute sense is rooted in a transcendental causality, the limits of which and the inter-relatedness of which to all other Divine Ideas cannot be subjectively determined. This complex and time-spanning interrelation of the Divine Ideas could only be described as *Divine Consciousness*. Our consciousness is the product of this infinite power. There is a beautiful Latin phrase that captures something that happens when our souls are moved by the grace and power of this infinite force. *Anima vice* (pronounced anima veche) means the turning of the soul. (Walker Percy refers to this as "rotation".) Our souls can only be "turned" by an actuality greater than what they themselves possess. When the soul turns, it moves like a man slowly remembering something long forgotten—an echo of light or the distant song of something so vast as to be incomprehensible.

The New Age thinking of Edgar Cayce and the trans-temporal entity known as Seth attempts to capture the extraordinarily complex nature of the soul in a time-spanning and multi-dimensional matrix that is similar, in many ways, to the present theories of physics regarding super strings.[19]

---

19 "According to [string] theory, the fundamental constituents of reality are strings of the Planck length (about 10–33 cm) which vibrate at resonant frequencies. Every string, in theory, has a unique resonance, or harmonic. Different harmonics determine different fundamental particles. The tension in a string is on the order of the Planck force (1044 newtons). The graviton (the proposed messenger particle of the gravitational force), for example, is predicted by the theory to be a string with wave amplitude zero." https://en.wikipedia.org/wiki/Superstring_theory

"Both Edgar Cayce and Jane Roberts speak of multi-dimensional reality where all our past and future are being lived now, each in its own dimension, and say that each personality in each dimension is a part of an expression of a greater soul or greater being. According to Roberts, we can penetrate into these other dimensions or lives to bring knowledge and understanding for transformation. By doing this, this dimension or our present lives can transform our other lives and dimensions. Or, said in more popular terms, how we live now in what we call this life affects both our past and future lives. All of these things are quite hard to understand, but they serve to help point out and challenge the limitations in our thinking about the nature of reality." [20]

This kind of thinking for many atheists and some religious would simply be psychobabble. The idea of multiple lives, past, present and future is still far off the charts for the modern mind. The kind of static universe imagined by the ancients, which is being eroded by modern physics and linguistic deconstruction, needs to be reconstructed in a newer, more flexible paradigm that takes advantage of all discoveries—metaphysical and scientific.

Alfred Korzybski in his 1933 book, *Science and Sanity*, illustrates some of the problems that occur when only partial knowledge is available through the senses. Korzybski, like many pre-World War II intellectuals, opposed the notion that there was an objective reality maintained by an exterior intelligence by claiming that the Kantian "thing itself" (the noumenon) or the reality of any object is always assigned by both "time binding" and assertion by way of mental "tagging". In other words, what a thing *is* was simply related to both labels of perception and assigning an object its place in time—all without any connection to an eternal ordering principle—aside from stochastic relativism. What Korzybski referred to as the "structural differential"

---

20 Roberts, Jane, *Dreams, Evolution and Value Fulfillment*, Prentice Hall Press, 1986, pgs. 169-170

was Kant's "noumenon" fleshed out in greater detail. The definition of the structural differential makes this abundantly clear. "The structural differential consists of three basic objects."

"The *parabola* represents a domain beyond our direct observation, the sub-microscopic, dynamic world of molecules, atoms, electrons, protons, quarks, and so on; a world known to us only inferentially from science. Korzybski described it as an 'event' in the sense of "an instantaneous cross-section of a process." Thus the 'event' or parabola represents the sub-microscopic 'stuff' that, at any given moment, constitutes an apple. In other words, the parabola represents the "external" cause of what we experience.

The *disc* represents the *non-verbal* result of our nervous systems reacting to submicroscopic "stuff", e.g., the apple that we see, hold, bite into, all on the non-verbal levels of experience. The disc represents what we *experience* of our surroundings versus what our surroundings actually *are*.

The *labels* [usually seven or eight are linked together in a chain, with the last one attached back to the parabola, but here we see just one] are shaped like suitcase labels, and represent the static world of words, e.g., "apple", giving imperfect accounts of dynamic reality. An object called an "apple" left in a jar for months becomes a putrid liquid (because of its underlying, dynamic, sub-microscopic structure), but the label "apple" does not change...

The holes in the figures represent the characteristics that exist at each level. The characteristics that are abstracted to the next level are indicated by the attached *strings*. The strings that don't make it to the next level represent characteristics left out of our abstractions, as do the holes without strings at all. More is left out of our abstractions at each level than was there at the previous level."[21] Note that there is no unifying principle of existence or even the notion of an external intelligence that might hold or form what is perceived *before* human perception is engaged. When things are viewed as processes their essential "thing-

---

21 [WP]

ness" or realness is devalued. Likewise, any thoughts you might have about morality or spirituality are simply abstract processes caused by grasping only a small part of the universe that is available for perception. (See the image[22] of the structural differential below.)

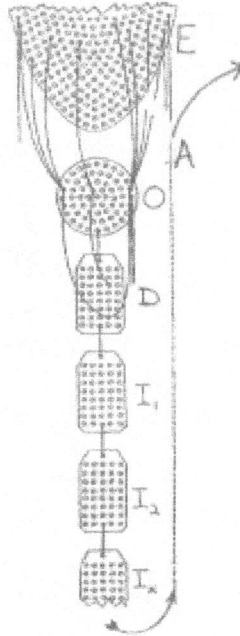

So was Korzybski right or was he barking up the wrong tree? He was fond of repeating: "Say whatever you like about a pencil but never say it is a pencil."[23] What Korzybski is correctly pointing to is that the word pencil is not the same thing as the actual pencil but he makes the mistake of dismissing it merely as a sign and not as a symbol that can be known, relative to our consciousness in space and time, by our becoming that item on the *plane of the act of knowing*. Fr. Joseph Ow-

---

22 Image courtesy of Milton Dawes. http://miltondawes.com/formal-essays-handouts/using-the-structural-differential/

23 Percy Walker, *The Message in a Bottle*, pg. 154, Picador, (Farrar, Straus and Giroux), New York, NY

ens, as noted earlier, was fond of saying that God is the pencil but the pencil isn't God. Both men have intuited and intellectually grasped the distinction between essence and Existence but have interpreted it in a different way. Korzybski, despite his brilliant analysis, failed to advert to what kind of existential knowledge his structural differential described. The act of knowing, as understood by metaphysical realists, is not the same thing as knowledge about something, which is a secondary phenomenon. The structural differential also tends to reduce the notion of soul and by extension, form or essence, to an unknown perceptual or mental anomaly that should be looked upon with suspicion.

The structural differential perfectly describes existence as energy that is neither created nor destroyed. It is a secular hymn, so to speak, to the First Law of Thermodynamics. We can never know, from this perspective, how all the parts are connected because the parts we see are merely abstractions of larger processes. This is, of course, true in one sense but once Existence is introduced as the living God, then existing things are granted their own charter of existence in the process of contingent being, which they do not have in an endless process of discontinuity.

Korzybski and many of the thinkers, who were both his contemporaries and intellectual successors, continued with the deconstruction of reality in a manner that would have been approved by the sophists of ancient Greece. The Greek philosopher Xeno, if you recall, argued that an arrow could never reach its destination because it would have to traverse an infinite number of points to get to its destination. Deconstructionists such as Jacques Derrida in the 1960's and Richard Rorty have only continued mining this same intellectually and morally destructive vein of reasoning that like a sweet ant poison is brought into the hive and results in unwitting death and destruction.

The realists, (the Rationalists) on the other hand, including Plato, Aristotle, Aquinas and even the author(s) of the Upanishads maintained that the form of an entity is knowable in itself. The science of how we know things is called epistemology. This kind of knowing is

significantly different than the camera imagery and operations posited
by empiricism as the way we know reality. A camera does not know
what it sees; it simply records images. It is true that the brain receives
sensory impressions but receiving sensory impressions is meaningless
without a simultaneous interpretation of what is received.[24] How is
this done? It might be noted that the most difficult task in developing
a true Artificial Intelligence (AI) is due to the inability of empirical
science to reproduce, in code, the process whereby human being come
to know reality.

Machines can record visual images much in the same way that the
brain may record images, i.e., as data that can be retrieved but that is
only part of the process. Empiricists refuse to acknowledge that scientifically unknown epistemological processes may be in involved in
how human beings know reality. In the metaphysics of Aristotle and
St. Thomas, we know things by *becoming them* on the plane of intentionality. This piece of epistemology was completely lost during the
Reformation, when the notion of participation in God's life was simply stated but not explained as it was in the metaphysics of Aquinas.

Unlike Kantian metaphysics, where the noumenon (the thing in
itself) is never fully known, reality is knowable in Aristotelian metaphysical systems. The 1949 science fiction book by A.E van Vogt entitled, *The World of Null A*, was a celebration of knowledge that defied
the Aristotelian notion that A = A. Vogt was the product of a culture
that was already equating empirical science with Aristotelianism when,
if anything, Aristotle represents the rationalist tradition. The publica-

---

24 "Rationalists generally develop their view in two ways. First, they argue that there
are cases where the content of our concepts or knowledge outstrips the information
that sense experience can provide. Second, they construct accounts of how reason
in some form or other provides that additional information about the world. Empiricists present complementary lines of thought. First, they develop accounts of how
experience provides the information that rationalists cite, insofar as we have it in the
first place. (Empiricists will at times opt for skepticism as an alternative to rationalism:
if experience cannot provide the concepts or knowledge the rationalists cite, then we
don't have them.) Second, empiricists attack the rationalists' accounts of how reason is
a source of concepts or knowledge." http://plato.stanford.edu/entries/rationalism-em-
piricism/

tion of this book and Heinlein's *Stranger in a Strange Land* in 1961 and others was a symptomatic indication that science was not answering the complex questions involved in understanding the mind/body interface. The rapid growth of fantasy and science fiction over the past fifty years might be thought of as an unconscious protest against the strictures[25] of empiricism. Rationalism, in the form of access to hidden or lost knowledge, is often featured in works of fantasy. The wonderful symbolism of the one ring in Tolkien's *Lord of the Rings* is a powerful metaphor for the enduring power of rationalism. What sort of empiricist could have even come up with the notion of linking rings to ancient and hidden powers—except as a form of sentimentality?

Knowing, from the point of view of realistic epistemology, involves a one-to-one correspondence with the form or *haeceity* of the thing itself. The agent intellect and passive intellect cooperate to produce abstractions that match what the senses perceive. The passive intellect, like a piece of wax, receives the form and the agent intellect abstracts the form. This does not mean that we have exhaustive knowledge of the thing or its historical process but rather a realistic

---

25 "The dispute between rationalism and empiricism takes place within epistemology, the branch of philosophy devoted to studying the nature, sources and limits of knowledge. The defining questions of epistemology include the following:

1. What is the nature of propositional knowledge, knowledge that a particular proposition about the world is true?

To know a proposition, we must believe it and it must be true, but something more is required, something that distinguishes knowledge from a lucky guess. Let's call this additional element 'warrant'. A good deal of philosophical work has been invested in trying to determine the nature of warrants.

2. How can we gain knowledge? We can form true beliefs just by making lucky guesses. How to gain warranted beliefs is less clear. Moreover, to know the world, we must think about it, and it is unclear how we gain the concepts we use in thought or what assurance, if any, we have that the ways in which we divide up the world using our concepts correspond to divisions that actually exist.

3. What are the limits of our knowledge? Some aspects of the world may be within the limits of our thought but beyond the limits of our knowledge; faced with competing descriptions of them, we cannot know which description is true. Some aspects of the world may even be beyond the limits of our thought, so that we cannot form intelligible descriptions of them, let alone know that a particular description is true. The disagreement between rationalists and empiricists primarily concerns the second question, regarding the sources of our concepts and knowledge." http://plato.stanford.edu/entries/rationalism-empiricism/

simulacrum provided by the senses of something that actually exists in the here and now. We know that a chair or a bullet exists with the same certainty that we know that we exist.

> *Think of the form or essence as a multi-dimensional pattern existing within the Reality Dysfunction that enables quantum and other mechanics of the sub-atomic order to form the visible universe that we are familiar with. These patterns can be accessed by the quantum machine that we call mind and in turn be imposed on matter via the four causes.*

The Aristotelian understanding of how we know the forms is very similar to *Tat Tvam Asi*: "that thou art or I am that" of the Upanishads. What we see in realistic epistemology is what we get. The disclosure of any entity in time is what it is now, in its present matter, as in-formed by the multi-dimensional vibration[26] of essence or form. The realist, in other words, knows reality as a non-local participation in God's own Being. Walker Percy noted that:

"The modern notion of the symbolic character of our awareness turns out to have a very old history, however, the Scholastics, who incidentally had a far more adequate theory of symbolic meaning in some respects than modern semiotics, used to say that man does not have a direct knowledge of essences as to the angels but only an indirect knowledge, a knowledge mediated by symbols. John of St. Thomas observed that symbols come to contain within the themselves the thing symbolized *in ali esse*, in another mode of existence."[27] This is, of course, the becoming of the thing itself on *the plane of the act of knowledge* referred to in earlier chapters. The agent intellect impresses, so to speak, the nature of the thing that *we become* in the potential intellect much in the same way as an impression is made in hot wax.

---

26 When we refer to forms or essences we can link the concept to the notion of super-strings or vibrations occurring in the many dimensions of hyperspace.

27 Percy Walker, *The Message in a Bottle*, pg. 156, Picador, (Farrar, Straus and Giroux), New York, NY

If you were to pick up a common rock and be able to see back a million years that rock or the atoms that constitute it might have been in a liquid form in the earth's mantle. Go forward 50,000 years and that rock may have been pulverized and made into road material. Go further into the future and some of those rock atoms might be part of an animal. What is it given the full spectrum of time involved in the lifetime of the rock? 'Rockness' as substance is only a formal determination that exists in the present. This is what Korzybski means when he says that we only see part of the process and not all of it. For the realist, the rock is what it is now regardless of what it was in the past or will become in the future. When the process is seen as contingent it has a form or vibratory pattern that is intelligible in the here and now.

Forms, like Ken Wilber's holons, can become building blocks for more advanced forms. Forms subsume the formal causes of other forms into a larger formality. The ultimate meaning of *rockness* (looked at over the full spectrum of time) isn't necessary for its present disclosure. What 'rockness' is in the final sense or whatever form it will ultimately take, can only be known and shared by a causality or consciousness, which englobes all other forms of causality. This is the final, ultimate causality and consciousness of the Divine. The Upanishads finger the mystery.

"*What cannot be seen with the eye, but that whereby the eye can see: know that alone to be Brahman the Spirit and not what people here adore.*

What cannot be heard with the ear but that whereby the ear can hear: know that alone to be Brahman the Spirit and not what people here adore.

What cannot be thought with the mind, but that whereby the mind can think: know that alone to be Brahman the Spirit and not what people here adore."

—Kena Upanishad

God is not some sort of cosmic administrator. The demiurge or Universal Mind/ Overmind is really only a way of trying to understand how the universe is ordered by a Being for whom order is an expression of a complete and finished understanding. Aristotle's concept of the Unmoved Mover or "that which moves without being moved" is much closer to the reality than almost all other metaphysical or theological formulations.

CHRISTIANITY AND THE SOUL

The most distinctive feature of Christianity is its teaching on the soul. The care of the soul, attested to by Socrates and celebrated by Cicero is given extraordinary new meaning and importance in the teachings of Jesus Christ. Christ identifies Himself with all men and to such a degree that the care of their souls affects Him personally. Furthermore, He teaches that His heavenly Father (much like Socrates taught) is more concerned about the quality of men and women's souls than He is with their earthly status. Additionally, we are told that those who do not care for their souls will not only lose them but may also be punished in a place of eternal torment.

Jesus is short on metaphysics but speaks with authority and almost all who hear him are impressed with the manner and power of his presentation. Jesus adds a new virtue to the inventory developed by the Greeks. *Faith,* which He speaks about on numerous occasions, is the transcendent virtue, *whereby mankind shares in the excellence and freedom of God.* Faith, like knowing, hoping and loving is an act of the soul. Furthermore, the virtue of faith gave Jesus and his disciples all manner of unusual powers. The dead walk, the sick are cured, thousands are mysteriously fed, and the powers of nature, in general, obey the men of faith. Jesus states in the Gospel of Matthew:

> *"If you had faith, you could say to the mountain, uproot yourself and throw yourself into the sea and it would be done".*

The theological virtues of faith, hope and love are those virtues that are activated in some mysterious way, by the Divine. This hidden and subtle call to spiritual virtue is called grace and is the work of the Persons of the Divinity. Faith participates in the freedom of God; it is profoundly unlimited. Thought of in this way, faith, hope and love are joint operations of God and man. There is also the notion of the infusion of gifts by God directly. If the notion of proper proportionality is extended, then it must be said that the Divine gives in proportion to our capacity to receive, which in turn is based on accepting greater spiritual consciousness as opposed to resisting it. Those who say something cannot be done or must always be done in a certain way are missing the notion that human freedom is ultimately bound up with divine freedom. The energy that supports the universe and everything that is in it is beyond our comprehension to limit.

Aquinas' teaching on moral and spiritual virtue was not merely a restatement of Aristotle's teaching on excellence; it was and is something new. Aquinas understood that Christianity involved a participation in God's life through grace and the sacraments. The morally and spiritually transformed life, which involves a kind of blending of divine and human consciousness is utterly lost to modern society. The notion that sexual and appetitive restraint might be required in order acquire a more spiritual life is not even on the radar of the average man on the street today.

Duns Scotus maintained that only seven virtues were required to perfect a human being: the three theological virtues of faith hope and love, together with the natural virtues of the ancients: justice, temperance, courage and prudence, or what we call today the cardinal virtues.[28] All of the virtues are on a continuum, so to speak, with Divine intentionality, which is oriented towards the return of man to God. This powerful teaching is complementary to that of Socrates, Plato and Aristotle, and adds to it a rich dimensionality that was apparently, very attractive to the mindset of the period.

---

28 Pinsent, Andrew, *The Second Person Perspective in Aquinas's Ethics*, Routledge Books, an imprint of Taylor and Francis, 2012, New York, NY, pg. 5

The Christian understanding of God and the soul spread throughout the ancient world with such speed and power that western civilization, as we know it, arose as a result of the adoption of these new
moral, spiritual and personal values built on the ashes on the older
civilizations of Greece and Rome. The center of the Catholic Church
has continued to persist in Rome, as the last living remnant of the glory
that was once the Roman Empire.

THREE DIMENSIONS OF VIRTUE

The theological virtues of *faith, hope and love* are consistently confused
and intertwined in our culture, with the notion of morality in general.
This is as it should be in the absolute sense but due to the religious plurality of our culture, the theological virtues need to be *relatively separated*
from the moral virtues. There is nothing to prevent our schools from
teaching the moral virtues, as opposed to teaching the theological virtues. Due to the specifically religious content of the theological virtues,
and due to the separation of Church and State, the theological virtues
need not be taught in the public schools. The relative separation of
the three dimensions of virtue into: *intellectual, moral* and *spiritual* habits
might help clarify the rhetoric surrounding the issue of teaching values
in the schools.

THE NEED FOR A SCIENCE OF THE SOUL

What does this admittedly truncated history of the concepts of being,
form and causality, mean for the purposes of our inquiry? If we understand Existence as simply energy, without beginning or end, then
the particular manifestation that constitutes the world is simply an accidental or stochastic aggregation not subject to metaphysical inquiry.
Within this context, consciousness is simply an ongoing development
of energetic relations between particles carrying different charges. If
however, Existence is conceived of as God or as a conscious, eternal

Entity, then everything that is linked to Existence may be thought of as being conscious. The soul, in this context, is directly linked to Existence.

If the soul might be understood in the most general sense, as a specific actualization of living matter and not necessarily as a religious concept (although the two are obviously and by no means, incompatible), then it might be easier for different cultural and religious groups, to accept the care of the soul and the actualization of human potential (a form of efficient causality) as both a goal and part of a common, metaphysical inheritance. Understanding that the Reality Dysfunction[29] is an invitation to use the moral navigation system of virtue and vice to bridge what God understands with what we understand enables us to grasp the nature and difficulty of the political and spiritual task before us.

Secondly, we must have a science that deals with the care and development of the soul directly. An ethical psychology of the soul is sorely needed but even more importantly, a discipline that unifies psychology, philosophy, physics and natural theology into a readily understandable discipline is required. The original meaning of the word 'psychology' means, *soul study*. How marvelous it would be to have such a discipline promulgated as a Public Philosophy, in every school in the country.

Certain schools of psychology, with simplistic explanations for human behavior do our culture a great disservice by locating the origin of behavioral dysfunction solely in either an individual's family history or in his or her genetic structure. The fact remains that whatever our neuroses or psychoses happen to be, we are not solely at the mercy of our own history. Personal limitations can be overcome through the application of the moral virtues (i.e., those virtues that govern the appe-

---

29 The Reality Dysfunction, refers to God's self-limited knowledge of Himself in time; i.e., God's knowing Himself, *relationally*, outside the Divine Essence in the theophanies. As part of the spectrum of Existence it is, like light, capable of being viewed in different colors but there is only one Light. The Reality Dysfunction might be thought of, for example, as violet light relative to the light of Existence and nothing more.

tites) and common sense. The proper province of psychology is those areas of human behavior which are genuinely not rational, such as the influence of the subconscious on our rational behavior.

Psychology should be used as a tool to help the ill, not as a methodology for determining the behavior of those individuals who are not sick. This is the proper province of morality and ethics. Unfortunately, many schools of Psychology utilize psychopathology as the basis for predicting normal behavior. What we need is a discipline which studies the behavior of healthy and successful individuals. Realistic Philosophy (philosophy with an Aristotelian base) is the only discipline that is properly equipped to begin this task, as it studies man in the context of the totality of his aspirations, by examining what we now understand to be the non-local structure of his nature.

CHAPTER 15

THE SOUL: WHAT IS IT?

"Since therefore God is the effective cause of things, the perfection's of all things must pre-exist in God in a more eminent way...Inasmuch as He knows His own essence perfectly, He knows it according to every mode in which it can be known... Now it can be known not only as it is in itself, but as it can be participated in by creatures...God does not understand things according to an idea existing outside Himself. Thus Aristotle (Metaph IX) rejects the opinion of Plato, who held that ideas existed of themselves, and not in the intellect. God is the similitude of all things according to His essence; therefore, an idea in God is identical with His essence."

—Aquinas,
Summa Theologica, Q. 15, Art 3, Pt.1

THE SOUL IS A BRIDGE

The soul is a non-local bridge between time and eternity; it is the entity beyond the future. (The brain is the wet interface between locality and non-locality.) The soul, known non-locally by God, shares in His eternity, for what God knows is one with His Nature. There is a crucial distinction that allows this not to be pantheism. God does not exist, non-locally, as a consequence of His nature or essence, He is that Existence. We exist as a consequence of His nature, of His knowing Himself locally, in all the ways that He might be known. God's knowing of Himself, as He might be imitated, necessarily involves the notion of time, for He knows Himself as He might be imitated by creatures who do not live in eternity as their primary reference. Time is necessarily involved in His notion of humanity. There is a profound paradox at work here. We are eternal from the perspective of God's nature but we only begin to exist in time. God is not waiting around for us to die; from His point of view, the end is no different from the beginning. Our existence in time is accidental from God's point of view; it involves a change in me, rather than in Him.

THE DUAL NATURE OF THE SOUL

The soul appears to have a dual nature that mirrors Divine consciousness; one temporal, one eternal. This is similar to the African notion of *real time* and *mythical time,* and more specifically, the "Ba" and "Ka" of the Egyptians. The Ka was the eternal manifestation of the soul much like the *Atman* of Indian Philosophy. The temporal manifestation of the soul is, from the perspective of this book, a necessary consequence of immortality for a creature that has been known, or decohered, as other than the Divine Essence. Our individual egos might be considered ephemeral, much like the "Ba" in relation to the deeper substrata of our existence (the "Ka") as it comes from the mind of God.

God cannot know Himself (if such a thing can be said) as He might be imitated, without knowing Himself in some way, as other than Himself. This knowing of Himself, as He might be imitated (or as other than Himself) involves the entire temporal order of things. One could argue that in order for God to know Himself as imitated, He must know time, for time would be involved in Him knowing anything as other than Himself. Since there can be no temporality in God, time and relation to God must exist outside of God as we do. God's knowing of Himself, *as other than Himself,* represents in one way, a new or virtual and "local" creation of Himself, *in time.* We are part of this local manifestation of something that is fundamentally non-local in nature.

TIME AND GOD'S NATURE

All things known as *imitable* in the Divine Essence are, therefore, part of the very creation of time itself. God has always known Himself without addition or diminution, therefore time has always been known and may have always existed. This is why Aristotle argued that the universe was eternal. The key to understanding the paradox lies in God's perspective. God is not waiting for anything to happen that He knows. He is so radically outside the limitations of time that we can only surmise that time exists as a manifestation of his thoughts.

The limitations of both time and matter are limitations only with respect to the Divine Nature. *Time appears to have no beginning because there was never a time when time was not known by God.* There is, however, a state which is so far beyond our imagination's power to conceive, that we must say that with respect to this state of existence, all other things including time are secondary or contingent. What this primary state is like is part of the mystery of divine consciousness.

Aquinas argues that God's knowledge of something in a sense makes it be. He calls this the *knowledge of approbation.* God's knowledge of time can rightly be said to make it be. This is, from the perspective of physics, the decoherence of quantum reality that an eternal observer makes possible. The fact that God might not make all of the things that He knows is part of the mystery of the Divine Consciousness. The necessity of time and matter's existence however can be inferred from God's necessary knowledge of Himself as He must know Himself, as Himself, outside of His own Existence.

Indeed, it might be inferred that God's perfection might in fact be limited, if He could *not* know Himself, as other than Himself— if He so chooses. Such a knowing could only occur as a kind of *kenosis* or emptying of Himself for a purpose. We have a metaphor for this in the birth of Christ. How could it be argued that the birth of Jesus, who according to theologians assumed a human nature, could be anything other than God knowing Himself as other than Himself? Arguing that all perfections are included pre-eminently in God, in such a way as to preclude God from knowing Himself, outside Himself, might render the Incarnation a Docetist[1] illusion.

As noted in *Authority, Creativity and the Third Imperium,*[2] "if we consider elements of the Old and New Testament as a metaphor for something not fully understood, we might say that what the Trinity is doing in the creation, from start to finish, is establishing the heavenly kingdom, including Father, Son and Holy Spirit, in an entirely new order of participated being." This is not for God's benefit but for our benefit. Creation, in this respect, is roughly analogous to what we might describe as a virtual, evolving reality. The entire order of participated and contingent being, including time, might be thought of, simply, as an artifact of eternity. All of creation, as we know it, occurs within this artifact, or secondary level of created being, existing contingently just outside the Divine Essence.

---

1 A heretical sect dating back to Apostolic times. Their name is derived from dokesis, "appearance" or "semblance", because they taught that Christ only "appeared" or "seemed to be a man, to have been born, to have lived and suffered. Some denied the reality of Christ's human nature altogether, some only the reality of His human body or of His birth or death.

2 O'Reilly, Sean, *Authority, Creativity and the Third Imperium: Why God's Knowing Himself, Outside Himself, Matters,* House of a Thousand Suns, pg.28

This means that there are only two things in the universe: what is created and what is uncreated. The notion of what is created may be in need of some extension.

Some have referred to this second level of creation as, *aveternity*, or a kind of secondary eternity that had a beginning but no end. Others, like the Greek Orthodox monk, Gregory Palamas (1296-1359 A.D.) referred to a distinction between the divine essence and the "divine energies."[3] The teaching on the divine energies is well established in Eastern Orthodox theology and has a long tradition going back more than 1,700 years, likely originating in the mystical teachings of Plotinus.[4]

"The divine energies might be described as that mode of existence of the Trinity which is outside of its inaccessible essence. God thus exists in His essence and outside of His essence."[5] The divine energies are what we are calling Dimensionally Interactive Cyber Kinesis due to the multi-dimensional nature of consciousness and matter once created within the Reality Dysfunction.

However described, the artifacts of eternity or everything that exists within our virtual universe, as part of the Reality Dysfunction, is based on the common assumption and conclusion that there can be no before and after in God, therefore any consideration of quasi-temporal events involving God, such as the Incarnation or the Light on Mount Tabor, during the Transfiguration, or even relations between the Persons of the Trinity must be re-considered from within a virtual construct that allows the mediation of time. This is similar to Plotinus's doctrine on the One[6] with everything that is not the One being

---

3   http://orthodoxinfo.com/phronema/florov_palamas.aspx
4   http://en.wikipedia.org/wiki/Plotinus
5   Lossky, as quoted in A. N. Williams, *The Ground of Union: Deification in Aquinas and Palamas*, Oxford University Press, 1999, page 140
6   The One is not just an intellectual conception but something that can be experienced, an experience where one goes beyond all multiplicity. Plotinus writes, "We ought not even to say that he will *see*, but he will *be* that which he sees, if indeed it is possible any

an "emanation" or a secondary order of existence from that of the One, which is identified as God."

Aquinas, for example, in discussing the four relations of the Trinity: Paternity, Filiation, Spiration and Procession makes it clear that these are ways for us to understand something that is an expression of a greater unity than metaphysical discussion can allow. Without evaluating the theological meaning of these four relations, it is sufficient to say that Aquinas specifically states that "it is manifest that relation really existing in God is really the same as His essence and only differs in its mode of intelligibility...thus it is clear that in God relation and essence do not differ from each other but are one and the same." [7] It is not possible, when discussing God, to take eternity and timelessness out of the equation and then add it back in for purposes of distinguishing orders of being. The limits of the construct must always be acknowledged as being a four dimensional description of an Act that is not only multi-dimensional but also un-dimensional to Itself.

SATCHITANANDA

"When the sun has set, and the moon has set, and the fire has gone out, and speech has stopped, what light does a person here have? The soul, indeed, is his light, said he, for with the soul, indeed, as in the light, one sits, moves about, does one's work, and returns."

—Brhadaranyaka
Upanishad, IV 3.6.

The Aristotelian notion of the soul as an Unmoved Mover that has its effect in the nature of its cause through imitation is, perhaps, an ear-

---

longer to distinguish between seer and seen, and not boldly to affirm that the two are one." http://en.wikipedia.org/wiki/Plotinus

7   Aquinas, Thomas, *Summa Theologica, The Blessed Trinity,* Q. 28, Art. 4, Pt. 1, pg. 153, Benziger Brothers Edition, 1947

ly iteration of the later doctrine of Aquinas that the soul was an entity that participated in God's inner life. The Hindu concept of *Satchitananda* (existence, consciousness and bliss) most clearly indicates the kind of imitative force that divine consciousness has in nature and in ourselves. Our very being is made up of *existence, consciousness and bliss*. The soul is manifested in time but known from eternity. We are the children of the Unmoved Mover, who englobes time non-locally within eternity. Our existence in time is the local end of eternity. Imagine a gateway which opens onto infinity on one side and finitude on the other.

How do we understand the notion of existence, consciousness and bliss in relation to ourselves and to God? We are part of the many worlds of *satchitananda*. The explosion of creation in the compression of eternal energy that results in time and space as a by-product of God's necessary knowledge of Himself, *known as other than himself*, must have produced a cataclysmic explosion of energy, matter and time that erupted out of nothing—the so-called Big Bang.

This fusion of knowing that occurs *only within time* is already part of God's eternity—a mental relation, from our frame of reference—

relative to the Act of His Existence. This is not, as has been previously noted, a real relation to God as the relation is already subsumed within the Actuality of His Existence. Christian theologians, consequently, argued that the creation didn't add anything formally to God. God is not even outside of time. God doesn't exist in relation to time; time exists in relation to God. Time is the local manifestation of a profoundly non-local entity or entities. We keep trying to put God "here", as a concept, and time "there" in relation to "it". There is no "there" with God—only a "here" that constitutes the relation to something that does not Itself exist in any way that we can conceive. The words of the common Christian prayer are applicable here.

> *"Glory be to the Father and to the Son and to the Holy Spirit, as it was in the beginning is now and ever shall be, world without end, amen."*

What we see in time, space and matter is a sequential realization of something that is already complete from the perspective of eternity. Time, space and matter are radical products of a self-subsisting Divine Consciousness and in the same instance cannot be univocally identified with that Consciousness. Time, space and matter emerge not from something visible but from the higher dimensions of a transcendental consciousness. They appear as suddenly as does the *interference pattern* of a hologram. They are relational but only in relation to something that already exists.

Time, as Wilhelmsen suggests, may be prime matter.[8] We can speculate, on the other side of the coin that time may be a "form" itself. If prime matter[9] is understood as the radical potency of anything to become something else, then time might be thought of as a form or Divine Idea, as it is already understood from the larger perspective of God's Existence. Prime matter, in other words, might be thought of as a function of the Reality Dysfunction, whereby the nexus for possibility and potentiality is created. This is similar, in a very general and analogous way, to the notion of locality and non-locality. Prime matter, *as matter without a form*, cannot exist in any particular location because it lacks either a specific form(s) or the aggregated laws of physics to differentiate it in time or in locality.

The relationship of time to "form" is too complex to further develop in this volume; nonetheless, postulating the relationship as originating in the mind of God and being part of the *Reality Dysfunction,* manifested as Dimensionally Interactive Cyber Kinesis, might provide an interesting avenue of inquiry for future thinkers. What we can say with some certainty is that the forms are derivatives of the Divine Ideas or represent ways in which God knows Himself, outside Himself. Forms are limits that the Divine Intelligence imposes on

8   Frederick Wilhelmsen, College Lectures, University of Dallas, 1970-1974
9   "Prime matter is matter with no substantial form of its own. Thus, it can change into various kinds of substances without remaining any kind of substance all the time." (An earlier form of prime matter was the Greek notion of Aperion or something that was completely unlimited. The earlier notion of form was simply that of a limit on the unlimited.)

Itself in knowing the universe as other than Itself.

> *What we see as actuality and potency in time is one point in the unfolding of a continuum that from God's perspective is a whole. From the point of view of the First Law of Thermodynamics, the continuum is simply an aggregation formed without purpose within the "laws" governing physics. The notion of laws without a lawgiver is a peculiarity of the modern mind's penchant for engaging discontinuity with the same rigor that previous thinkers reserved for continuity.*

The reason that God intervenes so indirectly in human affairs is due to the Reality Dysfunction. The limits by which Infinity considered Itself were also infinite, resulting in a barrier between time and eternity that is not easily crossed. God, having once considered and observed, in one eternal moment, the entire history of the universe, including its return to Him, has also once and for all, and without predetermining, superordinated all things and all possibilities to Himself. The kinds of changes or interventions we think that God should be engaging, at our request, are not how God operates. Within the Reality Dysfunction and due to Dimensionally Interactive Cyber Kinesis there are many possibilities for the manipulation of matter that do not involve the direct action of God.

Given that all matter is conscious to a greater or lesser degree in the Reality Dysfunction, the co-ordination of reality in terms of both providence and evolution is guided by immanent, multi-dimensional principles that ultimately reside in a more perfect formulation in the Mind of God. The decoherence of quantum reality in the Reality Dysfunction, by an eternal observer, is not disordered but it is limited.

No one, besides Jesus Christ, has claimed to have risen from the dead and there is probably good reason. The dead can't come back because their souls have already been united to what is beyond time and space. What are occasionally seen as ghosts or departed spirits are simply higher level, virtual mock-ups of the body that are referred to as astral bodies.[10] The Resurrection, on the other hand, was potentially established from the first moment of time and is, so to speak, part and parcel of the reality that we inhabit. It does not represent something new on the part of God, except relationally, within the Reality Dysfunction.

Using David Bohm's hypothesis of implicate and explicate orders, we can say that the explicate order is simply the unfolding of the implicate order, which is a translation of what is in the mind of God. The Reality Dysfunction actually creates the implicate order or what is other than God's nature. Now it would be unfair to attribute the these kinds of conclusions entirely to David Bohm but it is incontrovertible that he was seeking to re-establish a similar continuity that the ancients saw between the finite and the infinite.

> *"Bohm believes that the bizarre behavior of the subatomic particles might be caused by unobserved sub-quantum forces and particles. Indeed, the apparent weirdness might be produced by hidden means that pose no conflict with ordinary ideas of causality and reality...Bohm believes that this hiddeness may be reflective of a deeper dimension of reality. He maintains that space and time might actually be derived from an even deeper level of objective reality. This reality he calls the Implicate Order. Within the Implicate Order everything is connected; and,*

---

10 "The term 'astral', 'etheric', or even 'dream' body, refers to the theory that human consciousness can become completely separate from the body, and in this form be free of the limitations the body has. The astral body is said to appear very much like the physical body, with all the features and limbs, but be made of subtler material, or even of thought and emotion. This concept of a finer body most likely arose out of two basic human experiences in the earliest period of human thought. Because while dreaming it is common to be in places far distant from where one is asleep, it was thought that the dreamer actually visited that place while they slept, or that a finer spiritual body had travelled away from the corporeal self and gone to a heavenly or spirit world. Also early human beings, just as occurs today, experienced impressive out-of-body events which at face value again show a distinct self-moving at a distance from, and having a life completely independent of, the physical body." Provided by Tony Crisp (Dreamhawk)

in theory, any individual element could reveal information about every other element in the universe." [11]

The analogy of a point on a line might be helpful here. A geometric point has no mass, it is referential only. An infinite line without a beginning is composed of an infinite number of possible points. Each one of those points is technically part of the line but is not literally so. The sum totality of the line cannot be measured because it is infinite. In fact, if you rotate such a line about an axis point, in an infinite number of dimensions, you would have something approximate to a transdimensional sphere that would be infinite both inside and outside and have no point of origin, as the origin would disappear into an infinity of all directions—even within time. Origin collapses in the transdimensional reaches of higher spaces where meanings refold upon themselves as they approach the event horizon[12] of each infinite Act of the Divine Intelligence.

THE NO POINT AND THE COLLAPSE OF THE QUANTUM WAVE

Blaise Pascal (1623-1662) was a French mathematician, physicist, inventor, writer and Christian philosopher. Pascal defined space as "having its center everywhere and its circumference nowhere." At first glance this does not seem possible, if we think of space as we typically do, as being confined but upon reflection, imagining the universe composed of an infinite number of local space "bubbles" created by a non-local center that is everywhere, makes for some very interesting questions. Are both ends of the bubble the same, i.e., if one end of the bubble is *local* and the other end is *non-local* what would that mean? (This might be thought of as a practical way of thinking about both superpositioning and superstrings.) Is there a continuum of space be-

---

11 *The Cosmic Plenum: Bohm's Gnosis: The Implicate Order*, (http://www.bizcharts.com/ stoa_del_sol/plenum/plenum_3.html)

12 In general relativity, an event horizon is a boundary in space-time beyond which events cannot affect an outside observer.

tween the "bubbles"? If so, is it possible to move in the non-local (higher dimensional) spaces between the "bubbles" that form part of the circumference that is nowhere?

Eternity is not at the end of time, nor at the beginning of time. Since eternity is nowhere, evidence for it is as easily looked for inside as well as outside, or up as well as down. The point at which time emerges from eternity is nowhere. The point at which non-being emerges into being[13] might be thought of as a hyperspace gateway or a *no point*. The no-point shares in the characteristics of locality and non-locality; it is, like all forms, an artifact of the Reality Dysfunction. Physics refers to the collapse of the quantum wave, through observation, as "decoherence". Given that all that is quantum is also observable by God, the mechanics of the Reality Dysfunction become relatively more apparent. Everything that is quantum is "decohered" by the mind of God, relative to God's knowledge of it, relative to Himself.

> *This means that decoherence takes place according to a schedule within the Reality Dysfunction and according to no schedule within Eternity. Within eternity what God knows is One with the Divine Nature. It is not decohered. Decoherence can only be managed, so to speak, by some intermediary quantum effect that has not yet been identified.*

The emergence of be-ing from Being (if it could be seen) might look like a crack in space. Imagine it analogous to a sheer plane of nothing, out of which comes something, at an infinite right angle to it. The crack would be a distortion in space and time created with the emergence. Visualize all created things as rays with no origin. Go back to the point of origin and what do you find? Nothing.

Let's hypothesize that gravity is the signature of an incalculable number of no-points[14] or the massive decoherence of spatial reality

---

13 This is, essentially, the metaphorical point in space-time at which something that might be said to be non-local manifests or becomes something local.

14 The idea of the "no point" anticipates, to some extent, my later use of the idea of

caused by the Reality Dysfunction. If this is the case then we might argue that the presence of these no-points, like marbles dropped onto the surface of water, creates curvature or bubbles in space-time. Einstein would understand this as mass bending space and creating time. However, in order for mass to bend space, mass itself must first exist, it must be created or brought into existence as an energy conversion. But why would energy ever coalesce into mass without some reason or guiding principle? The Reality Dysfunction creates mass, space and time through God's infinite knowing of Himself outside Himself.

We might hypothesize that no-points are organized into gateways in the space-time continuum. Personal gravity, derived through conception, which might be described metaphorically and imaginatively as, *the falling*, emerges as a possible concomitant of the larger particulars of space, time and gravity that may take us to a possible and original *no point* of emergence.[15] Gravity, if understood from the perspective of superstring theory, as the "note" of a superstring rotating and vibrating at the speed of light in multiple dimensions might lead to the discovery of a kind of signature equation that would allow a conversion back to the *no point* of entry or a particular hyperspace gateway. The curvature of space may, in fact, be an inverse representation of hyperspace energies dropping down into three dimensions. The well-known lines of T.S. Eliot come to mind here:

> *"We shall not cease from exploration*
> *And the end of all our exploring*
> *Will be to arrive where we started*
> *And to know that place for the first time.*

Superstrings, which at the original time of writing, I was unfamiliar with. It just goes to show that metaphysical ideas can move in tandem with science or sometimes anticipate science.

15 This is pushing the speculative envelope but is an attempt to get some additional traction on ideas that are very difficult to express in three and four dimensional language. A Thomist theologian would look at this argument and, invoking Avicenna and Averroes, say that you can't exist before you exist but the argument can be made that God's knowledge of us from eternity constitutes something that is not nothing. Duns Scotus referred to this as the "ens diminutum" or little being.

Through the unknown, remembered gate
When the last of earth left to discover
Is that which was the beginning
At the source of the longest river
The voice of the hidden waterfall..."

The notion of a hyperspace conversion point or delta for the emergence of being from nothingness suggests that at the conversion point, between phase changes in matter, the essence or nature is already fully formed in terms of potentiality within the non-local structure of quantum wave forms. When matter is converted to energy or energy is converted to matter, the conversion is a result of an exchange between locality and non-locality. The notion that mere observation creates the possibility for change seems curiously incomplete to the rational mind. E=mc2 or energy equals mass times the speed of light squared is a possibility that is made possible by something that must contain more energy than what it gives. We can realistically ask what the reverse of that proposition might be. Energy less the speed of light squared = mass. Perhaps the idea of a ray appearing from nowhere is not so far-fetched after all. Mass or matter is just slowed down energy and creation may only be the local *appearance* of what already exists in quantum form. Physicists have been arguing that this is the case for many years.

The speed of light squared or times itself (even though such a speed has not yet been proven to exist) would yield a value so enormous, that for human senses, most movement would appear to be instantaneous. The following questions can be asked again, which were introduced in the beginning of this book: "so why would you have to multiply the mass by the speed of light to determine how much energy is bound up inside it? The reason is that whenever you convert part of a walnut or any other piece of matter to pure energy, the resulting energy is by definition moving at the speed of light. Pure energy is electromagnetic radiation—whether light or X-rays or whatever—and electromagnetic radiation travels at a constant speed of 300,000 km/sec (186,000 miles/sec)."[16]

"Why, then, do you have to square the speed of light? It has to do with the nature of energy. When something is moving four times as fast as something else, it doesn't have four times the energy but rather 16 times the energy—in other words, that figure is squared. So the speed of light squared is the *conversion factor* that decides just how much energy lies within a walnut or any other chunk of matter. And because the speed of light squared is a huge number—90,000,000,000 (km/sec)2—the amount of energy bound up into even the smallest mass is truly mind-boggling."[17]

Let's call this hypothetical figure *trans-light velocity*. Anything that dropped out of a speed at least four times that of light and manifested as mass, in local space, would simply appear, *as if* out of nothing. We could also argue that anything that moved at trans-light velocities could be said to be in almost all places at the same time and all times at the same place. In other words, imaginative notions such as trans-light velocity and hyperspace are another way of looking at the structure of non-locality. This is not to say that there are no solid scientific objections to the notion of trans-light velocity. There are those who will claim and with good reason that Maxwell's Equations would be violated.

> *"Maxwell's four equations describe the electric and magnetic fields arising from distributions of electric charges and currents, and how those fields change in time. They were the mathematical distillation of decades of experimental observations of the electric and magnetic effects of charges and currents, plus the profound intuition of Michael Faraday. Maxwell's own contribution to these equations is just the last term of the last equation—but the addition of that term had dramatic consequences. It made evident for the first time that varying electric and magnetic fields could feed*

16 http://www.pbs.org/wgbh/nova/einstein/lrk-hand-emc2expl.html#fea_top
17 Ibid

off each other—these fields could propagate indefinitely through space, far from the varying charges and currents where they originated. Previously these fields had been envisioned as tethered to the charges and currents giving rise to them. Maxwell's new term (called the displacement current) freed them to move through space in a self-sustaining fashion, and even predicted their velocity–it was the velocity of light!" [18]

However, Maxwell's equations were calculated using our common four dimensional world as a baseline for the behavior of electric current and magnetic fields. How these equations might fare or be subtly adjusted within multi-dimensional matrices is largely unknown. Even now, reactionless engines and observations of cold fusion occurring at room temperatures may indicate that the laws of physics, as we know them, may be subject to a correction based on new understandings provided by multi-dimensional and string theory. We know, for instance that light interacts with matter in novel ways that we are now only beginning to understand.

"In the mysterious microscopic realm where the electromagnetic fields of light and matter intimately intermingle as they exchange energy, plasmons, excitons, and other particles with unexpected and usual properties abound. Now physicists have created a new set of energy-carrying particles to add to this range. Dubbed "topological plexcitons," these new particles show promise in greatly enhancing energy flows for solar cells and nanoscale photonic circuitry. Scientists at UC San Diego, MIT and Harvard University have engineered these particles to help improve a process known as exciton energy transfer (EET). Created as a conjunction of plasmons (a quantity of collective electron oscillations) and excitons (excited electrons bound to the hole produced by their excitation), topological plexcitons specifically aid better direct energy flows in the EET."[19]

---

18 http://galileoandeinstein.physics.virginia.edu/more_stuff/Maxwell_Eq.html
19 http://www.gizmag.com/topological-plexciton-energy-particles-mit/43786/

"When light and matter interact, they exchange energy," said Joel Yuen-Zhou, assistant professor of chemistry and biochemistry at UC San Diego. "Energy can flow back and forth between light in a metal (so called plasmon) and light in a molecule (so called exciton). When this exchange is much faster than their respective decay rates, their individual identities are lost, and it is more accurate to think about them as hybrid particles; excitons and plasmons marry to form plexcitons."[20] If we think about the interface of light and matter as having these almost evolutionary qualities, it is not difficult to imagine that dimensionally amplified or augmented constructs may be able to perform tasks that are currently almost beyond our imagination. Engaging metaphysical speculation is a little bit like science fiction.

Imagining possibilities in a universe that operates on decoherence is essential for progress. Every new reality begins with the personal decoherence of quantum reality rendered by imagination.

Let's speculate, then, and say that one major difference between angels, God and men might be gauged by the speed at which they move. A stone, for example, does not appear to move but perhaps it does in stone time. Similarly, God may move in such a way that we are like stones in reference to Him. It might be said that we "move" faster in a state of virtue than we do in the context of vice. As our vibratory status comes closer to what the Divine offers us, we gain in power. Jesus' insistence on having faith and having the power to "say to the mountain uproot yourself and it would throw itself into the sea" makes more sense in this context.

*Time is what occurs when Existence "enters" space or "does" what is not eternal. In other words, time **occurs** because of something that Existence eternally does, by superordinating all things to Itself, locally, based on its own eternal and non-local knowledge*

---

20 http://www.gizmag.com/topological-plexciton-energy-particles-mit/43786/

of how it might be imitated. Time is one superordinated and decohered aspect of the Divine Act, as it might be thought of as relation, or its local existence outside of the Divine Nature in Tsimtsum or what we are calling the Reality Dysfunction.

This preserves the unchangeable nature of eternity and shows that time is a relation only in reference to the eternal. One way of thinking about this is to say that aside from the Divine Mind, there is no way of thinking about eternity without time. There is only the astonishing light of the Trinity without time.

TRANS-LIGHT ENTITIES

Gravity viewed from the 'speed' perspective represents part of the spectrum of tremendous energies that must be compressed at 16 times the force of the speed of light[21] when a trans-light object appears (moving down from 4 times the speed of light) in the space-time which we are familiar with. How are these energies accounted for causally by modern physics? It is one thing to have the equation $E=mc2$, which explains the convertibility of matter and energy and quite another to explain how and why those compression numbers exist.

Gravity might be postulated, metaphysically, as a local phenomenon created by the Reality Dysfunction. The creation of energy and mass represents an original distortion of God's eternal knowledge of Himself within the simultaneous creation of time and space required for God to know Himself as other than Himself. The compression of matter at sixteen times the power of the speed of light[22] may be what is responsible for the curvature of the universe and gravity.

---

21 http://www.pbs.org/wgbh/nova/einstein/lrk-hand-emc2expl.html#fea_top
22 Ibid

The original non-local unity of human potential in a trans-light existence might be such that entering normal space and time would be a painful experience. Does the soul, *as a decohered entity,* remember its paradoxical unity in the decohered mind of God and seek it? Is not the 'good' in one sense, an attempt to restore an original condition? Hillare Belloc in his book, *Path to Rome,* touches briefly on the memory of the soul.

> *"In very early youth the soul can still remember its immortal habitation and clouds and the edges of hills are of another kind from ours, and every scent and color has a savor of Paradise. What that quality may be no language can tell, nor have men made any words, no, nor any music, to recall it—only in a transient way and elusive the recollection of what youth was, and purity, flashes on us in phrases of the poets, and is gone before we can fix it in our minds—oh! My friends, if we could but recall it! Whatever those sounds may be that are beyond our sounds, and whatever are those keen lives which remain alive there under memory—whatever is Youth—Youth came up that valley at evening, borne upon the southern air. If we deserve or attain beatitude, such things shall at last be our settled state; and their now sudden influence upon the soul in short ecstasies is the proof that they stand outside time, and are not subject to decay."*

If we say that there is a conversion at the *no point,* whereby trans-light energy, associated with God's knowledge of Himself, becomes decohered as mass, then it is not unreasonable to assume that the probability of a conversion point, at the collapse of the quantum wave, could be mathematically determined. Let's say that there is a hyperspace time-coordinate that would be analogous to our conception in time. The particular collapse of the quantum wave that comes from a kind of handshake between time and eternity is moderated by the Reality Dysfunction. Would it not be safe to assume then that the soul contains the register of this information, inasmuch as the soul is a decohered entity?

> *The soul is who we are. It is our non-local, yet decohered (local) connection to eternity. We are dialed into God, so to speak. We can no more get away from Him than we can get away from ourselves. Our minds translate non-locality into locality and vice-versa. God's paradoxical thinking is expressed in terms of an absolute freedom seeking its origin outside Itself. God knowing Himself, outside Himself, in the Reality Dysfunction is what makes the human mind possible. This is an extraordinary gift. We are made out of God's own spirit and life. This is consonant with Teilhard de Chardin's observation: "You are not a human being in search of a spiritual experience. You are a spiritual being immersed in a human experience."*

What then is the purpose of *trans-light reduction* in local space or what is commonly referred to as birth or creation? There must be some purpose involved, some meaning for the earth and matter, for such travail to have taken place over the centuries. Creation, looked at as a trans-light reduction or decohered reality, looks more and more like a shipwreck, but this cannot be. The trans-light existence of the soul must be complimented by birth rather than un-complimented, otherwise we would live in a purposeless universe run by an insane God.

The ultimate meaning of freedom might be found in the notion that we come into this life as part of the vision of God and that possibly, we come in order to make something of it that it cannot be without us. Doesn't the Bible state that Jesus Christ was the firstborn of all creation and that through Him all things were made? It is possible for God to be entirely God and entirely man from the perspective of many dimensions. Time is the guardian and our protector from the enormous trans-dimensional creativity of a God whose sheer, conscious actuality could not be matched by the energy of one hundred trillion suns.

WHERE DOES ALL THAT ENERGY COME FROM?

Time is a form of potentiality and is necessarily involved in the unfolding and manifestation of locality as it is translated, so to speak, from God's non-local Existence through the *no point* or what might also be thought of metaphorically as, a *trans-dimensional gateway*. Time measures the enormous energy potential of the soul, in relation to an origin that is eternal and infinite.

> *The substantial form of time is the Reality Dysfunction caused by God's own knowledge of Himself, outside Himself. What we can say is that the entire essential order, including God as a concept, or God as known or decohered is a function of the exteriorization of contingent reality that occurs within the Reality Dysfunction.*

God cannot not know what He knows, according to His own nature, but even He cannot make His creation into what only He Himself Is. As the ultimate trans-light entity (or entities), God appears to be sharing the radicality and energy of His Nature with us, inasmuch as it is possible for Eternity to enter time and share Itself with what is finite.

> *What can be hypothesized is that when God imposes some sort of local limit on Himself, by allowing the rest of the universe to participate in His non-local excellence, there is an enormous compression that takes place. Infinity placed under limits, by infinity Itself, is still infinity and the enormous energy[23] that creates limits or essences is reflected in the Big Bang and the magnificence of the entire cosmos.*

The energy output of hundreds of millions of galaxies is a record of this enormous instant of self-limitation that leaves as its evidence, mat-

---

23 As indicated previously, this compression factor between Existence and essence/finitude can be hypothetically calculated at 16 times the power of the speed of light within the equation $E=mc2$

ter and energy on a titanic scale. What are billions of blazing suns but an attempt of matter to mirror the blinding life of the Infinite? A Oneness beyond oneness can only be expressed, it seems, by the profusion of the many. No one has expressed this more vividly and beautifully than Sri Aurobindo (1872-1950 AD) in his epic poem *Savitri*.[24]

> *"There is the secrecy of the House of Flame,*
> *The blaze of godlike thought and golden bliss,*
> *The rapt idealism of heavenly sense;*
> *There are the wonderful voices, the sun-laugh,*
> *A gurgling eddy in rivers of God's joy,*
> *And the mysterious vineyards of the gold moon-wine,*
> *All the fire and sweetness of which is hardly here*
> *A brilliant shadow visits mortal life.*
> *Although are witnessed there the joys of Time,*
> *Pressed on the bosom the Immortal's touch is felt,*
> *Heard are the flutings of the Infinite.*
> *Here upon earth are early awakenings,*
> *Moments that tremble in an air divine,*
> *And grown upon the yearning of her soil*
> *Time's sun-flowers' gaze at gold Eternity:*
> *There are the imperishable beatitudes.*
> *A million lotuses swaying on one stem,*
> *World after colored and ecstatic world*
> *Climbs towards some far unseen epiphany."*

This universe, seen from this poetic perspective, is a temporal expression of eternity, or God taking a look at or knowing Himself, outside Himself. This "look" is eternal from God's point of view and this is why Jesus Christ is said to be the "first born" of all creation. How could the eternal Son not be there from the beginning of this astonishing enterprise?

---

24 Savitri, in the Vedas, is the Divine Word, daughter of the Sun, goddess of the supreme Truth who comes down and is born to save.

Using the notion of *infinite compression*, as one of the primary effects and metaphors of the Reality Dysfunction, it can be asserted that infinite consciousness is also compressed or limited when God knows Himself as other than Himself in time. Whether this is considered as the mechanics of *Tsimtsum* or the Reality Dysfunction, the effects are the same. Consciousness that is limited by time is experienced as potency and act, and as such, is limited in terms of what it can recollect about Itself. The Divine consciousness, limited by its own eternal choice in time, is forgetful of its own origin. If it were in full possession of its origin and consciousness, in the way that we understand possession of consciousness, then it would, likely, wipe out space and time by its very presence. There is scientific evidence for this assertion as noted earlier.

"When physicists calculate the minimum amount of energy in a wave form, they find that every cubic centimeter of space has more energy than the total energy of all the matter in the known universe." [25]

This means that a nearly infinite, albeit derivative, force may be driving the dynamics of the visible universe. The hypothetical energy of the wave form has been called by some enthusiasts of free energy, for example, the Zero Point and this energy as Zero Point Energy. Some scientists claim that Zero Point Energy (ZPE) would violate the laws of physics, as we know them, but the economic advantages of the possibility of being able to harness this almost infinite energy are almost incalculable. The ZPE has also been referred to as the Dirac Sea.[26] Metaphysically speaking, the ZPE or the Dirac Sea, is simply part of the Reality Dysfunction and occurs as a result of the extraordinary quantum decoherence that results from God knowing Himself, outside Himself.

---

25 Talbot, Michael, *The Holographic Universe*, Harper Perennial 1991, pg. 51.

26 The so-called Dirac Sea was a theoretical model of the vacuum as an infinite sea of particles with negative energy. It was first postulated by the British physicist Paul Dirac in 1930 to explain the anomalous negative-energy quantum states predicted by the Dirac equation for relativistic electrons. [WP]

If Zero Point Energy is ever scientifically proven to exist, then such a discovery might to be the first step in understanding the algorithms of Existence, as they apply to the material order. Here, and at this juncture, where some indication of what ZPE might be, a discipline that could be called Transcendental Physics, might be undertaken.

The energy released by the atom bomb was based on knowing that there were tremendous forces at work holding the atom together and that those forces could be released. Imagine being able to release the binding energy of space and time that occurs within the Reality Dysfunction. The potential for both harm and benefit is almost beyond what we can imagine. The Zero Point and the No Point, no matter how they might be formulated, are ideas that are at the very frontiers of both metaphysics and physics. These are exciting times for both disciplines.

NEW AGE IDEAS AND PROCESS THEOLOGY

There is an analogy to the effects of the Reality Dysfunction in our own "lived" experience of potency and act. We experience our sense of "I-ness" as pure actuality but who we may become is hazy and more undefined; it is experienced as the shimmering of potential. Our sense of self then is deeply related to the potential of our souls, which in turn have the infinite knowledge and act of the Divine Mind as their source of origin. This is why it is possible to imagine Jesus Christ as not being fully cognizant of His Divine Nature—not in terms of not knowing Who He Is—but having that knowledge in all its fullness in the present moment. What was pertinent to him as a man with flesh and blood would, likely, be different from what would be fully understandable to God as the Second, Eternal Person of the Trinity.

The difference might have been interpreted by Jesus the man as a kind of higher understanding, which would be obscured (as it should be) by the natural limitations of the human form. He would have experienced this limitation, perhaps, as a kind of deference to the will of the Father. If this were not the case why would He ask, as He did in the Garden of Gethsemane, "for this cup to pass"?

There is an infinite gradation of being between God's Actuality and our own. Indeed, there may be discarnate beings who may be composite intelligences. In the same way that a husband and wife become an almost separate entity, these composite intelligences may inhabit the higher spaces of transdimensional gateways. The new age entities that various individuals claim to be in communication with may in fact be such creatures, or for that matter, so could angels.

Jane Roberts, in conjunction with the Seth entity, expresses the relationship between what has been traditionally referred to as the contingent actuality of form to existence, in terms of a relationship between the potentiality of matter and the actuality of Divine Consciousness:

> "Now I call the building blocks of matter CU's—units of consciousness. They form physical matter as it exists in your understanding and experience. Units of consciousness also form other kinds of matter that you do not perceive. CU's can also operate as particles or waves. Whichever way they operate, they are aware of their own existence. When CU's operate as particles, in your universe, they build up a continuity in time. They take on the characteristics of particularity. They identify themselves by the establishment of specific boundaries. They take certain forms, then when they operate as particles, and experience their reality from the center of those forms. They concentrate upon, or focus upon, their unique specifications. They become in your terms individual...
>
> When CU's operate as waves, however, they do not set up any boundaries about their own self-awareness—and

when they operate as waves...CU's can indeed be in more than one place at one time. I understand that this is somewhat difficult material to comprehend. However, in its purest form a unit of consciousness can be in all places at the same time. It becomes beside the point, then, to say that when it operates as a wave a unit of consciousness is precognitive, or clairvoyant, since it has the capacity to be in all places and all times simultaneously." [27]

CU's, the consciousness/force ratio of Sri Aurobindo and the notion of Dimensionally Interactive Cyber Kinesis[28] are all ways of making what was formerly described, as the distinction between essence and existence, more cause and effect based, in terms of the formal cause inhabiting the effect as both its source of existence and its limit. The limit that the difference between matter and form expresses is known by the Divine Mind as part of the Reality Dysfunction. Contrast and compare the New Age formulation of CU's with one of the essential tenants of Process Theology.

"God in His concrete pole is God as He actually exists at any given time in the process.' Therefore, time—or succession as the world exemplifies it—is real to God.' God constantly changes with each successive prehension[29] of all actual occasions. He ever increases and actualizes his abstract potential in the concrete...[30] The world is God but only in His experience, [not in His essence]. Hence God includes everything but everything is not God. God's essence is not exhausted by the world's prehension of it." [31]

27 Jane Roberts, *Dreams, Evolution and Value Fulfillment*, Prentice Hall Press, 1986, pg. 21

28 Sean J. O'Reilly, *How to Manage Your D.I.CK: Redirect Sexual Energy and Discover Your More Spiritually Enlightened, Evolved Self*, Ten Speed Press and the Auriga Publishing Group, 2001

29 Prehension: an interaction of a subject with an event or entity that involves perception but not necessarily cognition. [WP]

30 *Does God Change?* by Thomas Weinandy, OFM Cap., St. Bede's Publications, pg. 133, 1984, Still River, MA

31 David Griffin, *A Process Christology*, Philadelphia: Westminster Press, 1973 as quoted

"Prehension" is used as a concept to explain the interaction of the Divine Mind, which is the source of all causality, and its affect/effect on all created things. Rather than using the language of potency and act, or essence and Existence, *prehension* attempts to grasp the universe as we might experience it in relation to God's activity. *Prehension* might be described as a kind of gerundive[32] form of God's knowing Himself, outside of Himself. Prehension, much like the concept of Scottus Eriugena's *theophanies* or Aquinas's concept of *relation* is a way of describing how Existence can come to know Itself in a derivative or limited manner within time. Like Heidegger's concept of *dasein* (being there) or Dimensionally Interactive Cyber Kinesis, it is an attempt to reformulate the relationship between Existence and what was formerly called the essential order in a more organic and comprehensive manner. The multiple dimensions of hyperspace, within the context of the Reality Dysfunction, are simply a partial result of the quantum decoherence that occurs when God knows Himself, outside Himself.

Jane Roberts and Seth might be accused by realist philosophers of reinventing Plotinus (a 205-270 AD mystic and philosopher) but it must be stated that in Plotinus' system all being emanated from the One, in an almost infinite series. What is suggested (and which Roberts seems to be implying) is that *being* does not emanate at all from the One Being but rather is a fusion of Existence and contingent existence, or of Eternity and time that is expressed *in time* but cannot be considered as emanating out of anything at all.

The notions of creation, emanation and prehension are limited concepts that do not adequately address the nature of the relationship between time and eternity in the Divine Intelligence; neither do they address the full dynamism and reciprocation that

---

in Does God Change? by Thomas Weinandy, OFM Cap., St. Bede's Publications, pgs. 132-133, 1984, Still River, MA

32 A gerund is a noun made from a verb by adding "-ing." The gerund (ive) form of the verb "is" is "is-ing." If I might be kind to the process philosophers, prehension is a 'process' description in time of what God does personally from eternity.

*a deeper understanding of the relationship and signification be-
tween essence and Existence points to. A relation in reference to
non-local Existence is an essence or a simple limit created by the
Divine Intelligence as it knows itself locally, outside Itself, in the
Reality Dysfunction. All essences are, fundamentally, a result of
quantum decoherence by an eternal observer.*

God did not invent time in a moment of thought, in the sense
that at one moment there was no time and in another there was time.
God has always known time and known it in such a way that it is *equi-
primordial* with (to use a word invention of Heidegger) and simultaneously englobed by the radical trans-temporality of His Divine Nature.

Much of Hegelianism, Process Philosophy and New Age thinking is, in hindsight, an attempt to recover the existential dynamism
of Aristotle and Aquinas, which was poorly understood to begin with,
and to further explain what they both might have overlooked in their
focus on God's absolute independence. God's absolute transcendence
can obscure the importance of the primary reason for creation. Understanding that God's ability to know Himself, as other than Himself,
is part of Divine Consciousness is enormously clarifying. It explains
the meaning and form of Divine Love without in any way exhausting
it. Without attributing too much good will to process theologians, it
would be unfair to say that they do not have a bone to pick with some
knee-jerk forms of scholasticism.

The brilliance of Aristotle and Aquinas, whose breadth and depth
of metaphysical thinking have yet to be equaled in modern times,
reminds me of physicist John Wheeler's comment to the effect that
String Theory was something that really should not have been discovered for another century. Aquinas' concept of "relation" in respect to a
self-caused Existence was so advanced that it anticipated what process
philosophers, centuries later, attempted to harvest with the notion of
prehension. It is, perhaps, an easier enterprise to think of the entire
created universe as being a *virtual relation* with respect to the Divine

Essence than to enter into the subject-object dichotomy of classical contingency.

THE PHYSICS OF CREATION

Much of classical, standard model physics, ultimately, ends up focusing on particle spin and angular momentum. Even quantum mechanics does the same, albeit bumping everything up into higher dimensions to make even more complex calculations. Equations using Hamiltonian variables that interpret the total kinetic and potential energy of a system, to Einstein's Light Quanta Hypothesis in 1905, which states that the energy E of a photon is proportional to the frequency V^{33} and the Schrödinger Equation, which measures change over time in a quantum state or waveform—all focus on energy and mass that is characterized by rotation in some way shape or form. (The persistence of π in both mathematics and physics is an additional indication that this assumption is moving in the right direction.)

The astonishing question which comes to mind is this: why is everything we see in the microscopic and macroscopic universe apparently dominated by rotation and spin? An opaque answer to this might be that mass curves space and so energy is required to behave within certain constraints but the question from a larger perspective remains. Why? From the metaphysical perspective put forth in this book, which invokes God knowing Himself, outside Himself, *as form or essence*, a fascinating interpretation can be made.

Imagine infinite energy, force and consciousness *knowing Itself as other than Itself*. How would this non-local "rotation" get translated in space and time? The Divine Mind, in order to know Itself as knowledge about Itself, instead of a unity of timeless knowledge and act, knows Itself within a derivative order outside of eternity. The Divine Mind knows itself, locally, within limits; in order to do that it creates time and space **but the force with which it creates limits is infinite in re-**

---

33 angular frequency w = $2\pi v$ with w indicating the wave packet

lation to its own Nature. Imagine creation as a kind of one-way street in which what is created is made with such infinite force that the energy cannot escape and cannot return to its source. This is the Reality Dysfunction, whereby the Infinite and the Eternal understands Itself through time. This also functions as a very handy metaphysical way of explaining superstrings, which might be thought of analogically, as hadrons vibrating through all dimensions at the speed of light. Let's look at physicist Michio Kaku's definition of what a superstring is again.

Any given particle (hadron) is made of a string that vibrates and rotates [through all dimensions] at the speed of light.

God's understanding of Himself, outside Himself, in the Reality Dysfunction can be translated into a metaphysical analog of String Theory. In order to better understand the relationship between String Theory and the Reality Dysfunction, imagine a bucket without an exit, even by way of its "mouth" that cannot be penetrated by any kind of projectile having infinite velocity. What would such projectiles do if they entered the bucket? Some of them would just squish against the sides but others would ricochet around the bucket forever. This is what the ancients called "form" or a kind of "brane"[34] of superstrings; it is, so to speak, infinitely finite energy bound by infinite energy. Infinite energy that is *relatively contained* or compressed in this manner can only do one thing: it can move and rotate in an infinite number of states in three and four dimensional states, or as vibrating strings in hyperspace. Infinite energy creates infinite pathways, as it seeks to return to its Source.

Modern scientists think that energy is neither created nor destroyed. The real reason for this is that energy and time manifest *ex ni-*

---

34 Branes are mathematical objects created by superstrings. "In string theory and related theories such as supergravity theories, a brane is a physical object that generalizes the notion of a point particle to higher dimensions. For example, a point particle can be viewed as a brane of dimension zero, while a string can be viewed as a brane of dimension one." [WP]

hilo or out of nothing, so they *appear* not to be created to minds habituated to thinking in terms of only four dimensions. This is why trying to understand the multi-dimensional dynamics of the entrance point (*the no point*) into space and time, whereby being seemingly emerges in various energetic forms might provide a deeper understanding of how the universe operates. When measurements are made, for example, in quantum physics, the observer changes the outcome of a quantum state because both the observer and the observed are linked in a way in which the observer becomes part of the overall dynamics of the Hamiltonian.[35] What happens if the observer is God? What would that do to every frame of reference?

> *The primary difference between ourselves and God is that God originates Himself and we do not. Our origination occurs in Him and not in ourselves. Look closer; it is like a hall of mirrors. The closer you look at yourself, the more you see and don't see God.*

We share in the existential radicality of God's Nature because he has conceived of us in His own mind, the contents of which are co-existent with Himself—yet mysteriously self-limited—as he chooses to know Himself outside Himself. We are truly sons and daughters of God. Let's be worthy of our high origins and act accordingly. Morality, accordingly, is an expression of God's wishes for humanity. Inasmuch as God, as Existence, has a much bigger picture of time and goodness than we do, it would behoove us to pay attention to Him and not pretend He doesn't exist. Insofar as the soul participates in God's nature by grace, which is a form of communication between Existence and being, the soul is empowered to do extraordinary things.

---

35 In quantum mechanics, the Hamiltonian is the "operator" corresponding to the total energy of the system in most cases. It is usually denoted by H. In physics, an operator is a function over the space of physical states. As a result of its application on a physical state, another physical state is obtained, very often along with some extra relevant information. [WP]

THE TIME WAR AS A NEW MYTHOLOGY

> *"You never change things by fighting the existing reality. To change something, build a new model that makes the existing model obsolete."*
>
> —Buckminster Fuller

Fables and myths tend to be part of a larger understanding of reality than a culture may afford or consciously advert to. Myth is often "located" in the past in order to mirror something of a future yet to be or yearned for. Fantasy, for example, may indicate a deep and powerful understanding of the future that is not quite disclosed in the present but that can be voiced in tales hinting of mysterious lands. How could a strict empiricist, for example, make rational sense of the poem, *The Golden Journey to Samarkand* by James Elroy Flecker, except as an exercise in mere sentimentality? For the rationalist it makes more sense, as knowledge is not assumed to be solely sensory-based, but rooted in something deeper and older than time.

I

"We who with songs beguile your pilgrimage
And swear that Beauty lives though lilies die,
We Poets of the proud old lineage
Who sing to find your hearts, we know not why,
What shall we tell you? Tales, marvelous tales
Of ships and stars and isles where good men rest,
Where nevermore the rose of sunset pales,
And winds and shadows fall towards the West:
And there the world's first huge white-bearded kings
In dim glades sleeping, murmur in their sleep,
And closer round their breasts the ivy clings,
Cutting its pathway slow and red and deep.

II

And how beguile you? Death has no repose
Warmer and deeper than the Orient sand
Which hides the beauty and bright faith of those
Who make the Golden Journey to Samarkand.
And now they wait and whiten peaceably,
Those conquerors, those poets, those so fair:
They know time comes, not only you and I,
But the whole world shall whiten, here or there;
When those long caravans that cross the plain
With dauntless feet and sound of silver bells
Put forth no more for glory or for gain,
Take no more solace from the palm-girt wells.
When the great markets by the sea shut fast
All that calm Sunday that goes on and on:
When even lovers find their peace at last,
And Earth is but a star, that once had shone."

Given that our knowledge of both God and the universe is not complete, the Time War caused by the *Reality Dysfunction* (or what is also known in the Jewish Kabbalah as *Tsimtsum*) might be used as a new way of understanding what has been called the Fall of Man. By relating the *Reality Dysfunction* and the subsequent Time War to an original, local condition of the created universe, the fall of mankind can be seen as an original ontological condition caused by God's own generosity. The Redemption of Christianity can then be interpreted as the correction of a defect brought about by the creation and not specifically a fault brought about through the actions of Adam and Eve. This was noted as early as the eight century AD by Scottus Eriugena who held that the Fall occurred within human nature at creation and not in a mythical paradise.[36] A revised understanding of the human condition through the lens of the Reality Dysfunction might enable

---

36 *John Scottus Eriugena*, Carabine, Diedre, Professor and Director of the Institute of Ethics and Development Studies, Uganda Martyrs University; Oxford University Press, copyright 2000

a greater shift towards participating in God's life, as He Is, and not in the insistent "do or die" manner we may have conceived as being necessary, religiously and politically, based on the metaphysics and algorithms of damnation.

In order for God to share Himself as a Divine Person with humanity, two possibilities can be asserted. One: God chose to know Himself, as other than Himself, in order to truly share His being with creation. Two: nothing related to the creation is necessary for God and attempting to postulate the Reality Dysfunction is simply an Avicenna-style metaphysical error.

Avicenna, if you recall, made creation a divine necessity due to God's foreknowledge of that same creation. While the Thomistic contention that the entire creation adds nothing new to God is largely true, St. Thomas, in my opinion, obscures the meaning of creation due to his necessary focus on and his magnificent defense of *Ipsum Esse* (an essence which is its own existence). The notion of the universe being simply a *relation* to the Divine Intellect borders dangerously close, based on our present understanding of physics, to the universe being an illusion. St. Thomas protects reality by asserting that the relation between God and the rest of the universe is real between the created and the creator but not real in reference to God Himself.[37] What is real for God (for St. Thomas) could only be real if God could consider something outside Himself as other than Himself. St. Thomas does not exercise this option as it would involve a before and after in God, which is not possible. Let's look at this quote from St. Thomas again as it bears repeating.

> *"Since therefore God is outside the whole order of creation, and all creatures are ordered to Him, and not conversely, it is manifest that creatures are really related to God Himself; whereas in God there is no real relation to creatures but a relation only in idea, inasmuch as creatures are referred to Him. Thus there is*

---

37 Aquinas, Thomas, *Summa Theologica*, Q. 13, Article 7

nothing to prevent these names which import relation to the crea-
ture from being predicated of God temporally, not by reason of
any change in Him, but by reason of the change in the creature;
as a column is on the right of an animal, without change in itself,
but by change in the animal. "[38]

The problem of an immutable and impassible God who enters his-tory can be better explained, in modern terms, as a virtual or decohered reality. In other words, God's entry (using Aquinas' understanding) into time is not a real relation to Him but it is for us. An additional way of grasping the complexity of this might be to say that the Kenot-ic[39] understanding of Christology points in the right direction—that of a virtual creation necessitated by God knowing Himself as other than Himself—*as His prerogative.* St. Paul indicates something similar in Philippians 2:5-11 when he says:

> *"For love of us He adjured the prerogatives of equality with God.*
> *By an act of deliberate self-abnegation, He so emptied Himself*
> *as to assume the permanent characteristics of the human and*
> *servile life: He took the form of a servant...Thus remaining in*
> *unchanged personality, he abandoned certain prerogatives of the*
> *divine mode of existence in order to assume the human."*

God cannot, it would seem, know Himself, as other than Him-self without the simultaneous creation of time. If we can imagine that God might choose for a moment *not to be God* and then know what that is like, *within time,* is a different experience than being this knowledge through the eternal act of the Divine Essence. It is the Divine Essence, self-limiting itself, in order to share Itself and be subject to the participated order of creation. Scottus Eriugena notes that there are four mysterious divisions of creation. That which cre-

---

38 Ibid
39 In Christian theology, kenosis is the 'self-emptying' of one's own will and becoming entirely receptive to God's divine will.

ates, which is uncreated, that which is created and creates; that which is created and does not create and that which is not created and does not create.[40]

Time then can be understood as an original relation of the Divine Essence to Divine Knowledge. It is a mixed relation in that it is *not* other than the Divine essence, outside of time, but within time and due to the complete comprehension of the Divine Mind, it exists as a temporal relation, limited much in the same way that an angelic nature is limited[41] only by the Divine Essence. This is the virtual reality of God knowing Himself as other than Himself—not as *Ipsum Esse*—but as a self-limitation of the essential order possessed, not in Act, but in a derivation of act using the relation of time.

None of this is easy to understand but the consequences o
f the positions taken on these issues are the basis for any new thinking about the nature of God and His relationship to mankind and the universe. Expressed in the context of both the *Reality Dysfunction* and the *reality function*, both expressions of the infinity differential, God's chosen self-limitation, in the decoherence of quantum reality, is the foundation for understanding the nature of the Time War.

There may, if the hypothesis of the *Reality Dysfunction* is correct, never have been a fall of man. Unable to attribute imperfection to God, the biblical writers had to attribute the initial fault to mankind. *God Has Skin In The Game* affords a different vision of redemption but not, ultimately, of salvation.[42] God's plan for the universe involves, from the beginning, the Rise of Man.[43] Jesus is part of this plan from the beginning and His coming is not just a redemption

---

40 *John Scottus Eriugena*, Diedre Carabine, Professor and Director of the Institute of Ethics and Development Studies, Uganda Martyrs University; Oxford University Press, copyright 2000, page 30

41 Angels are said to be limited, in Thomistic metaphysics, only by the Divine Essence and nothing else.

42 Salvation is being saved or protected from harm or being saved or delivered from some dire situation. In religion, salvation is stated as the saving of the soul from sin and its consequences. The academic study of salvation is called soteriology. [WP]

43 "Let us make them in our image." *Genesis 1:26*

of man's failures but a redemption of the negative aspects of the Reality Dysfunction. The Incarnation of Jesus is a continuation of the *reality function* of the Trinity, which in relation to mankind is always and everywhere putting pressure on humanity, non-locally, through grace.

St. Bernard of Clairvaux, (1090-1153 AD) and founder of the Cistercian order of monks, described the creation of the soul as two works, which illustrates the paradoxical difference between God's knowledge of Himself, in His Divine Nature, and God's knowledge of Himself in the Reality Dysfunction.

> *"In the first work He gave to me myself*
> *In the second work He gave to me Himself*
> *And when He gave to me Himself*
> *He gave back to me myself."* [44]

The assertion of a primordial Paradise needs to be understood as a reflection of the current imperfection of man as he strides towards God's future. Paradise is a metaphor for the journey of the human soul. Paradise is not behind us; it is ahead of us. God is not waiting for us; we are waiting for Him. God is around the corner of time.

Our waiting is part of a journey that has already been marked by final causality in the Reality Dysfunction. There may have been a time, perhaps, when man was closer to God and lost this relationship but it was, likely, not perfect to begin with. In the same way that we might say that the average French Catholic of the 13th century might have had a richer spiritual life than the 18th century Protestant Parisian, the localizing of a time when things "were better" always invokes the notion of a kind of paradise. It is this, perhaps, rather than an actual Paradise, sometime in the ancient past that ancient memories seek as a touchstone.

---

44 *De Diligendo Deo*

GOD'S SELF-LIMITATION AS CHRISTIAN THEOLOGY

The French theologian Jean Galot, cited by Weinandy, expresses the reasonableness of understanding God's self-limitation as a consequence of his inexpressible vitality. Understanding this self-limitation is key to understanding the new metaphysics and theology that the Time War invokes.

> *"God's immutable being cannot be conceived as necessarily closed in on itself, incapable of any action directed outside itself. God's immutability signifies permanence and perseverance in perfection, but does not signify immobility. The Bible presents God to us as the supremely Living Being. God is revealed to be full of vitality, an overflowing vitality that is deployed in creation and in his relations with men. Philosophical speculation has arrived at this notion of God by identifying the divine being as "pure act" Pure act is perfect in itself, **but it cannot be thought powerless to act outside itself.** On the contrary, the interior vitality of God implies an excess of vital capacity directed to creatures. It is in this sense that God's immutability is a capacity for mutability."* [45]

Donald Dawe, likewise cited by the theologian Thomas Weinandy, poses the problem of Jesus the man and Jesus the God, as an issue that traditional theology tends to gloss over with terms like the hypostatic union, in which two natures are perfectly respected in the unity of one Person in the Son of God.

> *"How could a limited human consciousness co-exist in a single person with the full actuality of the divine consciousness? Would not the presence of the infinite and impassible Logos vitiate the uniquely human personality which is limited and change-*

---

45 Jean Galot, *Who Is Christ?* Cited in *Does God Change?* by Thomas Weinandy, OFM Cap., St. Bede's Publications, pg. 181, 1984, Still River, MA

able?...How could a limited human person be conceived if the integrative or personalizing center of Jesus' person was the Logos which by definition is omnipotent, omniscient, and omnipresent?" [46]

The argument of the scholastics would be that of Aquinas—that only the human nature of Jesus Christ changes in the Incarnation. What the second Person of the Trinity does, as a man, does not add anything to the eternal Second Person that He does not already possess. One finds this formulation intellectually rigorous but emotionally un-compelling. Something seems to be missing. What is missing is that God, Who is outside of time, always retains His impassibility and immutability but His reason for assuming a human nature or helping mankind can never be even remotely understood without adverting to the possibility of the Reality Dysfunction. If God is love, then the fusion of personhood and love in an Infinite Nature is something that we can only approach with both the understanding that has been given to us and with wonder.

Charles Péguy captured something of the potential for a derivative God to be surprised (as we have attempted to do with the concept of the Reality Dysfunction) in his powerful 1912 poem, "The Gateway of the Mystery of the Second Virtue."

"The faith I love best, says God, is hope.
Faith does not surprise me.
It is not surprising.
I shine forth so in my creation.
I shine forth so in my creation.
So that in order not to really see me,
it would have to be that these poor people were blind.
Charity, says God, does not surprise me.

46 Donald Dawe, "*A Fresh Look at the Kenotic Christologies*," Scottish Journal of Theology, 15, (1962), 342 as quoted in: *Does God Change?* by Thomas Weinandy, OFM Cap., St. Bede's Publications, pg. 109, 1984, Still River, MA

It is not surprising.
These poor creatures are so unhappy that,
unless they had a heart of stone,
they could not help but love one another...
"What surprises me," God says, "is hope.
And I cannot get over it.
This little hope that seems like nothing at all.
This little girl hope,
Who is immortal...
It is she, this little one, who leads them all.
For Faith sees only what is.
And she, she sees what will be.
Charity loves only what is.
And she, she loves what will be.
Faith sees what is.
In Time and in Eternity.
Hope sees what will be.
In time and for eternity.
In the future, so to speak,
of eternity itself." [47]

How then would we describe the "future of eternity" unless it were not within a contingent reality that God Himself inhabits, albeit virtually or as a relation of reason in reference to the Divine Essence? How would we describe the mechanism whereby eternity engages time

---

47 "Charles Péguy's long poem, "The Gateway of the Mystery of the Second Virtue," (often translated in English as "The Portal of the Mystery of Hope") is the middle volume in a trilogy, surrounded on either side by "The Mystery of the Charity of Joan of Arc" (a play) and "The Mystery of the Innocent Saints." Written in 1912, the poem presents itself as an extended meditation on the theological virtue of hope. According to Péguy, hope is characterized by its ever-new quality, its ability to approach the same task as if it were to be accomplished for the first time. This makes hope, the frailest of the virtues, the virtue that vivifies the rest – which for Péguy is represented by "little girl hope" standing between her two "older" sisters Faith and Charity, drawing them forward." https://catholickungfu.wordpress.com/2010/11/26/the-gateway-of-the-mystery-of-hope/

out of nothing? The *Reality Dysfunction* and the corresponding *reality function*—both caused by God's ability and wish to know Himself, as other than Himself in creation, may provide a more nuanced accounting of what science, poetry and religion reveal.

IV

REFLECTIONS ON THE MORAL CONTINUUM

"Whenever we are planning for posterity, we ought to remember that virtue is not hereditary."

—Thomas Paine

CHAPTER 16

RELIGION, MASTURBATION, SAME-SEX ATTRACTION AND THE SOUL

"I want to see you game boys, I want to see you brave and manly and I also want to see you gentle and tender. Be practical as well as generous in your ideals. Keep your eyes on the stars but remember to keep your feet on the ground. Courage hard work, self-mastery and intelligent effort are essential to successful life. Alike for the Nation and the individual, the one indispensable prerequisite is character."

—Epigrams from the Roosevelt Memorial,
on Roosevelt Island, Washington DC.

THE PROTESTANT REFORMATION AND VIRTUE

The Protestant Reformation with its insistence on Faith alone as the indispensable tool of salvation, introduced a potential disregard of philosophical reason to western culture. Faith as a supernatural or spiritual virtue (the other two being Hope and Love) cannot be used to the exclusion of the other virtues in general. The writings of Thomas Aquinas bear powerful testimony to this understanding of the complementarities of the virtues.

The Protestant Reformers, however, in order to rid themselves from an overly *intrusive* rational structure in matters of faith and religion, zealously did away with the substantial intellectual and moral structure of the Catholic Church. This situation persists today, in that we have a tremendous intellectual vacuum among Christians, in regards to the proper use of reason in the formulation of a moral or ethical life style. The general notion of sin, for instance, when isolated from rational referents becomes a primitive form of mumbo-jumbo that few individuals can use comfortably as a means of self-control when confronted with the vast array of pleasures that our civilization has to offer.

Christianity's great success has, unfortunately, obscured the meaning of virtue in the minds of the average person. Rather than considering the natural consequences of certain actions, individuals today seem hell-bent on defying religious authority just for the sake of it. The common attitude seems to be: "I don't care if it's a sin, that's nonsense so I'll do it anyway." No further consideration seems to be necessary. The consequences to the *state of the soul* for instance are not considered because no one seems to know what such states might even consist of. Honor, self-respect and happiness have been reduced to feeling good about yourself, which has further been reduced to the torpor of satiation.

Honor and happiness are states of the soul that accrue to the man or woman who practices virtue, and particularly, moral and spiritual virtue.

The assertion that virtue is on a continuum with the consciousness or spirit of God (by way of both affect and effect) is, at its very heart, the idea that motivated Socrates to claim that all good that comes to man comes from the practice of virtue. The opposite is also true of vice. Dishonor, and frequently, depression is the result of excessive appetitive indulgence. There is also a kind of ennui or anomie that comes about from appetitive indulgence without limits.

"Anomie is the condition of a society in which there are no clear rules, norms, or standards of value. In an anomic society, people can do as they please; but without any clear standards or respected social institutions to enforce those standards, it is harder for people to find things they want to do. Anomie breeds feelings of rootlessness and anxiety and leads to an increase in amoral and antisocial behavior." [1]

As a coda for what follows, it must also be added that we are all greater, in one sense, than our vices or our virtues; we are even larger, in spirit, than our religious beliefs or what we might believe about ourselves. Nonetheless, the intellectual virtues can be conditioned by the moral virtues, and in such a way, as to make them more excellent than they would be without them. How many geniuses do you know, who are truly productive, who spend most of their time doing drugs, chasing women and partying? There are some of them out there but it is only due to natural and biological intellectual abilities that they are able to rise above, what would be for most of us, an appalling liability and an energetic drag on motivation.

---

1   Cited in Kyle Eschenroeder' article in The Art of Manliness at: http://www.artofmanliness.com/2016/08/15/what-do-you-want-to-want/? This, in turn, was a selection taken from Jonathan Haidt's book entitled, *The Happiness Hypothesis*

THE FAILURE OF ORGANIZED RELIGION

The current failure of many Christian organizations not to use centuries of rich metaphysical thinking and apply the solutions contained in those traditions to modern problems represents a radical failure of will. Those for whom religion has become a social nicety with no real relation to thoughts and actions are deceiving themselves. God is not interested in parrots or assembly line believers. Jesus stated in the gospels that "not all who say Lord, Lord will enter the Kingdom of Heaven."

The extraordinary failure of most Christian denominations to understand their own origins and their present difficulties, or even to reflect on them honestly is almost beyond comprehension. What person in his right mind could belong to the Church of England, for instance, without being suspicious of the immoral motives of its founder? The Anglican Church was founded by Henry VIII, who simply wanted to enjoy serial polygamy. There are other reasons to be a member of the Church of England but the founder was hardly representable of any kind of spirituality.

The Roman Catholic Church (of which I am a member) lays claim to being the one true Church of Christ and yet is so idiotically concerned with ritual that far too many Catholic churches in the United States offer Confession only on Saturdays—the officious and sanctimonious rational being that the hearing of confessions during Sunday Mass is somehow inappropriate to the Mass. How could it be inappropriate for Jesus to be forgiving people at the same time that He might be making His appearance in Church, under the auspices of bread and wine? How obtuse can these prelates be? They wonder why so few people go to confession and why they have so many difficulties getting anyone to pay attention to them, yet they hear confessions only once a week on Saturday. This is analogous to a football coach wondering why his team isn't doing so well, when he only practices once a week. If you only showered once a week, to take another tack on this, would you wonder why you might smell badly? You are, if you are normal, going to get spiritually "dirty" on a regular basis. Confession is a way to stay spiritually clean and healthy.

A number of years ago, there was a furor in ecclesiastical and art circles over the restoration of the paintings in the Sistine Chapel at the Vatican. What bothered some of the more hide-bound clerics and believers was the shockingly, bright beauty of the restored versions. The colors were so alive and modern looking that one could hardly believe that they were in fact part of the Sistine Chapel. The image that many of us have of God corresponds to the unrestored paintings in the Sistine Chapel; they are dark and smoky—full of a haunting beauty. The reality is that God is not dark or obscure but so bright and alive that we probably would not believe Him if we could see Him. We would likely say, this is not God. Where is the somber face, where is the sorrowful look? Where are the accusations, the laundry list of what we did and did not do?

What minister of the gospel in any Christian Church should not be concerned with the rising tide of immorality and apathy that engulfs their congregations? Unfortunately, many of these ministers are busy trying to adapt their churches to the collective appetites of both themselves and their congregations with grotesque results. What Christian (or non-Christian for that matter) in is his or her right mind could possibly imagine Jesus Christ sanctioning abortion, drug-taking, pornography and masturbation? Nonetheless, there are Christians who maintain that these things are compatible with Christianity.

Who could possibly imagine that the founder of Christianity who said, "If a man looks upon a woman with lust in his heart, he has already committed adultery with her"[2] would condone the practice of homosexuality or masturbation? Please don't be so willfully ignorant. Tell them you are liberal and proud of it but don't say you are a good Christian; it doesn't make any sense, it is a contradiction in terms, like a man or woman showing up for basketball practice in scuba gear. Go

---

2   Matthew 5:28

about your business and worship Gaia[3] or Zeus but don't say you are a practicing Christian. This idea that goodness was hard and that evil was easy was noted by the prophet Isaiah sometime between 720 and 681 BC.

> *"A highway will be there, a roadway, And it will be called the Highway of Holiness. The unclean will not travel on it, But it will be for him who walks that way, And fools will not wander on it."* [4]

Anton Levey, the former writer of *The Satanic Bible* and worshipper of Satan had the decency not to pretend that he was a Christian. He was consistent in his opposition to a religion of goodness. However, it is interesting to note that on his death bed his dying words were: "Oh my, oh my, what have I done, there is something very wrong... there is something very wrong..."[5] Stalin, on the other side of death bed repentance, was said to have been full of hate and malice at his death according to his daughter who was present with him. It is, however, not really possible to defy Existence or even to be angry at Existence. What most people react to, either by blasphemy or annoyance, is their concept of God, which is usually God the administrator, God the denier of their well-being, God the punisher, God the judge. God's Existence is beyond these limited concepts.

God is constantly turning us in the direction that we must look—towards Him—and the force with which we are turned might be thought of as an unmoved movement or grace. When this grace is resisted all manner of moral, spiritual and even physical devolution oc-

---

3   Gaia or Gaea, was the personification of the Earth and one of the Greek primordial deities. Gaia was the great mother of all: the primal Greek Mother Goddess; creator and giver of birth to the Earth and all the Universe; the heavenly gods, the Titans, and the Giants were born to her. The gods reigning over their classical pantheon were born from her union with Uranus (the sky), while the sea-gods were born from her union with Pontus (the sea). [WP]

4   Isaiah 35:8 OT

5   http://www.nairaland.com/746723/famous-atheists-last-words-before

curs. The human heart was made to be moved by God and not to move against it. "Hardening the heart" or turning away are good images for those who resist the truth and power of Existence, which is always aligned with goodness—whether or not we can clearly perceive why that goodness might take a form that is opposed to our appetites. This is why Jesus indicated that "all sins would be forgiven except the sin against the Holy Spirit", i.e., that the resistance to the clear speaking of the spirit within is evil. He also said:

> *"In everything, then, do to others as you would have them do to you. For this is the essence of the Law and the prophets. Enter through the narrow gate. For wide is the gate and broad is the way that leads to destruction, and many enter through it."* [6]

There is obviously a huge difference between those who make mistakes and regret their choices and those who know that what they are doing is wrong but continue to make such choices against their better judgement and contrary to the promptings of Spirit and grace. The culpability of many, in the present age of moral confusion, may be lessened in matters that involve notions of misaligned sexual identity or fetishes that many of us would find disgusting but that doesn't change the nature of bad choices that are not consonant with Natural or Spiritual Laws.

THE SAME-SEX REVOLUTION AND INCONTINENCE

The gay revolution provides all of us with food for thought on the consequences of "if it feels good, it probably is good" mentality that has propelled almost all aspects of the psycho-sexual revolution. Now, more than at any other time, it is critically important to be able to say why something must be considered morally wrong, or what conditions allow moral wrongs not to be ascribed to certain sexual actions. Ob-

---

6   Matthew 7:14

viously, the standard of self-interest that has been the mainstay of the liberal left has had severe social repercussions. What are the limits of self-interest, in regards to sexuality?

We see for example that transgendered individuals i.e., transvestites and transsexuals want to be included in the gay coalition. What about NAMBLA (North American Man-Boy Love Association) i.e., those who want to have sex with small boys? Do we let them in on the action? Where do we draw the line? What about those sorry individuals who enjoy sex with animals? Who are we to say it is improper? Obviously, some moral definitions are in order here.

Rather than starting with same-sex attraction, we can examine the problem from the perspective of bisexuality. Is there such a thing as a true bisexual or are we really just dealing with perverts? After all, if same-sex attraction is genetically based, why not have bisexuality exonerated in the same manner? *Getting off* is the biological prime directive of the genitals. What difference does it make; what species the orifice may belong to—never mind the gender? Surely something artificial is as good as something living—at least it doesn't talk back. How, in the future, will sex with robots be classified? Using your genitals as a moral compass for any attraction that passes through the mind may not be a good idea. Genitals don't think. The Romans used to refer to the male organ, as *mentullus* meaning 'little mind' and if we viewed our genitals as headless, then we might be able to get some perspective on same-sex attraction, sex with inanimate objects and other disorders.

Sexuality is the most incontinent (i.e., least easily controllable) feature of human embodiment. This is apparently due to the evolutionary imperative to reproduce at all costs. We are frequently out of control in sexual matters, and severely in need of exterior social constraints. Many of us would like to have sex with every attractive female that we meet (at least as a peripheral interest) but since most of us haven't been put in jail, it must mean that we have either successfully resisted these impulses or have never been caught. Obviously and sometimes, what we want, we can't have. Every civilized person recognizes this and many homosexuals exercise similar self-restraint in this matter. What we need to understand is that same-sex attraction, as a preference, is not just a moral disorder but also possibly a personal disorder, despite the fact that it may be rooted in a biological inclination.

PERSONAL DISORDERS AND MORAL DISABILITY

A personal disorder involves the consequences of moral choices an individual makes. Some moral choices will *allow* a person to let his or her disordered affections or biological inclinations rule their lives. For example, a man or woman who might have a strong disposition towards smoking or alcoholism may or may not be aware of any such particular orientation until it is too late. If they are aware of the problem, then a choice has to be made. Immorality occurs when an individual who recognizes what the "good" is (in relation to a higher standard) ignores it and proceeds along the easy path of the appetites. This is the essence of vice and it is the result of choosing a lesser "good" based on the limitations of personal perspective without adverting to a moral standard. Who could argue that human beings are configured to have sex with the same sex? Obviously, if the 'parts' aren't right, then something else is wrong. The question is what is it? Is it a genetic problem or a personal disorder caused by poor moral choices?

A very small percentage of the homosexual population (perhaps as low as one percent according to some studies) may be genetically disordered. These individuals need to be treated with compassion. They may have a simple moral disability based on either bad habits or genetic inclination. Many of the so-called homosexuals are, more than likely, sexually incontinent and may be simply just too lazy to act like normal human beings. It requires an effort to be a sexually self-possessed and self-restrained man or woman.

Our culture assumes that all men and woman have genetically fixed sexual identities. This is probably not the case. Our basic biological instincts, as indicated by the prime directive of "getting off" don't give a fig for sexual identity. Sexual identity is rooted in social and intellectual moral patterns that are cultivated in conjunction with a multiplicity of genetic factors. Heterosexuals in prison, for example, can easily lapse into homosexual relationships, as a matter of convenience, when there is an absence of available females. These men are not homosexuals; they are just doing whatever it takes to "get off". Those with unregulated appetites always serve themselves first.

THE DISJUNCTION BETWEEN OBJECTIVITY AND SUBJECTIVITY

Why is same-sex attraction only limited to those who have sex with members of the same sex? Why isn't masturbation considered a same-sex attraction? Masturbation is having sex with not only the same sex but the same person—a double exclusivity—even if the masturbator is focused on images of the opposite sex. My own opinion is that if someone can masturbate, they can engage in homosexual sex without too much difficulty. Such behavior might be viewed as analogous to killing in war. There are those who, at first, are horrified by killing but then later come to accept and even enjoy it. Particularly bothersome is the notion that an individual's sexual preferences should be considered the primary determinant of sexual behavior. There is something about this idea that is reminiscent of slavery. Pressed into service by our genitals, we had better march to the tune.

No individual should allow feelings based on appetite to completely determine a course of action. Imagine that you are walking down the street with a gun in your pocket and you see two men beating a young woman senseless—kicking her in the face, stomping on her head. What do you do? Suppose you have no appetite to get involved? Suppose you had a rough night and you just can't be bothered, or you are worried about being sued if you have to shoot one of the disturbing individuals in front of you...suppose you are afraid? Obviously, under these circumstances, character and prudence, and not feelings, need to determine the course of action.

Feelings provide the matrix or the elements for a decision based on character and the notion of honor. Most of us just don't want to get involved in the affairs of others and we certainly don't want to get hurt. The difficulty, as presented, shows that helping the woman who is being beaten is the moral thing to do, and that any cowardly or lazy impulses to do nothing must be resisted. The higher good of exercising courage and rendering assistance must be acknowledged by the intellect and chosen by the will. If this second step is not taken moral paralysis will likely be the result and you will do nothing.

The worst thing about doing what you feel like doing is that it *may* be wrong. The *disjunction* between feeling and moral action, and the acknowledgment of this disjunction is what distinguishes the cultured from the uncultured, the couth from the uncouth, the cowardly from the brave and the immoral from the moral. The cultured person understands that self-discipline is the action of an internal, moral editor against the pressure of immoral appetites. "Will you tell me," John Adams asks, "how to prevent luxury from producing effeminacy, intoxication, extravagance, vice and folly...I believe no effort in favor of virtue is lost." [7]

Someone may ask, "What about those people whose inclinations and feelings are naturally moral?" These are people whose first impulse is to help those who are afflicted or in danger. They are individuals whose emotions and intellects are more naturally ordered towards rational action and the 'good'. These fortunate individuals may find that doing 'good' comes more naturally than doing 'bad'. Why take issue with the fact that there are some who are more naturally disposed to take that road? However, even the naturally good have to make an effort to stay good and to become even better, despite their propensity towards reasonableness.

---

7   John Adams in a letter to Thomas Jefferson, cited in *America's God and Country*, William J. Federer, FAME Publishing, Coppell, Texas., page 13

LUST OR RESONANT LOVE?

"We are each of us angels with only one wing, and we can only fly by embracing one another."

—Lucretius

Sexual feelings present us with a fundamental problem that requires moral editing. All of us have experienced sexual desire for individuals whom we know would not be suitable for a long-term relationship. The one-night stand originates from this place of moral confusion. We just want to mount them, or be mounted—never mind about the relationship. Isn't it unpleasant though, when you wake up the next morning and barely want to speak to the other person? This *disjunction* between desire and reason is a common problem across all orders of sexuality and is the most frequent feature of incontinence. The rational solution is to find someone for whom you have both strong sexual desire and a complementary personal attraction. This can lead to a powerful resonance of intention and love that can be a solid basis for transcending the difficulties that occur in every relationship.

Unfortunately, large sections of the homosexual community, like the heterosexual community, find themselves with plenty of lust and multiple partners but little personal satisfaction. All individuals desire someone who is appropriate to their own perfection; that is the meaning of complementarities between lovers. If sexuality is perfected by personal complementarities, then the issue of same-sex attraction can, in some circumstances, be eclipsed by the more important moral quest for a lover whose soul is proportionately related to our own. There are huge numbers of people who marry those whose natures are not proportional to their needs or identity. Divorce is a direct consequence of a metaphysical failure to identify the nature and habits of the person we are marrying.

Many heterosexuals are impressed by the devotion that many gays show towards life-long partners. Nonetheless, the perfection of human nature would not seem possible in homosexual relationships. Homosexuality is, more likely, a temporary way station for those who have lost their moral or psychological compass. Many homosexuals, just like 'straight' people, are looking for someone whom they can love without reservation.

No one should doubt that some homosexuals love their partners but it is highly unlikely that these relationships can lead to moral or spiritual perfection. This is why those who argue that same-sex attraction is a genetic phenomenon and nothing else, are not looking at the whole picture. The condition of a homosexual orientation is real enough, but unfortunately, like alcoholism, the choice of staying with it may be a form of moral and spiritual illness.

As Charlie Allnut (Humphrey Bogart) says to Rose Sayer (Catherine Hepburn) in the 1951 Movie, *The African Queen*: "What are you being so mean for, Miss? A man takes a drop too much once in a while, it's only human nature." Catherine's response as Rose Sayer is profound in its brevity and its wisdom: "Nature, Mr. Allnut, is what we are put in this world to rise above." This sort of statement may be largely incomprehensible to the true empiricists (the mantle that is now worn by current liberals) who embrace only the totality their senses; for the rationalist, who accepts sources of knowledge and information beyond the senses, Rose's statement may ring as clear as a bell.

PREFERENCES AND MORALITY

Enrique Rueda, author of *The Homosexual Network,* argues that:

> "*An almost universal theme within the homosexual movement is the idea that homosexuals are in no way responsible for being the way they are. In the process of growing up, homosexual movement writers assert, a person discovers that he or she is homosexual. The acquisition of a homosexual consciousness is, therefore, seen as a process of self-discovery and maturation rather than as involving*

*conscious choices on the part of the homosexual. It must be kept
in mind however...this statement is ideological rather than scientific in nature, i.e., that it has been formulated for the purpose of
serving the goals and objectives of the homosexual movement."* [8]

Congressman William Dannemeyer, in his book, *Shadow in the
Land: Homosexuality in America* argues along similar lines, in attempting to show that homosexuality is chosen behavior. He cites a work
by a once noted (now deceased) pro-homosexual researcher, Deryck
Calderwood, in which Calderwood states:

*"There are no sexual instincts in man...human sexual behavior
is entirely dependent on human conditioning. The individual's
pattern of sexual behavior is acquired in the context of his unique
experiences and are in no sense innate or inherited."* [9]

Despite the fact that Calderwood inadvertently buttresses the idea
that homosexuality is a moral choice, his notion that 'acquired behavior' has no moral connotation or connection to higher principals is also
consistent with moral relativism. The idea that 'choosing' just floats in
the waters of whimsy represents a radically different morality than that
upon which western culture has traditionally been based. Is what you
choose simply related to The First Law of Thermodynamics, where all
choices are as discontinuous as reality or are moral choices related to a
bigger picture of existence?

Aristotle, for example, points out that there are three moral states
to be avoided: *vice, incontinence and brutishness.* The incontinent man
knows that what he does is bad but does it as a result of passion.[10] The
continent man, knowing that his appetites are bad, restrains himself
and acts properly.[11] Brutishness results when vice is unopposed by rea-

8   Rueda, Enrique, *The Homosexual Network*, pg. 92
9   Calderwood, Deryck, *Lovemaking: Heterosexual, Bisexual and Homosexual*
10 Aristotle, *Nichomachean Ethics*
11 Ibid

son. Take a cruise to your local ghetto and observe brutish behavior at its finest, or better, watch Bruce Jenner (Caitlin) for a display of both moral confusion and emotional incontinence.

The virtue of Temperance is essentially self-restraint in reference to bodily pleasures. Is there *any* notion of this in pro-homosexual writers? Show me. The assumption of all those who maintain that sexual choice is based on preference are simply not going far enough in their conclusions. So what if someone has bad preferences? We all do. The issue is what we do with our bad preferences, whether it is smoking, over-eating, drinking to excess, engaging a bad temper or mounting whatever we feel like, whenever we feel like it. The quasi-rational statements of the apologists of pleasure are dismissed by Aristotle in striking language:

> *"It is plain then that incontinent people must be said to be in a similar condition to men asleep, mad or drunk. The fact that men use the language that flows from knowledge proves nothing; for even men under the influence of these passions utter scientific proofs and verses of Empedocles, and those who have just begun to learn a science can string together its phrases, but do not yet know it; for it has to become part of themselves, and that takes time; so that we must suppose that the use of language by men in an incontinent state means no more than its utterance by actors on the stage."* [12]

Excessive or unrepentant masturbation, like homosexuality may be considered incontinent behavior and as such, should always be resisted as a moral dysfunction, like any other bad habit. The notion that sexual preference is somehow innate and cannot be changed is based on a limited understanding of human adaptability. If masturbation is uncritically accepted as the gold standard for "getting off" then whether you have sex with a man, a woman or even a dog is irrelevant; it becomes a matter of preference, or as they say, of "orientation".

12 Aristotle, *Nichomachean Ethics*, Bk. 7, Chapter 3

The idea that it is unhealthy not to masturbate is an idea that has been promoted by sexual researchers who have not done their homework. "When sex educators claim masturbation in men is healthy, they are referring to research about *ejaculation*. One study, cited earlier, from the Journal of the American Medical Association, says, when you look at the various studies on this subject, the results are quite mixed. Some show a positive correlation to reducing prostate cancer risks, some a negative correlation, some no correlation at all."[13] The article goes on to say that:

> *"Conclusions from the research about ejaculation are mixed because researchers often assume all orgasms are created equal."*[14]

All orgasms aren't, apparently, created equal. Even the makeup of semen is different when you compare masturbation to vaginal intercourse. Once researchers started differentiating between masturbation and vaginal intercourse, they noticed more consistent trends regarding health benefits. Compared to sexual intercourse, Dr. Stuart Brody says masturbation is correlated with fewer health benefits—or even increased health risks—for the following conditions in men:

- Satisfaction with one's mental health
- Relationship satisfaction
- Self-rated happiness
- Lower depression scores
- Less likely to have schizophrenia
- Improved erectile function
- Faster recovery from stress
- Fewer prostate abnormalities
- Less prostate cancer risks

---

13 http://www.covenanteyes.com/2015/04/13/the-great-masturbation-hoax-is-not-masturbating-unhealthy-for-you/
14 Ibid

Dr. Brody says masturbation is actually associated with more symptoms of depression and more prostate abnormalities than not. In short, there *are* a few distinct health problems associated with masturbation, and whatever physiological benefits masturbation claims to have, it is only because of its distant relation to its healthier cousin: *sexual intercourse.*" [15]

Given that the statistical evaluation of masturbation indicates that it may be morally and physically problematic, how can we understand masturbation as a questionable activity on a continuum with perversion? Unfortunately, there is simply no way to discuss perversion unless there is an existential standard against which to measure what might pass as sexual 'normality'. How can we talk about homosexual pederasty, for example, unless it is simply the age of consent that would make such sexual acts moral or immoral? Consent, by itself, cannot determine the morality or immorality of sexual activity otherwise adultery, for example, between consenting adults would be completely moral.

There are very few homosexuals and nearly as many heterosexuals, as of this writing, who believe that there is anything wrong with masturbation. If masturbation is perfectly acceptable then who you 'get off' with becomes morally irrelevant, which is the situation today. Masturbation has simply become a toilet function. Sexual continence requires continuous effort for all people no matter what "orientation" or set of habitual preferences they might have. There is also the additional consideration that immorality may result in *soul displacement* or the derangement of self-esteem and self-motivation. Strong appetites that have gone unchecked can shoulder aside what used to be called conscience or the inner voice of the higher self. The notion of a higher self is based on a conscious and volitional identity with the soul.

Most of us have a profound sympathy for those with same-sex attractions and respect the honesty of those who acknowledge who and what they are. The issue, however, is not one solely of honesty, which is commendable and indeed virtuous, but is one of moral di-

---

15 Ibid

rection. If I acknowledge that I am an alcoholic, a kleptomaniac, a compulsive masturbator, pederast or a homosexual, then that is the first step towards solving the problem. One of the worst things that a homosexual can do is to go and set up housekeeping in a homosexual love relationship or gay "marriage". Likewise, the worst thing that a compulsive masturbator can do is engage in the frequent viewing of pornography. As C.S. Lewis once said, this is like having a harem with no responsibilities. Viewing porn, whether you are gay or straight, just cements bad habits.

The recent Irish and American votes, in favor of gay marriage, are like locking an alcoholic up in a liquor store, as part of the cure for alcoholism. Under these circumstances, homosexuality ceases to be mere incontinence and becomes vice. Brutishness lives just around the corner from vice, so don't be surprised if some of those who indulge in homosexuality *or* excessive forms of heterosexual behavior don't also take drugs and possibly indulge in pederasty and other forms of self-destructive and immoral behavior.

PLATO AND HOMOSEXUALITY

Plato, who believed that the philosopher had a 'holy duty' to speak the truth, despite any opposition he might meet, clearly stated his position against homosexuality in his book, the *Laws*, despite its prevalence in his culture.

> *"These institutions (gymnasia) seem always to have had a tendency to degrade the ancient and natural custom of love below the level, not only of man but of beasts...I think that the pleasure is deemed natural which arises out of the intercourse between men and women; but that the intercourse of men with men, or of women with women, is contrary to nature and that the bold attempt was originally due to unbridled lust."* [16]

16 Alice von Hildebrand, *Plato and the Homosexuals*, Homiletic and Pastoral Review,

There may be those apologists for homosexuality who will point to the *Symposium* as a celebration of homosexual love but they forget that Alcibiades who apparently 'swung both ways' lauded Socrates for his sexual continence:

> *"And yet not withstanding all, he (Socrates) was superior to my solicitations, so contemptuous and derisive and disdainful of my beauty—which really, as I fancied, had some attractions—hear O judges: for judges you shall be of the haughty virtue of Socrates—nothing more happened, but in the morning when I awoke (let all the gods and goddesses be my witness) I arose from the couch of a father or elder brother."* [17]

The cure for same-sex attraction begins when the homosexual individual accepts who he or she is and then starts to search for ways to overcome the problem. There are too many stories of those who have been homosexual and then become successfully heterosexual, to ignore the possibility that same-sex attraction may be a psychological and moral defect. Indeed, AIDS, Hepatitis C (almost worse than AIDS) and 35 million dead[18] worldwide from AIDS makes the cure for same-sex attraction and incontinence, rather than a focus on just curing the symptoms of the disease, a more natural agenda for the medical and political community.

December 1981, pg. 23
17 Ibid
18 This figure can probably be doubled or tripled based on statistics from WHO (World Health Organization) that show that many AIDS patients succumb to tuberculosis before they succumb to AIDS.

CHAPTER 17

ABORTION AND ANTI-CONCEPTS

"The purpose of anti-concepts is to obliterate certain concepts without public discussion; and as a means to that end, to make public discussion unintelligible, and to induce the same disintegration in the mind of any man who accepts them, rendering him incapable of clear thinking or rational judgment."

—Ayn Rand,
Capitalism: The Unknown Ideal

CHOICE

There is no issue which has divided Americans in recent years like the abortion issue. Both sides have equally passionate advocates and both sides have taken to the streets to express their respective beliefs. There is also no issue which is more in need of metaphysics and no issue in which metaphysics is less suitably employed. The notion of 'Choice' is clearly an anti-concept, as it is offensively obfuscatory. The term 'Pro-

Life' (although true) is redundantly sanctimonious. Indeed, these two phrases contribute to the difficulty and polarization of the very issues in question.

Choice begins before sex, not just after. You have a choice, albeit a difficult one; either cross your legs or keep it zipped. Clearly, many individuals don't think about the moral consequences[1] of sexuality, but there is still little or no excuse for labeling the abortion issue as one of 'choice.' One might as well say that you have a choice to execute two-year-olds. Unfortunately, the other side of the coin, which claims to be 'Pro-Life' ascribes an anti-life mentality to those who support abortion. While this may be true in the literal sense of the word, it does not contribute to a resolution of the problem. Obviously, the supporters of abortion are concerned with the quality of human life and with ex-utero human beings. Unfortunately, they are unable to see the larger issues involved. The delusion that life begins at birth is a grotesque bias. Life begins when it begins—how about at the beginning?

The notion that a fetus isn't human, because it can't be seen is a product of a mind-set that has no understanding of the soul. If in fact a soul is the first act of a body having life-potential as Aristotle argues, then indeed, whether the fetus looks like a full-sized human baby is completely irrelevant. Indeed, it might be argued that by not engaging the concept of soul, the entire abortion issue is reduced to one of self-interest politics which as we have seen, reduces all moral choices to personal preference. Hence the obscene bumper sticker that says, "If you don't like abortion, don't have one." This is the ultimate expression of subjective values.

Even the Aztecs and the Mayas, with all of their bloody rituals and wretched beliefs in gods who would annihilate them, believed that women who died in childbirth, along with warriors who died

---

1   Sean J. O'Reilly, *How to Manage Your D.I.CK: Redirect Sexual Energy and Discover Your More Spiritually Enlightened, Evolved Self,* Ten Speed Press and the Auriga Publishing Group, 2001 addresses the full dimensionality and moral spectrum of sexuality.

in battle, would enjoy eternal gladness in the Maya paradise.[2] Why isn't giving a child up for adoption considered the height of womanly courage and honor? No need to be troubled by either courage or honor with abortion; if you've chosen it, then it must be good. Unfortunately, many women's' experience of abortion is exactly the opposite. Many (not all) feel a wrenching sense of moral dislocation and no amount of 'feel good' therapy can take away the hidden knowledge that something is not quite right. Without a philosophy of soul, all the misgivings about abortion remain just that. The ultimate legacy of abortion is depression and a sense of spiritual dishonor that is hard to shake.

The very worst thing about abortion is that it separates us from any consideration of the importance of the human soul and its historic and moral significance. All of us might as well be recyclable plastic products, with no more usefulness than a milk carton, when it comes to the choice of abortion. Are there no morally evil people who will step forward and have the guts to say, "I don't care if abortion is wrong, I want it and will accept the consequences?" Give me an honest, bad person any day, as opposed to these mindless, plastic people who prattle on about choice and have no more understanding of the word than a pigeon. (Ayn Rand is probably turning over in her grave over my use of her quote in this context. She was an early supporter of abortion rights.)

DEMONS

Late-term abortion procedures have been produced by truly warped minds.[3] Look at what these morally ill individuals put into practice:

---

2   Eliade, Mircea *Encyclopedia of Religion*
3   Recent video and audio tapes of Planned Parenthood officials discussing the alleged harvesting of body parts produced by abortion makes this report, written in 1993, all the more relevant. The relative truth or falsity of the assertions, we can leave to the courts…

"They open the cervix, which is the opening to the womb, over a two-day period. On the third day, with the mother on the operating table, the surgical assistant places an ultrasound probe on the mother's abdomen. This enables the 'doctor' to see the baby on a screen and find the baby's legs. The doctor inserts forceps, or pliers, with sharp grasping teeth into the mother's womb. When the instrument appears on the screen, the surgeon is able to open and close the instrument's jaws and firmly grasp a lower extremity. The surgeon applies firm traction to the instrument...and pulls the extremity into the birth canal. Then the doctor pulls the baby's other leg, torso and both arms into the birth canal...The baby's head is too large to pull through the opening and stays in the womb. The 'doctor' then slides Metsenbaum scissors along the baby's spine up to the base of her head. He forces the scissors into the base of the skull or into the foramen magnum, having safely... entered the skull, he spreads the scissors to enlarge the opening. The surgeon removes the scissors and introduces a suction catheter into the hole and evacuates the skull contents. He sucks out the partially born baby's brains." [4]

This is mind numbing. Can you imagine a trained medical doctor allowing himself to sink to such a sub-human level? This brings to mind the notion of demons. A demon is an individual who has allowed his or her appetites to take the position of reason. Such individuals invert the moral order of appetites being ruled by the intellect. A "demon" is an inverted person. Such people think and do inverted things. Some child molesters and mass murderers may be demons. Some of your Congressmen may be demons. Arguments with demons are not possible because they have forsaken the common rational ground upon which humanity attempts to stand. The only thing you can do with a demon is to lock it up or shoot it.

---

4   *Right to Life Newsletter*, date unknown

The notion of repentance and conversion is particularly appropriate with demons. Hitler and Stalin for example were both demons. You do not negotiate with a demon. This is why Churchill and Roosevelt were mistaken in trying to 'deal' with Hitler and Joseph Stalin. A demon will never change unless either forced to or a change from within allows the higher values of the soul to be reinstated. Malcolm X, for example, was once considered so bad in prison that his cellmates called him Satan. At one point, he decided to embrace Islam and in a passionate search for truth, he transcended his demonic and devolved state and became a statesman for the black community.

The most contemptible pro-choice advocates are those Christians who maintain that abortion is compatible with Christianity. They are out of their collective minds. How could they possibly imagine that a man like Jesus, who frowned on all manner of earthly attachments could approve of abortion? This goes beyond an intellectual error, this represents a governing of the brain by the appetites, an immoral and demonic brutishness barely exceeded by Hitler's desire to cleanse the Aryan body of Jewish political and social thinking. Hitler failed to understand that differences in opinion are not racially or even just culturally at odds. Dramatic differences in opinion are a direct result of how our collective relationship with God and the universe is conceived and put into practice.

Hitler, despite what the Richard Dawkins Foundation might advocate in its overwrought, *The Atheist Atrocities Fallacy*, was operating on an implicitly atheistic agenda that mistakenly located the origin of social devolution and moral corruption in a people instead of a set of ideas. The Dawkins Foundation presents the following statement from Hitler in its attempt to link Nazism to Christianity.

"Besides that, I believe one thing: there is a Lord God! And this Lord God creates the peoples. We were convinced that the people need and require this faith. We have therefore undertaken the

fight against the atheistic movement, and that not merely with a few theoretical declarations; we have stamped it out. "[5]

While it may be true that Hitler believed in some sort of God, the inescapable fact is that he behaved as if God did not exist. Who, besides the ethically and morally retarded, could possibly believe that God would desire the violent deaths of millions of his children? The reality is that both atheism and religion are used as a justification for ideas that are both intellectually superficial and morally retrograde. It is disingenuous not to advert to the negative consequences or tendencies of any belief system, whether it religious or atheistic in nature. Both religion and atheism (which is really just another kind of religion) can be used in support of violent means for rationally justifiable ends.

Conservative social critic, Dinesh D'Souza,[6] notes that "Hitler was born Catholic just as Stalin was born into the Russian Orthodox Church and Mao was raised as a Buddhist. These facts prove nothing as many people reject their religious upbringing, from an early age." Quoting historian Allan Bullock, D'souza points out that "Hitler had no time at all for Catholic Teaching, regarding it as a 'religion fit only for slaves' and detesting its ethics." [7]

Hitler was, clearly, possessed of what might be described as a confusing blend of rational and irrational ideas. He had inherited unexamined Christian values from his childhood, which he merged with a psychopathological and racial hatred of the Jews, which quite frankly, had been promoted by some segments of the Christian Church for many centuries. Hitler, who was more lucid in his early life than he was towards the end, could only be described as metaphysically and demonically confused by his own appetites.

"There is no worse death," as John Scottus Eriugena notes, "than ignorance of the truth." The vast bloodshed of the 20th century and

---

5   *Atheist Atrocities*: https://richarddawkins.net/2014/10/the-atheist-atrocities-fallacy-hitler-stalin-pol-pot/ by Michael Sherlock
6   D'souza also attended my alma mater, the University of Dallas in Irving, Texas
7   From Dinesh D'Souza's article: *Was Hitler a Christian?*

what might still be more to come with the anarchy of pseudo- Islamic groups such as ISIS, makes it imperative that we have a new moral philosophy that understands that the near infinite power that we have been given for goodness and creativity also has the capacity for evil on a colossal scale. If the idea of Satan has merit, outside the traditional understanding of a separated evil entity, it is that the enormous power that has been given to us in the Reality Dysfunction can be misused. Satan is, in this context, a metaphor for the negative aspects of the Reality Dysfunction, a symptom of an original ontology that comes into being and possibility due to God's eternal knowing of Himself, as other than Himself.

The unexamined life that resists the intellectual interrogation of bad impulses based on an atheistic moral and intellectual schema that claims there are no objective moral values, related to Divine intentionality, is not without disturbing political and social consequences. The algorithmic limiting of moral and intellectual pathogens,[8] normally established by rational laws rooted in an understanding of human nature, can only be effectively re-introduced to American culture via a deeper legal and metaphysical understanding of morality and its relationship to the human enterprise. The current climate of moral relativism is a cultural pathogen that is in need of an antivirus that can only be provided by Natural Law and philosophical reflection.

Unless we have a serious re-evaluation of the intellectual, moral and spiritual ideas, which our country was founded on, we are likely to see a plague of demons unlike anything seen before. Just read the daily headlines and the future, in which a destructive and morally vicious lawlessness spreads across America, is already in evidence.

---

8   The notion of intellectual and moral pathogens was taken from a lecture by Tim O'Reilly given at the Long Now Foundation in 2012 and more than likely has its origins in Jared Diamond's book, *Guns, Germs and Steel.*

CHAPTER 18

AMERICA NEEDS A PUBLIC PHILOSOPHY

"Diodorus began to brood on modern Rome again, and made a face. The armchair generals who could direct, petulantly, the campaigns of hardened commanders in distant fields, and devise tactics and strategies as if they knew anything about them! The soft pale senators in their molded togas, buying and selling in their stock exchange, after a long morning in the baths recovering from a night of debauchery, and partially restored by skilled slaves with lubricated hands who had massaged their flabby muscles! Buying and selling, the fatted dogs, what other men had given their lives to obtain for Rome, and wafting perfumed kerchiefs in their faces as they languidly bargained and bid and outsmarted each other, and in between bids related the latest obscene gossip of the city! Their whorish women, their concubines, their depraved wives who bore the noblest names in Rome and committed adultery as if it were a fashionable pastime— which it was. The parasites, the Augustales, who moved in and

out of the Palatine, as aristocratic as statues, with rottenness in
their bodies and harpies in their souls! The golden litters, the
pampered boy slaves kept for shameful purposes, the raping and
licentiousness of a once disciplined and frugal society, the slow
disappearance of a sound middle class, a disappearance delib-
erately designed! The shining city, the mistress of the world—
become a sewer of corruption, treason, greed, plotting, pleasure
and decay, a stench of foulness from which wafted the fevers,
madness and disease which were polluting the
farthest reaches of the Empire."

—Taylor Caldwell,
Dear And Glorious Physician

America needs a Public Philosophy. This is clearly evidenced by the endless newspaper accounts of senseless violence over drugs, shoes or popular items of clothing. The 1992 Los Angeles riots and the later, 2015 riots in Ferguson, Missouri provided viewers with graphic examples of massive social disorder. The continuing, multiple accounts of on-going white collar crime only complement this dismal picture. The newspaper articles and TV shows that report on these items usually have similar explanations for the unfortunate event which they are reporting. The favorites seem to be poverty, the cutting back of government programs, social injustice and a culture that stresses acquisition as an end in itself.

These partial explanations are part of the problem. No solution will be found until the real issues of freedom and moral accountability are addressed. There are numerous countries much poorer by comparison than the United States which have far less crime and violence than this country. Americans with liberal tendencies tend to ignore any explanation which involves God or the decline of religious belief as the primary cause of the moral decline of our nation's youth. I believe that this explanation is not without merit but I am convinced that there is a better answer which will satisfy both the liberal penchant for excluding religion, and the conservative desire to include religious values in any instruction of the young.

We cannot teach one religion in the public schools for good reason. Whose religion would we teach? Religion *should* be taught as history but religious prejudice is so strong that impartial points of view are impossible without a common perspective from which to evaluate all religions. We can however, teach an updated and modified Aristotelian ethics and philosophy to students, to provide this common perspective which would provide real freedom of choice, when evaluating religious claims. The teaching of religion as history makes much more sense with Aristotle's teaching on causality as the referee.

Why a moral code based on Aristotle's philosophy and not someone else's? Why Philosophy at all—isn't the freedom we cherish in America based on different points of view, none of which can be absolute, so as to preserve that freedom? The paradox between freedom and responsibility that most of us are aware of, contains within itself the answer to the reason why we must have a Public Philosophy. There is a tension between freedom and moral responsibility in Western civilization, which has never been properly articulated, due to the intrusion of improperly formulated non-religious and religious values. Aristotle's sophisticated distinctions, coming as they did prior to the advent of Christianity and Islam, and having also been utilized by Jewish theologians are a logical choice for the task. A neo-Aristotelianism that would pare away the outmoded aspects of Aristotle's thinking and present the clarity of his understanding of causality for modern readers is not a difficult task.

The time has come to *relatively separate* intellectual, moral and spiritual values, in a way that might make them universally accessible and acclaimed by the majority. The minority of the offended will have to be ignored, if the attempt is to succeed. There are those for whom reason does not occupy any position of honor, those for whom ideas are merely instruments for obtaining self-satisfaction, at anyone and everyone's expense. The time has come to say no to those simple things which are clearly wrong; honesty is required as never before. Everyone may have to yield a little, in order to reintroduce the foundations of morality.

One example of such a compromise would be our response to the homosexual agenda. Give homosexuals their constitutional rights to the extent that the morality of others is not compromised but don't allow their behavior to be considered normal until it is proven to be genetically based. Same-sex attraction is an unfortunate liability for those afflicted. Classify it as a moral disability, and exclude homosexuals, transvestites, pederasts and those who prefer animals, from various activities, on that basis. Job discrimination against homosexuals should only be allowed by religious organizations, departments of moral education and the military. Same-sex attraction as a disability[1] could be used to exclude avowed homosexuals from some areas of military service, teaching and from marriage on the basis of an inability to act in accordance with natural law. Understanding any moral disability as being on a continuum with an impairment to non-local access might help to make this distinction more acceptable.

Furthermore, this moral impairment might exclude homosexuals from some forms of insurance coverage as a self-induced medical liability. Let gays be free to develop their own medical insurance services if they insist upon engaging in 'risky' practices. The upside of this position would be that homosexuals might qualify under the Americans with Disabilities Act for certain benefits not available to the general population.

Same-sex pairings should not be described by the word 'marriage' but should be referred to as 'domestic partnerships' and taxed accordingly.[2] Domestic partnership legislation would have to be carefully crafted to disallow homosexuals' child-rearing privileges or other positions of moral authority, except under unusual circumstances. This

1 I am indebted to David Foster for this concept.
2 These words were written in the early 1990's and, in my opinion are still appropriate, although outdated by current affairs.

may seem harsh given that many homosexuals treat children as fairly and kindly as any parent might but the ultimate goal of same-sex activists is to completely legitimize the gay agenda and all that it entails. The heterosexual community has a legitimate interest in setting a standard for moral behavior. Just as Americans have the right to demand that anyone who settles in this country make an attempt to learn and speak English, they have the right to insist on certain standards of sexual behavior. Given the financial and health problems caused by AIDS, this is not an irrational or homophobic position.

Thirty five million deaths worldwide due to AIDS and millions more from those with weakened immune systems who have contracted tuberculosis[3] is not something to be discounted by the morally obfuscatory word "homophobia". Viruses are opportunistic but given that "opportunities" for infection within most biologically normative, single partner relationships are not available, it might be suggested to the homosexual community that nature has already cast a negative vote in the direction of same-sex activity. The same principle applies to "swingers" with multiple sexual partners within the straight community who are, from the perspective of virtue and vice, on much the same level as homosexuals with multiple partners.

A political compromise between the left and the right in regards to gay marriage might be just the thing to initiate the moral dialogue required for the enactment of a Public Philosophy. Nowhere is the breakdown in our understanding of morality more self-evident than in our discussions of sexual morality. Sexuality without any understanding of continence is a free-for-all. While it is certainly true that there are many moral homosexuals, in reference to behavior outside of sexuality, it is also true that homosexuals have a different view of what might constitute sexual excess than those adhering to the common spiritual and moral heritage of the West.

This is why maintaining the distinction between gay marriage and

---

3   WHO (World Health Organization) statistics indicate that some 135 million people a
    year die worldwide from tuberculosis.

civil unions is so important: it allows for a continuing discussion of what sexual immorality might consist of. Having said this does not mean that the position stated in this book is correct; it only means that if God exists and desires human goodness that homosexuality is, likely, at variance with God's goodness. While no one can entirely presume what goodness might be to the Creator, some congruence with the natural order in regards to sexuality might be expected. Understanding that a morally uncritical attitude towards masturbation might be a sexual behavior on a continuum with homosexuality may help facilitate the conversation between the gay and straight communities.

THE PROBLEM OF AGNOSIS

We are far too accustomed to hearing words like soul and virtue and equating them immediately with Christianity. These are concepts that antedate Christianity and must be re-understood in relation to both Greek and older philosophical systems, in order to better understand what Christianity both achieved and obscured. Virtue as a concept, and its relation to happiness, cannot be understood unless it is located in the far larger concept of human nature, its place in the natural order, and those natural laws which may apply to human nature.

The Classical Greek definition of moral virtue was: *an activity of soul in accordance with right reason.* The Christian definition of virtue is activity in accordance with the intentionality of God, which by definition, orders all things perfectly both in reference to God and to ourselves. What this suggests is a corollary: that there are ways of behaving that are not in accordance with right reason or Divine intention, and that proper moral and psychological function cannot be clearly determined without an understanding of the structure of human nature. The moral virtues are those deliberated *acts*, those modalities of reasonableness, which enable men and women to control the irrationality of their appetites and exercise some rule over the emotions. In a deeper sense, moral virtue is a non-local pivoting of the soul and an aligning of the will and spirit with the non-local and local power of the Divine. The opposite of virtuous deliberation is what Aristotle calls incontinence, or lack of self-restraint which when indulged habitually, becomes *vice* or an absolute lack of reasonableness in behavior and choice.

Vice is the doorway to both brutishness and evil. Think of it as a moral pathogen.

The Greeks, the Jews and later, the Christians understood these distinctions and utilized them in the creation of useful moral precepts and religious observances. For example, the Four Cardinal Virtues of the medieval Christians were: Prudence, Temperance, Justice and Fortitude. Compare these with the Platonic formulation of: Wisdom, Temperance (self-restraint), Justice and Courage. Another example would be the Socratic and Christian vision of the soul, as something to be *attended to* and the good life as the happy consequence of the cultivation of moral and intellectual excellence. The Aristotelian and scholastic concept of the five powers of the psyche or soul and their respective operations being ordered by formal, material, efficient and final causality (the four causes) is a rich field for study—even today.

Political thinking which does not consider the 'good' from the perspective of natural law, as presented by both Socrates and Aristotle, will artificially polarize both politics and religion. Separation of Church and State should not mean antagonism between Church and State. One can live a moral life without religion but one cannot live a normal life without morality. A life without morality is a life closed to the soul or spirit, and subject to the vicious whims of our biological nature.

Our culture is in a state of chaos due to our inability to formulate clear solutions to moral issues. The problem goes deeper, however, than a mere inability to focus on the issues. There is sometimes a willful indifference to known problems on the basis of a kind of moral laziness known as *agnosis*. Agnosis is defined as indifference to or an ignoring of defective knowledge. If evil is a defect or "the absence of a good which could and should be present" then agnosis, as the practiced indifference to evil, needs to be pointed out when it is visibly displayed in the discourse of public figures. When Hillary Clinton or Nancy Pelosi, for example, express outrage at the way in which Planned Parenthood members were "tricked" into exposing business practices that were redolent of the Nazi's callous disregard for human life, they are engaging *agnosis* as a mental habit. Likewise, when the Bush administration failed to think through the possible consequences of deposing Saddam Hussein, not only were they engaging in wishful thinking they were allowing agnosis to cloud their vision. The State Department's failure to react swiftly to the Benghazi incident and the death of a US ambassador represents a particularly repugnant form of agnosis. The apparent inability to adequately prepare for and respond to violent contingencies with necessary force and protection for American personnel is vice in the form of imprudence, and at the very least, indicates a lack of moral resolve.

Political scientist Dr. Paul Eidelberg refers to agnosis as "a moral inability to recognize certain human acts as downright evil."[4] This is, of course, part and parcel of the obfuscation that occurs when the appetites override intellectual virtue in the shredding machine of legal positivism when it is divorced from a moral code. This moral confusion in our culture can and will end, when the common language of a Public Philosophy is used to dispel the extremes of moral relativism. Since the time of Socrates, this has been the honorable and necessary task of philosophy.

---

4   The Maccabean Online: Political Analysis and Commentary on Israeli and Jewish
    Affairs, August 2012, *Obamagnosis: A Sickness Unto Death* by Professor Paul Eidelberg,
    The Israel-America Renaissance Institute

V

THE FOUNDERS' CODE

"We have staked the whole future of American civilization, not upon the power of government, far from it. We have staked the future of all of our political institutions upon the capacity of mankind for self-government; upon the capacity of each and all of us to govern ourselves, to control ourselves, to sustain ourselves according to the Ten Commandments of God."

—James Madison,
Father of the U.S. Constitution

"If the citizens neglect their duty and place unprincipled men in office, the government will soon be corrupted; laws will be made, and not for the public good so much as for selfish or local purposes; corrupt or incompetent men [and women] will be appointed to execute the laws; the public revenues will be squandered on unworthy men; and the rights of the citizen will be violated or disregarded."

—Noah Webster, the Father of American
Scholarship and Education

CHAPTER 19

MORAL PATTERNS AND POLITICAL THINKING

"The idea that biological crimes can be ended by intellect alone, that you can talk crime to death, doesn't work. Intellectual patterns cannot directly control biological patterns. Only social patterns can control biological patterns, and the instrument of conversation between society and biology is not words. The instrument of conversation between society and biology has always been a policeman or a soldier and his gun. All the laws of history, all the arguments, all the Constitutions and the Bills of Rights and Declarations of Independence are nothing more than instructions to the military and police. If the military and police can't or don't follow these instructions properly they might as well have never been written."

—Robert Pirsig,
Lila: An Inquiry into Morals

BIOLOGY AND VALUES

What Pirsig broadly defines as 'biological patterns' of value, we can affirm as a different way of speaking about appetite. "Good" appetites are socially acceptable and are the basis of what he terms *social patterns*. "Bad" appetites are, generally speaking, those aspects of biological patterns of value that are not socially acceptable and consequently, may be immoral or at variance with the goals of a good society. The two ideas are not uncomplimentary as both can be used as ways of defining certain activities of *being* in relation to the soul.

Pirsig's notion of biological crimes not being entirely answerable to reason echoes anthropologist A. E. Hooten's observation, who wrote in *Apes, Men and Morons,* published in 1937:

"The only valid reason for trying to improve the biological status of man is that he be made a better animal—more honest, more unselfish, more decent and considerate in his human relations. I think that a biological purge is the essential prerequisite for a social and a spiritual salvation. Let us temper mercy with justice and dispense charity with intelligence. We must stop trying to cure malignant biological growths with patent sociological nostrums. The emergency demands a surgical operation."[1]

We have only to recall police cowering behind shields as rocks and bricks were thrown at them in the recent 2015 Baltimore riots, to understand the power of this observation. Biology, frequently and more often than not, answers only to force. A few well-placed gunshots into the crowd of brick-throwers would have had an immediate and salutary result in terms of a cessation of violence. If not, a few more rioters shot in order to maintain order would not have been an inordinate response—given the millions of dollars' worth of property damages caused by the looters.

The pattern that emerges, in any observation of society, values and appetites, is that it is possible to *be* bad. This can very simply be

---

1   A. E. Hooten, *Apes, Men and Morons*, page 295, GP Putnam and Sons, 1937

understood as choosing those values (or 'goods') which are more bio-logically primary, than socially or intellectually primary. What rioters may choose in a state of inchoate rage or self-indulgence could hardly be described as acts of reason.

Pirsig's observations on the meaning of value in relation to his four divisions of value: *Inorganic, Biological, Social and Intellectual* are invaluable. Pirsig argues that the four basic patterns of value are aug-mented by something that he calls Dynamic Quality.[2] Dynamic Qual-ity is what many or most classical philosophers would call *Existence*. What Pirsig has done, is to clearly indicate that *Dynamic Quality* is responsible for the thwarting of the Second Law of Thermodynamics, which is what life does best. Pirsig has many wonderful descriptions of dynamic quality that are worth savoring.

> *"The explanation of life as a migration of static patterns toward Dynamic Quality not only fitted the known facts of evolution, it allowed new ways of interpreting them. Biological evolution can be seen as a process by which weak Dynamic forces at a sub-atomic level discover stratagems for overcoming huge static in-organic forces at a super-atomic level. They do this by selecting super-atomic mechanisms in which a number of options are so evenly balanced that a weak Dynamic force can tip the balance one way or another. The particular atom that the weak Dynamic subatomic forces have seized as their primary vehicle is carbon. All life contains carbon..."[3]*

What Pirsig is describing as dynamic quality is analogous to what has been described in this book as Dimensionally Interactive Cyber Kinesis. Dimensionally Interactive Cyber Kinesis is multi-dimensional energy fused with intelligence or information in the Reality Dysfunc-tion, whereby Existence infuses the virtual reality we call creation with

2   Pirsig, Robert, *Lila: An Inquiry into Morals*, Bantam Books, 1991
3   Ibid

negentropic motion and intelligence. What we see within the context of evolution is dynamic quality or Dimensionally Interactive Cyber Kinesis at work. What Pirsig has done is quite extraordinary: by postulating that Dynamic Force, (which may be thought of as an effect of Existence) could be an unknown vector influencing matter, he has given science a new tool to investigate the effects of Existence. What he describes as the ratcheting and manipulation of carbon, which on the face of it could be thought of as a product of stochastic forces, ultimately, would make no sense without the guiding principles of the Fifth Law of Thermodynamics.

GOD AND EVOLUTION

This is great stuff for all those who are interested in a more rational explanation of the Theory of Evolution, than the fairy tales for adults that the scientific establishment is currently propagating. The question is: how does this relate to the soul? The soul can be considered, from an Aristotelian perspective, as an invention of *Existence* or *Dynamic Quality*, or from a Chinese perspective, as the activity of the Tao. What Pirsig sees as an apparently person-less process, may be seen as the result of something so personal that it only appears to be impersonal, and by that we mean the Reality Dysfunction.

Existence, knowing Itself, outside Itself results in a concatenation of being from the smallest particle to the farthest star. This "knowing" expresses Itself in evolution, whereby Dimensionally Interactive Cyber-Kinesis, as patterns of energy, combine and recombine in ever more extraordinary ways in order to more fully mirror and meet their transcendent Source in a new and different order of participated being. What Indian sage, Sri Aurobindo, described as the Overmind[4] is nothing more than Existence Itself in the derivative format of the Reality Dysfunction.

---

4   Between the Eternal and temporal manifestations is the manifestation in aveternity, which corresponds to the Plane of Overmind. This closely corresponds to the Demiurge of the Gnostics.

VALUES AS MORAL PATTERNS

Pirsig's ideas about *Dynamic Quality* are also extremely useful in looking at social and biological issues from a larger perspective than we have allowed in the past.

> *"A Dynamic advance is meaningless unless it can find some static pattern with which to protect itself from degeneration back to the conditions that existed before the advance was made. Evolution can't be a continuous forward movement, it must be a process of ratchet-like steps in which there is a Dynamic movement forward up some new incline and then, if the result looks successful, a static latching-on and then another Dynamic advance, then another static latch..."* [5]

Virtue might be thought of as having some of the same operational characteristics as *Dynamic Quality*. Virtue involves the aspects of a *social* no and a *dynamic* yes. We say 'No' to something bad in order to say 'Yes' to something good. This is a form of "latching" or an affective pattern and can be the basis for an understanding of the way that the moral virtues work. The moral virtues are those social patterns (using Pirsig's terminology) that are used for the controlling of biological patterns, which have their own evolutionary agenda, at everyone and everything else's expense.

Pirsig advances the notion that patterns of value cannot be understood solely in terms of other patterns. He uses the example of machine "thinking" versus human thinking:

> *"Trying to explain social moral patterns in terms of inorganic chemistry patterns is like trying to explain the plot of a word-processor novel in terms of the computer's electronics. You can't do it. You can see how the circuits make the novel possible, but they do*

---

5   Pirsig, Robert, *Lila: An Inquiry into Morals*, Bantam Books, 1991

not provide the plot for the novel. The novel is its own set of patterns. Similarly the biological patterns of life and the molecular patterns of organic chemistry have a machine language interface called DNA but that does not mean that carbon or hydrogen or oxygen atoms possess or guide life. A primary occupation of every level of evolution [is] offering freedom to lower levels of evolution...as the higher level gets more sophisticated it goes off on purposes of its own."[6]

Using Pirsig's model of a machine interface, we might analogously suggest that the soul functions as a non-local interface between matter and spirit or be-ing and *Being*. The soul is, ultimately, a product of the infinite algorithms of the Reality Dysfunction, which is the negentropic power and intelligent design behind evolution. The soul can no more be explained by matter, than can the novel on the word-processor be explained by the electronic hardware.

The soul is a construct as is the word-processor or computer. Cultures and religions might be likened to various software packages. The soul is 'user friendly' and is compatible with all such 'software', whether good or bad. It is the job of the intellect, in conjunction with the will, to throw out the worthless and outdated software of either bad culture or religion in the formation of worthwhile political structures. For this reason, cultural relativism is only marginally useful, when considering the need for universal moral standards.

---

6   Pirsig, Robert, *Lila: An Inquiry into Morals*, Bantam Books, 1991

CHAPTER 20

EDUCATION AND POLITICS

"Education is the soul of a society as it is passed on from one generation to the next.

—GK. Chesterton

VIRTUE AND EDUCATION

If a society ceases to believe in the existence of the soul is it possible to transmit any kind of education at all? The evidence indicates that without the soul, there is no real education but rather an imposition of data on unhappy brain cells. Ask any high school student about the quality of his or her education and you will frequently pick up on the lack of meaning in it all. What is the purpose of study, if it is just to get a job? Some students are able to get well-paying jobs without much formal education and are consequently uninterested in school. What

447

really galvanizes students is the idea that education has some relevancy to their personal lives. Students are not fooled by the vague prescriptions for good behavior doled out by both educators and parents. They want to know why they should be good, as opposed to being bad or even indifferent to moral values.

How could any parent or teacher explain the necessity of excellence and its relation to goodness, without an understanding of the concept of virtue? Furthermore, without the distinctions between the intellectual, the moral and the spiritual virtues, how could there be any intelligent discussion of the problems facing education today? It is one thing to have separation of church and state or what should be separation of the moral and intellectual virtues from the spiritual virtues; and it is quite another thing, to have separation of moral and intellectual development. How can you have excellent citizens without rational moral development?

Our current concept of separation of Church and State is based on a false equating of religion and morality. The Founding Fathers were not interested in separating God and the moral law from politics, only specific religious formulations. There is no more pernicious idea at work in our society than this—that separation of Church and State means separation of God and State. The universal moral values that can be extracted from Christianity were those that Thomas Jefferson had in mind in crafting the Declaration of Independence.

The moral virtues can and must be taught separately from the spiritual virtues of faith, hope and charity.[1] The distinction is critical, if our culture is to remain even half rational. How can we distribute condoms in high schools and yet forbid the discussion of life's purpose,

---

1   There were, additionally, in the pantheon of Christian virtues, modalities of being that could be "infused" directly by the Holy Spirit. The seven infused gifts of the Holy Spirit are: spiritual wisdom, understanding, counsel, knowledge, fortitude, piety, and wonder (AKA fear of the Lord).The notion of "gifts" that the Divine could infuse into the soul of an honorable man or woman is so far off the register of modern man's empirical consciousness as to be invisible. An understanding of The Aristotelian world of acquired virtue enables an understanding of the kind of participation in Divine life that infused virtue and other spiritual gifts signify.

or the history of the soul? A curriculum that revolves around an understanding of virtue will provide adequate protection for all religious faiths by showing what is common to all.

One of the most overpowering sensations that I get when I visit most public high schools is one of boredom coupled to a kind of moral vacancy. Long, empty halls, lockers and classrooms are designed, it seems, primarily to warehouse bodies; any sense of soul has long since been abandoned, even though the intellectual virtues are cultivated to some extent. Individuals learn to read and write, speak properly and perform mathematics and geometry with varying degrees of complexity and success but there seems to be no overall sense of high purpose or excitement about the process. What is missing? Aristotle poses the question, whether what makes a man a good citizen is necessarily the same thing that makes an individual good:

> *"And the things that tend to produce virtue taken as a whole are those of the acts produced by the law which have been prescribed with a view to education for the common good. But with regard to the education of the individual as such, which makes him without qualification a good man, we must determine later whether this is the function of the political art or of another; for perhaps it is not the same to be a good man and a good citizen of any state taken at random."*

—Aristotle,
Politics

Our schools' emphasis on the intellectual virtues, as opposed to the moral virtues makes one wonder if in fact there is a difference between what might be considered a good person by a society or educational system, and someone who really is good intellectually, morally and perhaps spiritually. Public schools might view the well-adjusted football star or the National Science finalist as good students but they might in fact be rotten to the core without some notion of moral goodness. Suppose the 'grade A' student values conservation but is a thief or the football star indulges in date rape. No one would doubt the intellectual or physical excellence of our two imaginary students but are they, in fact, good human beings? Have they cultivated moral or spiritual excellence?

Do public schools teach any moral values and if so, what are they? If you might have a hard time finding anything that is taught directly, what might be the implicit values taught? Lying, cheating, stealing, murdering and taking drugs would probably make the list. What makes them bad? Does anyone know? Are there any other bad things? The response that many students will make, when asked about a moral issue, is based on the notion that if something doesn't hurt anyone, it is probably okay. Pleasure and pain (without any reference to a moral structure) are the ultimate determinants of morality for many students. Pretty high grade stuff huh?

The fundamental problem that high schools face today is that they have no curriculum for morality or personal accountability. Not only is there no curriculum for morality, the education establishment is hopelessly deadlocked over the teaching of values in the schools for fear of devaluing anyone else's values or beliefs. Furthermore, as I have indicated earlier, most individuals in positions of leadership would not know how to define virtue or vice, even if their lives depended on the answer. Mark Twain summed up the problem a long time ago. He said, "For practice God made an idiot, then he created the school board."

What is needed is an acceptable defining, formatting and presentation of what morality is in relation to the individual person and society. Until morality is *relatively separated* from religion, the problems facing our system of secondary education are bound to grow in leaps and bounds. Keep in mind that while the level of reported crime in America's high schools is extremely high—that is only the tip of the iceberg, when considered in relation to the additional level of intimidation and disrespect that exists between various groups of students and teachers.

SCHOOL VIOLENCE, RESPECT AND THE NEED FOR FORCE

News reporting indicates that the cursing of teachers by students has become relatively commonplace in some of our schools. Statistics show that there are approximately 16,000 violent and criminal acts a day in our schools.[2] That equals one such incident every six seconds. Students claim they want respect but they don't want to earn that respect in any traditional way. They want to be respected for simply existing. I think that if we look at part of the problem as originating from a disrespect of the educational system, then we will get a better handle on where the students are coming from. Who could respect teachers and institutions who don't stand for anything?

Surely the approximately 50,000 assaults[3] on teachers a year shows us that there is a serious problem with respect for teachers and institutions. What is there to respect in an educational system that treats students not to respect either themselves or moral ideas? What is there to respect in administrators who are morally incompetent to lead and do not believe in anything other than their jobs? Why do football coaches and athletes command respect? Coaches and athletes represent an unyielding standard of excellence that doesn't require much thinking to respect—they command respect.

How do we command respect from high school students? The first thing that commands respect is a system that stands for something. Almost everyone respects the military because it stands for order and justice—whether or not you like the military, or the individuals in it. High school students will never respect their institutions or their

---

2   *The Washington Times*, February 10, 1993 (these figures represent old data from the first edition of this book, and while the numbers may have changed, they represent a growing trend towards institutional anarchy glossed over by charges of racism.)

3   Ibid

teachers, unless they uphold standards that are lofty and worthy of respect. Having standards alone won't do it, however. What ultimately commands respect is the judicious use of force to back up the system.

Let me furnish a simple example of how well force can be applied to ensure compliance with rules. I spent two and half years in a Catholic seminary studying for the priesthood, before I left to pursue a more unfettered lifestyle. The rector of the seminary had a written policy that all students had to be in chapel at 5:30 AM sharp or you washed dishes for a week. Needless to say, after a week of washing dishes, not many students were late for chapel. What is most instructive about this episode is that all of the students were in the seminary of their own free will and you would think that they would be highly motivated for things like chapel and morning Mass. Nonetheless, the judicious use of punishment was required to get even the high-minded aspirants to the priesthood to church on time.

O'REILLY'S THIRD MORAL LAW

Force or discipline is required in proportion to the level of moral disorder to restore order. Incontinence answers only to force—either self-imposed or external. The greater the virtue in a people, the less external force will be required.

Discipline, including corporeal punishment is required for moral order at all levels of society. If seminarians, who are well motivated have trouble getting to chapel on time, imagine how difficult it will be to get public school students to come to class on time or behave in general without some form of coercion. The Justice Department, for example, estimates that over a 100,000 students carry a gun to school on a daily basis, to intimidate or deter those who would coerce them. Let us stop pretending that all people are well-intentioned or are sufficiently motivated to learn and exercise self-restraint without some socially imposed moral limits and effective punishments. Unless morality is considered from the perspective of right and wrong actions, in relation to our existing nature and appetites, then we will never have the tools to adequately express what either the problem is or the solution.

EDUCATORS AND EDUCATION

"It is difficult to get a man to understand something, when his salary depends on his not understanding it."

—Upton Sinclair,
The Jungle

The distribution of condoms in high schools represents a moral failure of academic thinking, despite its practical function in preventing disease and pregnancy. Educators might as well distribute prophylactics against rational thought while they are at it. Fornicating and study do not go well together for high school students. High school students should be encouraged to date and look for someone they can fall in love with, instead of being encouraged to hump like baboons, whenever they feel like it. Teenagers will always feel like having sex but is it really good for them outside the context of marriage or a committed relationship? Academics and laymen alike would do well to reflect daily on the Socratic dictum that not everything which appears to be good is actually good.

Perhaps if we made self-control the most honorable activity for high school students instead of over-emphasizing sex, cars, sports, cheer leading and high fashion clothing, we would have a higher grade of student than some of the loathsome reptiles that seem to hang out at our local schools. Did Wayne Gacey, the convicted homosexual mass murderer of young boys attend a school that encouraged continence and self-discipline? More than likely, he attended a school that had no ideas about morality on its curriculum and most likely, he had teachers who were morally no better than the vegetables to be found at the local supermarket. Perhaps he had teachers who told him that it was not good to repress his desires. Such people are not able to discern incipient moral problems in their students because they live in the fog of incontinence.

I might add that there are probably countless students who have been rescued by caring teachers and professionals who recognize that morality is an important dimension in the development of the young. Unfortunately, these teachers and professionals are in the minority due to the union thugs who run our nations educational system. A former head of the American Federation of Teachers is one such moron. I once heard him say on national television, in discussing teaching poor, inner city children that: *"We just don't know how to educate these kids..."* He might as well have said that he was incompetent. How is it that the majority of private schools, especially Catholic and Nation of Islam schools know how to educate these children and this gentleman doesn't? I might suggest that this 'educator' does not understand either morality or metaphysics and that if he did, he might not profess his ignorance so readily.

The teaching of a metaphysics of virtue has to do primarily with morality and is not religion. Such a teaching is open to spirituality, inasmuch as truth is open to greater truth. The concept of virtue, as a derivation of Natural Law is the ideal educational vehicle for giving students the foundation for ethical values without resorting to religion, and yet will allow those who wish to serve God to better understand their respective faiths. If we think of virtue as an exercise in excellence in the three areas of intellect, appetite-desire and spirituality, then we might be able to get a better handle, on how to relatively separate the intellectual and moral virtues, from the spiritual virtues.

Our public schools might have a legitimate ideological difficulty teaching students about faith, hope and charity (the theological or spiritual virtues) but they could certainly teach the moral as well as the intellectual virtues. For example, what is religious about the moral virtues of self-restraint, courage, wisdom and justice? Indeed, it might be argued, that to deny a student some knowledge of moral virtue constitutes an infringement of human freedom and liberty, by unnecessarily condemning students to the harsh slavery of mindless appetites. As Owen Wister so keenly observed in his 1902 best-seller, *The Virginian*:

"I thought there should in truth be heavy damages for malpractice on human souls." [4]

Twenty years ago, I had an amusing conversation with a member of the US. Department of Education. I asked her if there was an expert there who was familiar with the ideas behind moral education and virtue. "We don't have anyone who deals with that," I was told. I laughed out loud and said I could not believe that the Department of Education, which was charged with the education of the nation's youth could not find me someone who knew about virtue. The lady to whom I was speaking also laughed. What a sad commentary on our society. If I had asked for an expert on political liaisons for education, or a sex education expert, I probably would have been given the phone numbers of entire departments. But virtue? *"We don't deal with that."*

Virtue or excellence, in all the forms that it takes, is given a new meaning when seen as a useful application of natural law. Furthermore, the Socratic and Aristotelian concept of psyche or soul, as both a life force and an innate principle of the actuality and potentiality of matter, fits well with New Age interests in holistic healing and the spirituality of the self. These concepts are universal in scope and application. Most of us have no difficulty with the premise that it is better to be reasonable than irrational or that there are principles of matter which science has not yet discovered.

Such teachings, as part of a Public Philosophy could do much to mitigate the vicious subjectivism of appetite or desire which is a

---

4   *The Virginian*, Wister, Owen, 1902 Heritage Press, NY, page 185

major cause of the vast increase in crime and disorder that has taken place in our nation over the past thirty years. The Greek concept of excellence or virtue and its antecedent and posterior metaphysical history should be taught in its entirety, as part of a newly formulated national curriculum in our nations' schools and colleges.

CHAPTER 21

TOWARDS BUILDING A
CULTURE OF HONOR

*"A rational society, be it a corporation or a country, can only
maintain itself if personal responsibility and accountability are
at its core; that is, from top to bottom, every agent or citizen
must be empowered to conduct her or his role and to be fully accountable for its performance. To the extent that this is
done, there is order, freedom, efficiency and progress, but when
personal accountability is diffused, the ultimate result is license,
confusion, backbiting, and finally a frightening and destructive
anarchy. As Plato wrote in the Republic, in such a
society even the dogs become arrogant."*

—James L. Fisher,
The Baltimore Sun

THE QUANTUM CONTINUUM

Have you ever carefully planned a day only to have it completely unravel as the day proceeds? I like to plan in advance but frequently something comes up that captures my attention. That something could be as simple as suddenly desiring to go to the store instead of mowing the lawn. Who can explain why—on occasion—that something suddenly feels better put off or exchanged with another task? Often, it might be the subconscious (or supra conscious) mind at work doing some subtle organizational work for us by foreseeing consequences that we are not consciously aware of.

Suppose however, using our example of going to the store, that you avoid a nasty mowing accident or perhaps even more curiously, you avoid an auto accident two weeks down the road. If this is possible, it shows that there may be a kind of quantum[1] or non-local exchange between being and existence that allows the future to be felt in the present in much the same way that a ship's prow sends out waves ahead of itself. The potential of the future may be known to us, in a subtle way, by elements of the subconscious or supra-conscious mind that bridges all dimensions.

The mind, Aristotle claimed, is the *place of the forms*. Indeed, the mind as a power of the soul, is a witness to forces beyond the observable dimensions of space and time. If actuality determines past, present and future, then it would behoove us to be aware of *time shifts*, various shades of intuition and sudden senses of disproportion between what we want to do and what we subtlety feel we should not do. The 'place', as it were, where this occurs, might be called the *Quantum Continuum* or the *Tao*. (The Chinese Ta-Hua or *Great Becoming* is an early model for this concept.)

"Tao (pronounced "dao") means literally 'the path' or "the way." It is a universal principle that underlies everything from the creation

---

1   A discrete quantity of energy proportional in magnitude to the frequency of the radiation it represents.

of galaxies to the interaction of human beings. The workings of Tao are vast and often beyond human logic. In order to understand Tao, reasoning alone will not suffice. One must also apply intuition."[2]

> *At any given moment there is an energy ratio between ourselves as we presently are and the actuality or existence that is part of our infinite and non-local future. This actuality has already posited our existence as a structured and local potential that is based on an infinite relationship with Eternal Existence. There is a ratio at all times between ourselves and this non-local actuality of Existence that is our potential self or soul. Every decision we make or do not make alters the space-time fabric of the universe and Existence responds and adjusts the manifold accordingly. Put more simply: our input/output connection to the universe is based on a power and freedom that has been given freely to us as an output of something much larger than we can grasp. At any given instant, the future can change. Remember that superstrings and their note-like particles vibrate at the speed of light in multiple dimensions. The notion of a higher self is what you are in both your relation to the Divine and to these higher dimensional spaces. Virtue, in this respect, is an art like surfing; you must constantly pay attention and make adjustments to your position in space and time. As your skill and power of observation increases, the more you will enjoy living.*

This quantum continuum (or Tao) is a hadron sea, and our interaction with this ocean of light is often experienced as strong intuition, or sometimes, as the feeling of being at a fork in the road, or as described earlier, grasped as *anima vice,* or a turning of the soul. Intuition or the turning of the soul is a rotation into a future that is one step ahead of our three- and four-dimensional sense of space and time. Think of it as attending to and being changed by the in-

---

2   http://www.taoism.net/articles/what_tao.htm

finite notes of hadrons as they vibrate and rotate at the speed of light through all dimensions. The hadrons that compose your body are continuously bathed in this sea of light. Alternatively, it is like listening carefully to a song that you do not want to miss a single note of, or "hearing" the speaking-togethering that Heraclitus spoke of so many centuries ago.

Imagine yourself getting ready to argue with a colleague about an important business decision. There is a moment when doing this is just right and another when it just doesn't work as well. We can sense the difference if we are paying attention to the vibratory patterns that confront us. Our choice of action or lack of action shifts the continuum—changes the future. Whenever this ratio becomes unbalanced, a series of quantum shifts, resulting in apparently random events, may take place to bring us into balance.

Unfortunately, if we are unaware of the process, such a quantum shift may result in destructive behavior (or a downshift instead of an upshift) as we desperately seek an internal balance. Each step of our own unfolding involves an ever-widening connection between ourselves and all existing things. Our sense of identity becomes larger, the more we actualize our potential. Our sense of identity can also become weaker the more energy we expend on self-gratification.

Physicist Edward Teller, as mentioned earlier, asserted that "the extinction of the human race will come from its inability to understand the exponential function."[3] Exponential growth occurs when the rate of change itself is exponentially changing. Hadrons vibrating and rotating at the speed of light are what make exponential growth possible when we engage in creative activity. In other words, this kind of change is not fixed and does not progress in simple steps but in huge, multi-dimensional leaps that in turn create new directions for even greater exponential growth. "Look closer," Lam Kong, a Chinese doctor told me. "Everything [is] connected."

---

3   Some say this is not solely attributable to Edward Teller but to Al Bartlett. This is, however, Teller's formulation.

What has been missing from many of the discussions about the meaning of virtue is that virtue is not simply like the Newtonian application of force against an object. Who you are, for example, changes with right action and it can change exponentially when linked to the infinite force of Existence. The Divine Essence exponentially affects the virtual creation in time and dimension and it is also this exponential change that constitutes the basis for movement within the Reality Dysfunction.

The Divine intelligence, as derived or as a secondary entity, cannot mirror the changes made by the Divine Essence rapidly enough in time because time is a self-limiting factor, which is accidental to the Divine Nature. Dimensionally Interactive Cyber Kinesis or being is the first function of the infinity differential and it takes many forms. The notion of a Demiurge might be thought of as an older way of understanding the infinity differential and the Reality Dysfunction.

The Demiurge is God knowing Himself infinitely, as a reflection in time, of His own Act of Existence. In other words, He knows Himself "locally" *by way of possession*—meaning external to His own non-local Act of Existence—as the delta of managed change that we call God. God seeing and seeking His Divine Nature in time, as an expression of the Reality Dysfunction, is ultimately represented by the Incarnation of Jesus Christ. God really and truly has skin in the game in the local manifestation of the Second Person of the Trinity in time.

Socrates insisted that the greatest good and, indeed, all human good comes from virtue of one kind or another. We become what we do and only partially become what we know. This is why someone who knows all about something may not be as effective as someone who is actually doing and putting into practice what they know. Virtue helps us move more rapidly and stay in tune with the exponential function of the Divine Essence, which is not simply based on knowledge but on doing.

Wisdom is the progressive awareness of a greater sense of the interconnectedness of all causality with who we are. Machine-augmented intelligence, via complex networks of server linked information, enables human beings to cooperate on a hitherto unforeseen scale. Leveraging cooperative intelligence needs to move beyond harnessing the delivery of goods and services, including nearly unlimited porn for the masses, to promoting wisdom that can free human beings from the tyranny of biological impulses. Machine augmented intelligence is somewhat like a multi-cellular organism that is evolving.[4]

The "Singularity," described by Ray Kurzweil and AI (Artificial Intelligence) enthusiasts "is an era in which our intelligence will become increasingly non-biological and trillions of times more powerful than it is today—the dawning of a new civilization that will enable us to transcend our biological limitations and amplify our creativity."[5] This is, of course, not the "naked" singularity of physics but the notion of the singularity used metaphorically to describe an event that will be exponential in nature. What makes the Singularity of Kurzweil so interesting is that it is the reverse process of the Reality Dysfunction. Inside of Kurzweil's singularity, we might say that knowledge of and about the universe will accelerate until it approaches or reaches the same speed at which the Reality Dysfunction was created. We need to make sure, however, that it does not evolve into a morally bankrupt Frankenstein.

Wisdom is the badge of those who have surfed their baser impulses and found them lacking. Courage is the force that is required to bridge the gap between how we are and what we are called to be—both individually and culturally. Courage, as a virtue, is the call of the heart and will to the Divine. "Come forward, help me to be what you have made me." Courage is the seizing of the future—a leap into greater actuality and power by the soul. Prudence, Temperance (self-restraint), Wisdom and Justice are the necessary tools to reach this future.

This is why vice is so destructive. Vice tends to prevent us from attending to the development and understanding that is offered to us

---

4   This insight comes from Tim O'Reilly.
5   http://singularity.com/

on a daily basis. Vice focuses on the narrow time frame of pleasure and pain and constricts individuals from clearly seeing the future to which they are called by their own nature and the Nature of the Existence that has brought them into being. Those who make war upon themselves, or upon their own biology, have little or no time to make war on others. This is the fundamental shift that needs to be engaged in order for humanity to move beyond the Time War.

An exchange between being and Existence (Being) in our lives, or a balance between our potential and the timely actualization of that potential by forces that are larger than our ability to completely describe, is critical to self-development. Without the actualization of personal potential, life stagnates. When we are attentive to our own inner awareness in this regard, we become active participants in the process of our own actualization. Author Sheila Graham has described this most beautifully:

> *"You can have anything if you want it desperately enough. You must want it with an inner exuberance that erupts through the skin and joins the energy that created the world."*

All morality and all virtue begins with a sense of the disparity between the potential and the actual. Happiness consists in actualizing our potential for goodness and when this brings us closer to the infinite Actuality of Existence, suffering and disappointment is flooded with light. Morality in particular is based on the awareness of a disproportion between what we want to do and what we feel we might or should do. Moral responsibility begins when we allow ourselves to become accountable for our failure to act on what we feel we *ought* to do.

This is a far cry from feeling a vague sense of guilt. Guilt begins with the disquieting thought that we might not be acting as we should. Frequently individuals who feel guilty about something don't have the language to describe why they feel guilty or to put their fingers on the exact nature of the problem. Sometimes, guilt begins with unexamined motives for behavior that might come from family or friends and not be self-generated. A conscious understanding of the non-local nature of morality is the best way to deal with a nagging sense of guilt. There is obviously good guilt and bad guilt, with good guilt being based on the soul's awareness of the good and bad guilt consisting of unexamined motives and drives. Modern psychology is useful for examining bad guilt but not very useful for understanding good guilt.

> *The idea that life might consist of a continuum or virtual exchange between being and Existence suggests that moral and political accountability, based on Natural Law, is one way of acknowledging that such an exchange exits. This "exchange" can also be thought of as the Tao on one hand, or a manifestation of a scientifically unknown algorithm between what is spiritually non-local and what is local.*

If, in fact, there is a hierarchy of "goods" to be deliberated upon, this non-local hierarchy must be reflected in our political and moral values. The denial of this hierarchy of "goods" has allowed self-interest politics to determine what is morally acceptable and what is not acceptable. At the same time, we must acknowledge that each individual has a unique relationship with Existence and that political and moral structures must not be so tightly developed that personal responsibility and self-awareness are obscured. The liberal insight that values must be acquired and possibly clarified must be balanced with the conservative notion that values really exist and are not merely subjectively determined.

Aristotle ultimately failed to grasp the spiritual meaning of existence and in so doing left his understanding of virtue in a vacuum. This is why the concepts of virtue and honor have only periodically taken root in Western culture. Virtue makes no sense unless it can be related to Existence, Consciousness and Bliss or to metaphysics as a whole. If virtue doesn't bring us closer to joy or to the full development of our potential, then it is not worth pursuing. Satchitananda or Existence, Consciousness and Bliss is the Agape of the Greeks or the overflowing love at the heart of existence. It is to this arbor of transcendence and honor that virtue leads.

CHARACTER DEVELOPMENT

If, as Aristotle and the Chinese sages have argued, that virtue is a state of character, how might we go about developing the concept of virtue into a philosophy of character for modern man? What is it about good character that we like? Don't we admire courage and fair play? Aren't we impressed with people who are able to exercise self-restraint and who seem to be happier for doing so? Does anyone admire a coward or a glutton, or someone who exposes himself to young children? Why not? These are things that most of us feel are undesirable traits and yet we are often unable to express the why in terms of a philosophy. We are almost afraid to call something a vice for fear of offending someone who is unfortunately vice-ridden.

The public equality of self-interest prohibits our saying that anyone else's values are less than our own. A moral philosophy allows us determine why some actions are good and why some, relatively and objectively speaking are bad. This is not the same thing as standing in moral judgment of anyone. If an objective moral code exists, the vice-ridden are guilty before the code. They stand self-convicted by reason. Cicero describes this with great power and beauty in his treatise *On the State*:

> "*True law is Reason, right and natural, commanding people to fulfill their obligations and prohibiting and deterring them from doing wrong. Its validity is universal; it is immutable and eternal. Its commands and prohibitions apply effectively to good men, and those uninfluenced by them are bad. Any attempt to supersede this law, to repeal any part of it is sinful; to cancel it*

entirely is impossible. Neither the Senate nor the Assembly can exempt us from its demands; we need no interpreter or expounder of it but ourselves. There will not be one law at Rome, one at Athens, or one now and one later, but all nations will be subject all the time to this one changeless and everlasting law."

Virtue or moral and intellectual excellence is humanity's way of relating itself to the law of Reason or Natural Law. This is just another way of saying that virtue connects us to the non-local structure of the universe in all the right ways.

In the Middle Ages, the virtues were primarily divided into the Four Cardinal Virtues (or excellences) of: prudence, temperance (self-restraint or continence), fortitude and justice. These virtues had parts which consisted of other lesser but nonetheless important virtues. For example, patience might have been considered part of temperance and courage a part of fortitude. Although some medieval theologians made courage a part of fortitude, it makes more sense, sometimes, to reverse the order. Fortitude is defined as a strength of mind to encounter adversity without wavering—in short: guts. It sometimes requires courage to exercise fortitude. Likewise, it makes more sense to make prudence a part of wisdom. Is it not wise to be prudent?

Similarly, Benjamin Franklin's virtues of frugality, order, silence and resolution, for example, represent useful combinations of the traditional classifications of virtue. These variants involve the application of will and intellect in different forms. How we are "present" to ourselves and understand our natural deficiencies will determine which virtues resonate the most.

A formulation of the cardinal virtues that might make sense for modern man would be the **four primary values**: Courage, self-discipline (continence), wisdom and justice. All other values might be thought of as being derived from these four primary values. The two results of having and practicing these values are *honor* and *happiness* which should be the two pillars of any civilization.

Who, in the present age, with the exception of the morally confused, could argue with Cicero's basic definition of the three kinds of moral goodness presented in Chapter 5? If you recall, Cicero held that moral goodness fell into **three** basic categories:

The **first** was the ability to distinguish truth from falsity and to understand the relationships between one phenomenon and another, and the causes and consequences of each one. The **second** was the ability to restrain the emotions and to make appetite or desire amenable to reason. The **third** was the capacity to behave with consideration and understanding towards other people. These virtues of honesty, self-restraint, consideration and understanding are basic to the formation of any culture. We simply cannot afford *not* to teach our young people how to cultivate these aspects of good character. Do you understand that this is seldom, if ever, taught at the public school level of education? What sort of moral and intellectual blindness would lead many educators to think that students would become moral and law abiding without even understanding what morality is?

There are many individuals in our society who are depressed and suffering because they have no sense or understanding of honor. Every human being craves both happiness and honor. Indeed, some are willing to fight to the death over a matter of honor or personal happiness. How much better then to have a clear idea about the meaning of honor and happiness, by locating them inside a metaphysics of moral excellence. Happiness, like moral excellence, makes little sense unless it is understood as a state of the soul. The significance of happiness becomes clearer when it is understood as a *product* of moral and intellectual excellence or what might be loosely termed "good character". Good character is produced by the pursuit of honor and the desire for excellence. Honor is the hidden image of itself that the soul longs for. The quest for honor and excellence produces happiness by fulfilling the soul's eternal desire to come forward and express itself more completely in time. Happiness is a manifestation of the soul's knowledge and power in the present, a window as it were on the infinite.

The relationship between happiness, honor and personal power constitutes a moral paradigm of the highest order. I call this the *Venus Paradigm*. The Venus paradigm states that happiness, like honor is a product of the love of moral and intellectual excellence and that such virtue leads ultimately to a deeper knowledge of the soul and a greater participation in the non-local life of the Divine.

The Stoics of Cicero's time for example, believed that all men shared in the divine spark of God's existence and that virtue brought humanity closer to God. These same Stoics also believed in a *progression towards virtue*. They understood that there was much stumbling on the path of virtue but that all human beings should continue to make the effort. This was a cosmopolitan and pre-Christian view of morality that we would do well to adopt in the present age. As Aristotle noted:

> *"Even if happiness is not sent by the Gods but is the result of virtue and of learning a discipline of some kind, it is apparently one of the most divine things in the world for it would appear that which is the prize and end of virtue is the supreme good, and its nature divine and blessed."*

There is no good reason that the four moral values or Aristotle's moral and intellectual virtues could not be taught in depth, as part of an established and rational moral curriculum, in primary and secondary schools. How could anyone argue that moral excellences such as courage, self-restraint, wisdom, justice, generosity and kindness are not useful and necessary for the preservation of a society? Let the religious issues surface. Who really would be hurt by frank discussions of religion and moral values? As Benjamin Franklin said of his own pursuit of excellence:

> *"Though I never arrived at the perfection I had been so ambitious of obtaining, but fell far short of it, yet I was, by the endeav-*

*or, a better and a happier man than I otherwise should have been
if I had not attempted it."* [6]

There is a kind of territory that is created by an interior self-awareness that cultivates a relationship with Existence that has profound
cultural implications—whether it is absent or present. Have you ever
seen, as is common in some Midwestern American cities, vast numbers
of cars and trucks parked on wide boulevards with young men and
women just "hanging" or "chilling" during the early and late hours of
the evening? These are the tribal children of a culture that promotes
vice. They are sexually impulsive with little or no interiority—desper-
ate for something to happen to titillate their jaded senses. If we do not,
as a culture, provide programs for young people to help them develop
an interior landscape that acknowledges ontic[7] realities, we will end
up with mindless hordes who will be subject to the whim of whatever
impulse seizes the collective mind. Some of those collective impulses,
as we have seen in various inner city uprisings, are not by any means
benign. Much worse will come, unless we take offensive action to create a culture of moral responsibility.

THE QUEST PROGRAM

Our young people today not only have a need to be noticed but a desire
to contribute to society and learn how to be better human beings. We
should have a rite of passage, some ritual coming of age that would be
preferable to gang-fights, graffiti making, sexual excess and the general
juvenile delinquency that constitute the current transition from youth
to adulthood. Why don't we take some of the funds that are being
wasted on the excessive bureaucracy of the teachers' unions and create
character development programs? These programs might be designed
by a commission or wisdom council made up of Aboriginal, African

6   Benjamin Franklin, *Autobiography*, New York: Derby & Jackson, 1859
7   "of or relating to entities and the facts about them; relating to real as opposed to phe-
    nomenal existence"

and American Indian tribal elders along with military training officers. Although this might seem like an unlikely mix, each group has centuries of cultural experience in developing rites of passage.

Our understanding of both human psychology and motivation has come a long way since the Middle Ages but what was true then is still true now. Moral and intellectual excellence should not contract but expand. Motivational speakers such as Tony Robbins have explored human dynamics from a modern perspective in a way that can shed fresh light on ancient teachings. Tony Robbins, for example, has articulated six basic human needs,[8] which conceptually enhance the meaning of virtue and vice in a social and personal context. The **Six Basic Human Needs** are:

1. **Certainty:** This need involves physical survival and psychological and spiritual needs.

2. **Uncertainty:** We need uncertainty for novelty and surprise. Note that both the Reality Dysfunction and stochastic energy systems indicate a uncertainty as being "baked into" the system.

3. **Significance:** Men, being testosterone-driven, seek significance and will die or kill others for significance or to be "somebody". Robbins uses examples of men beating and killing others to achieve some level of significance that is otherwise missing from their lives. There are, consequently, negative and positive ways to achieve significance. Without an understanding of intellectual and moral excellence, negative ways of achieving significance will continue to be a problem among the disenfranchised.

---

8   The Six Basic Human Needs are taken from a Tony Robbins podcast on *Why We Do What We Do*, which was modified from an original TED talk given in 2006.

4. **Connection or Love:** Some folks choose "connection" rather than love because it is familiar or safer. This is why many people stay in abusive relationships because some connection or familiarity is often viewed as being better than none.

5. **Growth [and Creativity[9]]:** Growth is life and creative progress equals happiness.

6. **Contribution**: to step out of ourselves and share, which makes sharing even bigger)

An awareness of the six human needs gives us a very good example of how the intellect can make excellent distinctions that need to be followed up by moral decision-making (moral excellence). Understanding the six basic human needs and their relationship to how human beings really experience the world might be enhanced through a participation in Outward Bound or military style boot camp programs. For lack of a better label, let's call this the **Quest Program**. This program might work as follows:

Phase One: The Quest. All freshman and sophomore students would be allowed to study religion *as history* for a period of two years with the classes being taught by representatives of the world's major religions. The six basic human needs would be taught as the context for intellectual and moral virtue as the right solution for these needs. The teachers would be not be at liberty to convert students to any particular set of religious beliefs and all students would be encouraged to critically compare religious systems based on the six human needs. (Religiously neutral Neo-Aristotelian ethics and metaphysics would be an adjunct require-

9 Tony Robbins does not, as far as I know, link growth and creativity but it can certainly be assumed that he would do so.

ment for all four years.) The First Amendment would
not be violated because no religion in particular would be
established through the program. This would represent a
wholesome moving away from moral empiricism towards
rationalism and forms of knowledge beyond sensory data.

Phase Two: The Delphi Analysis. The motto of the Oracle
at Delphi was: *Know thyself.* At the beginning of the junior
year, each participant in the program would be required to
analyze themselves in relation to their understanding of the
moral virtues and pick ways in which they might be more
courageous, more self-restrained, wiser, more just, etc.
These matters would be discussed with their classmates
and even though this might seem a bit of a 'stretch', just
raising questions about basic impulse management might
be beneficial. Each student would be required to help
develop their own one-year agenda for self-improvement
in conjunction with an established program structure. This
might involve community service, boot camps or even participation in athletics for those who would not ordinarily
play sports.

Phase Three: The Rite Of Passage. At the end of their junior
year, participants would be required to declare and defend
their moral or religious beliefs in the context of the six
basic human needs. They would also be free not to have
any beliefs. A student could just as easily profess atheism
or agnosticism, as well as profess belief in various Christian, Hindu, Jewish, Moslem or oriental sects. The point is
that the students would have the opportunity to declare an
affiliation, to choose a moral or religious code, or not, after
three years of study. As Aristotle noted, "It is the mark of
an educated mind to be able to entertain a thought without accepting it." A rite of passage then might be thought

of as a more formal way of joining the adult community than by simply graduating from high school.

Phase Four: Guidance. Seniors would be responsible for conducting the Quest Program for the three classes under them as associate guides in conjunction with teachers.

The most extraordinary result of such a program would be astonishingly simple. By giving students a moral and psychological framework from which to conduct their thinking, the overall tonality of consciousness would be changed from simple moral floundering to at least a level of intelligent inquiry and boundary making. By giving young people a moral map—particularly in regards to impulse management—the moral equivalent of literacy might be achieved.

A PUBLIC PHILOSOPHY

"Virtue, morality, and religion. This is the armor, my friend, and this alone that renders us invincible."

—Patrick Henry

America desperately needs a moral code that is applicable to all peoples and that will serve as a basis for cultural development. By harnessing the unifying principles of the Reality Dysfunction, we can overcome the splintering effect of that same dysfunction. A Public Philosophy, employing the principles of the Founding Fathers, might do much to establish a common basis for the future direction and prosperity of the United States. No lasting civilization can be built without some ethos or code of honor. There is no more honorable political document than the Declaration of Independence and the principles upon which it was built are the foundation of the Founders' Code.

The Founders' Code, like the Code of Hammurabi or the Ten

Commandments, is a simple statement of ten principles now and for the current millennium. America is still the operative model of democracy for the rest of the planet. What we do will be adopted by others. The world, no less than America, needs such a public philosophy, which our Declaration of Independence and Constitution were based on. A Founders' Code will also act as counter-balance to the growing influence of Sharia Law in the western world.

THE FOUNDERS' CODE

1. Existence is the ultimate force in the universe and source of all religion.

2. The soul or life-force is a dynamic link between Existence and all living things.

3. Moral law is based on a relationship between Existence and the soul.

4. Responsibility and accountability are based on a hierarchy of moral and intellectual values.

5. There are five intellectual values: Science, Wisdom, Understanding, Prudence and Art.

6. There are ten moral values: Courage, Self-Restraint (Continence), Liberality, Magnificence, Magnanimity (selfless generosity), Honor, Gentleness, Friendship, Truthfulness, and Justice.

7. The vices or bad habits, such as gluttony, greed, laziness, intemperance, lack of self-restraint (incontinence), cowardice, injustice, lying, parsimony

(cheapness), rudeness, ill-temper, impatience, violence and hatred are the doorway to evil.

8. Honor and happiness come to those who practice moral and intellectual excellence.

9. The family is the first school of the soul.

10. All things return to Existence. This is the basis for the mystery of life.

HOW TO CHANGE AMERICA IN TWELVE STEPS

"Somehow strangely the vice of men gets well represented and protected but their virtue has none to plead its cause—nor any charter of immunities and rights."

—David Thoreau

In the late 1700's, the government adopted by the Thirteen Colonies was in danger of self-destructing under the centrifugal force of economic self-interest run amok. Under the Articles of Confederation, states were entitled to issue their own money and levy multiple tariffs. National and business development was hampered by having an insufficiently strong central government and the nation's affairs were in serious disorder. The Constitutional Convention of 1787 was convened in Philadelphia to address the problem. The final result of this convention was the Constitution of the United States, which is now the oldest living constitution in the world. The Constitution and the Declaration of Independence are, essentially, a collection of well-thought out algorithms, designed to limit the propagation of moral and intellectual pathogens in society.

Comedians have noted that "America was founded by geniuses so that it could be run by idiots." We have only to look around us to see the truth of this proposition. Words and definitions have become so elastic and porous under the constant pressure of legalists schooled in positivism that the Constitution and the Declaration of Independence have almost ceased to have real meaning. Much like the Ten Commandments, which have become the "Ten Suggestions," the political meaning of the Constitution, separated from the Declaration of Independence, has become degraded in regards to important moral and legal considerations. Given that America was founded by rationalists and not by empiricists, a return to the Rationalist basis of the Constitution and the Declaration of Independence would be in keeping with our common heritage.

America is in need of another Constitutional Convention. Our nation has some very serious problems with education, crime and the economy that will not be mended by grinding out more legislation. As it is, there are more laws on the books than we know what to do with. Most Americans realize that there are some very disturbing trends in our society. Our schools don't seem to be able to produce students with sound intellectual or moral values, and crime has assumed a more casual and random appearance than many of us can sometimes believe. Social issues such as gender identity and various kinds of sexual attraction, masquerading as normality, create new forms of confusion that muddy the waters of conventional morality.

We are also aware that our economy is not providing the safe harbor that it used to. We have a profound sense that all is not well. Where can we begin? There are many economic and social prophets warning us of dire consequences should we fail to begin the process of reform. But where can we really begin the process of moral and political change? We can begin by realizing that our problems are not going to go away and that a much more serious approach, based on the ideas of the Founding Fathers, is needed to resolve them. The ballot box can only accomplish so much.

"The notion of good and evil cannot be resolved by universal suffrage. It is not given to a ballot to make the false become the true and the unjust the just. The human conscience cannot be put to the vote."

—Victor Hugo

The Founders' Code, as a working concept, focuses on America's problems in a way that will make change possible under the rules of the Republic. The notion that a pure democracy can arrive at moral solutions is like arguing that a body without a head can think. At first glance, the Founders' Code may appear to be something out of a New Age manual but in reality, these ideas are based on established principles that are over 2,000 years old. The Founding Fathers were familiar with and used some of the key ideas of the Code in framing the Constitution and Declaration of Independence.

Clearly, it is difficult to imagine America ever adopting such a public philosophy but the failure to make the attempt will likely result in the further degradation of this country as a functioning and transformative political entity. We would do well to heed the prescient warning of John Adams: "Have you ever found in history, one single example of a Nation thoroughly corrupted that was afterwards restored to virtue...And without virtue there can be no political liberty." [10]

The process to establish the Founders' Code might begin with the call for a Constitutional Convention. Such a Convention would make it possible to address a number of issues that have been degraded and confused by the actions of moral and legal deconstruction over the past fifty years. There is nothing, other than a knee-jerk reaction to change, that should prevent a good faith analysis of the algorithms of good governance and the Constitution in order to make sure those

---

10 *The Works of John Adams—Second President of the United States,* Boston, Little and Brown and Co., 1854, (Harper Brothers edition, 1958)

algorithms are still serving the purpose they were intended for. The following twelve action steps should be proposed and acted upon.

1. A Constitutional Convention as Allowed Under Article V of the Constitution

Article V of the U.S Constitution states:
"The Congress, whenever two thirds of both Houses shall deem it necessary, shall propose Amendments to this Constitution, or, on the Application of the Legislatures of two thirds of the several States, shall call a Convention for proposing Amendments, which, in either Case, shall be valid to all Intents and Purposes, as Part of this Constitution, when ratified by the Legislatures of three fourths of the several States, or by Conventions in three fourths thereof, as the one or the other Mode of Ratification may be proposed by the Congress; Provided that no Amendment which may be made prior to the Year One thousand eight hundred and eight shall in any Manner affect the first and fourth Clauses in the Ninth Section of the first Article; and that no State, without its Consent, shall be deprived of its equal Suffrage in the Senate."

The primary purpose of the Constitutional Convention would be to establish an American public, moral philosophy to be called the Founders' Code, in honor of the Founding Fathers, and to sever relations with the established or defacto public Church of Atheism subscribed to by education and the legal system as a violation of the First Amendment. The secondary purpose of the Convention would be to address a multitude of evils that have crept into our legal and political system that are at odds with the understanding of the Founding Fathers.

2. Re-establish the Meaning and Significance of the First Amendment without Ideological Distortion.

The First Amendment simply says:
"Congress shall make no law regarding the establishment of religion or prohibiting the free exercise thereof; or abridging the freedom of speech, or of the press; or the right of the people peaceably to assemble, and to petition the government for a redress of grievances."

The concern of the drafters of the First Amendment was that Congress not enact legislation favoring the development of one religion at the expense of all the others. Our modern understanding of this as a prohibition on the teaching of any religious or moral values in public education is a result of self-serving special interests that utilize the notion of a plurality of religious values as a way of denying moral values altogether. There is a fundamental difference between the reasonable separation of Church and State and the separation of God and State, which this idea has morphed into. The First Amendment should guarantee that *access* to religious and moral information should be provided by public education. This is not to say that providing this information would be easily separated from the formation of intense religious opinion but the effort must be made to ensure impartiality. A bias towards scientific materialism is as dangerous as any other form of religious intolerance.

3. Clarify the Meaning of the Eighth Amendment and the Death Penalty.

The Eighth Amendment states:
"Excessive bail shall not be required, nor excessive fines imposed, nor cruel and unusual punishments inflicted." Cruel and unusual punishment will vary from age to age. Indeed, what is cruel and unusual is the injustice meted out to the victims of violent crime, when the guilty are not appropriately punished. Cruel and unusual punishment has been inflicted on our society as a whole, by the failure to carry out justice in a swift and timely manner. Furthermore, the failure of our government to ensure domestic tranquility is a constitutional violation of the highest magnitude.

Despite all those who claim that the death penalty doesn't work, it does. Those who think that the death penalty does not deter crime are simply confused. The penalty by itself doesn't deter anyone. What deters violent crime is swift and certain execution or punishment for crimes committed. The hands of thieves are chopped off in Saudi Arabia as are the heads of convicted murderers. Would any rational person wonder why theft and murder are extremely low in the Kingdom? The death penalty in the US should be no different in effect, despite our repugnance at the harshness of punishment in other countries. Certitude of swift and immediate punishment does, obviously and clearly, deter certain kinds of behavior.

The death penalty, however, needs to be implemented fairly and with adequate safeguards for those who have truly repented of their crimes. If we executed several thousand unrepentant criminals a year, we might conceivably reduce the violent crime rate substantially and in a self-evident manner. U.S. Disaster statistics[11] show approximately 15,000 thousand murders per year in the US and over a million assaults. We might, conceivably, prevent 150,000 murders over a ten-year period with the institution of swift punishment. A few marginally innocent people (those wrongly convicted of crimes they did not commit) executed for the good of the many, over a ten-year period, versus 150,000 saved should be an attractive number to almost anyone who seriously reflects on criminal statistics.

Large numbers of criminal executions a year might also result in incarceration savings of many millions dollars a year. (This figure is based on a national average of $25,000 spent per year on each prisoner in Federal prison.) Additionally, prison populations would be reduced, as would building and facilities maintenance. According to estimates by Armstrong Williams, the black conservative, crime overall costs the American public 425 billion dollars a year in direct and indirect costs.[12] A savings of any substantial portion of these costs would mean a huge increase of available funds for worthwhile public works and other programs.

Humane forms of corporal punishment need to be devised. There is nothing quite like fear to motivate people. It is astounding that we continue to pretend that fear is not a powerful motivation. Are we not afraid to lose our jobs or our health? Are we not all afraid to some extent of violent crime? Why? We are afraid because we might be victims of violence. Let's turn the table around and put fear to work for us. Criminals should be desperately afraid of getting involved with the police. We really need to get away from the knee-jerk reaction to this kind of proposal that says, "do we really want to create a police state?" The notion, for example, that police need de-escalation policies, put forth by Elizabeth Warren, is on the face of it reasonable but what about de-escalation behavior, via a public code of morals, for the communities that need it the most?

---

11 (http://www.disastercenter.com/crime/usc)
12 These figures were derived from 1990's Justice Department statistics. The potential savings would, likely, be much higher now than Armstrong indicated.

Let's be realistic, many unfortunate Americans live in a state of moral and social anarchy and have gotten used to it. Which is worse, a bandit state, or a police state? We don't have to have either, if we return to the notion of an authoritative, Republic based on moral values. A state that is not afraid to put the common good above self-interest or ideological lunacy will help America restore its greatness.

4. Comprehensive Education Reform

Education reform is currently in the hands of those who have an atheistic moral agenda. This is like having the fox guard the chicken house. The public's funding and support for teachers' unions needs to be phased out. Education is far too important to be left to those whose agenda is based primarily on financial reward or left-leaning ideologies. School vouchers need to be mandated by Federal Law to stimulate competition. The failure to provide school vouchers for parents represents a First Amendment violation by allowing the Religion of Secular Humanism (or all values are good values) to be promulgated with Federal funds. Programs such as the Quest Program should be tested locally, then nationally. How could anyone be seriously hurt by the teaching of either religious or moral values in an amoral atmosphere where children carry guns, take drugs with frequency and fornicate at lunch time?

The importance of teaching some semblance of moral values based on a traditional understanding of virtue and vice might do much to stimulate discussion of what is important and what is not important in life. Currently we teach many different kinds of intellectual excellence but without a teaching on moral excellence, the moral character of the young is left to the Darwinian forces of natural selection, which will almost always select appetite as their point of entry into the evolutionary process. Politicians like to talk about safety nets but the most important safety net of all is one that protects the young from the vicious biological rule of only the strong or intelligent rising to the top. The vast majority of young people need protection from violent alpha predators and the morally compromised.

5. Judicial Reform

The current policy of Supreme Court judges serving lifetime terms that cannot be abrogated seems to be at odds with the stated wording of Article III, Section I of the Constitution which states: "The judicial Power of the United States, shall be vested in one supreme Court, and in such inferior Courts as the Congress may from time to time ordain and establish. The Judges, both of the supreme and inferior Courts, shall hold their Offices [*during good Behaviour*], and shall, at stated Times, receive for their Services, a Compensation, which shall not be diminished during their Continuance in Office." Clearly judges, *including Supreme Court justices,* who might vote for issues not supported by the Constitution or common decency might be removed under the definition of "good behavior."

David Josiah Brewer, a Justice of the United States Supreme Court in the 1892 case of *Church of the Holy Trinity v. United States* (143 U.S. 457-458, 465-471, 36 L, ed., 226) stated categorically that: "Our laws and our institutions must necessarily be based upon and embody the teachings of the Redeemer of mankind. It is impossible that it should be otherwise; and in this sense and to this extent our civilization and our institutions are emphatically Christian."[13] If this

---

13 *America's God and Country*, William J. Federer, FAME Publishing, Coppell, Texas, page

might be considered as even being remotely true, then Roe v. Wade and the recent Supreme Court decision supporting gay marriage are simply repugnant to the moral foundation of American jurisprudence.

6. Tort Reform

"Torts include all negligence cases as well as in-
tentional wrongs which result in harm. Therefore,
tort law is one of the major areas of law (along with
contract, real property and criminal law) and results
in more civil litigation than any other category."[14]

The astonishing proliferation of lawsuits designed by compen-
sation-seeking lawyers has done much to make large sections of our society less civil and less reasonable. Tort-free medical facilities, for example, with strict oversight, administered by medical boards empowered to grant reasonable compensation in the event of malpractice or stupidity, might do much to reduce medical costs—if administered with moral instead of merely legal intent.

7. The Marriage Amendment

An Amendment stating simply that marriage is a state
that can only be attributed to a man and a woman
and that anything else, while it may be privately held
as marriage, is not marriage but rather a contractual,
civil arrangement between consenting parties. The
distinction is necessary to maintain the moral continuum between the values of the last several millennia
and the evolution of values such as the future might
bring. Words must be connected to reality in a way

> that truly reflects what is. We do not, for example,
> refer to two dogs or two birds as being "married"
> except metaphorically to indicate loyalty or duration
> of relationship.

Marriage between a man and a woman might be likened to alloying carbon and steel—it is a melding of two dissimilar metals to create something stronger. Gay "marriage" is like trying to alloy steel with steel or carbon with carbon; it cannot be done, except by way of pooling or mixing the two similar materials together. Gay "marriage" simply represents more of the same—not something ontologically different and new. This "pooling" of resources and sexuality that is characteristic of gay unions is merely a civil contract that is difficult to imagine as being sanctified or approved by a higher power. The civil union or CU is the appropriate designation for such relationships. Inheritance rights, adoption, custody, power of attorney and other legal issues can easily be assigned by law to civil unions as they are in marriage.

8. The Human Life Amendment

> Human life begins at conception and must be protect-
> ed. All men and women, born or unborn, are entitled
> to life, liberty and the pursuit of happiness in accor-
> dance with what we understand to be the will of the
> Creator, who seeks goodness for all mankind. Excep-
> tions may only be made in cases of rape and incest.
> No one can be compelled to the kind of heroism that
> having a child under those two circumstances would
> require. It is, however, a noble thing to bear a child
> under such adverse circumstances and women choos-
> ing this option should be well-supported by gov-
> ernment funding and held in high public esteem for
> bravery.

9. Declare that a State of War Exists Between the People of the United States and the Criminal Community.

The US. Military is being highly underutilized to fight crime. We have gotten into such a mind-set over international warfare that we fail to realize that crime, in the form of the alpha predators described by Hillary Clinton, poses a far more dangerous threat to the security of the United States than does any foreign body. How is it that we can kill 100,000 Iraqis over oil and territory in one month and we can't shoot a few of our own criminals without endless arguments about civil rights and due process? Where was the due process for the two wars against Iraq? The answer was that it was deemed not necessary.

The same should be true for the war on crime. Crime, on the scale that it exists in the United States, is a form of war. There is a hidden fear that many people seem to have in this regard and it goes like this: if we use the military against our own population, it might cause widespread civic unrest. This may be partly true but the end result of a firm attack on crime, *coupled* with public works projects, (targeted at low-income areas) should result in a widespread support for the program by all members of our community.

10. Public Works Projects and Free Enterprise Zones

Massive public works projects and other creative and co-operative enterprises might be undertaken with the substantial savings realized by lower crime. Free enterprise zones, where companies are incentivized through tax breaks and local hiring regulations to invest in poor communities, would improve employment prospects in these areas. Low income neighborhoods might be targeted for public works projects and free enterprise zones first, since many would complain that these communities would suffer a disproportionately large number of executions. This would help generate enthusiasm for the program. Additionally, safer neighborhoods would likely generate a business renaissance in areas long-suppressed by crime.

An organization much like DARPA (The Defense Advanced Research Projects Agency) which was designed for the US Military in the late 1950s so that America would never be at a technological disadvantage by a foreign power could be utilized for this purpose. A department of Advanced Economic Projects (AEP) might be utilized to insure that economic development is never derailed by morally backwards or intellectually retrograde environmental concerns.

11. Establish a Wisdom Council as a Counterweight to the Executive, Legislative and Judicial Branches of Government.

A Wisdom Council could be used to consider the feasibility and format of a Public Philosophy based on the Code. The Wisdom Council should consist of members of major religions, tribal elders, military leaders and philosophers with the primary requirement being that all members be conversant with the epistemological difference between Empiricism and Rationalism. It is interesting to note, in this regard, that the Founding Fathers initially wanted the members of the Senate to be chosen by the House legislature in order that the best men might be chosen. Clearly, this would not prevent partisanship entirely but something like a Wisdom Council might be a useful start:

A senatorial vote for members of the Council might be an appropriate way of selecting members. The Wisdom Council should report to and advise the Supreme Court as an independent entity. The Wisdom Council should be empowered to over-ride the Department of Education when necessary.

12. Establish a Public Philosophy, as an Amendment to the Constitution, to be Called the Founders' Code.

Once the content and structure of the Public philosophy is decided upon, this set of rules and values must be implemented and taught at all levels of public education. The domestication of appetite, much like the domestication of fire in ages past, could ignite the potential for a truly just and fair society.

The Declaration of Independence and the Constitution gives us the authority to re-organize the social order into something more profound than the dog-eat-dog world of capitalism or the superficial moral vision of the advocates of self-interest at all cost. Recovering the notion of not only intellectual excellence but moral excellence is an absolute requirement for the re-vitalization of America. No set of laws can help us establish a just social order without some acknowledgement of the need for both moral and intellectual excellence. One form of excellence without the other is like standing on one foot instead of walking on two feet.

EPILOGUE

"We hold these truths to be self-evident...that whenever any form of government becomes destructive of these ends, it is the right of the people to alter or abolish it, and to institute new government, laying its foundation on such principles, and organizing its powers in such form, as to them shall seem most likely to effect their safety and happiness." [1]

No nation can survive without clear principles and definitions. As Aristotle stated: "a definition shows what something is and words tell what the definition means." [2] Without definitions that connect causes with effects a culture cannot survive. The current enterprise of empirical atheism, in its many forms, tends to sever the connection between an objective moral order and human behavior. The extent to which it has succeeded is evidenced by the extraordinary level of intellectual confusion and moral paralysis that we see all around us.

If the right hand of good governance is adherence to the law, then surely the left hand is the guidance provided by a sensible and univer-

---

1   *The Declaration of Independence*
2   This was brought to my attention by Fr. William O'Kielty

sal moral code. The right hand must, so to speak, know what the left hand is doing. The current separation of Church and State was never intended to become a separation of morality, or even God, from the State as it has become today. America's birthright is moral greatness. "We hold these truths to be self-evident" cannot be translated by empiricists, who are unwittingly destroying America, into: "We hold no truths to be self-evident."

The moral enterprise of the current millennium will be made in America or it is likely not to be made at all. We tend to forget that part of the uniqueness of the Declaration of Independence was that it did not seek to create new, previously non-existing rights but to secure existing, God-given rights. As Cicero noted over twenty centuries ago, "In all probability the disappearance of piety (duty) toward the gods will entail the disappearance of loyalty and social union among men as well and of justice itself, the queen of all the virtues."

The effort to reclaim our country as "One nation under God" and the sound principles established by the Founding Fathers will be difficult but the failure to make the attempt may result in the long-anticipated and predicted fall of the West. What we do now in regards to instituting a constitutionally sound and moral society can and will make the deciding difference in the course of America's influence on the world to come. If we can take steps in this direction, then Virgil's prophetic lines regarding an empire that will endure may yet come true.

> *"Then one...will inherit the lines and build the walls of Mars...*
> *On them I set no limits, [of] space and time;*
> *I have granted them power, empire without end..."*

—Virgil, *The Aeneid*

∞

AUTHOR'S NOTE

"We must conceive of this whole universe as one commonwealth
of which both gods and men are members."

—Cicero

I don't wish to suggest in any way that the absolute transcendence and eternity of God is compromised in the Reality Dysfunction but I do think that what might be called the theology of polarization, between man and God, needs to be more carefully examined. God's *affect* is univocal but His *effects* are, clearly, equivocal. This is the basis for the Reality Dysfunction or, if you prefer, the Reality Disproportion. The disproportion between God and creation is not "perfect" in that there is a fundamental disproportion between what exists perfectly, in and of Itself, and what exists contingently in a limited manner and in time. "Relation" is a way of expressing the difference between a Being who does not exist in any way that we can really grasp and those things, which we can understand that "have" existence. Relation is the lens

491

through which that which does not exist is revealed. There is no such lens in the mind of God.

The great mystery, as was put to me by the Reverend Cornelius O'Brien, is why God is not closer to us than His power and omnipotence might indicate. Perhaps this is an illusion. As St. Augustine indicated, God is closer to us than we are to ourselves. If this is true, it is more likely that we are filtering out His Presence, by blindly adhering to a familiar but limited understanding of what is possible between God and man. The insistence of Jesus on the importance of faith is an indicator that there is an exponentially immediate, two-way relationship (of affect and effect) between God and humanity that is available and not fully utilized.[1] Faith is akin to a medium of exchange between ourselves and God; it is the transcendental virtue that completes and fulfills all excellence.

What we can say with some confidence is that Existence, considered equivocally, is relational in some fundamental manner that we do not yet understand but must make the effort to do. The Eternal englobes time and seeks to bring about a perfect proportionality between Itself and everything that exists. This is, as stated earlier in the book, is the real basis for evolution. The entire universe is being moved by the image of a perfect proportionality that exists as an "end" in the Divine Mind as a derivative and relational entity within the interference patterns that constitute the Reality Dysfunction.

The Reality Dysfunction is also not a back door attempt to immanentize the eschaton[2] but rather a re-examination of the grounds upon which the present state and destination of mankind might be considered. If current Christian soteriology is wrong, it is likely to be wrong only by degree or because its context, while large, doesn't reflect the full reality of God's dynamic Nature and generosity. Theology

---

1 The descent of the Infinite is, perhaps, resisted in general by the material order.
2 "In political theory and theology, to *immanentize the eschaton* means trying to bring about the eschaton (the final, heaven-like stage of history) in the immanent world. It has been used by conservative critics as a pejorative reference to certain utopian projects, such as socialism, communism, and transhumanism." [WP]

and metaphysics cannot be put in a box. God, as One or Trinity, is simply too vast for any construct—analogical or otherwise. The Reality Dysfunction, much like a prism, shows how reality is part of the larger spectrum of the great light that is Existence. What we have with such metaphysics are tools for understanding His ways but the final approach will always be on our knees.

St. Joseph of Cupertino (1623-1663 AD), an Italian Franciscan, once noted that all of humanity's great evils and difficulties have no more weight with God than children battling with toy guns. What we perceive as being immensely difficult is easy for God. As Mother Theresa used to say: "God has plenty of money."

What we are, however, *in relation* to the Act of Existence, is paradoxically, more than nothing. Like the *ens diminutum* (the little being of Duns Scotus that may exist in the Mind of God (in the Reality Dysfunction), we are part and parcel, so to speak, of an eternal story. All that we have ever dreamed of, both in this life and the next, is based on something that is supremely real. This is what makes the Reality Dysfunction and the other Transcendental Algorithms so compelling. While they illuminate much of what humanity is struggling to understand, these algorithms also point back to the Divine. We live in a universe that is interpenetrated by the hidden wonders and mysterious realms of Existence. We are, in this sense, part of the "skin" Existence has in the game.

We are free, within the Divine gift of our sovereignty, to come to understand what we are called to be. This "calling" from eternity is often obscured by our misinterpretation and misunderstanding of the God who brings us into being. Napoleon once remarked, "What magic liquid is it that keeps us from the things we love?" We are, for the most part, the only ones who keep ourselves from what we love by asserting an unnecessary dichotomy between what we want and what God may "want".

We have, in a way, the world that we have imagined because we have not worked harder to imagine a better world. God is not waiting for us to change the world; He does, however, provide us with the tools needed to fulfill, as the Chinese say, the mandate of heaven. The finish will be up to God but humanity, collectively, has to step up to the plate and attempt to build a civilization of honor.

The saints and the New Age sages are entirely correct in asserting that alignment of the personality with the soul and consequently with the will of God is what, ultimately, leads to personal happiness and good order in society. The relevance of God to politics, if God's Nature is understood in such a way as to not polarize those who are at different levels of appreciation of His Existence, is paramount.

Mohammed, who "did not at first intend to establish a new religion, but rather to reform the belief in Allah which already existed, and to show what this belief truly signified and rightfully demanded"[3] would, likely, have approved of an approach that emphasizes the Oneness of God and a universal formulation of behavior based on dynamics attributable to Existence rather than to the short-sighted expectations of humanity based on acquisition. The growing evangelization of Christians by Muslims and the growth of atheism are indications of how important it is to reintegrate politics and religion in a new synthesis that will help all religious and other groups to have a better appreciation of each other's positions. If this book might be helpful in creating conditions to augment that process, I will have been richly rewarded.

---

3   *Mohammed: The Man and His Faith*, Tor Andrae, 1936, Translated by Theophil Menzel, 1960, pgs. 13-30

ABOUT THE AUTHOR

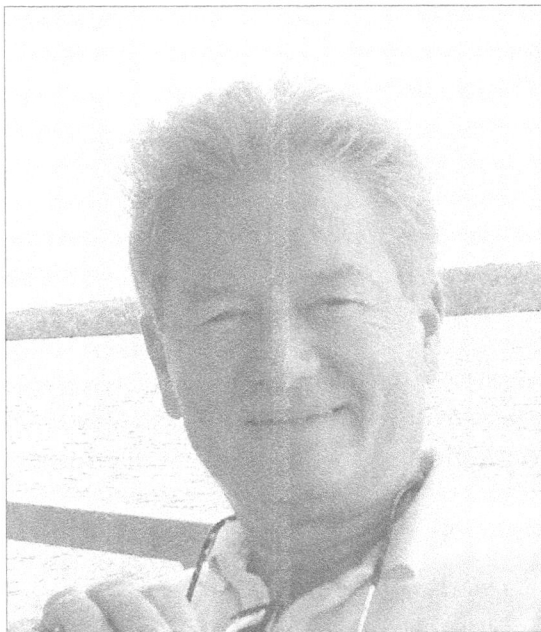

Image taken at Mount Vernon, Virginia

Sean J. O'Reilly was born in 1952, in England, and educated in the UK and the United States. He graduated from the University of Dallas in 1974-75 and attended the Braniff Graduate School for advanced studies in Theology. He is a former seminarian, stockbroker, and prison instructor with a degree in Existential Phenomenology and Psychology. Currently CEO and Founder of the Auriga Distribution Group, Redbrazil.com, Johnny Upright, House of a Thousand Suns and the nascent Fifth Access Foundation, he is an advocate for a return to the wisdom of the past as it might be re-interpreted by science. A patented inventor, he is a devotee of good humor and all things sacred and profane. A former member of the Naval Reserve intelligence community and a long-time editor for Solas House and Travelers' Tales, he is also the author of a number of controversial non-travel books, including:

- *How to Manage Your Destructive Impulses with Cyber Kinetics* (AKA: *How to Manage Your D.I.C.K.*)

- *Fifth Access: Cyber Therapy and Quantum Cyberdynamics*

- *Authority; Creativity and the Third Imperium: Why God's Knowing Himself, Outside Himself, Matters*

- *God Has Skin in the Game: How a New Understanding of Politics and the Soul Could Change America.*

His editorial credits, with James O'Reilly, Larry Habegger and Tim O'Reilly, include many award-winning travel books.

- *The Road Within*

- *The Best Travel Writing 2015*

- *Travelers' Tales China*

- *Travelers' Tales France*

- *Hyenas Laughed at Me and Now I Know Why*

- *Travelers' Tales American Southwest*

- *Travelers' Tales Greece*

- *Travelers' Tales Ireland*
- *Travelers' Tales Grand Canyon*
- *Traveler's Tales Danger!*
- *Travelers' Tales 30 Days in the South Pacific*
- *Travelers' Tales Paris*
- *Travelers' Tales San Francisco*
- *Pilgrimage*
- *The Spiritual Gifts of Travel*
- *The Ultimate Journey*
- *Testosterone Planet*

Widely traveled, Sean has wandered through Argentina, Australia, Chile, China, Europe, Israel, Kenya, Mexico, New Caledonia, New Zealand, Fiji, the Seychelles and other islands of the South Pacific, Southeast Asia and forty-nine of the American states. He lives in Virginia, in sight of the Blue Ridge Mountains, with his wife Brenda, three of his six children, two dogs, three pigs, a horse, a steer, three cats and one python.

INDEX

www.ingramcontent.com/pod-product-compliance
Lightning Source LLC
Chambersburg PA
CBHW021551270326
41930CB00027B/119